rietveld's universe

Edited by
Rob Dettingmeijer
Marie-Thérèse van Thoor
Ida van Zijl

NAi Publishers
Rotterdam

rietveld's universe index

8, De 224

a

Advisory Committee for Fine and Applied Arts 51
AEG 177, 182
Ain, Gregory 81, 83
Akademie der Künste, Berlin 32
'All-Russian association for cultural relations abroad' 224
Alma, Peter 56, 224
America 252-256
Amsterdam 21, 32, 33, 38, 51, 53, 54, 56, 57, 60, 106, 117, 124, 126, 131, 137, 176, 176-178, 188, 203, 216, 217, 219, 233-235, 239, 244
Amsterdam General Extension Plan 32
Amsterdam School 25, 170, 173
Antilles 115
Antwerp 170, 178
Architectura et Amicitia 53
Arkin, David E. 225
Arnhem 84, 87, 106, 114, 115, 117, 120, 124, 130, 131, 156, 246
Art Nouveau 170
Arts & Architecture 79, *80*, 81
A.S.B. 57
Athens Charter 32

b

Bakema, J.B. (Jaap) 21, 29, 32, 155, 159
Banham, Reyner 16, 23-25, 29, 33
- *Age of the Masters* 16
- *Theory and Design in the First Machine Age* 23
Barcelona 178
Baroque 25, 170, 261
Barr, Alfred 28, 30, 234, 244, 254
Bauhaus 23, 24, *26*, 41,*132*, 133, 139, 173,189,*191*, 253, 254, 256

Baumeister, Willy 208
Beeren, W.A.L. 32
Begeer, Anthonie 53
Begeer, Carel J.A. 51, 56, 99
Begeer, Cornelis L.J. 51, 53, 56, 99, 100
Behne, Adolf 40, 41
- *Eine Stunde Architektur* 41, *41*
Behrendt, Walter Curt 41
- *Der Sieg des neuen Baustils* 41
Beltman, G. 116, 119
Bendien, Jacob 54
Benevolo, Leonardo 29, 32
Bergdoll, Barry 83
Bergeijk 28, 71, 84, 88, 90, 91, 116, 117, 119

Berghoef, J.F. 28
Bergvelt, Ellinoor 33
Berkovich, Elmar 63
Berlage, H.P. 23, 35, 84, 99, 100, 103, 170, 173, 253
- Villa Santpoort 100
Berlin 139, 182, 195, 208, 216
Bertoia, Henry 227, *230*
- Steel wire chair *230*
Besnyö, Eva 57
Best 71
Betsky, Aaron 28
Bijvoet, Bernard 67
Bilthoven 104, *104*, 144
Birdseye, Clarence 191
Birza, J.W. 56
Blake, Peter 75
Blake, William 24
Bless, Frits 33
Blotkamp, Carel 32, 34
Bock, Manfred 32, 33
Boeken, Albert 202
Boks, Joost 155, 159
Bolland, G.D.J. (Gerard) 38, 40
Bons, Jan 159, 162, 163, 167
Boon, A.A. 102
Braat, company 131
Bredero, Adriaan 106
Bredero's Bouwbedrijf 57, 90, 104, 106, 110
Breuer, Marcel 24, 83, 139, 144, 173
- Model no. B6 *139*, 144
Breukelen 28, 104, 123, 227
Brinkman, J.A. 67, 133, 175, 176, 254
Brinkman and Van der Vlugt 133, 175, 176, 254
Van Nelle Factory, Rotterdam 133, *133*, *176*, 254
Britten, Benjamin 159
Brno 65, 66, *68*

Brom, Leo 56, 63, 189
Brown, Theodore M. 16, 26, 35, 254
Brugman, Til 208, 209
Brussels 63, 155, 158, 160, 166, 167, 170, 178
Buchholz, Erich 208
Buijs, Jan Willem Edward 178, 182, 183
- De Volharding 178, 182, *183*

c

Case Study House Program 72, 76, 79, *80*, 81
Centraal Museum Utrecht 14, 15, 21, 22, 29, 53, 54, 56, 60, 144, 163, 172, 173, 256
Chicago 133, 136, 137, 254
CIAM 23, 25, 35, 43, 63, 224
Cold War 233
Colenbrander, Bernard 26, 29
Colonial Exhibitions
- Antwerp 178
- Paris 178
Colquhoun, A. 23
Committee to erect a war memorial for the city's fallen resistance fighters, Utrecht 51
Communal Work 219
Compagnie Internationale des Wagons-Lits 71
Constructivism 182, 213, 216
Constructivists 217, 219, 225
Le Corbusier 23-25, 33, 65-67, 72, 75, 103, 155, 159, 163, 166, 167, 173, 178, 213, 225, 256

- *Le poème electronique* 159
- Villa Garches 25, 65
- Villa Savoye 65, 66
- Villa Stein-de Monzie 65, *65*
Cottage movement 66
Creman, Jurjen 17, 151
Cubism 25, 29, *30*, 234, 254
Cultuur der U.d.S.S.R. 213, 224, 225
Curaçao 114, 115, 227
Cuypers, P.J.H. 35, 103, 170

d

Dada 29, 32, 47, 54, 173
Dal Co, Francesco 29, 32
- *History of World Architecture* 32
Darley, Gillian 175
De Bazel, K.P.C. 53
De Gemeenschap 59, 60
De Gruyter, W. Jos 57, 60
De Hollandsche Revue 201
De Ligt, Bart 207, *209*
De Maasbode 56
De Rook, G.J. 34
De Stijl 17, 21, 23-26, 28-30, 32, 33, 35, 37, 53, 65-67, 71, 83, 170, 173, 182, 195, 196, 198, 202, 207, 208, 211, 213, 216, 225, 227, 233-236, 238, 239, 242-244, 249, 253, 254, 256, 261
De Stijl 23, 24, 28, 32, 37, *37*, 38, 40, 196, *196*, 198, *198*, 201, 254

De Vrije Bladen 47
De werkende vrouw 46, 47, *47*
De Wilde, E.L.L. 32
Delft 131, 155, 175, 227, 244
Delft College of Technology 35, 104, 117, 225
Detroit 63
Deutscher Werkbund 40, 57
Die Form 175
Doesschate, G. ten 54, 56
Doesschate, Jurriaan ten 54
Domela, César 207
Dudok, W.M. (Willem) 21, 106, 110, 173, 182
Duiker, J. 67
Dunster, David 23
Düsseldorf 175

e

Eames, Charles and Ray 81, 227, 228
- Chair of curved wood 227, *228*

Edison lichtweek *176*
Eerste Algemene Begraafplaats Soestduinen 51
Elffers, Dick 57
Elling, Piet 54, 56, 57, 199
Ellwood, Graig 81
Engelman, Jan 53, 60
Engels, Chris 115
Engels-Boskaljon, Lucia 115
Entenza, John 79-81
Eschauzier, F.A. 28
Eskes-Rietveld, Elisabeth 163
Exhibitions
- 'American National Exhibition' 233
- 'Americana' 32
- 'Architectura' 32
- 'Contemporary Dutch Art' 224
- 'Cubism and Abstract Art' 254
- 'Die neue Wohnung' 188
- 'First Russian Art Exhibition' 216
- 'Les Architectes du Groupe "de Styl"' 208
- 'Modern Architecture – International Exhibition' 254
- 'Neues Bauen' 57
- 'Socialistist Art Today' 219
- 'Style. Standard and Signature' 26, 29
- 'Tomorrow's Small House' 83
Exhibitions dedicated to Rietveld (see also De Stijl, exhibitions)
- 'Gerrit Rietveld 1888-1964' 256
- 'Gerrit Rietveld. A Centenary Exhibition' 256
- 'Rietvelds ranke ruimtedieren en andere creaturen van de avant-garde' 21, *22*

f

Fanelli, Giovanni 32
Filler, Martin 81
Filmliga see Utrechtsche Filmliga
Fischer, Max 41
Fles, Etha 56
Forster, Kurt W. 23
Fraenkel, E.M. 56
Frampton, Kenneth 23, 29
Frankfurt kitchen 46
Freedman, Barry 254, 256
Functionalism 29, 173, 254
Futurists 23

g

Gabo, Naum 63
Galerie L'Effort Moderne 53, 208
Galleria Nazionale d'Arte Moderna 239, *242*, *243*
Gan, Aleksei M. 216
Geleen 106, 110
Gemeentemuseum, The Hague 32, 54
General Electric 177
Genootschap Nederland-Nieuw Rusland 56, 57, 213, 233
Germany 38, 40, 46, 141, 175, 177, *179*, 213, 233, 239
Giedion, Sigfried 25, *26*, 28, 29, 244
- *Mechanization Takes Command* 25, 28
- *Space, Time and Architecture* 25
Ginzburg, Moisei 216, 222, 225
Gispen, Willem H. 139
Glushenko, Gleb I. 219
goed wonen 81, 90
Goed Wonen, Stichting 81, 83
- *Mens en ruimte* 83
Gorinchem 110, 113
Granpré Molière, M.J. 28
Greek pavilion, Venice 21
Groep '53 181
Gropius, Walter 24, 25, *132*, 133, 173, 189, 191, 195, 213, 225, 254

- Bauhaus, Dessau *132*, 133, 191
Guggenheim (Family) 83

h

Haarlem 198
Hammacher, A.M. (Bram) 57, 196, 201, 239
Häring, Hugo 182
Harrenstein, A. 56
Harrenstein, Reinder Johan 54, 217, 219
Harrenstein-Schräder, An 63
Harris, Harwell Hamilton 81
Harrison, Wallace 133
- United Nations Building 133
Hartog, A.M. 23, 54, 56, 140, 141, 189, 190, 254
Hausbrand, Franz 63
Heerlen 71, 90, 94, 104, 133
Hegel, G.W.F. 38
Hermitage 224
Hilberseimer, Ludwig 225
Hirschhorn Museum and Sculpture Garden 254
Hitchcock, Henry-Russell 24, 25, 254
- *The International Style* 254
- *Modern Architects* 254
Holland (Michigan) 233
Holland Fair 167
Hollandse Patent Metaalindustrie, N.V. (Hopmi) 144, 148-153
Hood, Raymond 175
Hoogstraten & Zoon, D. 115
Hopmi see Hollandse Patent Metaalindustrie
Huis ter Heide 100
Huszár, Vilmos 57, 195, 208-211, 216
Hyman, Isabelle 254

i

i10 38, 39, 40, 41, *42*, 43, 46, 47, 216, 219
Ibelings, Hans 28
IBM 155
Idea House 83
Ikonnikov, Andrei V. 225
Ilpendam 28, 71, 73, 90, 93, 122, 124, 244

Industrial Art School 99
Institute for Applied Arts Education 124, 233

International Style 25, 81, 254
Italy 239
IZORAM 219, 224

i

Jaffé, H.L.C. (Hans) 24, 28, 35, 234, 235, 239, 244
Jena 207
Jencks, Charles 29, 30
Jesse, Nico 60, 185
Jones, Quincy 81
Johnson, Philip 24, 25, 234, 254
- *The International Style* 254
- *Modern Architects* 254
Junkers factory 139
Juryfreie Kunstschau Berlin 208, 216

k

Kahn, Louis 29, 32
Kalff, L.C. 155, 159, 163, 167, 177, 178
Kant, E. 38
Karfík, Vladimír 178
- Bata shoe shop *178*
Katwijk aan Zee 207
Kharkiv 224
Kholostenko, Mikola (Nikolai) V. 217-219
- Agitation centre 217, *218*
Khrushchev, Nikita 233
Kiev 217, 219
Kiev Art Institute (KHI) 217
Kiljan, G. 57
kitchen debate 233
Klaarhamer, P.J.C. 37, 57, 99, 100, 253
Klapheck, Richard 175
Koch, Pyke 63
Kochküche 46
Koenig, Pierre 81
Kok, Antony 195
Kolthoff, Mark 56
Koninklijke Bibliotheek 55, 63
Koninklijke Van Kempen & Begeer 51
Koolhaas, Rem 29
Korn, Arthur 213
Krasheninnikova, Nadezda L. 225
Krefeld 72
Kröller-Müller Museum see Rijksmuseum Kröller-Müller
Krop, Hildo 56, 219
Kuiler, Kees 57
Kultermann, U. 25, 28
Kultuurkamer 110
Kunstliefde, Genootschap/Society 51, *51*, 56
Kuper, Marijke 29

l

Lange, Hermann 71
Lanjouw (Family) 144, 149, 151, 153
Lao-Tse 173
Laren 63
Lehning, Arthur 40, 63
Leiden 38
Leningrad 219, 224
Lightolier 189
Lissitzky, El 54, 195, 208, 213, 215, *216*, 217
- *Proun* 213
- *Prounen-Raum* 216
Louis Styles 170
Loosdrechtse Plassen 227
Lootsma, B. 155
Los Angeles 81, 84, 95
Lürsen, Joan B. 178, 183
- De Volharding 178, 182, *183*
Lunsingh Scheurleer, D.F. 234
Lyndon, Maynard 63

m

Maarssen 54, 106, 141, 190, 254
Maas, Willem 57, 60, 63
Maatschappij tot Exploitatie van de Staatsspoorwegen 53
Mácza, Ivan (János) L. 225
Malevich, Kazimir S. 25, 213, 216
- *Architekton* 25
- *Bèta-Architekton* 213
- *Zèta-Architekton* 216
Markelo 110
Maronier, J.H. 53, 54, 63
Marseille 224
Masthoff, Sienna 208, *209*
May, Ernst 182, 225
Meier-Graefe, Julius 175
Merkelbach, B. 81, 159, 173, 224
Mertens, H.F. 57, 149
Metz & Co 144, 151, 152
Meulenbelt, J.C. 73, 178

Mexico 115
Mexico City 162, 163, 170
Meyer, Erna 46
Mies van der Rohe, Ludwig 16, 17, 24, 65-67, 68, 71, 72, 74, 75, 90, 120, 133, 136, 137, 139, 185, 186, 188, 189
- Adam Department Store, Berlin 185, *186*

- Bank building, Stuttgart 185
- Farnsworth House, Plano 74
- Federal Center, Chicago *136*, 137
- Gericke House, Berlin 71
- Lake Shore Drive Apartments, Chicago 133, *136*, 137
- Lange House, Krefeld 71
- Seagram Building, New York 189
- Tugendhat House, Brno 65, 66, *68*
Minimum subsistence dwelling 46
Minneapolis 33, 254
Mock, Elizabeth 83
Modern Movement 16, 17, 23-25, 28, 30, 32, 33, 56, 65, 67, 75, 120, 216, 227, 253, 254
Moholy-Nagy, László 139, 195, 225
Mondrian, Piet 23, 32, 33, 38, 40, 54, 195, 198, 244
- *Compositie met kleurvlakken* 198
- *Kompositie B* 198
Moneo, Rafael 23
Montreal 29, 202
Morris, William 24
Moser, Karl 63
Moscow 213, 215, 217, 219, 220, 222-225, 233
Mulder, Bertus 34, 35
Museum Boijmans Van Beuningen 32
Museum Meermanno 52, 53, 55, 60
Museum of Modern Art, New York 21, 25, 28, 83, 188, 233-235, *238*, 254

n

Nagele 28, 167
Nazi Germany 233
Nederlands Documentatiecentrum voor de Bouwkunst 32

Nederlandse Spoorwegen 53
Neoplasticism 29, 195, 198, 254
Netherlands Architecture Institute 14-16, 28, 256
Netherlands (Dutch) Biennial Pavilion, Venice 115, 155, *157*, 244, *244*
The Netherlands Information Bureau 234
Netherlands-New Russia Society 43, 56, 213, 219, 224, 233
Neutra, Richard 63, 72, 81, 95, 225
- 'Hoe bouwt Amerika?' 63
- Lovell Health House, Los Angeles 95
- VDL Research House 81
New Objectivity 23, 47, 57, 100, 170, 173
New York 21, 25, 28, 83, 133, 134, 182, 189, 233-235, 238, 244, 254
Nieuwe Beelding 33, 198
Nieuwe Bouwen 17, 28, 32, 33, 35, 56, 79, 120, 216, 227
Nieuwe Rotterdamsche Courant 40
Nieuw Rusland 213, 223, 224
Nijland, E. 51
Nijland, J. 60
Nixon, Richard 233
Nolte, H.J. (Henk) 114, 115

o

Ob'edinenie Sovremennykh arkhitektorov (OSA) 217, 219, 225
Obolenskii, L. 219
- *Albidum* 219
Olbertz, system 106
Oorthuys, Gerrit 225
Opbouw 57
Osram 177
Otterlo 32, 33, 35
Oud, J.J.P. 21, 25, 29, 32, 35, 37, 40, 41, 43, 46, 57, 67, 159, 173, 195, 196, 198, 202, 207, 208, 211, 213, 216, 225, 233, 234, 239, 253, 254, 256
- *Holländische Architektur* 35, 41
- Oud-Mathenesse, Rotterdam 41
- Werkbund Exhibition, Stuttgart 46,185
Overy, Paul 28, 195,
Oxenaar, R.W.D. 32
Ozinga, M.D. 35

p

Paris 53, 144, 178, 195, 208, 233, 244, 248, 256
Pastoe 149
Perez Gomez, Carlos 23

Petit, Jean 159
Peutz, Frits 133, 159
- Schunck Building, Heerlen 133, *133*
Pevsner, Nikolaus 24, 25
- *An Outline of European Architecture* 24, 25
- *Pioneers of the Modern Movement from William Morris to Walter Gropius* 24
Philadelphia 167
Philips 155, 159, 162, 163, 164-166, 167, 170, 177, 178
- Gloeilampenfabriek *177*
- Office for Lighting advice 177
- Philips Pavilion 155, 159, *162*, 163, *164-166*, 167, 170, 178
- Woningbouwvereniging 83
Planjer, J.I. 57
Plano 74
Poissy 65
Polano, Sergio 33
Porphyrios, Demitri 23
Postmodernism 29, 33, 256
Praktische Studie, Civil engineering and architecture student society 47
Pugin, A.W.N. 24

r

Radermacher Schorer, M.R. 56, 60, 62, 63
Rand, Ayn 233
- *The Fountainhead* 233
Rasch, Heinz and Bodo 139, 151
- *Der Stuhl* 151, *151*
Rebel, Ben 33
Renaissance 32, 120, 167, 170
Reich, Lilly 185, 188
Rietveld, Bep 63
Rietveld, G.Th.

- Armchair 'First Model' 144, *144*
- Armchair A.M. Hartog 140
- Armchair Metz & Co 144, 151
- Birza Chair 144
- Chair SS Nieuw Amsterdam 145
- Children's chair *37*, 41
- Cinema seat Vreeburg 149
- Crate Chair 144, *150*, 152
- Danish Chair 227, *229*
- Dutch pavilion Brussels 155, *160*
- Highchair Schelling 53, 54
- Lanjouw (Hopmi Chair) 144, *148*, 149, *149*, *150*, 151, 152, *153*
- Military chair 151
- Rattan chair 232
- Red-Blue Chair 14, 16, 23, 144, 195, *197*, 198, 202, 253, 256

- Slatted armchair 249
- Steltman Chair 249
- Tube-framed chair 54, 141, *142*, 144, 151, 152
- Upright chair *143*, 144
- Wire Chair 227, *231*
- Zigzag Chair 54, 144, *147*, 151
Conversions
- Goud- en Zilversmids Compagnie, Amsterdam 51, 202, *203*, 244
- Jewellery shop Cornelis Begeer, Utrecht 51, 99, *100*
- Jewellery shop Steltman, The Hague 249, *249*
- Lanjouw garage 144
- Lunchroom and ice-cream factory Van Beurden, Utrecht 185, *187*
- Record, Utrecht 245
- Verrijn Stuart House, Utrecht 24, 75, 189, *189*
- Vreeburg Cinema 60, *61*, 104, 149, 182, *184*, 185, *185*, 178
- H. van der Vuurst de Vries garage, Utrecht see chauffeur's dwelling
- E. Wessels & Son, Utrecht 219
- Zaudy, Wesel 178, *179*

Exhibition design
- 'Architectuur Schilderkunst Beeldhouwkunst' 57
- 'Así es Holanda' 162, *163*
- 'Centenary Holland' 234
- 'De Stijl 1917–1928' 21, *236-239*, 254
- 'De Stijl 1917–1930' *242*, *243*
- Dutch pavilion, Brussels 155, *160*
- 'Expositie van Utrechtsche jongeren' 56, 57, *58*
- 'Factoren van het Zichtbare' 155, *167*, *168*, *170*, *171*, *173*
- 'Juryfreie Kunstschau Berlin' 208, *209*, *210*
- 'Rietveld. Bijdrage tot vernieuwing der bouwkunst' 21, *172*, *173*
- Venice Biennale, Greek Pavilion 21
Exhibition pavilions
- Dutch Pavilion, Venice Biennale 115, 155, *157*, 244

- Philips Pavilion, Brussels 155, *162*, 163, *164*, *165*, 167, 170, 178
- Sonsbeek Pavilion, Arnhem 24, 28, *114*, 115, 155, *156*, 244, *246*
Furniture
- Cradle Johanna Karin Schelling 53
- Cupboard 72, 100, 191, 216, 239
- Radio cabinet for M.R. Radermacher Schorer *62*, 63, 191
- Room and furniture for G. ten Doesschate 54
- Sideboard and two armchairs for P. Elling 56
- H.J.M. Weve 54
Graphic design
- Birth announcement Anne Schelling *52*, 53
- Birth announcement Hendrikus Johannes Witteveen 53, *55*
- Bookplate J.H. Maronier 53
- Cover *De Gemeenschap* 59, 60
- Exhibition poster 'De Stijl' exhibition Rome 239, *242*, *243*
- Invitation 'Expositie van Utrechtsche Jongeren' *58*

Holiday home, see Summer house
Houses
- Bláha, Best 71, 72
- Chauffeur's dwelling, Utrecht 28, 54, 90, 100, 104, *105*, 106
- Driessen, Arnhem 84, *87*
- Hillebrand, The Hague 28
- House for an architect 28
- Lommen, Wassenaar *102*, 103, 219
- Nijland, Bilthoven 51, 60, 104, *104*
- Rapsodie House, Santpoort 104
- Schröder House, Utrecht 14, 16, 21, 23, 25, 28, 29, 33, *34*, 35, 46, 54, 57, 63, 65-67, *70*, 71, 72, 75, *77*, 79, 95, 100, 119, 120, 124, *124*, *125*, *197*, 204-206, *207*, 216, *216*, 219, 225, 239, *240*, 244, 253, 254

- Slegers, Velp 84, *86*
- Stoop, Velp 83, 84, *85*
- Theissing, Utrecht 90, *92*, 104
- Van Daalen, Bergeijk 71, 90, *91*
- Van Dantzig, Santpoort 71, 72, *73*
- Van den Doel, Ilpendam 28, 71, 72, *73*, 90, *93*, 121, *122*
- Van Slobbe, Heerlen 71, 90, *94*, 104
- Visser, Bergeijk 84, *88*, *89*, 90

Housing
- Erasmuslaan, Utrecht 29, 54, 57, 67, *70*, *78*, 79, *141*, 189
- Gorinchem 110, *113*
- Public housing 32, 43, 227
- Robijnhof, Utrecht 110, *110*
- Schumannstraat, Utrecht 29
- Small houses 42
- Standardized dwellings 38, *39*, 40, 43, 47, 106
- Utrecht-Hoograven 51, 84
- Utrecht-Tolsteeg 51
- Wiener Werkbundsiedlung 29, *78*

Interior design
- Bathroom L. Brom 189
- Cabin *SS Nieuw Amsterdam* 144
- Consultation room A.M. Hartog 23, 54, *140*, 141, 189, *190*, 254
- R.J. Harrenstein 54, 217, 219
- Press room UNESCO building 244, *248*
- Room Truus Schröder-Schräder 54
- Show interior ideal flat Expo '58 *158*, 159

- Julianahal Utrecht Royal Trade Fair 167, 178, *181*
- Lamp designs 54, 189, *190*, 191, 217

Lectures
- Centraal Museum Utrecht architecture exhibition 173
- Honorary Degree TH Delft 29, 35
- 'International Course in New Architecture' 47
- *Voordracht gehouden door architect G. Rietveld op 20 februari 1959 te Delft* 155, 170

Museums
- De Zonnehof, Amersfoort 115
- Van Gogh Museum, Amsterdam 14

Nagele, sketches 28, 167
Portrait Anthonie Begeer 53

Publications
- 'Inzicht' 40
- 'Nieuwe Zakelijkheid in Nederlandse architectuur' 47, 170
- 'Nut, constructie: (schoonheid: kunst)' 38, *39*
- *Periodiek in briefvorm* 43, 45, 56

Schools
- Applied Arts School, Amsterdam 117, 124, 233
- Fine Arts Academy, Arnhem 117, 124, *130*, 131

- Gerrit Rietveld Academy, Amsterdam *117*, 124, *126*, *128*, *130*, 131, *137*, *137*, 233
- Music School with two apartments, Zeist 54

Schrale Beton, office 115, 178, *180*
Stereoscopic cinema 185, *185*

Summer houses
- De Braamakkers see Verrijn Stuart
- Lanjouw, Loosdrecht 144
- Markelo 110
- Van Ravesteyn-Hintzen, Breukelen 104, *123*
- Verrijn Stuart, Breukelen 28, 227, *227*

Textile Factory De Ploeg, Bergeijk 28, 90, *116*, 117, 119, *119*

Mgr. M.I. Verriet Institute, Curaçao *114*, 115
Rietveld, J.C. (Jan) 21, 158, 159
Rietveld, Wim (brother) 38
Rietveld, Wim (son) 158, 159
Rijksmuseum Kröller-Müller 32, 33, 239
Risselada, Max 71, 225
Rodchenko, M. 219
Rodijk, G.H. 29, 83, 84, 100, 103, 104, 115, 189
Roosenburg, Dirk 177
Rosenberg, Léonce 25, 208
Rothuizen, E.J. (later Rotshuizen) 120
- *Het dak* 120
Rotterdam 25, *26*, 32, 41, 53, 55, 106, 133, 141, 175, *176*, *208*, 234, 254, 256
Rotterdamsche Kring, De 213
Ruskin, J. 24, 99

S

SA (*Sovremennaia Arkhitektura*) 217, *218*, 219, *220*
Saarinen, Eero 81
Sandberg, Willem 233-235
Santpoort 73, 100, 104
Sartoris, A. 25, 28
Schaafsma, H. 21
Schama, Simon 90, 95
Scharroo, P.W. 99
Schelling, Anne *52*, 53
Schelling, H.G.J. 51, *52*, 53, 54, 56, 63

- Amstel Station 53
- Muiderpoort Station 53
- Naarden-Bussum Station *52*, 53
Schelling, Johanna Karin 53
Schellink, Sam 56
Schilp, Cor 57
Schindler, Rudolph 81
Schopenhauer, A. 38, 40

Schräder, An 54, 63, 217
Schröder, Binnert 117
Schröder, Frits 54, 56
Schröder, Han *240*
Schröder-Schräder, Truus 35, 43, 51, 54, 56, 63, 66, 67, 72, 77, 106, 117, 151, 189, 191, 195, 197, 202, 219, 225, 233

Schuitema, Paul 57
Schwitters, Kurt 54, 195
SDAP 182
Second World War 14, 24, 25, 29, 32, 33, 51, 53, 77, 79, 81, 83, 106, 115, 219, 224, 227
Segal, Walter 24
Shell 155
Shirokov, Grigorii P. 219
- *Kak ty zjivesch* 219
Siemens 177
Singelenberg, Pieter 35, 244
Skidmore, Owings and Merrill see SOM
Slegers, Piet 84
Smithson, Alison and Peter 32, 202
Socialist Artists' Circle (SKK) 219
Sokolov, Boris A. 215, 217
SOM 133, 134
- Hanover Manufacturer's Trust 189
- Lever House 133, *134*
Soriano, Raphael 81
Spinoza, B. 38
Staal, Arthur 202
Stam, Mart 23, 24, 53, 54, 57, 67, 133, 139, 141, 176, 216, *216*
- Model S33 *139*
Standardmöbel 144
Stedelijk Museum, Amsterdam 21, 32, 33, 54, 57, 144, 216, 219, 233-235, 236, 239
Steel-tube furniture 25, 28
STICUSA 115
Strens, Eugène 53
Stroitel'naja promyshlennost' 214, 216
Stroitel'stvo Moskvy 215
Stuttgart 46, 144, 185, 188
Stuttgart Werkbund 46, 185

Struve Gallery 254
Suprematism 213, 216
Surinam 115
Switzerland 144
Szénássy, I.L. 23, 26
Székely, Zóltan 104

t

Tafuri, Manfredo 23, 29, 32
- *History of World Architecture* 32

Tagore, Rabindranath 40, 53
Taut, Bruno 54, 57, 195, 225
- 'Wollen und Wirken' 57

Ter Braak, Menno 60
Tessenow, Heinrich 39-41, 43
- *Hausbau und dergleichen* 39, 41
- *Handwerk und Kleinstadt* 41

The Hague 28, 32, 54, 147, 178, 182, 183, 208, 209, 249
Theissing, E.M. 104
Tolstoy, Aleksei N. 224
Toorop, Charley 54, 56, 57, 60, 63
Trachtenberg, Marvin 254
Treib, M. 155, 159
Troy, Nancy 207, 256
Tube chairs 23, 54, 60, 139, 141, 144, 149, 151
Tubular-steel/steel-tube furniture 25, 28

u

Uiterwaal, Jo 54, 56
Uiterwaal, Stef 56
UMS see Utrechtse Machinale Stoel- en Meubelfabriek
Unilever 155
USA 25, 63, 120, 177, 191, 233-235, 253, 254
Utrecht 16, 21, 28, 29, 37, 51, 53, 54, 56-58, 60, 61, 63, 65, 70, 77-79, 84, 90, 92, 99, 100, 104, 105, 110, 124, 144, 149, 167, 172, 173, 178, 181, 182, 184, 187, 189, 195, 201, 202, 204, 206, 207, 213, 216, 219, 225, 240, 245, 253, 254, 256, 260

Utrecht Beautification Committee 51
Utrecht Museum Committee 51
Utrecht Royal Trade Fair 167, 178, *181*
Utrecht University 14, 16, 54, 196
Utrechtsch Dagblad 57
Utrechtsche Algemeene Brandwaarborg Maatschappij 60
Utrechtsche Filmliga 60, 213
Utrechtsche Kunstkring 53, 57, 60, 63
Utrechtse Machinale Stoel- en Meubelfabriek (UMS) 149

v

Van de Velde, H. 173
Van den Broek, J.H. (Joop) 29, 106, 155, 159, 234, 235
Van der Kaa, H. 106
Van der Kloes, J.A. 99
Van der Leck, Bart 195, 202, 213
Van der Leeuw, C.H. 81
Van der Vlugt, L.C. 67, 133, 175, 176, 254
Van der Vuurst de Vries, H. 54, 56, 106
Van der Woud, Auke 35
Van der Zweep, Douwe 54, 56
Van Dijk, Hans 249
Van Dillen, J. 29, 104, 126, 128, 130, 131, 137, 170
Van Doesburg, Theo 17, 21, 23-25, 28, 29, 32, 33, 38, 40, 54, 83, 195, 196, 198, 201, 202, 207, 208, 209, 211, 213, 216, 234, 235, 244, 254

- Hôtel Particulier (with C. van Eesteren) 208, 216
- Monument for Leeuwarden 216
- *Tot een beeldende architectuur* 23
- Villa Rosenberg (with C. van Eesteren) 21, 25, 208

Van Eesteren, Cornelis 21, 25, 32, 40, 207, 208, 216, 234, 235, 239

- Hôtel Particulier 208, 216
- Villa Rosenberg (with Th. van Doesburg) 21, 25, 208

Van Eyck, Aldo 32, 84, 88, 90, 202
Van Leusden, Willem 54, 56, 63, 202
Van Loghem, J.B. 103, 106
Van Lohuizen, Th. K. 32
Van Luijn, Dick van 56
Van Ravesteyn, Sybold 53, 54, 56, 57, 60, 63
- Chair 53
- Interior for M.R. Radermacher Schorer 60, 63

Van Ravesteyn-Hintzen, Dora 56, 104, 123
Van 't Hoff, Robert 24, 37, 100, 195, 216, 253
- Stair Pole 216
- Villa Huis ter Heide (Villa Henny) 100
Van Tijen, W. 63, 81, 106, 185
Van Tricht, J. (Johan) 29, 126, 128, 130, 131, 137, 170
Van Velzen, Th. 32
Van Vriesland, Victor E. 56
Van Walsem, H.F. 155, 159

Van Weerden-Griek, Hans 234
Van Zijl, Ida 29
Vantongerloo, Georges 195, 198, 211
Varèse, Edgar 159, 167
Velp 83, 85, 86
Venice 21, 115, 155, 156, 244
Vereeniging Het Utrechtsch Museum van Kunstnijverheid 99
Verrijn Stuart, C.A. 56
Vienna 29, *78*, 79
Viollet-le-Duc, E.E. 99
Visser, Martin 84, 90
VKhUTEIN 217
Vkhutemas 217
VOKS 224
Voor de Kunst 51, 54, 56, 57, *58*, 60, 63

Vygodskii, L. 219

w

Wadsworth Atheneum Museum 254
Walker Art Center 33, 254
Wassenaar 102, 103, 219
Weissenhof 144
World's Fair
- Barcelona 178
- Brussels 155, *160*, 178
Wesel 178
Weve, H.J.M. 54, 56
White, Michael 28
Wiener, company 131
Wiener Werkbund 29, 78
Wiessing, H. 56
Wijdeveld, H. Th. 253
Wils, Jan 21, 25, 38, 195
Wisconsin 83
Witteveen, Hendrikus Johannes 53
Witteveen, W.G. 53-55
Wölfflin, Heinrich 25

Wohnküche 46
Wright, Frank Lloyd 16, 66, 75, 81-84, 173, 225, 253, 254
- Fallingwater, Mill Run 83
- Herbert Jacobs House, Madison *82*, 83
- Johnson Wax Building, Racine 83
- Kaufmann House see Fallingwater
- Prairie houses 66
- 'Tomorrow's small house' 83
- Usonian Houses 83, 84
Wuster, William 81

Xenakis, Iannis 163, 166, 167, 178

Zadkine, Ossip 159, 167
Zanstra, P. 106
Zeist 21, 54, 115
Zevi, Bruno 23, 25, 26, 28
Zwart, Piet 57
Zwolle 114, 115, 117, 178, 180

Contents

14 Foreword

Rob Dettingmeijer, Marie-Thérèse van Thoor, Ida van Zijl
16 Every Generation Gets the Rietveld It Deserves

Rietveld in Theoretical Perspective

Rob Dettingmeijer
20 Rietveld and the Writing of Architecture History

Dolf Broekhuizen
36 An Awakening Consciousness. The Early Development of Rietveld's Theoretical Approach

Social Context: Clients and Commissions

Roman Koot
50 Rietveld's Network in Utrecht

Wolf Tegethoff
64 Rietveld's Residential Concepts. From Manifesto to Domestic Privacy

Maristella Casciato
76 Dutch 'Case Study' Houses. Rietveld's Contribution to Modern Living in Perspective

Articulating Space: Materials, Techniques and Mass Production

Marieke Kuipers
98 Materialization in Rietveld's Architecture

Hielkje Zijlstra
118 Flat Roofs and Open Corners

Jurjen Creman and Otakar Máčel
138 The Hopmi Chair and Rietveld's Other Pre-War Tubular Furniture

Marie-Thérèse van Thoor
154 Factors of the Visible. Rietveld's Ideas about the Renewal of Architecture

Dietrich Neumann
174 Artificial Lighting as a Design Task for the Modern Architect

De Stijl and Styles

Marijke Kuper
194 Rietveld and De Stijl

Ivan Nevzgodin
212 Perspective from the East: Rietveld's Impact on the Soviet Union

Ida van Zijl
226 De Stijl as Style

Approaches to Rietveld

Anthony Alofsin
252 Rietveld's Influence in America: the Chair and the House

Ole Bouman
258 Honest Designs

Foreword

Gerrit Rietveld (1888-1964) was a 'study-artist'. By studying goals, forms and materials, he had the ability, time after time, to further master beauty and function and to define it anew. This is the essence of his innovative designs. To study is also to discover oneself, or as Rietveld put it, to realize one's own existence. Swimming against the current of social and political circumstances during the economic crisis of the 1930s in the Netherlands, the Second World War, post-war reconstruction and the recession in the 1950s, Rietveld nevertheless kept on experimenting, as if this were exactly what enabled him to go beyond circumstances and eventually surmount them. What's more, experimenting became second nature to him, he gave modernisman extra dimension with it, an interpretation of his own that we nowadays call 'social design'.

Rietveld imparted new élan and quality to simple and modest living. His designs for furniture, interiors and buildings are equally simple, but this is precisely the source of their grandeur and grace. Seldom do artists realize such a unique series of works in their lifetime. With Rietveld, that series is incredibly rich, beginning with the famous Red-Blue Chair and the Schröder House and ending with the Van Gogh Museum. Between the realization of these works were short and long phases of technical and practical research, which Rietveld combined with theory and reflection as he went along. Alongside Rietveld himself, and perhaps even more than Rietveld himself, others who admired him attempted to give his work a place within the developments in art, design and architecture.

Starting in 2006, collaborators at Utrecht University, Delft University of Technology and the Centraal Museum Utrecht conducted a collective investigation into 'Rietveld's Universe'. In order to draw a more nuanced and complete picture of Rietveld, they related his work and methodology to his immediate surroundings and colleagues and placed it within the broader context of the social developments of his time. The project has resulted in the publication of this book, to which scholars from the Netherlands and abroad have contributed, and in an eponymous exhibition that is opening in parallel to it that has been organized in close collaboration with the Netherlands Architecture Institute.

Our combined efforts to place Gerrit Rietveld's oeuvre within his time also makes it possible to draw that line to our own time and perhaps even continue it into the future. We want to formulate themes and topics that make our time intelligible, inspired by the work and views of individuals from previous eras. The world, our industrial culture, and the art, design and architecture within it have become more complex because of the nature of the processes in which they are manifested, not because of the artists, designers and architects themselves. In fact, artists intuitively seek and find a way to understand this complexity and make it comprehensible. Rietveld was a pioneer in this. His work evokes the function and essence of art, design and architecture. He has influenced the development of these disciplines all over the world. This book and the accompanying exhibition make his oeuvre newly accessible.

Our thanks go to Ida van Zijl, the initiator and project leader of 'Rietveld's Universe', Rob Dettingmeijer, Marie-Thérèse van Thoor and Linda Vlassenrood, who are responsible for the substance of the exhibition and/or book. Furthermore, we would like to thank authors Anthony Alofsin, Dolf Broekhuizen, Maristella Casciato, Jurjen Creman, Roman Koot, Marieke Kuipers, Marijke Kuper, Otakar Máčel, Dietrich Neumann, Ivan Nevzgodin, Wolf Tegethoff and Hielkje Zijlstra for their contributions and also for their valuable advice and suggestions, whereby we also wish to commemorate Paul Overy, who was involved in the project from the start until his death in 2008. Vera de Lange, Nora Leijen, Joris Roovers, Froukje Vermeulen and Yao Zhou have contributed as student trainees in various ways, but all with great enthusiasm. Finally, we wish to thank members of the recommending committee Wiljan van den Akker, Carel Blotkamp, Hubert-Jan Henket, Wytze Patijn and Aleid Wolfsen; public and private lenders; foundations and sponsors, our partner the Municipality of Utrecht and the Ministry of Education, Cultural Affairs and Science.

Ole Bouman, Director of the Netherlands Architecture Institute
Edwin Jacobs, Director of the Centraal Museum Utrecht

Every Generation Gets the Rietveld It Deserves

'From now on, the question as to the position Rietveld deserves in history can be expected to get a well-founded answer,' wrote the directors of the Centraal Museum and the Netherlands Architecture Institute in 1992 in the foreword to the catalogue on his oeuvre, *Gerrit Th. Rietveld 1888-1964. The Complete Works*. Almost 15 years later, that challenge was taken up with the starting of an investigation into 'Rietveld's Universe'. For two days in November 2006, experts from the Netherlands and abroad discussed questions and departure points for a research project to result in a book and an exhibition. The title indicated that we, the initiators, defined the subject broadly and wanted to give an answer to a question that had already been raised in 1975 by Reyner Banham, on page 69 of his *Age of the Masters. A Personal View of Modern Architecture*: 'No-one, not even his official biographer, Theodor M. Brown, has yet been able to suggest why this very competent, but otherwise unremarkable provincial figure should *twice* [the Red-Blue Chair and the Schröder House] have contributed such symptomatic objects to the rise of the Modern Movement, and at his death in 1964 he still remained an enigmatic but revered figure.'

In the research and study devoted to Rietveld in the following years at Utrecht University and Delft University of Technology, his universe was investigated as broadly as possible. While social developments, technological innovations and historic events were considered relevant, attention was also given to Rietveld's personal universe, his background, his network and his worldview. The last of these became the central focus of the project: How did Rietveld experience his world, how did he react to his environment, and how did he manifest this in his ideas and work? The key element in this approach was the creative process. Using that as a starting point, the authors, many of whom had participated in the first discussion in 2006, could give a new analysis of his work. This book starts off with an exploration by Rob Dettingmeijer of the existing historiography on Rietveld: How and where did the image arise of a simple furniture maker who dumbfounded the world with one chair and one house? Next, by contrast, comes an essay by Dolf Broekhuizen, who describes the early development of Rietveld's ideas. Broekhuizen does what Brown, Banham and most writers on Rietveld refrained from doing: he takes Rietveld's words and writings seriously and relates them to his oeuvre. Following this, other authors examine various influences and phenomena that are important for Rietveld's work. Roman Koot points out that a rich world of the arts existed in the secluded provincial city of Utrecht. Perhaps that art scene at the beginning of the twentieth century was so lively because at that point Utrecht was breaking out of its isolation with growing fervour and developing into a national traffic junction, industrial city and university centre. Rietveld's first clients lived in this environment. Possibly this is the origin of the 'search for space', an important theme in Rietveld's work. As the essay by Dietrich Neumann shows, the light in the dark grew increasingly brighter, literally and figuratively, due to the new possibilities provided by electric lighting, in which Rietveld was intensely interested as a designer. Figuratively, Rietveld's universe expanded through new scientific discoveries that inspired many artists, designers and architects. Maristella Casciato and Wolfgang Tegethoff show that Rietveld was very specifically searching for a new kind of housing. In this regard, he measures up to other greats of modern architecture such as Ludwig Mies van der Rohe and Frank Lloyd Wright.

Other essayists in this book investigate how Rietveld used the technologies of his day in order to come up with innovative designs. Rietveld's approach has as little to do with a furniture maker's handwork as Mies van der Rohe's work and ambitions have to do with the profession of bricklayer. Rietveld continually tried to create space in a manner that is not possible (or not yet), sometimes at the expense of the client, while someone like Mies van der Rohe primarily offered his clients luxurious perfection, which he sometimes could only surpass with the greatest difficulty in the next commission. Marieke Kuipers, Hielkje Zijlstra and Marie-Thérèse van Thoor each give a part of the answer to questions on Rietveld's attempts at innovation in architecture. That experimental approach is also the basis of Rietveld's artistry in his designs for furniture, as Jurjen Creman and Otakar Máčel make clear in their joint contribution.

The form that Rietveld chose for his designs was both innovative and a product of its times. His name is connected with De Stijl and the *Nieuwe Bouwen* (the Dutch manifestation of the Modern Movement in architecture), although De Stijl is no longer to be defined unequivocally. As the result of more research having been done on this movement, it appears that the idea of De Stijl as a coherent international avant-garde is primarily the construction of one person, Theo van Doesburg.

After their first, comprehensive inventory of Rietveld's oeuvre in 1992, Marijke Kuper and Ida van Zijl now each have individually tried to place Rietveld in De Stijl and examine his relation to that movement. Ivan Nevzgodin convincingly shows that in the countries of the former Eastern Europe, Rietveld's specific interpretation of De Stijl attracted many followers. The question that inevitably rises during an investigation into Rietveld's significance is the relevance of his work for this day and age. At the end of the book, two authors give their view of Rietveld's topicality. Anthony Alofsin concludes with the assumption that Rietveld's innovative qualities could be of great significance for the future, and Ole Bouman suggests that the moral dimension of Rietveld's modernism might gain in currency in the twenty-first century.

In the Netherlands, many people still find Rietveld's work inspiring. For others, he represents a phase of modernism from a far-off past. Wanting to write the history of someone who aimed to serve the future and only saw his work as a contribution to a development would seem a paradox. That is why this book and the accompanying exhibition examine the fragile, the experimental and the tentative aspects of his work.

Rob Dettingmeijer
Marie-Thérèse van Thoor
Ida van Zijl

Schröder House, Utrecht
14, 16, 21, 23, 25, 28, 29, 33, *34*,
35, 46

'Nut, constructie: (schoonheid: kunst)'
38, *39*

i10
38, *39*, 40, 41, 42, 43, 46, 47

Barr, Alfred
28, 30

Rietveld in Theoretical Perspective

Van Eesteren, Cornelis
21, 25, 32, 40

Brown, Theodore M.
16, 26, 35

De Stijl
23, 24, 28, 32, 37, 37, 38, 40

Rob Dettingmeijer

Rietveld and the Writing of Architecture History

H. Schaafsma, *Gerrit Rietveld. Bouwmeester van een nieuwe tijd*, Utrecht 1959 Published by Utrecht city council on the occasion of Rietveld's 70th birthday

[1] Schaafsma, 1959, 62.

[2] Bakema et al., 1958.

[3] This had its origins in a discussion about design that Rietveld had for a short time with Jan Wils, Cornelis van Eesteren and Theo van Doesburg, and in the creation of a scale model of a Villa Rosenberg, which played a crucial role in the beginning of what is sometimes called the early period of De Stijl. For the most complete description with the widest range of bibliographical references, see K. Somer and V. van Rossem, 'De Stijl en de stad' in: Bock 2001, 53-208:106-130; 166-179. Several key exhibitions were held in 1951 and 1952 at the Stedelijk Museum in Amsterdam, the Greek pavilion at the Venice Biennale, and the Museum of Modern Art in New York, where Rietveld not only made suggestions about the layout, but also produced replicas of his own work and models for other people, including models of the Villa Rosenberg and of designs by J.J.P. Oud. See Küper and Van Zijl 1992, 251.

[4] A top-100 list of buildings after 1940 compiled by Van Santen et al. 2007 includes three designs by Gerrit and one by his son J.C. Rietveld. The latest edition of Groenendijk and Vollaard 2006 includes 27 structures associated with the name of G. Th. Rietveld, only two less than for W.M. Dudok, the leader in this respect. J.C. Rietveld is also well represented, with four structures to his name.

[5] For instance, J.B. Bakema, *Van stoel tot stad. Een verhaal over mensen en ruimte*, Zeist/Antwerp 1964, is about sitting, standing and walking, but not actually about chairs. This little book, based on a television series, is a fine example of a history that examines the broad sweep from the first primitive hut to the megastructures of the future. Bakema also provided much of the text for the Rietveld birthday exhibition at the Centraal Museum Utrecht in 1958.

[6] Most recently, H. Engel, 'Theo van Doesburg & the Destruction of Architectural Theory, in: Fabre and Wintgens 2009, 36-43: 39. In 2008, the same observation led the Centraal Museum to title its summer display 'Rietvelds ranke ruimtedieren en andere creaturen van de Avant-garde' (Rietveld's slender spatial animals and other creatures of the avant-garde), 5 July-16 October 2008. Another example

He hesitated for a long time before he said yes, since there was so much other work to be done. But because the exhibition could convey an impression of the entire development of the new architecture, he finally agreed.[1]

De Stijl was mentioned only briefly, almost offhandedly, in Rietveld's 70th-birthday retrospective 'Rietveld. Bijdrage tot vernieuwing der bouwkunst' (Rietveld. Contribution to the renewal of architecture) at the Centraal Museum in Utrecht in 1958, an event staged largely by Rietveld himself.[2] Nonetheless, Rietveld's reputation has grown ever more tightly interwoven with narratives and views about De Stijl. This is partly because he was involved in all the De Stijl exhibitions held during his lifetime, even developing new versions of historic designs for them.[3] Likewise, the Schröder House is included on the World Heritage List as an icon of 'De Stijl architecture'. In cultural heritage management and the art trade, Rietveld's star is still on the rise. He is seldom left out of travel guides, and some are even devoted entirely to his buildings.[4] His furniture, which is at least as well known as his architecture, is still in production, in an ever-expanding range of models and variations. Although there are other architects who designed furniture, in Rietveld's case, the transition from chair to city seems especially fluid.[5] As early as 1920, Van Doesburg remarked on how exceptional Rietveld's furniture was, saying that it formed a separate category between sculpture and architecture.[6]

Rietveld's towering reputation is not nearly as visible in late twentieth-century historical writing about architecture. The attempt to write one grand narrative about the modernization of society and architecture, as the expression of a *Zeitgeist* or the inevitable march of history, was then seen by some as a failed project and by others as dangerously misguided. The age of the grand narratives seemed to have ended, and in the historical

21

Affiche 'Rietvelds ranke ruimtedieren + andere creaturen van de avant-garde', Summer exhibition Centraal Museum, 2008

Th. van Doesburg, 'Schilderkunst van Giorgio de Chirico en een stoel van Rietveld', *De Stijl* 3 (1920) 5, 46

dat zij maar met één wezenlijke beeldingswaarde te doen hebben: harmonie door verhouding. En ieder geeft aan dit ééne wezenlijke en universeele der beeldende kunst uitdrukking met zijn kunstmiddel. Eén en hetzelfde dus op steeds andere wijze.
De schilder: door kleurverhouding. De beeldhouwer: door volume-verhouding. De architect: door verhouding van omsloten ruimten. De meubelontwerper: door onomsloten (= open) ruimteverhouding.
Het ontwerp van Oud is gebouwd op een (in enkele onderdeelen gewijzigd) grondplan van den architect S a a l. De opbouw was daarmede reeds eenigermate vastgelegd.
Voorzoover het ontwerp van Oud nog aesthetisch opzet vertoont (b.v. in de détailplastiek) is het nog decoratief en niet onopzettelijk uit den platten grond (die wij in een der volgende nummers zullen afdrukken) ontstaan. Elke behoefte naar détailplastiek zal verdwijnen wanneer algemeen begrepen zal worden, dat slechts het vlak en de rechte lijn het maximum van plastische uitdrukking mogelijk maken.
Boog tegenover rechte lijn, schuine lijn tegenover boog enz., zijn nimmer bij machte evenwichtige verhouding, zoo bepaald en onveranderlijk tot uitdrukking te brengen als vlak en rechte lijn. Ook dit besef komt in de eenheid der werken op bijlagen II, V, VI en VII tot uitdrukking.

SCHILDERKUNST VAN GIORGIO DE CHIRICO EN EEN STOEL VAN RIETVELD.

Verschil en overeenkomst.
Verschil in bedoeling, in expressie, in middelen.
Overeenkomst in metaphysische aanvoeling en mathematische aanduiding van ruimten.
In beide: ruimten door ruimten begrensd.
Ruimtedoordringing.
Ruimtemystiek.
Bij Chirico's schilderkunst, opzettelijk — vervloeken wij toch elke kunst met voorbedachte rade! — bij Rietvelds stoel onopzettelijk, noodwendig, klaar, reëel;
'N RANK RUIMTEDIER.
In de „Solutidine" van de Chirico (Zie: Chirico-album No. 12):
op den voorgrond de mathematische mensch — ruimten beheerschend en door ruimten beheerscht. Met elk vlak, hoek of punt daarom, daaraan of daarneven een ruimte-afmeting g e s y m b o l i s e e r d.
RUIMTE-ANATOMIE.
en als contrast tot den mathematischen mensch in het ruimteweb gevangen:
een nuchtere open ruimte met fabriek en rechthoekige pijp daarbij.
Rietvelds stoel: onopzettelijke, maar onmeêdoogende verwerking van open ruimten met als contrast: **NOODZAAK** **ZITTEN** **STOEL**
materieele beperking tegenover rijke, onverholen en vaste beelding van open ruimten.
STOEL
stomme welsprekendheid als van een machine.   Th. v. D.

46

literature Rietveld was portrayed, at best, as one more designer in one design movement among many.[7]

Modern Movements in Architecture

The above-mentioned attitude towards Rietveld is exemplified by Kenneth Frampton (b. 1930) in his 'critical history'. In the book *Modern Architecture. A Critical History*, many copies of which are still being sold, he traces the development of contemporary architecture: its roots in the nineteenth century, its maturation in the twentieth, and the continuation of the tendencies in question in our own day. Frampton supports his narrative by reference to a spectrum of movements and tendencies, including some that he argues still have present-day potential and others that are purely of historical interest. Ever since its first edition in 1980, this book has treated Rietveld primarily as a member of the historical movement De Stijl.[8] Yet the message of current research seems to be that – in contrast with the minor role allotted to him by Frampton in his chapters 'New Objectivity' and 'The Vicissitudes of Ideology: CIAM and Team X' – Rietveld in fact also played a considerable role during his life and even after his death in these movements and periods.[9] Frampton reserves most of his praise for the iconic Red-Blue Chair, but also mentions other 'modest pieces of furniture' and includes an illustration of Rietveld's sideboard (1919). He suggests that it would have been difficult to anticipate just how much influence Rietveld's furniture would have on architecture. Frampton also writes very admiringly of the consultation room of the family doctor A.M. Hartog (1922), commenting that as in later work by Mondrian, it evokes 'an infinite series of coordinates in space'.[10] Surprisingly, he goes on to call the Schröder House 'in many respects a realization of Van Doesburg's *Tot een beeldende architectur* [sic] (16 points of a Plastic Architecture)', and does not examine it in relation to the further development of Rietveld's household objects into architecture.

The description of the Schröder House as a unique architectural example of what was primarily an avant-garde movement is found as early as 1960 in the book *Theory and Design in the First Machine Age* by Reyner Banham (1922-1988). He contends that the house 'was, and remains, the only Elementarist structure to be built in permanent form'.[11] This claim is part of an argument that might be described as a 'history of the immediate present', as defined by Anthony Vidler in 2008: a description of the present from the perspective of the past, rather than the other way round.[12] Banham's evaluation of the significance of De Stijl contains a note of irony: 'The spirit of the times in the plastic arts was largely the creation of an interaction of Cubist forms and Futurist ideas . . . , as were most of the movements it encountered or allied itself to. Much of *de Stijl's* importance lay in its being first in the field with an organised body of ideas, a magazine and an energetic impresario [Van Doesburg].'[13] Throughout this book, the futurists are the true modernists, because they were the only ones to recognize the importance of technology as the literal and figurative dynamo of the modern age. Banham accuses De Stijl, the Bauhaus, and even Le Corbusier of not really understanding the technology of the first machine age.

Rietveld is the object of still greater scorn. Banham argues that Rietveld led modern furniture design into a dead end, which it escaped only when Mart Stam came along with his Steel-Tube Chair.[14] Banham says that he

is Szénássy 1969, 8-15, 8, 9. In view of space limitations and their different pattern of historiographical development, it proved impossible to deal with all the individual articles about Rietveld's chairs and other non-architectural designs in this article. For a survey of his non-architectural objects, see Vöge 1993. For Dutch-language publications by Vöge and many others with useful notes containing further references, see the CD-ROM or website *Jong Holland Index* 1984-2000, http://www.jong-holland.nl/engindex.htm, www.jong-holland.nl/engindex.htm, and on the possible continuation of this website as an e-magazine, see http://www.jong-holland.blogspot.com, www.jong-holland.blogspot.com (accessed 2 January, 2010); for references to the literature, see Byars 2004, 626-627; in Dutch, see Huygen 2007/2008.

[7] For discussions concerning my contribution I would like to thank the 'Rietveld team' – M.-Th. van Thoor, I. van Zijl, and the students in the research working groups for the BA in Art History, 2007-2009 – for many inspiring conversations. I used the most recent book on historiography with much pleasure and admiration: D. Arnold, E.A. Ergut and B.Turan Özkaya, *Rethinking Architectural Historiography*, London/New York 2006. The fragmentation of history in general and architecture history in particular has coincided almost completely with the emergence of contemporary architecture theory. See K.M. Hays (ed.), *Architecture Theory since 1968*, New York 1998, X-XV.

[8] Frampton 1980, Part II: A critical history 1836-1967, chapters 15, 16. Early in his career, Frampton appreciated the difficulty of tracing a continued line of development in modern architecture. In the 1960s, he even considered giving up on his historical surveys. See *Architectural Design* 52 (1982) 7/8, 4, for which he was the guest editor, contributing several essays of his own but also inviting Alan Colquhoun, David Dunster, Kurt W. Forster, Rafael Moneo, Carlos Perez Gomez, Demitri Porphyrios, Manfredo Tafuri and Bruno Zevi to offer their critical reflections on his project. Frampton saw Rietveld as part of De Stijl rather than the New Objectivity. On the meeting where CIAM (Congrès Internationaux d'Architecture Moderne) was established, he wrote, 'in the curious company of Rietveld and Berlage, Stam represented Holland at the foundation meeting'. Frampton 1980, 136.

N. Pevsner, *Outline of European Architecture*, Baltimore, MD 1960 (sixth anniversary edition), 674-675

[9] Frampton 1980, Part III, chapter 3. One exception among general surveys is P. Gössel, *Moderne Architektur A-Z*, also published in an English edition, vol. 2, Cologne etc., 2007, which includes images of the Verrijn Stuart House and the Sonsbeek Pavilion, but shares in the general lack of appreciation for the post-Second World War houses.

[10] Frampton 1980, 144.

[11] Banham 1972, 197.

[12] Vidler 2008, XIV-XV.

[13] Banham 1972, 199.

[14] Ibid., 198. He claims that in fact all Marcel Breuer and Le Corbusier did was to translate Rietveld's chairs into steel and leather. In his view, it was not until some time later that the field found its way out of the dead end, with the cantilever chairs of Mart Stam and Mies van der Rohe.

[15] Ibid., 149: 'This study of de Stijl is heavily indebted to Dr H.L.C. Jaffé's book de Stijl 1917-1931 (Amsterdam, 1956) as all future studies of the movement will be, and also to the personal narratives given me by Rob van 't Hoff, Mart Stam and Walter Segal.'

[16] Letter on the letterhead of *The Architectural Review*, 4 December 1956, typescript, RSA.

[17] Banham 1972, 12 (foreword); he is, of course, referring to the book that – with many, many revisions – nevertheless remained a much-used manual in educational programmes in design and art history. Pevsner 1936; in the title of the second edition (1949) 'Movement' was replaced by 'Design'; the revised, expanded 2005 edition is still in print. On the relationship between Banham and Pevsner, see Vidler 2008, 114-125.

[18] Pevsner 1943. Still available in various editions in many languages. This finds clearest expression in the recurring visual themes of the more lavishly illustrated anniversary edition, 1960, 674-675. Pevsner was also associated with *The Architectural Review* for many years.

369 Utrecht Villa by Gerrit Rietveld, 1924

370 Paris Pavillon de l'Esprit Nouveau at the Exhibition of 1925, by Le Corbusier and Pierre Jeanneret

371 Garches Villa by Le Corbusier and Pierre Jeanneret, 1927

Boulogne-sur-Seine (1926), Garches (1927) as much as to the excellent J. J. P. Oud's working-class housing at and near Rotterdam (1924-30) and to Gropius' Bauhaus buildings at Dessau on which more will be said later. The parallelism to the problems of the cubists in painting is clear, especially in Le Corbusier, who is a painter himself and among those architects who allowed fantasy more play than Gropius and Oud (Rietveld in Holland, c. 1924, Mendelsohn in a pair of semi-detached houses at Berlin already in 1921, Robert Mallet Stevens in Paris c. 1927 etc.). Fantasy of a higher architectural order kept Le Corbusier safely from making a manner out of the cubism of his villas. Already in the Pavillon de l'Esprit Nouveau at the Paris Exhibition of 1925 he allowed a tree to stand inside the house and rise through the roof, and already in his Swiss Students' Hostel in the Cité Universitaire in Paris of 1930 random rubble – a natural, only roughly-treated material – appears side by side with glass and the white concrete and plaster. Nature in the sense of the irrational claimed a re-entry. But for this the time was not yet ripe – and on the whole there is reason to be thankful for that.

based this vision of De Stijl (and presumably that of Rietveld's work as well) on a 1956 study of the movement by the art historian Hans Jaffé (1915-1984) and on personal conversations with Robert van 't Hoff, Mart Stam and Walter Segal. He devotes admiring words to Jaffé in particular.[15] Those conversations and that book did slightly diminish the reputation of the Bauhaus and enhance that of De Stijl. During Banham's stay in the Netherlands, he had started out with loftier ambitions. In a letter to Rietveld in 1956, he asked to see one of the architect's early houses:

> I am at present working on a book on architectural theory in the early part of the century (roughly from 1907 to 1927) in which I hope to afford the Dutch contribution to modern architecture a less prejudiced and more fair-minded treatment than it has received so far, and I want, particularly, to learn from these who were connected with *de Stijl* what part they think van Doesburg *really* played.[16]

The main objective of his research was to dispel the image that modern architecture was essentially 'an international style' and redefine it as an attitude towards modernization and mechanization.

Canonization

Throughout his career, Banham contested the canonization of a single modern architecture by Pevsner, Hitchcock and Johnson. They saw the architecture of the 1950s as a logical extension of the progressive developments of the nineteenth century, which had not yet fully taken shape. Nikolaus Pevsner (1902-1983), author of *Pioneers of the Modern Movement from William Morris to Walter Gropius* (1936), was Banham's primary target:

> The human chain of Pioneers of the Modern Movement that extends back from Gropius to William Morris, and beyond him to Ruskin, Pugin and William Blake, does not extend forward from Gropius. The precious vessel of handicraft aesthetics that had been passed from hand to hand was dropped and broken.[17]

Banham classified Rietveld's furniture as 'crafts', having nothing to do with the sister term 'arts'. This is consistent with his view of Rietveld's chairs as an obstacle to the emergence of truly modern steel-tube furniture.

In Pevsner's *An Outline of European Architecture* (1943), probably the most-read survey of architecture history ever, Rietveld is mentioned almost in the same breath as Le Corbusier. Pevsner saw the Schröder House as an indispensable step on the way to the 'true modern movement'. Yet its design was too whimsical and artful for his taste. He suggested that Le Corbusier displayed the same whimsy but was able to pull it off more effectively, thanks to his exceptional artistic talents. Pevsner's sympathies lay instead with J.J.P. Oud, Walter Gropius and the other figures generally acknowledged as central to the 'International Style'.[18]

In the International Style exhibition at the Museum of Modern Art in New York (1932) and the accompanying catalogue, Philip Johnson (1906-2005) and Henry-Russell Hitchcock (1903-1987) saw no need to mention Rietveld (in contrast to Oud). It was not until the International Style had been pronounced dead that a new perspective began to take shape. In the introduction to the 1966 edition of his book, Hitchcock wrote: 'Hindsight suggests that Holland might have been better – or also – represented by Rietveld than by Oud.'[19]

Hitchcock was also one of the first to offer an informed and thorough discussion of Rietveld's contribution to modern architecture. Yet Rietveld's name remained tied to the word 'also':

> Despite the continuing vitality of the Amsterdam School through the mid twenties, the new Dutch school associated with Rotterdam rose rapidly in national and international significance. Oud, indeed, brought the new architecture to maturity in Holland in precisely the same years as Le Corbusier and their German contemporaries; Rietveld and several others made signal contributions *also* [emphasis added], in Rietveld's case equal in importance to Oud's.[20]

Absolute Authority

Sigfried Giedion (1888-1968), long known to architecture historians (and even longer to designers) as the ultimate authority, depicted the history of modern architecture and design as an almost inevitable line of development from the baroque to the present day.[21] With training as an engineer and a doctoral degree in art history, Giedion commanded a wide range of subject matter.[22] His best-known book, *Space, Time and Architecture*, based on a series of lectures given during the Second World War, attributed great importance to De Stijl. For Giedion, De Stijl is primarily Theo van Doesburg, along with Cornelis van Eesteren and J.J.P. Oud. Rietveld is not mentioned in the book. Giedion saw Cubism, especially as it was transformed within De Stijl, as a form of liberation from the material, transforming architecture into a purely spatial art. He writes that in the model for Léonce Rosenberg's villa, it seems as though the blind surfaces of a Malevich *Architekton* have gained the power of sight.[23]

It was not until 1956 that Giedion acknowledged the profound importance of the Schröder House, but even then he grouped it with Le Corbusier's villa at Garches, at the dawn of the first stage of the true

[19] On the occasion of the first exhibition on architecture at the Museum of Modern Art in New York: Hitchcock en Johnson 1932; the additional words 'Since 1922' were left out of later editions, Hitchcock, Foreword to the 1966 edition, X-XI.

[20] Hitchcock 1969, 506.

[21] Giedion was the secretary of CIAM and a close friend of Le Corbusier's. For Giedion's background, and for a bibliography and biography, see J. Bosman et al., *Sigfried Giedion 1888 – 1968. Der Entwurf einer modernen Tradition*, exhib. cat. Zürich, Museum für Gestaltung 1989; S. Georgiades, *Siegfried Giedion. Eine intellektuelle Biographie*, Zürich 1989.

[22] In addition to the sources in note 21, see also S. von Moos, 'Die zweite Entdeckung Amerikas' in Giedion 1987 (1948), 781-816: 781. Giedion's best known titles, *Space, Time and Architecture* (1941) and *Mechanization Takes Command* (1948), were published in the USA during or soon after the Second World War. The German manuscript of the latter book is in the Giedionarchiv at the Institut für Geschichte und Theorie der Architektur / Eidgenössische Technische Hochschule, Zurich.

[23] For a historical account, preliminary studies, and a model, see Bock 2001, 151-180. At an early stage, Van Doesburg, Wils, Rietveld, and Van Eesteren discussed the design. Wils was removed from this group at Rietveld's request, and subsequently Rietveld waited for the final design and produced the model only after considerable delay. Rosenberg was deeply impressed with the beauty of the model and compared it to the grandeur of Assyrian art. Reprint letter by Van Doesburg in Ottevanger 2008, 601.

[24] Giedion 1956. There are two copies at the RSA. On the crucial role of this little book in Giedion's personal development, see Georgiades op. cit. note 21, 183-186.

[25] Giedion 1956, 31. Sartoris 1957 and Zevi 1953 based most of their accounts on the work of the Swiss art critic Heinrich Wölfflin (1864-1945), For more about Zevi, see A. Oppenheimer, *Bruno Zevi on Modern Architecture*, New York 1983, with transcripts of hours of audio tape. Kultermann and Sartoris corresponded with Rietveld and/or Schröder, RSA letters Kultermann 1956-1960, Sartoris, 18 March 1939; 26 June and 3 July 1956, and included more and later work by Rietveld in their publications.

S. Giedion, *Architektur und Gemeinschaft*,
Hamburg 1956, 362-363
From Braque to Bauhaus, via De Stijl

Th.M. Brown, *The Work of G. Rietveld,
Architect*, Cambridge, MA 1958, 62-63

I.L. Szénássy, *Architectuur in Nederland
1960-1967*, Amsterdam 1969, 8-9

B. Zevi, *Poetica dell'architettura
neoplastica*, Milan 1974, 170-171
Left page after Theodore Brown

B. Colenbrander, *Stijl. Norm en handschrift
in de Nederlandse architectuur*
(Style, Standard and Signature),
Rotterdam 1993, 236
The only mention of Rietveld is in a
comparison with a private house by
Piet Elling

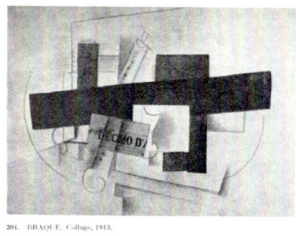
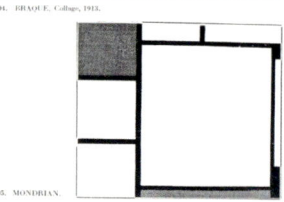

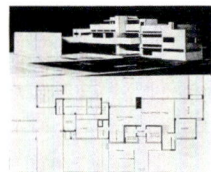

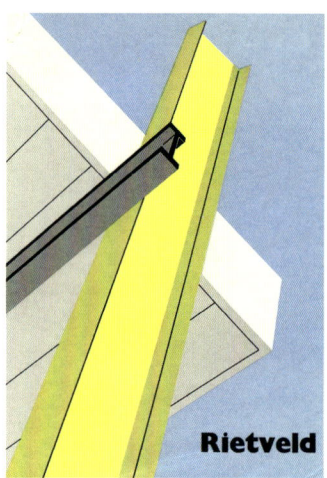
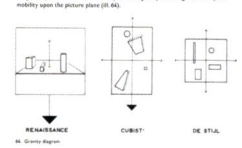

26 Rietveld in Theoretical Perspective

G. Rietveld 1888-1964

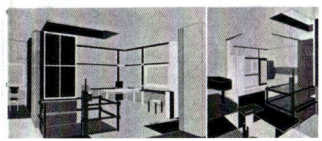

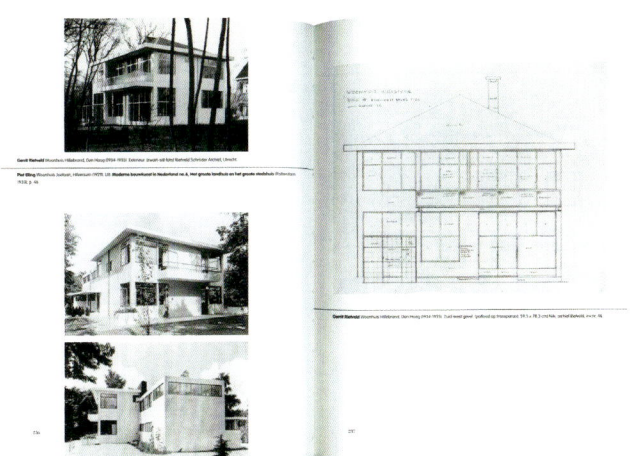

[26] Giedion 1948, 528-531: 528. Giedion considered Rietveld's contribution to steel-tube furniture and further developments in the 1930s to have been negligible.

[27] White 2003.

[28] Overy 1969, 17, referred to by White 2003, XIV.

[29] Overy 2007. Overy points out the important ritual role of washing, especially in his discussion of 'washing and watching', referring not only to the Schröder House, to which he also devoted a monograph (Overy et al. 1988), but also to the Hillebrand House and the study for a house for an architect.

[30] A. Betsky, 'Voorwoord, trek u eigen conclusies', in Ibelings 2005, 7. Ibelings 1995 was also published in English translation and as an accompaniment to the NAI's permanent exhibition. Ibelings was well aware of the arbitrary character of his project. Ibelings 2005, 6. A great deal of space is devoted to Rietveld; he is mentioned in three of the ten decade-based chapters, in connection with not only the Schröder House, but also the chauffeur's dwelling in Utrecht; the Verrijn Stuart House in Breukelen; Sonsbeek Pavilion; the Van den Doel House in Ilpendam; and the factory building De Ploeg in Bergeijk. The new publication for the NAI's new exhibition includes only a sketch made by Rietveld for Nagele, and Rietveld is only mentioned as part of the design team. Berg et al., 2004, 142.

[31] One noteworthy aspect of the opening exhibition at the Netherlands Architecture Institute was that chronology was subordinated to style and theme in a very loose sequence of 38 titles, showing the 'signature of one or more architects' and sometimes structures or objects that served to inspire them. Oddly enough, Rietveld was represented only in the section on restraint and plainness, by the Hillebrand House in The Hague, in the company of houses by Elling, Berghoef, Granpré Molière and Eschauzier. See Colenbrander 1993, 234-237.

Nieuwe Bouwen (the Dutch manifestation of the Modern Movement in architecture).[24] The warmer reception of Rietveld's work in this period is probably connected to the international exhibitions about De Stijl that took place in the 1950s and '60s. Publications by Kultermann, Sartoris and Zevi, who also admired work by Rietveld, may also have played a role. Bruno Zevi (1918-2000) even called De Stijl, and especially the work of Van Doesburg and Rietveld, a critical architectural idiom that retained its validity in his own day.[25] Earlier, in 1948, Giedion's book *Mechanization Takes Command* had declared the furniture maker Rietveld to be the earliest and greatest of the pioneering modern furniture designers. 'The Dutch were the first to project the new artistic vision into furniture . . . Rietveld did not stand alone. He was linked with the Dutch avant-garde.'[26]

The Dutch Avant-Garde
Whether there was a unified Dutch avant-garde, and what the relative importance of an avant-garde is in its own day, have been topics of increasing debate in recent years. This debate is a response to older narratives in which De Stijl is ascribed great significance as the Dutch contribution to the international avant-garde. In 1936, the first director of the Museum of Modern Art in New York, the art historian Alfred Barr, Jr, (1902-1981), was already pointing out the central importance of De Stijl in the development of abstract visual art. Later the movement was also recognized for its contribution to the plastic arts, still later for its role in design and architecture, and eventually even for its work in urban planning. At the same time, however, it was becoming less and less clear what De Stijl actually was: the group of artists who published and were discussed in the eponymous periodical, all those people who used a related formal language and presented themselves as belonging to the movement, or the individuals specifically mentioned by Van Doesburg as members of De Stijl who adhered to the group's principles.

A book by the British architecture historian Michael White, *De Stijl and Dutch Modernism*, is the most recent attempt to present a coherent picture of the Dutch avant-garde subsumed under the general heading of De Stijl.[27] White openly rejects Paul Overy's opinion that every author can create his own De Stijl and arrives at a much more subtle view that is essentially in harmony with Jaffé's. After Van Doesburg, Jaffé was the first to identify De Stijl as the one great Dutch contribution to modern art.[28] Furthermore, Overy (ironically enough) showed in 2007 that exploring the theme of modernity could help to elucidate larger issues.[29] But even as recently as that, fear and aversion to grand narratives still seemed to predominate.

The results of that aversion to grand narratives can be illustrated by the case of Hans Ibelings. After two books presenting first Dutch architecture and then Dutch urban design in terms of a sequence of decades, he edited a book that introduces the Dutch architects of approximately the past 200 years in alphabetical order. Aaron Betsky, who was the director of the Netherlands Architecture Institute (NAI) from 2001 to 2006, makes the relevant point very clearly in his foreword to this book:

> This seems to imply that Dutch architecture, as a clearly definable phenomenon, no longer exists. But did it ever really exist, or was it

a beautiful story, told in the form of history and analysis? This book does not draw any conclusions about that either.[30]

This is not merely an isolated case. At the NAI's opening exhibition 'Style. Standard and Signature' in 1993, it became clear that the institute's large collection of archives would not be used to construct grand narratives. According to architecture historian Bernard Colenbrander, who edited the exhibition catalogue, what was ultimately on display there was no more than the individual stylistic signatures of each architect and their personal sources of inspiration, loosely organized into 38 themes.[31] Rietveld plays a highly marginal role in this publication. This seems to be the final assault in a campaign launched by Rem Koolhaas and his friends several years earlier against Rietveld and the formal modernist tendencies in Dutch architecture. Koolhaas called the Schröder House 'full', writing that it could even be compared to a gypsy caravan, 'full of high purpose and sly intentions; it is full of wishes; it is full of things; it is full of colour, or at least of paint; it is full of abstract bells and full of sublimated whistles'.[32]

The discovery of more and more of Rietveld's oeuvre did not lead to new appreciation for his work, or even to a new perspective on it. A large number of previously unknown dwellings designed by Rietveld were published with detailed commentary for the first time by G.H. Rodijk in 1991.[33] Rodijk had been investigating the still largely disorganized archives of the firm of Rietveld, Van Dillen, and Van Tricht, which were transferred to the NAI soon afterwards. This fount of information also inspired Marijke Kuper and Ida van Zijl to undertake a vast and meticulous research project, culminating in the publication (in 1992) of an oeuvre catalogue with 681 entries, primarily based on the archival documents at the NAI and the more personal documents at the Centraal Museum Utrecht.[34]

This catalogue had been published too recently to play a major role in the colloquium 'Architecture and Cubism' held in Montreal in 1993, where renewed efforts were made to probe the connections between visual art and architecture that had seemed so self-evident to Giedion. The book that issued from that conference was described as 'an opportunity to deconstruct the conceptual limits within which cubist scholarship has most often operated.'[35] Again, the simplistic nature of some comparisons between visual art and architecture was a topic of discussion, but new subjects were also broached.[36] The deconstruction of grand narratives was the general theme, rather than the construction of new ones.

The attack on cohesive, evolutionary narratives, instigated by Banham, became increasingly fierce, even at the international level. Charles Jencks (b. 1939), a critic of both modernism and postmodernism, had shown by example how difficult it was to construct a single narrative of the modern after the Second World War. As the illustration shows he tried to save his evolutionary account by labelling 80 per cent of architecture 'unconscious' and identifying a variety of traditions that broke up, sometimes died out and then sometimes reunited. At this stage, it should not come as a surprise that he classified Rietveld solely as a member of De Stijl, along with Oud and Van Doesburg. It is also instructive to note that, according to Jencks, this style of architecture associated with Rietveld was the dominant one at that time in that historic stream. It transformed into a very thin line

[32] R. Koolhaas, 'Rem Koolhaas' in Leupen, Deen and Grafe 1990, 11-20: 14-15.

[33] Rodijk 1991.

[34] Küper and Van Zijl 1992.

[35] Blau and Troy 1997, XI. This book also includes an essay by Frampton in which he relates his views in Modern Architecture: A Critical History with the present-day architecture theories of Peter Eisenman et al.: 'Neoplasticism and Architecture: Formation and Transformation', in: Blau and Troy 1997, 99-123.

[36] Overy 2007, chapter 6, 'The Cell in the City', 117-140.

[37] Jencks 1973, 28.

[38] Benevolo 1960. Benevolo writes in his twelfth Italian edition (1985) that he wishes to take on the challenge issued by Jencks (1973), Dal Co and Tafuri (1979), and Frampton (1980). He accuses them of seeing contemporary architecture as an epilogue to the previous century, and in that edition he tries once again to extend the narrative up to the present rather than adding an ever-expanding appendix. Paraphrased from 'Vorwort' in: Benevolo 1988, vol. 3, 5.

[39] Vidler 2008, 183. He upbraids Tafuri for 'uniting Dada and de Stijl, Kahn and Rietveld, under this antihistorical umbrella'.

[40] Fanelli 1968. In the chapter on De Stijl and functionalism Fanelli 1978, 135, he writes: 'His most significant works (leaving aside his furniture) are the Schröder House – the most poetic and inventive application of the principles of De Stijl – the row of houses on Erasmuslaan (1930-1931) and Schumannstraat (1934) in Utrecht, and those at the Werkbund model housing estate in Vienna. These terraced houses show all the later characteristics of Dutch functionalism.' Another striking fact is that in the epilogue Van den Broek and Bakema are described as the true inheritors of the tradition of modern architecture that flourished between the world wars. Van den Broek was the promoting professor for Rietveld's honorary doctorate. Fanelli 1978, 177.

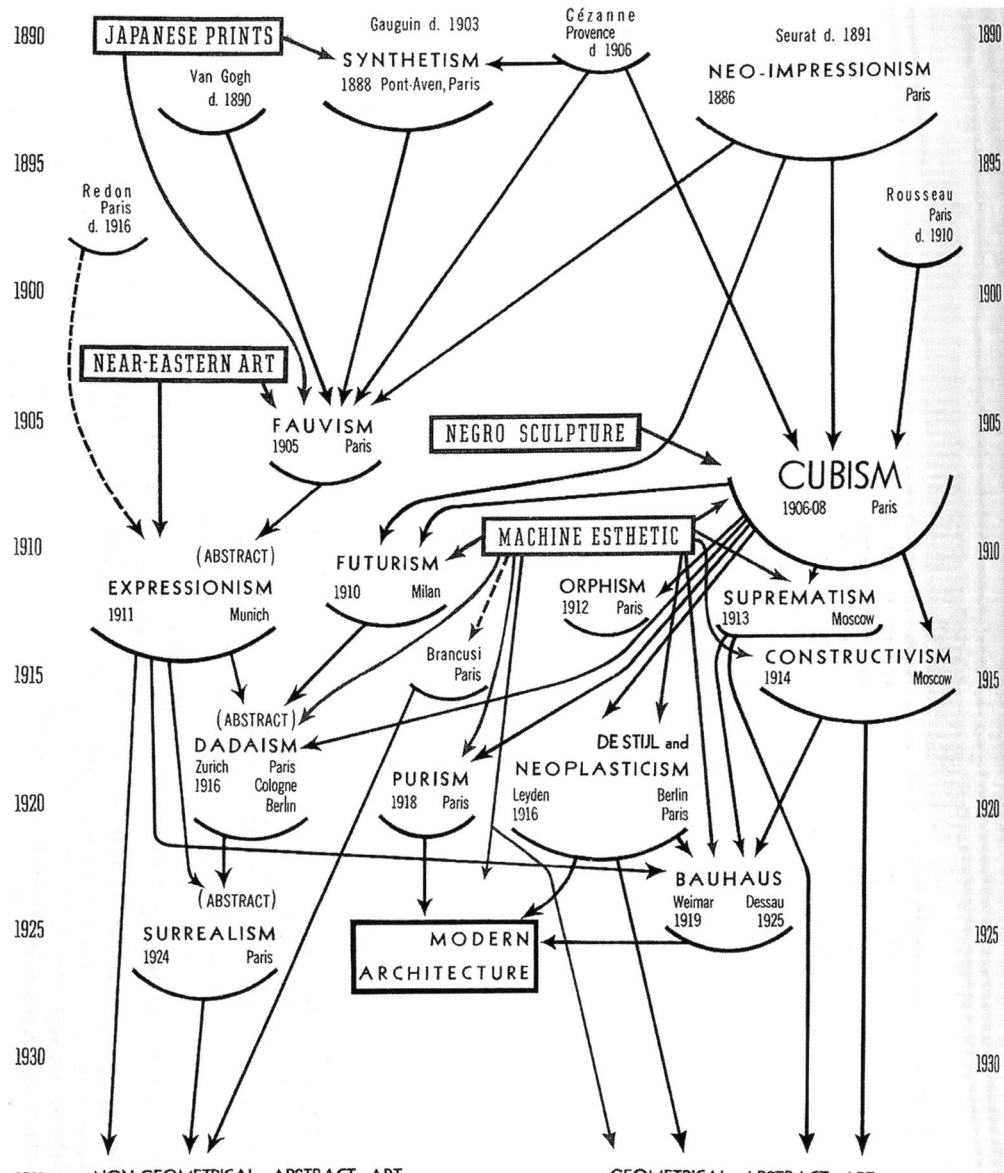

A. Barr Jr, The diagram, used on the cover of his book *Cubism and Abstract Art*, 1936, indicates the position of De Stijl in the development towards abstract visual art

Ch. Jencks, 'Evolutionary Tree', *Modern Movements in Architecture*, Harmondsworth 1973

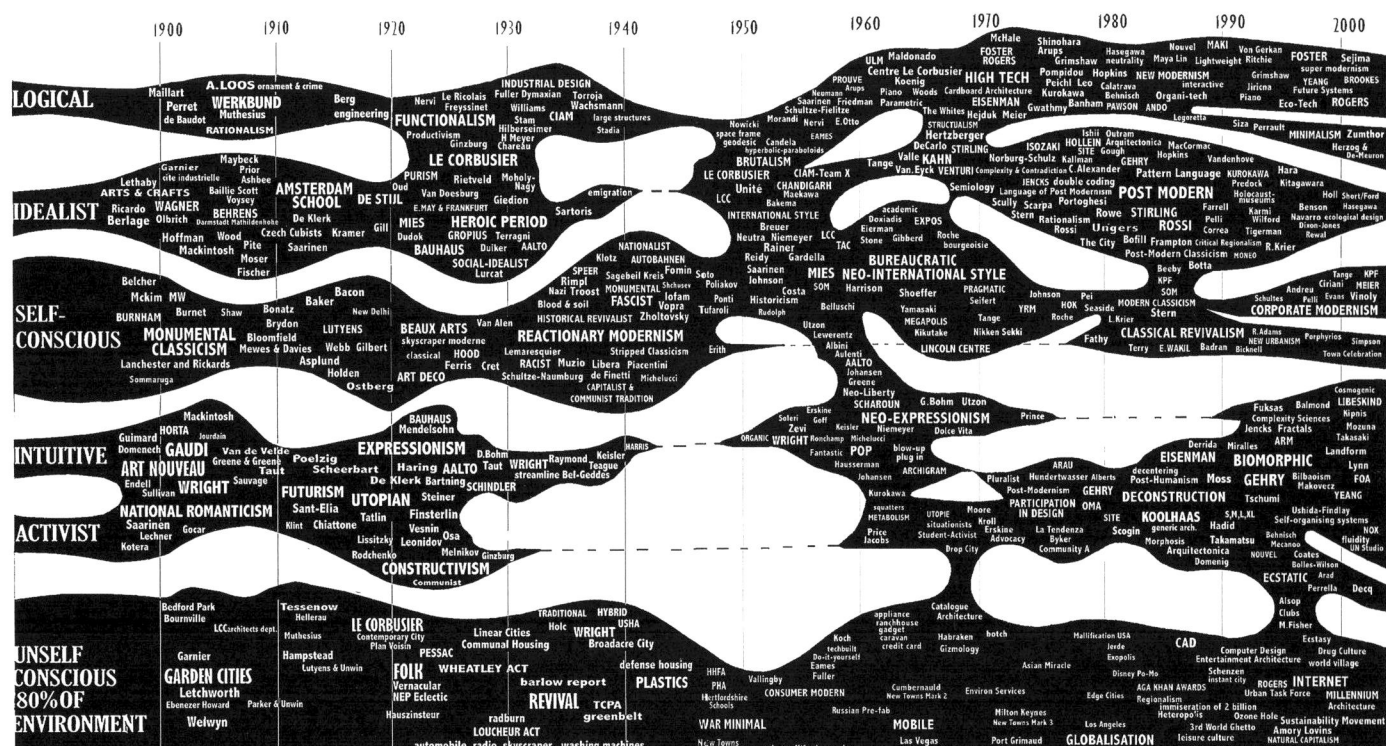

Rietveld and the Writing of Architecture History

in the architectural void of the Second World War, which broadened after the war to include such figures as the Smithsons, Bakema, and Van Eyck, all of whom Jencks outlined as emphatically keeping the Rietveldian tradition alive.[37]

The Italian architecture historian and critic Manfredo Tafuri (1935-1994) was an even more successful critic of the pretensions and motives of modern architecture. He disputed the image of a single, unified modern tradition – defined as inclusively as possible and originating in the French Revolution – that had been expounded in copious detail and with great tenacity by his compatriot Leonardo Benevolo (1923).[38] Rather than lumping together Dada, De Stijl, Kahn and Rietveld, Tafuri wanted to give history a central role again, a history of the relationship between design and utopia, a labyrinthine narrative claiming that since the Renaissance the architect's profession and field of action had grown ever wider-ranging and more ambitious, but had been plunged into an escalating series of crises in the age of capitalism and socialism.[39] When he wrote, with Francesco Dal Co (1945), the volume on modern architecture in the Electa *History of World Architecture*, Rietveld remained the man who had designed that one major house. In fact, they could easily have learned that it was Rietveld, even more than Oud, who formed the link between De Stijl and the *Nieuwe Bouwen*, since Giovanni Fanelli's précis of Dutch architecture from 1900 to 1940 had been published in Italian in 1968.[40] Yet Tafuri and Dal Co were both much more impressed by Van Eesteren, who focused his energies on urban design in Amsterdam, than they were by Rietveld.[41]

On the Dutch and international scene, it was Manfred Bock who first pointed out De Stijl's connection with urban planning and Rietveld's and Van Eesteren's linking roles in the development of Dutch modern architecture and urban planning. The icon of Bock's narrative is a map showing Amsterdam's General Extension Plan (AUP), created under the supervision of Cornelis van Eesteren (1897-1988), architect and urban designer, and Theodor Karel van Lohuizen (1890-1956), planner and urban designer, whose working method eventually led to the *Athens Charter* (1933-1943). The failure to fully execute the AUP, along with a profusion of half-understood references to the *Athens Charter*, led Van Eesteren's methods to fall out of favour both in the Netherlands and internationally. Yet this did nothing to diminish the legendary status of De Stijl, as Bock wrote:

> Even those who severely criticized the concept of the functional city after the war were not prepared to carry out a true iconoclastic fury. On the contrary, Mondrian's paintings, Rietveld's chair, Van Doesburg and Van Eesteren's designs . . . this cultural heritage was indispensable to the young people who criticized functional urban planning.[42]

It was not the critical architects to whom Bock was referring, such as Aldo van Eyck and Jaap Bakema, but art historians, led by Carel Blotkamp, who raised serious questions about the cohesiveness of De Stijl as a movement. Accounts of De Stijl as a movement or school culminating in Mondrian's pure abstraction gave way to loose sets of descriptions of personalities and products, some of which used the periodical *De Stijl* as a medium while others did not.[43]

---

[41] M. Tafuri, *Progetto e Utopia*, Bari 1973; although there were earlier translations in circulation, the book first made a real splash after its official translation under the title of *Architecture and Utopia: Design and Capitalist Development*, Cambridge 1976. On the influence of this book and for a few texts, see Hays 2000, 2-35, 143-146; Tafuri and Dal Co 1979, a translation of the original series in which this volume appeared in Italian in 1976, 250. Dal Co was also one of the contributors to the book M. Casciato, F. Panzini, S. Polano (eds.), *Architektuur en volkshuisvesting. Nederland 1870-1940*, Nijmegen/Milan 1980, in which a few of Rietveld's public housing studies were published for the first time: fig. 80, 220, 221.

[42] Bock 1993, 12. This view is expressed in an even more emphatic form in M. Bock, 'Vom Monument zur Städteplanung: Das Neue Bauen' in D. Honisch et al. (eds.), *Tendenzen der Zwanziger Jahre, 15. Europäische Kunstaustellung unter den Auspizien des Europarates*, exhib.cat. Berlin, Neue Nationalgalerie, Akademie der Künste und Große Orangerie des Schlosses Charlottenburg 1977, I, *Vom Konstruktivismus zur konkreten Kunst*, 1/26-1/41. The most detailed presentation of Bock's ideas, under his leadership, is Bock 2001, 1993, 1994, 2007.

[43] Blotkamp 1996.

[44] W.A.L. Beeren (Museum Boijmans Van Beuningen, Rotterdam), R.W.D. Oxenaar (Kröller-Müller Museum, Otterlo), T. van Velzen (Gemeentemuseum, The Hague), E.L.L. de Wilde (Stedelijk Museum, Amsterdam), D. van Woerkom (Nederlands Documentatiecentrum voor de Bouwkunst, Amsterdam (NDB)). Forewords to the five catalogues. There are considerable differences in the English and Dutch texts that were printed next to each other in every catalogue. Except in the case of Museum Boijmans Van Beuningen, this was the continuation of a partnership between the same museums in 1975, which related to four aspects of the period 1890-1960. Nieuwe Bouwen and De Stijl were mentioned only obliquely in the exhibition 'Americana' at the Kröller-Müller; the exhibition catalogue for 'Architectura' at the NDB was the only one of which a partial German translation appeared.

[45] Bless 1982, 'Verantwoording', October 1981, 7.

[46] Ibid., 148.

The years 1982 and 1983 were marked by a sudden explosion of publications, even though the source materials had yet to be fully organized. The most prominent of these were the exhibitions and accompanying catalogues about the *Nieuwe Bouwen* in 1982-1983. The directors of five major Dutch museums jointly wrote:

> The Nieuwe Bouwen now has a high profile in the Netherlands . . . The facts of the matter have been recognized for some time, and this recognition is also found in recent work in architectural history. But at the same time 'there is still a great deal to be done'.[44]

Rietveld was mentioned briefly in each of the catalogues, but no coherent picture emerged.

In the catalogue about the 'historical background', an essay on Rietveld was contributed by Frits Bless. Naturally, Bless referred to his 1982 monograph, in which he had tried to come as close as possible to Rietveld's perspective. He deliberately avoided lengthy descriptive passages, instead trying to reconstruct the designer's life and opinions in the most cohesive way possible. Only his new discoveries and interpretations were introduced in an 'art-historically descriptive manner'. Furthermore, the new discoveries served not only to add to the store of knowledge about Rietveld, but also to underscore his versatility.[45] Bless struggled most with the post-Second World War period. On the one hand, Rietveld had gone on doing pioneering work; on the other, like younger generations, he seemed to be looking back to the avant-garde period at the start of the century. Bless believed that this line of research should be pursued further, perhaps with special attention to Rietveld's work as an interior architect, a designer of exhibitions and stands at trade fairs, and, in the 1950s, a furniture designer whose pieces were produced only in small numbers. Studies of such topics, Bless said, would do greater justice to the international reputation of Gerrit Rietveld.[46]

Bless must have been gratified to see the essays on Rietveld in the Dutch and English-language catalogue *Het Nieuwe Bouwen, Amsterdam 1920-1960*, which included selected findings of a working group headed by Ellinoor Bergvelt. She and her co-authors later produced another publication about modern interior design. *Het Nieuwe Bouwen* included an article by Ben Rebel, which made many of the conclusions of his doctoral thesis accessible to an international audience.[47] An exhibition catalogue in the *Nieuwe Bouwen* series devoted entirely to De Stijl explicitly attempted to correct the picture that Rietveld and his circle painted in the 1950s.[48] Another 1983 event was an exhibition about De Stijl at the Walker Art Center in Minneapolis, which came to the Netherlands a year later.[49] In the catalogue for that exhibition, Sergio Polano wrote his famous words: 'A De Stijl architecture does *not* exist.'[50] He took almost as firm a position on the Schröder House as Ben Rebel, who argued that the house had not had any discernible influence on the *Nieuwe Bouwen*.[51] This reinforced the image of Rietveld as a historical figure who had once been important in the distant past.

[47] E. Bergvelt et al., 'Het Nieuwe Bouwen en het interieur/Nieuwe Bouwen and the interior' in K. Bosma et al., *Het Nieuwe Bouwen*, Amsterdam 1920-1960, exhib.cat. Amsterdam, Stedelijk Museum, Delft 1983, 112-141; in the same collection: B. Rebel, 'De Amsterdamse architectenvereniging "de 8"/The Amsterdam architects association "de 8"', 8-51. Rebel 1983, with English-language summary. On the later work of this group, see the literature cited in E. Bergvelt, F. van Burkom, K. Gaillard, *Van Neorenaissance tot postmodernism: honderdvijfentwintig jaar Nederlandse interieurs/From Neo-Renaissance to Post-Modernism: A Hundred and Twenty-Five Years of Dutch Interiors*, Rotterdam 1996.

[48] C. Boekraad, introduction in Boekraad et al. 1983, 5-15: 7. Boekraad says that the catalogue and the exhibition drew on the recent publication by. Troy 1983 and A. Doig, *Theo van Doesburg: Painting into Architecture: Theory into Practice*, Cambridge 1986.

[49] Friedman 1982. The exhibition then went on tour and also ran in the Stedelijk Museum, Amsterdam and the Kröller-Müller Museum, Otterlo. Bock contributed 'De Stijl and the City' to this volume.

[50] S. Polano, 'De Stijl/Architecture = Nieuwe Beelding' in Friedman 1982, 86-97: 87.

[51] Rebel 1983, 111. Polano op. cit. note 50 in: Friedman 1982, 97: 'But on closer scrutiny the Schröder house too turns out to be a fascinating but necessarily unique experiment.' This conclusion stands in sharp contrast to Banham's view, in which the 'cardboard Mondrian' is crucial precisely because of its dating: 'Here for the first time; in 1924, the aesthetic possibilities of the hard school of modern architecture were uncompromisingly and brilliantly revealed (no early house of Le Corbusier is comparable until 1926, his first vintage year).' Banham 1978, 68.

B. Mulder, G.J. de Rook and C. Blotkamp,
Rietveld Schröderhuis 1925 1975, Utrecht
1975

History and Creativity

Theodore Brown wrote in his dissertation in 1958, the year that Rietveld said he only wished to look into the future: 'The creator's view of his work is determined by a way of thinking quite different from that of a historian.' Through chronology and stylistic analysis, Brown sought to illuminate Rietveld's work in a way that the designer himself could not or would not. At the same time, Brown's book seems to have been strongly influenced by Rietveld and his partner Truus Schröder. That may be the reason for his strangely incoherent treatment of the Schröder House. On the one hand, it is presented as a development that at most parallels the paintings of De Stijl, but on the other hand, the diagrams and illustrations place so much emphasis on the similarities between the two that the reader becomes convinced they cannot be mere coincidence. Brown describes the result in ecstatic terms: 'The Schröder House is in an almost perfect state of visual equilibrium . . . the building sits gently upon the ground like a delicate white dove amid the leaden dodos of the neighbouring structures.'[52] Because Brown's main intention was to present the Schröder House as following on from earlier Rietveld designs, the preceding period of Rietveld's career is treated almost entirely as a prologue to 'the House'. Moreover, time constraints – perhaps in combination with limited understanding – weakened the analysis of the later work.

Ultimately, Brown's account was almost entirely compatible with the then dominant narrative,[53] the skeleton of which had been constructed in Oud's *Bauhausbuch* in 1926: first the chaos of eclecticism, then Cuypers, soon after that Berlage, and finally Oud himself, who completed the line of development.[54] Brown did argue that greater importance should be attributed to Rietveld's contribution to this historical process, but in later publications he presented Rietveld as a man with little formal training who largely relied on his natural talents, steered clear of conceptual debates, and distrusted history.[55] It is almost impossible to overstate the significance of Brown's compact study. For many years – alongside Jaffé's book, which called the Schröder House 'the first and foremost realization of the new trend in European architecture' – it was almost the only source of detailed information about Rietveld for an international readership.

Despite Brown's intentions, his book had precisely the sort of impact that Rietveld had dreaded: the designer's name was forever linked to that one exceptional chair and unique house, and he became a historical character in a past that some believed was already dead and buried. It did not help that, in the years just prior to his death, Rietveld continued to strive towards new solutions for contemporary problems with the techniques and methods of the future. Furthermore, he felt little need (even by modernist standards) to construct a history of his work, let alone his life.[56] Though many still draw inspiration from his example, he himself emphasized that his contemporary architecture should not be regarded as 'suitable for the future'.[57] He made this point most clearly in his acceptance speech for an honorary degree at Delft College of Technology on 11 January 1964: 'I feel defeated – a lost man, who believed he still had a very long journey ahead of him, but has suddenly found himself here at what seems to be the end of the line.'[58]

---

[52] Brown 1958, 62.

[53] A letter from Pieter Singelenberg, RSA, to 'Esteemed Mr Rietveld', 8 April 1959, is especially critical of the analysis of the 1924-40 period and remarks that there is too little attention to the later work: 'Ted [Theodore Brown – RD] realized that', but the dissertation had to be finished. This story was later confirmed by the dissertation supervisor, Prof. M.D. Ozinga.

[54] J.J.P. Oud, *Holländische Architektur*, *Bauhausbücher no. 10*, Munich 1926. The work of Auke van der Woud, since his contribution to the series of exhibitions on Nieuwe Bouwen, has been crucially relevant to the Dutch debate about the claim that historians have used source materials by modern architects in an uncritical fashion. A. van der Woud, *Het Nieuwe Bouwen Internationaal/ International, CIAM Volkshuisvesting Stedebouw/Housing Town Planning*, exhib.cat. Otterlo, Rijksmuseum Kröller-Müller, Delft 1983. Most recent English-language bibliography: Langmead 1996.

[55] Brown 1965; 1968.

[56] The special role of Bertus Mulder should be mentioned here. His place in historiography is unique because he refers to his conversations with and instructions of Rietveld. In his restorations, reconstructions, and accounts and analyses of the work of Rietveld, he has had the courage to develop a perspective all his own, which may now form a barrier to clear perception of the many building blocks that are still available for constructing other Rietveldian histories. In this context, the most intriguing development is the recent publication about 'the house': Van Zijl and Mulder 2009, with a survey of the literature. For more general observations about the writing of history and the Dutch situation, see E. Jonker, *Ordentelijke geschiedenis, Herinnering, ethiek en geschiedwetenschap*, Utrecht 2008.

[57] G. Rietveld, *Tweede min of meer herhaalde lezing tijdens de architectuur tentoonstelling in het Centraal Museum te Utrecht*, typescript, RSA.

[58] Short speech by G.Th. Rietveld on receiving an honorary doctorate in technical sciences from Delft College of Technology on 11 January 1964. Typescript, RSA.

Dolf Broekhuizen

An Awakening Consciousness. The Early Development of Rietveld's Theoretical Approach

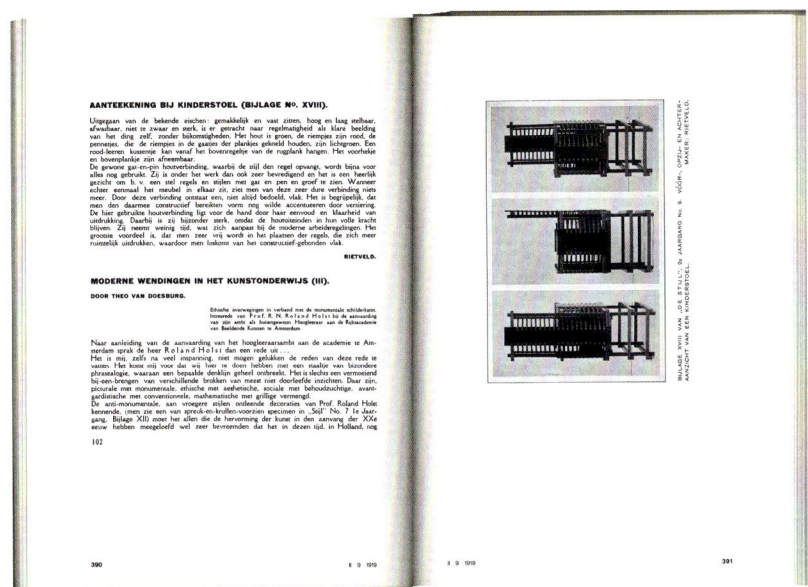

G.Th. Rietveld, 'Aanteekening bij kinderstoel (appendix XVIII)', *De Stijl* 2 (1919) 9, 102 and separate appendix XVIII (reprinted 1968)

[1] See e.g. M. Filler, 'The furniture of Gerrit Rietveld: Manifestos for a new revolution', in: Friedman 1982, 126.

[2] Early studies of Rietveld's texts include Brown 1965, 292-296; Bless 1982; Madge 1982, 37-43; translations of six of Rietveld's texts have been published in Küper and Van Zijl 1992, 22-55; for an extensive discussion, see Mulder 1994, with Rietveld's words, dating from 1958: 'As a boy I was a weak little dreamer, who found nothing more astonishing than that such a small chunk of life could be conscious of its own existence' (58).

[3] I. van Zijl, 'Het Rietveld-Schröder archief', in: Küper and Van Zijl 1988, 28, 31.

In the vast quantity of literature about Rietveld's designs, relatively little attention is paid to his writing. As a result, the popular image of Rietveld is that of a brilliant designer who underwent practical training but was scarcely interested in theoretical matters.[1] This picture does not do justice to Rietveld's interest in architecture theory. Research into the development of his theoretical approach has demonstrated convincingly that his practical work and theoretical interest may well have developed hand in hand.[2] But Rietveld seldom clarified his early work until later, in retrospect. In fact, in the early period, he even appears to have rejected the idea of explaining his work. By 1919, when he wrote his first short article for *De Stijl* to accompany photographs of a children's chair with a remarkable design, he had been working as a cabinetmaker for almost 20 years. When some of his other designs appeared in *De Stijl* later on, he again refrained from comment. In this sense he acted very differently from the architects J.J.P. Oud and Robert van 't Hoff, who used the journal directly as a platform from which to publicize their ideas.

In the 1920s, Rietveld started publishing articles and giving lectures more often. By the time of his death in 1964 he had produced a total of 270 lectures and written texts, most of them written after 1945, about one-third of which have been published.[3] The focus in this chapter is the early period from the time he first started working with furniture until he wrote his first lengthy treatise in 1932.

Broad Cultural Development

Although Rietveld did not start publishing his views with any frequency until he was 40, his early theoretical development was an integral part of his training and work as a cabinetmaker and eventually as a universal designer of whole urban neighbourhoods. His interest in theory gradually becomes noticeable. In terms of formal education, the architecture course he attended in 1911-1912, taught by the Utrecht architect P.J.C. Klaarhamer,

[4] Bless 1982, 12-14.

[5] Gerrit's brother Wim had attended philosophy lectures in Leiden since 1914. Bless 1982, 14. Bolland 1904 and Bolland 1906, in particular, were widely read.

[6] Van Doesburg's fundamental principles have been studied in detail, see, for example, the recent analysis by H. Engel, 'Theo van Doesburg and the destruction of architectural theory', in: Fabre and Wintgens-Hötte 2009, 36-45; it is far less well known that Van Doesburg drew his inspiration for the explanatory drawings from a design (which was never executed) by the architect Jan Wils for a kiosk in the IJ forest in Amsterdam from 1918. This design was published in Van Bergeijk 2007, 168-169.

[7] 'Klare beelding van het ding zelf, zonder bijkomstigheden', Rietveld 1919, 102.

was the most important. At these sessions, over ten years after he had started work in his father's cabinetmaking workshop in 1899, he learned about matters such as the relationships between design, art, politics, philosophy and literature.[4]

In 1914, Rietveld studied the work of diverse philosophers in greater depth. In the university town of Leiden, the charismatic philosopher and spiritualist G.P.J. Bolland lectured on Dutch thinkers such as Spinoza, and other – largely German – philosophers such as Hegel, Kant and Schopenhauer. These names occasionally crop up in Rietveld's early texts.[5] Some aspects of their ideas, such as Schopenhauer's remarks about visual perception, Hegel's focus on developing consciousness, and Spinoza's quest for essence and purification, became key ideas in Rietveld's thinking. But Rietveld was not alone in his bias towards German theories. Theo van Doesburg, for instance, would later (in 1919) draw a sharp distinction between the elementary modes of expression available to painting (colour), sculpture (plasticity) and architecture (space).[6]

In 1917 Rietveld was already translating such ideas into his designs for slat chairs; that same year, he set up his own cabinetmaking workshop. Rietveld's first article, in which he described the properties of a child's chair he had designed, was clearly based on contemporary philosophical and aesthetic ideas, but Rietveld did not indicate his sources. He justified the functional considerations as if they were self-explanatory; they were 'familiar requirements', like an adjustable seat, washable materials and a sturdy construction. The slats of which the chair's structure is composed do not fit together snugly; instead they cross and extend beyond the point of juncture. As a result, the emphasis shifts from the chair as a finished object to the slats of the chair as parts of a larger whole. The slat is sawn through to expose the crosscut end, so that the brain follows the slat through in thought and the space outside the chair is emphasized. This psychological effect has been analysed using the Gestalt theories of perceptual organization that were developed in Germany in the early twentieth century.

There is a second, more practical reason underlying the use of straight slats. In his text, Rietveld discusses the development from craftsmanship to factory production and to the influence of this innovation on design and style. The straight slats and planks of which the chair is composed are suitable for mechanized production, which would bring about a change in culture. The design of the residential environment (furniture, interior, building) therefore had to be brought into line with industrial production methods. This led to the 'pure representation of the thing itself, without extraneous details'.[7] The terminology corresponds to the use of words in *De Stijl*, in which, for instance, Mondrian had published his theories of neoplasticity.

Standardized Dwellings or *Normaalwoningen*
Ten years later Rietveld started to write at greater length about his ideas and designs. He published two more distinctly theoretical articles in the international avant-garde journal *i10* in 1927 and 1928. The one entitled 'Nut, constructie: schoonheid: kunst)' (Usefulness, construction (beauty: art)) was Rietveld's response to the style debate that was provoking fierce

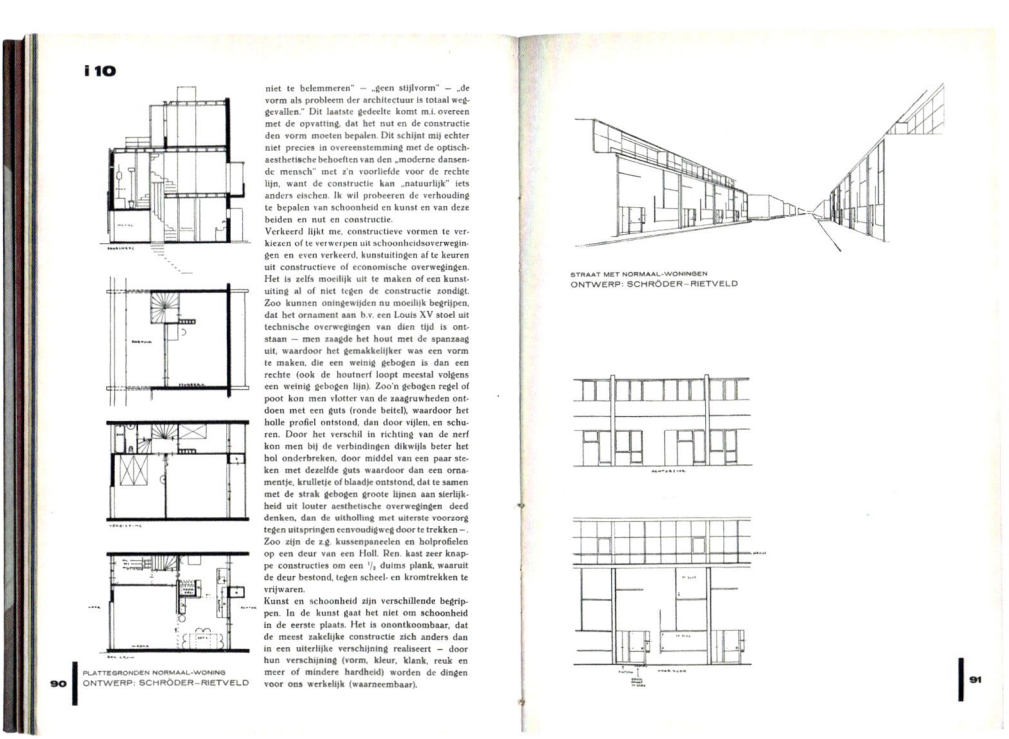

Presentation of the design for standard dwellings in the article G.Th. Rietveld, 'Nut, constructie (schoonheid: kunst)', *i10* 1 (1927) 3, 90-91

H. Tessenow, *Hausbau und dergleichen*, Munich c. 1928 (first edition 1916)

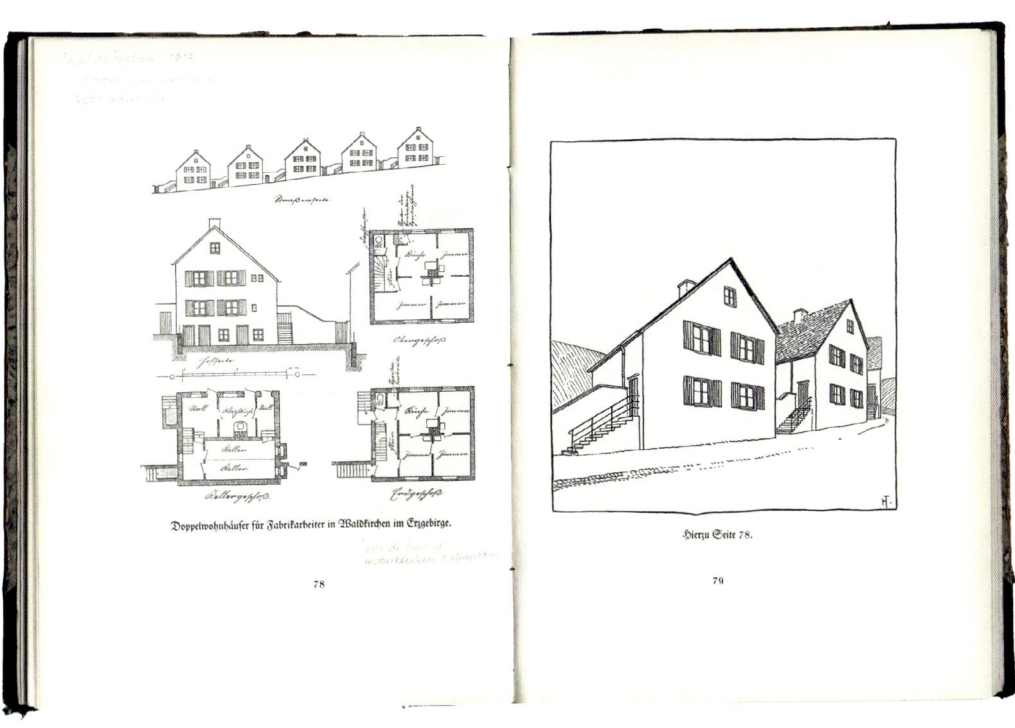

[8] Rietveld 1927 (a), 89-92.

[9] Rietveld 1928, 89-92.

[10] Rietveld 1927 (b), 46.

[11] 'Maar ik lees niet alles en kan dan ook eigenlijk niet schrijven. Ik weet ook heel goed, met schrijven kom je er niet, en het geschrevene wordt pas iets en zegt pas iets, als je het verwerkt tot wat wij een kunstwerk noemen. Maar je doet het omdat je toch niet alles goed kunt vinden.' NAI, Oud archive, letter from Rietveld to Oud, 9 February 1927.

[12] In 1924, for instance, a reviewer wrote a highly critical piece on his furniture in *Nieuwe Rotterdamsche Courant.* Huygen 2007, 283-285.

[13] In 1928, C. van Eesteren became a member of the editorial board of *i10* but Rietveld did not.

[14] For a discussion and translation, see Mertins and Mallgrave 2000.

[15] For an analysis of Behne's work: Haag Bletter 1996, 62-64.

[16] '. . . niet zonder geestigheid, echter zonder respect, noch voor 't nieuwe, noch voor 't oude . . . Dit boek van A. Behne lijkt me geforceerd modern. Zakelijkheid en doel en dan schelden op dingen waarvan hij het doel niet ziet.' NAI, Oud archive, letter from Rietveld to Oud, undated [c. 1928].

[17] 'Ik heb het boek van Tessenow gekocht en vind dat heel erg mooi. Men moest meer zoo als hij rustig overwegen in plaats van zoo in de eerste plaats modern te willen zijn.' NAI, Oud archive, letter from Rietveld to Oud, undated [c. 1927].

[18] See the monograph on Tessenow's work: De Michelis 1991 and the critical review of it in Hofer 2005, 41-55.

[19] NAI, Oud archive, letter from Rietveld to Oud, 10 February 1927.

controversy at this time. Reform movements in the Netherlands and for instance in Germany, in Deutsche Werkbund circles, were also struggling with tradition and innovation. In *i10*, Rietveld discussed the question of style, invoking the views of the Dutch artists Piet Mondrian and Theo van Doesburg and the architect J.J.P. Oud. From the painters he quoted suggestions that tauter, purer designs could counterbalance the busy life of the city. From Oud he derived the notion that contemporary culture should be the seedbed of architecture as well as its point of departure. The goal of architecture is to create space, and outward appearance, construction issues, and efficient modes of use are all subordinate to this. He identifies that goal, and the effect of space on human beings, as 'being' (*zijn*), which he clarifies by quoting from Gerard Bolland and the poet-philosopher Rabindranath Tagore – popular thinkers among artists in this period. Of the early texts, this is the one with the clearest references to his sources of inspiration. Rietveld demonstrates here not only his wide reading, but also the ways in which he applied his reading in his professional practice, in that the article can be interpreted as an indirect clarification of his design for standardized dwellings (*normaalwoningen*).[8]

In the article entitled 'Inzicht' (Insight, 1928) he posited his own position more boldly, where in his first *i10* article he had been somewhat evasive, largely referring to the views of others. This text is heavily based on observations about the operation of the sense of sight by the German philosopher Schopenhauer, for instance, although Rietveld does not mention him by name. Rietveld noted that everything we experience derives from our senses. He draws a sharp distinction between the experience of colour, plasticity and space. These experiences may be blurred, as in crowded rooms, where the impressions are full of superfluities. But objective architecture is not burdened with such superfluities. On the contrary: in such a building, life is simplified, and we experience the space more directly. Through that direct experience of reality, people live more consciously and as a result they grow as human beings. Any exaggerated technical design or colour will distract from that purpose. What is more, according to Rietveld, houses do not have to be large to function well. They can even be smaller. This conviction leads him on a search for a new typology of houses for the lower middle classes. Implicitly, Rietveld is also critical of the propertied classes, with their spacious houses and their elaborate furniture and interior design. He sees that abundance as a sign of spiritual poverty.[9]

Aversion to Propaganda

Why was Rietveld willing to publish in *i10* now, and not before? The architecture editor, Oud, had asked him to write about his designs in the new journal founded by Arthur Lehning back in 1926. But Rietveld still thought it unnecessary to provide any justification for his own work, as is clear from the beginning of the first article in *i10* and from a brief text published in *De Stijl* the same year.[10] He believed that a work of art must be capable of functioning without explanation. Indeed, it is only a work of art if it makes explanation redundant; if it can induce a change of consciousness.

He wrote to Oud that his articles were really responses to views expressed by others:

But I don't read everything and therefore can't really write. I also know very well that writing doesn't get you anywhere; the written word doesn't become anything or express anything until you process it into what we call a work of art. But you do it because you really can't agree with everything.[11]

In the last sentence he appears to be referring to critical reviews of his work. A highly disparaging article had appeared in 1924, for instance, in which the reviewer had pointed out that children could easily hurt themselves on the projecting pieces of wood in the children's chair.[12]

From correspondence we learn that Oud not only encouraged Rietveld to write, but that he also sent him books and asked him to react. He sent Rietveld his Bauhaus book, *Holländische Architektur* (1926), for instance, which included a large number of Rietveld's architecture projects. They also exchanged views about publications by the architect Heinrich Tessenow and the historian Adolf Behne. Oud may have been hoping that Rietveld might review them for *i10*, but this never happened.[13] However, Rietveld did express his opinion about them in his letter to Oud. Rietveld wrote that he would rather visit projects such as Oud's garden village Oud-Mathenesse in Rotterdam (1924) and analyse them in detail than write what would essentially be a kind of advertisement.

He had an aversion to propaganda, and detested *Der Sieg des neuen Baustils* (1927) by the German architect Walter Curt Behrendt.[14] Even more vehement was his reaction to Behne's book *Eine Stunde Architektur* (1928), which he considered utterly without value.[15] He considered the conscious propaganda and the collages intended as visual corroboration of Behne's assertions 'not without wit, but without respect, either for the new or the old'. He continued: 'This book by A. Behne seems to me to possess a contrived modernity. Objectivity and purpose and then railing at things the purpose of which he cannot see.'[16]

He greatly admired the work of Tessenow, because he believed that it reflected a careful, exploratory approach. Rietveld obtained one of Tessenow's recent publications about housing – probably *Hausbau und dergleichen* (1916) or *Handwerk und Kleinstadt* (1919), it is not clear which. In an undated letter to Oud, Rietveld wrote admiringly: 'I bought Tessenow's book and consider it a really fine piece of work. More people should consider things reflectively, as he does, instead of straining so hard to be modern.'[17] Tessenow's books analyse diverse aspects of types of dwellings, in text and image. These analyses led to designs in which regional differences or characteristics, archetypal shapes, and considerations of efficiency were forged into a unified whole.[18]

From the designs that Rietveld used to illustrate his articles, it is clear that he – unlike Tessenow – tended to generalize regional features. His goal was to provide for a freer way of life, without the application of individual differentiation, or of specific, regional shapes. Indeed, while Tessenow drew inspiration for elements such as window and door frames from regional features, Rietveld's design for the façade of his *normaalwoningen* included a ventilation slit for the bathroom that was so unusual, and made such an abstract impression in the appearance of the façade, that Oud was perplexed and had to ask what it was.[19]

A. Behne, *Eine Stunde Architektur*, Stuttgart 1928

A. Behne, *Eine Stunde Architektur*, Stuttgart 1928, 38
Collage by Max Fischer

G.Th. Rietveld, Isometric cutaway and floor plans for a design for small houses, *i10* 12 (1928) 17/18, 92

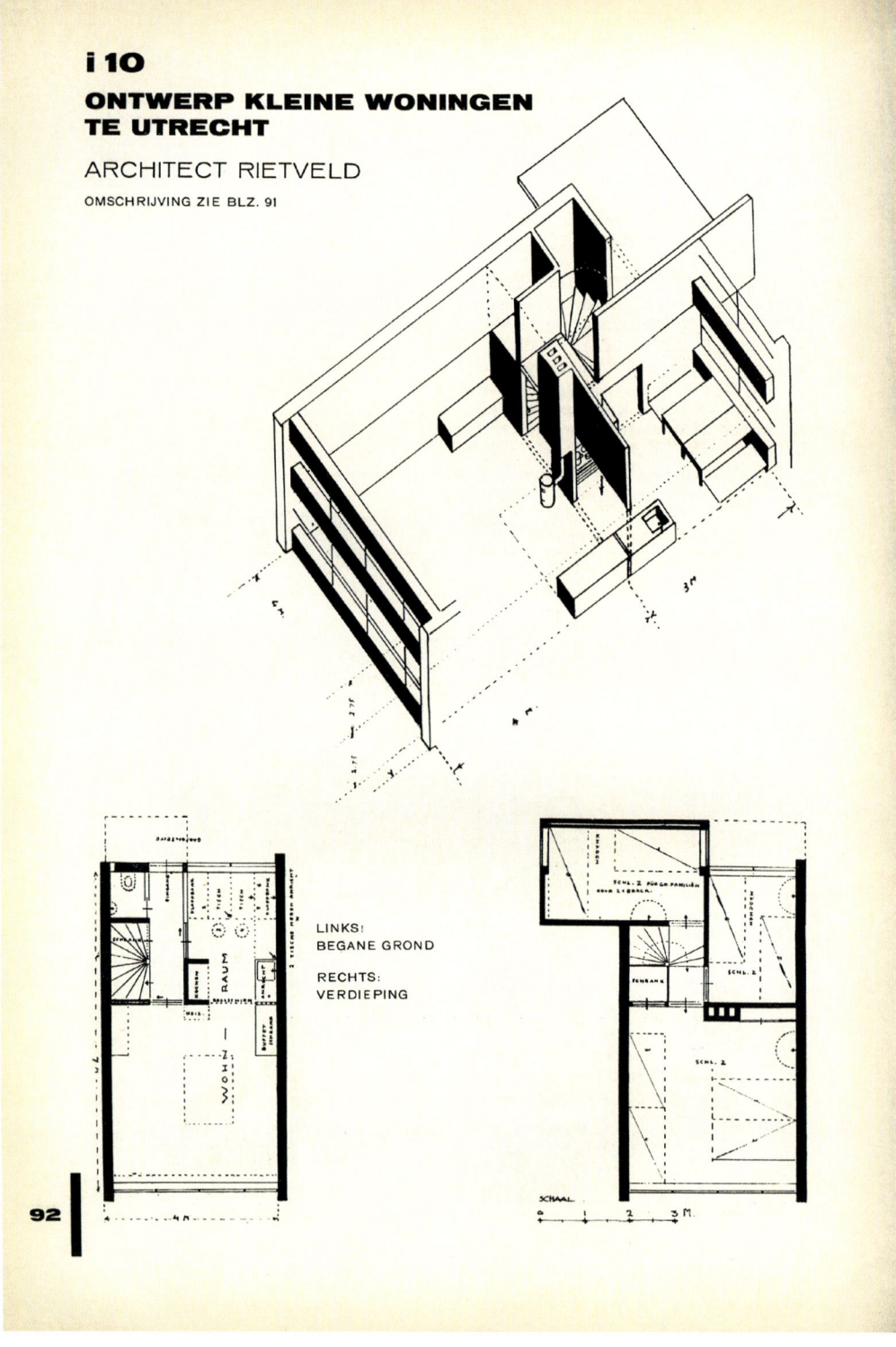

Even so, in Rietveld too, it is not always easy to distinguish objectively between advertisement and neutral information. In the late 1920s, he became the editor of the periodical of the Netherlands-New Russia Society, and was the second delegate of the International Congress of Modern Architecture (CIAM). In 1930 he even joined with others to launch a periodical: *periodiek in briefvorm* (epistolary periodical). This publication had none of the visual force of *i10* or of Tessenow's meticulous drawings. On the contrary, it appeared in the form of a newspaper with letters to the editor. In the opening statement and editorial preface, he called on others to commit their ideas to paper. 'This small periodical in epistolary form does not acknowledge a single preconception. It will be a free platform for every living idea, or it will disappear immediately after the first attempt. This freedom also applies to criticism.'[20]

Rietveld's idea was to create a wide-ranging cultural network, ranging from literature and religion to art. He wanted a cultural debate – through reading, thinking and writing – with the wider goal of achieving mental growth. The periodical was not very successful; it attracted few participants. In spite of Rietveld's repeated calls for contributions, only six issues appeared, and after about 12 months, the initiative quietly expired.

Questionnaire on Housing Preferences
Besides using the media to provoke exchanges of opinion, and to encourage others to express their ideas on paper (as in *periodiek in briefvorm*), Rietveld also saw his contributions to journals and periodicals as providing openings for his own research. He wanted to devise a questionnaire in *i10*, together with the interior architect Truus Schröder – with whom he often collaborated on projects – on the kinds of housing people wanted to live in. He did not expect the results to yield a few types, to cater for different family sizes and types of living arrangement, for instance, but hoped that they would lead to general floor plans that would be of universal application. He explained his idea to Oud:

> Couldn't we ask a few questions in *i10* . . . about living preferences for all kinds of people in order to arrive at a programme for a type of dwelling that we need . . . People must be able to make their demands without restriction, but they have to understand that if their demands are excessive, the most important thing will more or less escape their notice.[21]

This 'most important' thing was the impact of the space, which was closely related to the way in which people inhabited it. Rietveld tried to formulate a looser clustering of functions and a freer style of living than was customary in the Netherlands at that time. That can already be seen in the floor plan of the house built for Truus Schröder-Schräder, in which sliding walls make it possible for the mother and her children to use the space flexibly. Similar sliding walls were used in the floor plans for his standardized dwellings for the lower middle classes. Rietveld's principles here were not only completely at odds with the prevailing practice, but they also clashed with the views of most architects and those involved in providing public housing.

[20] 'Dit kleine periodiek in briefvorm erkent geen enkele vooropgezette mening. Het wordt een vrije tribune voor elke levende idee, of het verdwijnt direct na de eerste poging. Die vrijheid geldt evengoed voor de critiek.' G.Th. Rietveld, 'periodiek in briefvorm' (introduction in trial issue, June 1931), in: Van Beusekom 1991, 33-52.

[21] 'Zouden we in *i10* . . . eens eenige vragen kunnen stellen omtrent woningeischen voor allerlei soort menschen om te komen tot een program voor een woningtype dat we nodig hebben. . . . De menschen moeten onbegrensd hun eischen stellen maar daarbij weten, dat als ze teveel vragen, ze dat wat het voornaamste is meer of minder ontgaat.' NAI, Oud archive, letter from Rietveld to Oud, 10 February 1927.

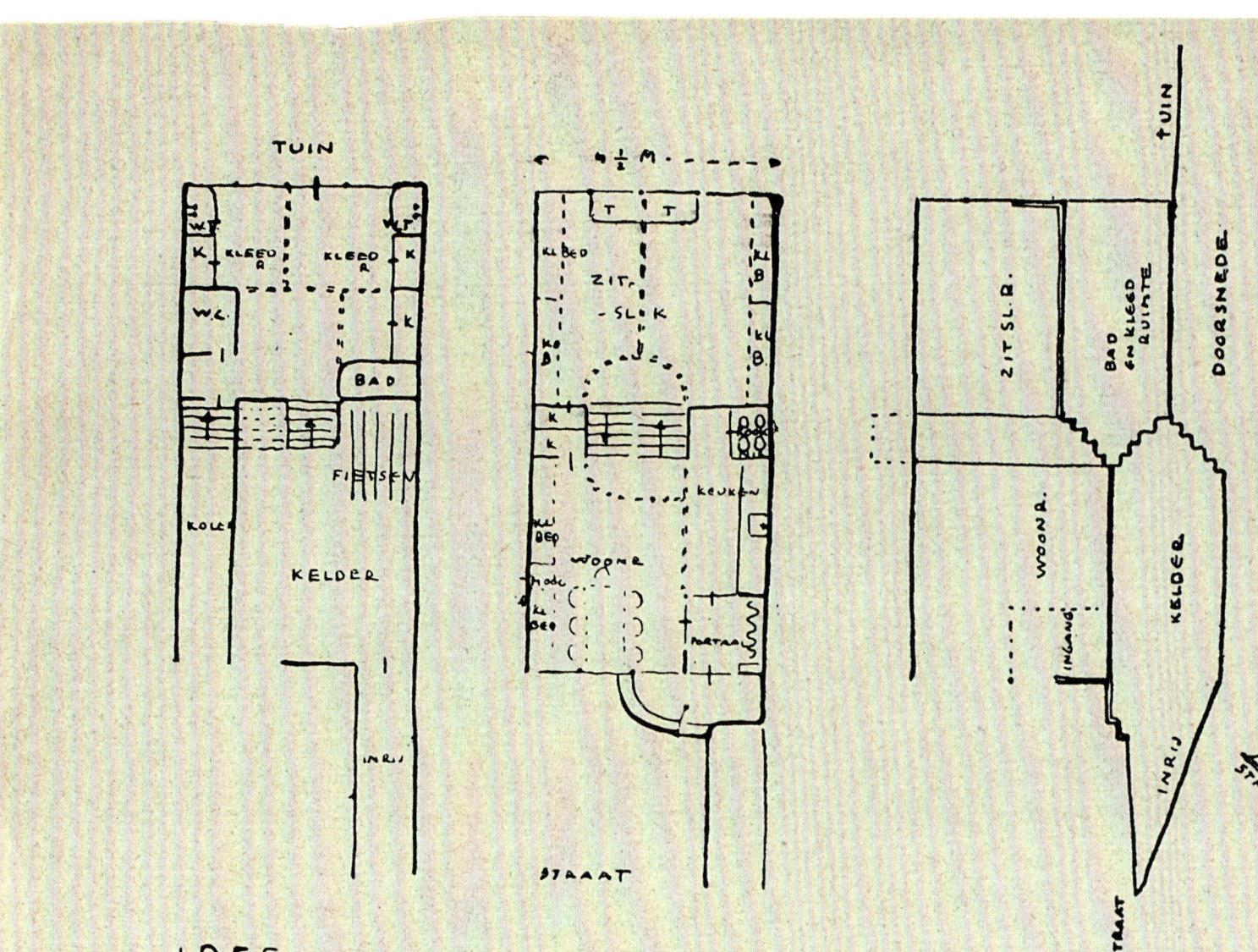

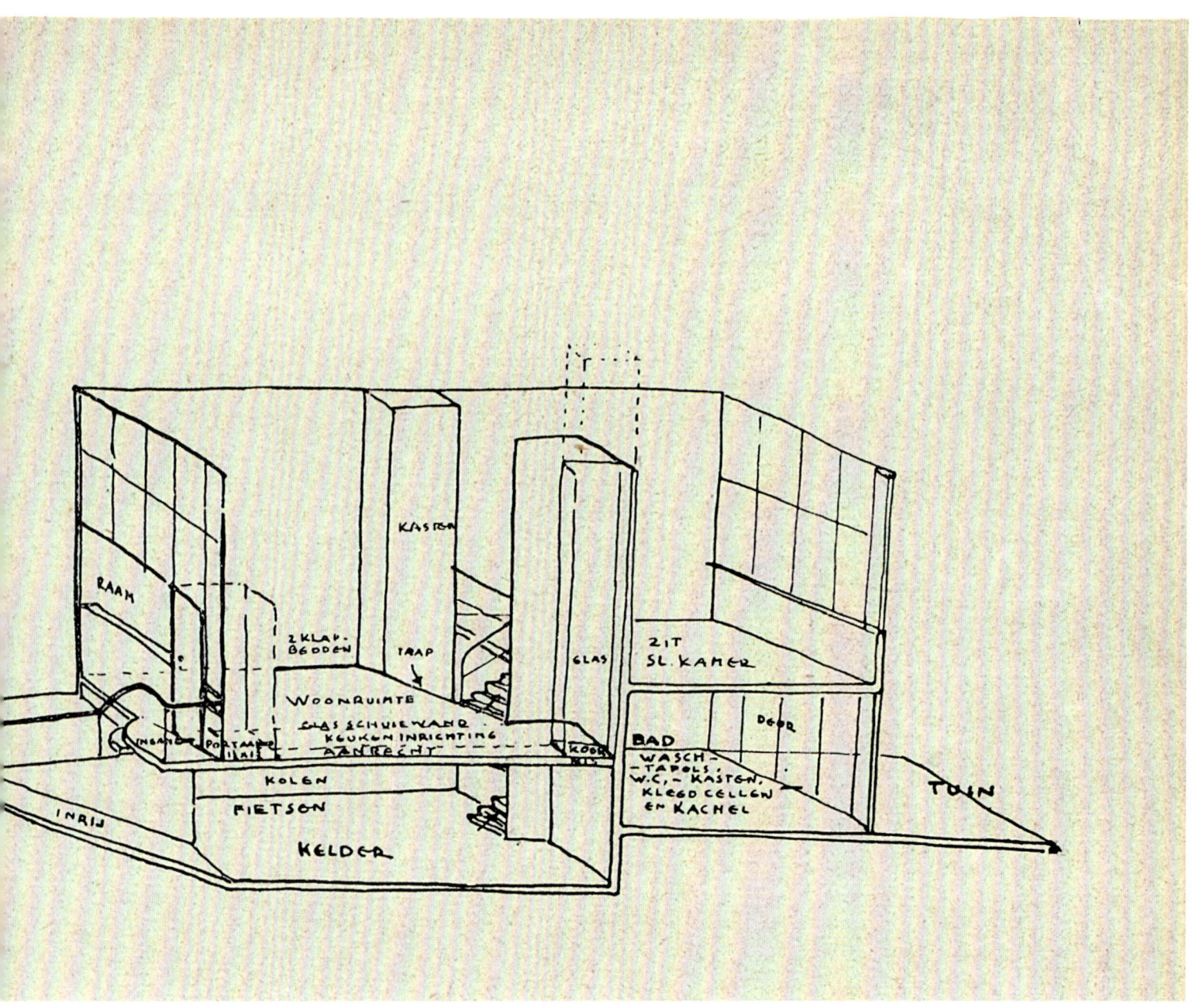

G.Th. Rietveld, 'Idee voor eenvoudige woning' (Idea for a simple dwelling), *periodiek in briefvorm* (July/August 1931), 1

[22] For the debate on the kitchen and the contributions of housewives' organizations, see Bullock 1994.

[23] In 1926, Erna Meyer published *Der neue Haushalt*, in which she extolled the Schröder House, because the large glass surfaces were easy to keep clean. See Küper and Van Zijl 1988, 19.

[24] NAI, Oud archive, letter from Rietveld to Oud, undated [c. 1927].

[25] Rietveld 1930 (a), 244.

[26] Rietveld 1930 (b), 316-318.

The chosen method for his questionnaire about housing preferences was largely based on the proposals for the rationalization of domestic life by associations of housewives. In Germany, the result was far-reaching rationalization, exemplified by parallel rows of minimalist housing blocks (*Zeilenbau*) and the minimum subsistence dwelling (*Wohnung für das Existenzminimum*). It acquired its clearest form in the Frankfurt Kitchen, in which the kitchen's design was attuned to a completely objective analysis of the way it was used.[22] Oud would design a rationalized kitchen of this kind for his model dwellings at the Werkbund Exhibition in Stuttgart (1927), aided by Erna Meyer, a specialist in progressive housekeeping.[23]

Rietveld had nothing good to say about this rigorous functional separation of the *Kochküche* (cooking-based kitchen). On the contrary, he favoured the *Wohnküche* (kitchen-diner), in the Netherlands sometimes known as the 'Brabant kitchen-diner', in which preparing food, and eating and living together, were combined in an integrated whole – and a single space. In 1928 he published a floor plan in *i10* that included two moveable tables in the kitchen. While meals are being prepared, these tables are pushed against the kitchen-sink unit and used as a worktop. During meals they are moved back and serve as dining tables. Later on, they are moved to the living area to be used in a variety of ways. With his preference for the kitchen-diner, which was rejected by numerous modern architects in the Netherlands and Germany, Rietveld favoured lively enjoyment of the home above dry rationalism and a Taylorist household.

New Simplicity

No study of housing preferences was ever published in *i10*, since Rietveld's questionnaire was never actually carried out. In a letter to Oud around 1927, he wrote that he no longer wanted to fulfil individual housing preferences; instead, he sought to define universal needs.[24]

In successive articles, published in 1930, Rietveld discussed his ideas on types of dwellings at greater length. He published these texts in the periodical *De werkende vrouw* (Working Women), which promoted the emancipation of women. In the first one, he discussed the influence of mechanization on the design of the interior and of houses. He posited that in the search for the right design of the chair, it was time to bid the past farewell: with the 'new mechanical methods, new materials and new construction-based inventions', a chair would be created that would possess a kind of natural quality – as natural, say, as a spoon. It should be a functional form, pried loose from the 'complicated past', with a range of diverse forms.[25]

The quest for 'a universal form' was also at the centre of his following article in *De werkende vrouw*. Rietveld felt that commercial contractors working in the construction industry had brought about the necessary standardization, but that the change was accompanied by an impoverishment, with little regard for demands for sunlight, comfort and efficiency. Rietveld adopted a different angle. In his opinion, people living in a busy world needed a peaceful living environment. For that sense of emotional wellbeing, he wanted to simplify the home – in fact he labelled this endeavour 'new simplicity'.[26]

De werkende vrouw 1 (1930) 9

G.Th. Rietveld, 'De stoel', *De werkende vrouw* 1 (1930) 9, 244

Two years later, in the full-length article 'Nieuwe Zakelijkheid in Nederlandse architectuur' (New Objectivity in Dutch Architecture, 1932), Rietveld formulated his view of the innovative trends in architecture for a general readership. Interestingly, he accorded significant influence to Dadaism, which he felt had done far more than contemporary movements to pave the way for modern forms. At the end of the article he argued in favour of flexible uses, drawing inspiration from Dadaism:

> Since at our best moments we are happier sitting on a table than a chair, or indeed have no need whatsoever of a house, table, or chair, the house for the future (that is, the house for the next generation) cannot, and should not, completely satisfy the prevailing concept of 'dwelling'.[27]

Studying the early development of Rietveld's theory, it becomes apparent that his views were based on theories of aesthetics, observation and philosophy developed long before 1920.[28] He was entirely conscious of the ways in which he was following in that tradition, and he was equally convinced of the need to break with design traditions.[29] By inducing psychological responses with his new products, which were preferably to be made in industrial production processes, he sought to neutralize the negative aspects of mass production. So his standardized dwellings or *normaalwoningen* were not familiar spaces reduced to a minimum, but products of a quest for a more conscious life, through new attitudes to space. Since he noticed that public support for this project could not be taken for granted, he started writing, providing public information, and giving lectures. He did so for fellow professionals, but he considered it at least as important to try to create a wider support base in periodicals such as *i10*, *De werkende vrouw* and *De Vrije Bladen*. By reaching out in this way, he hoped to expand the number of people for whom architecture could become an instrument of spiritual growth.[30] ◆

[27] 'Daar we in onze beste momenten beter op een tafel zitten, dan op een stoel of in 't geheel geen huis, tafel of stoel nodig hebben, zal het huis voor de toekomst (dit is het huis voor de nieuwe generatie) niet geheel het nu nog heersende begrip "wonen" mogen en kunnen bevredigen.' Rietveld 1932, 27. (for English translation of the text see Küper and Van Zijl 1992, 33-39). *De Vrije Bladen* was an independent monthly for art and literature. Most of its readers were probably familiar with the term New Objectivity (*Nieuwe Zakelijkheid*) in literature, but not in architecture. As was customary among modernist architects in this period, Rietveld presented the architecture of New Objectivity as a break with the past, in which abstract art had shrugged off limitations of style.

[28] See e.g. F. Bollerey, 'Innovation or "Nothing new under the sun"', in: Henket and Heynen 2002, 276-289.

[29] In an unpublished text about housing (1940), he described it as a 'space for cooking and eating in which both cooking and eating are a Bruegel-like pleasure'. G.T. Rietveld, 'Woningbouw', unpublished [1940]. Quoted in Küper and Van Zijl 1988, 67-68.

[30] In December 1930 Rietveld lectured to the architecture section of the civil engineering and architecture student society 'Praktische Studie' as part of the International Course in New Architecture: Rietveld 1930 (c), 507; in May 1931 he gave the opening address for an exhibition of work by Utrecht's youth: 'Openingsrede van den heer Rietveld', *Utrechtsch Provinciaal en Stedelijk Dagblad* 8 May 1931, RSA.

Begeer, Cornelis L.J.
51, 53, 56

Schröder-Schräder, Truus
35, 43, 51, 54, 56, 63, 66, 67, 72, 77

Bergeijk
71, 84, 88, 90, 91

Schelling, H.G.J.
51, *52*, 53, 54, 56, 63

Erasmuslaan, Utrecht
29, 54, 57, 67, *70*, *78*, 79

Social Context: Clients and Commissions

Radermacher Schorer, M.R.
56, 60, 62, 63

Vreeburg Cinema
60, 61

Witteveen, W.G.
53-55

Roman Koot

Rietveld's Network in Utrecht

On 5 July 1963, Gerrit Rietveld received the silver medal of the City of Utrecht. Awarded just a year before his death, it was a remarkably late acknowledgement of his importance to the city. Rietveld spent his entire career – indeed, his entire life – in Utrecht and left a profound mark on the city's development and image, through both his architecture and his active role in local artistic circles. It was not until the 1950s, after he had gained national recognition as an authority in architecture and design, that his own city offered him a few major commissions and he was invited to join a variety of local art committees.[1] Even then, it was mainly private individuals and a few building companies that gave Rietveld the opportunity to put his ideas to work.[2]

Nevertheless, from the earliest years of his artistic career, Rietveld's development was closely tied to the city where he lived. Most of his buyers and patrons came from Utrecht, had family there, or had other ties to the city, and Rietveld himself had a deeply rooted personal and professional network there. In this period, he played an active role in the main local organizations for modern art, either as a member or as an officer.

Rietveld's Earliest Patrons
At first, most of Rietveld's buyers and patrons belonged to Utrecht's social or cultural élite or to Rietveld or Truus Schröder-Schräder's personal circle of friends and acquaintances. They were open to new movements in art and society and wanted to make a contribution. Some of them worked at the local university or for the railways, and a considerable number of them were physicians. Many belonged to the association Voor de Kunst (For Art's Sake; see below), as did Rietveld himself. Apart from these forward-thinking individuals, most of the people who bought Rietveld's furniture, or (especially after the Second World War) asked him to design their homes, were fellow artists, architects and designers. For Rietveld, these contacts and commissions not only put bread on the table, but also provided opportunities to experiment.

The first of Rietveld's benefactors was Carel J.A. Begeer (1883-1956). Rietveld was employed in Begeer's silver workshop from 1904 to 1913, with occasional stints as a draughtsman or model maker. Carel Begeer designed silver ornaments and utensils. From 1910 until his death, he was the director of Koninklijke Van Kempen & Begeer, the leading Dutch precious metals company. For Rietveld – still a novice designer, who had just left his father's workshop and the local applied arts school – working for Begeer was a tremendously valuable experience. 'I have never forgotten your influence, which did so much to broaden my horizons,' he wrote in 1954, two years before Begeer's death.[3] Begeer put Rietveld into contact with patrons,[4] and probably encouraged him to join the Utrecht artists' society Kunstliefde (Love of Art; see below).[5] Carel's half-brother Cornelis L.J. Begeer (1869-1948) also gave Rietveld several major commissions, such as the renovation of the front of his jewellery shop in Oudkerkhof, a street in the centre of Utrecht, in 1919, and that of the headquarters of the Goud- en Zilversmidscompagnie (Association of Gold and Silversmiths) in Amsterdam in 1921. These were Rietveld's first architectural commissions.[6]

The architect H.G.J. Schelling (1888-1978) was another early and influential patron of Rietveld, and the two men were friends for many years.

Art appreciation society Kunstliefde electing new members, including 'G.Th. Rietveld, draughtsman', 26 October 1909
CMU, Utrecht

[1] Rietveld's largest Utrecht commission was the design of a new district, including several hundred single-family houses and flats, in the Hoograven and Tolsteeg areas between 1954 and 1958. Part of the extensive district was renovated in the period 2005 to 2009. See Edens 2009. In this period he was on a committee to erect a war memorial for the city's fallen resistance fighters (1948), as well as the Utrecht Beautification Committee (1948-1958), the City of Utrecht Museum Committee (1956-1957) and the Advisory Committee for Fine and Applied Arts (1960).

[2] For a list of all of Rietveld's buildings in Utrecht, see Van Zijl 2001.

[3] Begeer archive (part of the still uncatalogued Van Kempen & Begeer archives in the custody of the RKD in The Hague), letter from Rietveld to Carel Begeer, 15 July 1954. As quoted in Bless 1982, 258, note 5.

[4] In 1909, Begeer asked Rietveld to design a funerary monument for E. Nijland (headmaster of the Nederlandsch Hervormde Burgerschool, a secondary school in Utrecht) at the Eerste Algemene Begraafplaats Soestduinen. See Küper and Van Zijl 1992, cat. no. 8.

[5] From 1910 to 1920, Carel Begeer was on the executive committee of Kunstliefde and active in other capacities in the Utrecht art world. In 1910 Rietveld was admitted to the society as a 'draughtsman'. At the

H.G.J. Schelling, Naarden-Bussum Station, 1925
Picture postcard
Het Utrechts Archief, De Pater collection

H.G.J. Schelling family, July 1923
Daughter Anne on Schelling's arm
Schelling estate

H.G.J. Schelling (design) and G.Th. Rietveld (execution), birth announcement of Anne Schelling, 1922
Woodcut, 6.1 x 9.9 cm
Museum Meermanno Westreenianum, The Hague

Social Context: Clients and Commissions

Schelling was a civil engineer at the Maatschappij tot Exploitatie van de Staatsspoorwegen, later the Nederlandse Spoorwegen (the national railway company), and in 1942 he became the head of the company's architecture department for the north-eastern region. In conjunction with Sybold van Ravesteyn, who was in charge of the south-western region, Schelling was responsible for the construction of Dutch railway station buildings in the years immediately preceding and following the Second World War. His surviving work includes the station in Naarden-Bussum (1925) and Amsterdam's Muiderpoort and Amstel Stations (1939).

In 1916 Rietveld designed and produced furniture for the occasion of Schelling's marriage. Not a great deal is known about how Rietveld came to receive this and subsequent commissions from Schelling. The two men seem to have worked closely together on the cradle that Rietveld made for Schelling's daughter Johanna Karin in 1918. According to the heirs, Schelling had substantial influence over the design, especially with regard to the selection and the form of the quotations by Rabindranath Tagore. A review by Jan Engelman of a craft exhibition held by the Utrechtsche Kunstkring (a local art society; see below) in April 1924, where the cradle was on display, even describes it as 'Mr Schelling's cradle'.[7]

There are also other designs that seem to have been Schelling's work, with Rietveld responsible solely for their execution. Examples include an undated fir cupboard,[8] the announcement of the birth of Anne Schelling in 1922,[9] and a bookplate that Rietveld made around 1920 for J.H. Maronier, an artist who also worked for the Dutch railways.[10] A number of bookplates and New Year's cards attest to Schelling's talents as a graphic artist. He was also an authority in the field of small graphic works, of which he had a large collection.[11]

During this period, Rietveld had a similar working relationship with W.G. Witteveen (1891-1979), another railway associate of Schelling's and the later Rotterdam city planner.[12] The cover of a government committee report on traffic conditions in and around Rotterdam (*Mededeelingen der Staatscommissie betreffende verkeerstoestanden in en nabij Rotterdam*, n.p., 1921) bears a woodcut designed by the author, W.G. Witteveen, and carved by Rietveld. A stylistically similar birth announcement from the same year, for Hendrik Johannes Witteveen, is credited to W.G. Witteveen and may also have been executed by Rietveld.[13] It can hardly be a coincidence that in 1923, at Witteveen's request, Rietveld reproduced a highchair he had made for Schelling in 1918, again for Hendrik Johannes.[14]

Van Ravesteyn also had a design for a chair executed in Rietveld's workshop in 1921.[15] The interest shown in Rietveld's work by these civil engineers at the Dutch railways is striking, but their relationships with him were always one on one. They knew him from Utrecht's cultural scene, and through each other. No further ties were established between Rietveld and the Dutch railways.

Rietveld maintained a friendly relationship with Schelling (albeit from a distance). As he wrote in a letter on the occasion of Schelling's 70th birthday:

> You were actually my only true friend, Her [Schelling's first name], old boy, and as far as I'm concerned that hasn't changed, although we've happened to grow apart a bit. I hope I will never forget your enthusiastic

exhibition of work by members of Kunstliefde in the spring of 1912, he had four paintings on display, including a portrait of Anthonie Begeer, his employer's father. For more about Begeer and his forward-looking attitude toward the applied arts, see Krekel-Aalberse 2001.

[6] Rietveld also made traditional furniture for Cornelis Begeer's shop; see Vöge 1993, cat. nos. 32-35. In 1920, Rietveld received the bronze medal of the Utrecht division of Architectura et Amicitia (a national society of architects) for his renovation of the shop. The designs for the Amsterdam renovation were Rietveld's contribution to the De Stijl exhibition in Galerie L'Effort Moderne in Paris in 1923. See also the essay by Marieke Kuipers in this publication.

[7] 'In Mr Schelling's cradle, some parts of which are very fine, we encounter reminiscences of De Bazel. Its execution is somewhat ponderous and heavy, but also very precise.' Jan Engelman in *Het Centrum*, 26 April 1924. In 1909, the architect and designer K.P.C. de Bazel had designed the cradle for Princess Juliana.

[8] Included in the retrospective of Rietveld's oeuvre in 1958; see Bakema 1958, cat. no. 14.

[9] Küper and Van Zijl 1992, cat. no. 64, described as a Rietveld design. The birth announcement is described in the following terms in the collection of Museum Meermanno: 'design by H.G.J. Schelling, woodcut by Rietveld'. The source of Meermanno's attribution is the collector Eugène Strens, inv. nos. SAT 12969 and 12970.

[10] At the Centraal Museum, Utrecht, dated c. 1917-1920. The wooden stamp is in the collection of the Centraal Museum; see Küper and Van Zijl 1992, cat. no. 46. This bookplate (from the collection of Eugène Strens) is described as follows at Museum Meermanno: 'design by H.G.J. Schelling, woodcut by the architect Rietveld, Utrecht' (Strens' handwriting) (inv. no. SAT 12956). The one in the Schwencke collection, now at Meermanno, is also described as having been designed by Schelling and dated 1922, inv. no. SW 05563.

[11] His collection of more than 10,000 bookplates, New Year's cards and books was purchased by Museum Meermanno in 1978.

[12] On Witteveen, see Mens 2007.

[13] Birth announcement collection Museum Meermanno, inv. no. SCHEL 06908, from the collection of H.G.J. Schelling.

14 On the Schelling chair, see Küper and Van Zijl 1992, cat. no. 34. The version for Witteveen was discovered in 2008 and is in the collection of the Centraal Museum in Utrecht and the Stedelijk Museum in Amsterdam. See Van Zijl and De Roode 2009, 26-29.

15 An oak desk chair; see Scharlemann and Koudijs 2005, 35.

16 RSA, letter from Rietveld to Schelling, 19 October 1958.

17 It is unclear why so many purchasers of Rietveld's furniture were physicians. Overy has suggested that Rietveld's furniture forces users to assume an active posture that promotes physical and mental health. See P. Overy, 'From icon to prototype', in: Vöge 1993, 17. The modernist adage 'light, air and space' must also have appealed to medical practitioners.

18 The interior design, which included an initial version of the tubular lamp, has not been preserved and is known only from photographs. One solid wooden desk is now at the Gemeentemuseum in The Hague. Küper and Van Zijl 1992, cat. nos. 59-63.

19 Küper and Van Zijl 1992, cat. no. 151.

20 Signed and dated sketches at the NAI, Rietveld archive, inv. no. 472.

21 There were flaws in the construction of the roof, however, and in Utrecht the garage apartment acquired the nickname of 'the basket' or 'the sieve'. See also the essay by Marieke Kuipers in this publication.

22 Van Zijl and Mulder 2009.

23 Truus's older sister An was married to the paediatrician Rein Harrenstein. In 1926 and 1931, Rietveld renovated the sitting room and a number of other rooms in the house on Weteringschans in Amsterdam. The couple had a large circle of friends who were visual artists, including Jacob Bendien, Charley Toorop, Kurt Schwitters and Piet Mondrian.

24 During the Dada tour that Theo van Doesburg and Kurt Schwitters organized in the Netherlands in 1923, an evening reception for a select group of invitees took place in Truus's room in Biltstraat. Many international artists and architects, such as El Lissitzky, Bruno Taut, Mart Stam, Theo van Doesburg and Kurt Schwitters, stayed at the Schröder House at one time or another.

and idealistic attitude toward life, which had so much influence on my own views.[16]

Many of Rietveld's early purchasers and patrons were physicians and medical specialists, such as the general practitioner A.M. Hartog from Maarssen, who had his consultation room redecorated by Rietveld in 1922.[17] Rietveld – who may have known Hartog from Voor de Kunst – collaborated on the project with Willem van Leusden. Hartog gave them a very free hand, and the room became one of Rietveld's most striking early interiors.[18]

Hartog and Rietveld may also have been brought together by the Utrecht ophthalmologist G. ten Doesschate (1885-1964), who was an energizing force in the Utrecht art scene from around 1905 onward. J.H. Maronier, who in his student days had been Ten Doesschate's neighbour, had put him into contact with Rietveld. In 1930, Rietveld decorated a large front room in Ten Doesschate's home at Catharijnesingel 53. He designed a desk for two in the shape of a large question mark. The interior has been lost, but several pieces of furniture, including the desk, are still in the family's possession.[19] Other commissions from Ten Doesschate included a music school with two apartments in Zeist (1931-1932) and furniture for his son Jurriaan.

Ten Doesschate also put the ophthalmologist H.J.M. Weve (1888-1962), a professor at Utrecht University, in touch with Rietveld. There are design sketches dating from 1934 and 1935 for various pieces of furniture, including relatively luxurious versions of Rietveld's Zigzag Chair and tube-framed chair, both upholstered in green morocco.[20] A final major commission came from the physician and art collector H. van der Vuurst de Vries; in 1927-1928, Rietveld renovated his garage and designed an apartment above it for his driver. This project involved one of the earliest uses of prefab elements in housing construction and formed a step towards standardization.[21]

Involvement in the Utrecht Art Scene
One figure who loomed large in Rietveld's career was Truus Schröder-Schräder. In 1921 he redecorated her room in the house in Biltstraat, and after the death of her husband Frits Schröder (1923), she asked him to design a new house for her. This 1924 building, now known as the Schröder House, was the product of intense collaboration between the two.[22] Later, she took the initiative for the design of a row of houses on Erasmuslaan (1931). Truus Schröder was a sounding board for Rietveld and became his sometime partner in the design process. After the death of his first wife in 1957, she also became his life companion. Her social background was utterly different from Rietveld's, and she brought him into contact with patrons and, through her sister An, with artistic circles outside Utrecht.[23] In difficult times, she supported him and his family financially. Her door was always open for their artistic acquaintances and relatives.[24]

Rietveld was particularly active in Utrecht cultural life in the 1920s and 1930s. He knew many artists in the city and built up a large network. In his workshop, he received visits from such artists as Willem van Leusden (1886-1974), the sculptor Jo Uiterwaal (1897-1972) and the painter Douwe van der Zweep (1890-1975), as well as from architects, such as Van Ravesteyn, Schelling and Piet Elling (1897-1962).[25]

W.G. Witteveen (design) and
G.Th. Rietveld (execution),
Birth announcement of Hendrikus
Johannes Witteveen, 1921
Woodcut
Museum Meermanno Westreenianum,
The Hague

W.G. Witteveen (design) and
G.Th. Rietveld (execution), Cover
*Mededeelingen der Staatscommissie
betreffende verkeerstoestanden in
en nabij Rotterdam*, 1921
Woodcut
Koninklijke Bibliotheek, The Hague

[25] Piet Elling was a novice artist and architect at that time. He bought two armchairs and a sideboard from Rietveld in 1919, and a few other pieces of furniture at a later date. Schelling and Elling were among the earliest purchasers of Rietveld's work. See De Wagt 2008, 40-42 and passim. Many artists who were friends of Rietveld's made furniture in a Rietveld-inspired style around this period.

[26] Kunstliefde's collection of old master paintings from Utrecht formed the core of the collection at the city's Centraal Museum.

[27] This group of reformist artists also formed a drawing club together. Led by Willem van Leusden, they experimented with the abstraction of the human figure, reducing it to its most elementary lines. Rietveld probably attended the meetings of this club from time to time. On this subject, and for a detailed account of developments relating to it, see R. Koot, 'De crisis van 1929-1930', in: Van der Haar et al. 1997, 61-86, 94-95. For images and anecdotes, see Juffermans 1996, 49-66.

[28] Printed in facsimile with explanatory notes in Van Beusekom 1991, 33-51. See also the essay by Dolf Broekhuizen in this publication.

[29] Such as the officers of the Genootschap Nederland-Nieuw Rusland (Netherlands-New Russia Society), A. Harrenstein, H. Wiessing, I.E. Prins-Willekes Macdonald and Victor E. van Vriesland, and the visual artists Peter Alma, Hildo Krop, Mark Kolthoff and Charley Toorop. In this period, Rietveld was involved in the politically engaged movement, in part through his activities on the executive committee of this society.

[30] There was no journal devoted to the *Nieuwe Bouwen* (the Dutch manifestation of the Modern Movement in architecture) in this period.

[31] Carel and Cornelis Begeer, Leo Brom, G. ten Doesschate, A.M. Hartog, Dora van Ravesteyn-Hintzen, M.R. Radermacher Schorer, Frits and Truus Schröder-Schräder, C.A. Verrijn Stuart, H. van der Vuurst de Vries and H.J.M. Weve.

[32] This group also included Leo Brom, Willem van Leusden, Dick van Luijn, Sybold van Ravesteyn, Jo and Stef Uiterwaal and Douwe van der Zweep.

[33] Anon., 'Utrechtsche Jongeren', *De Maasbode* 2 May 1931.

Genootschap Kunstliefde

As early as 1909, Rietveld was admitted as a working member of the Schilder- en Tekenkunstig Genootschap Kunstliefde, a society of Utrecht artists that was the main venue for its members to exhibit and sell their work. That is, it played this role from 1807, the year it was founded, until the early 1920s, when the executive committee more or less threw in the towel, bringing an end to the society's programme of exhibitions and its group drawing sessions. By that point, its impressive art collection had been sold to the city.[26] In 1912, after exhibiting four paintings, Rietveld gave up on a career as a painter, and he was not involved with the society again until 1929, when a group of younger artists protested plans by Kunstliefde's executive committee to shut down the society. The initiators of this coup included the gold and silversmith Leo Brom (1896-1965), Willem van Leusden, Douwe van der Zweep and the brothers Jo and Stef Uiterwaal (1889-1960). At their request, Rietveld wrote a memorandum proposing the return of Kunstliefde to the centre of Utrecht's modern art scene, with a full programme of exhibitions and a library of its own. Ultimately, the reform of Kunstliefde was due in large part to the efforts of a new executive committee, whose members included Jonkheer M.R. Radermacher Schorer (1888-1956; see below), Sybold van Ravesteyn, Willem van Leusden and Cornelis Begeer. From 1931 to 1933, Rietveld was on the executive committee of Kunstliefde.[27]

One of his first initiatives in this role was to publish a curious, nameless magazine described as a 'periodical in epistolary form'. Between June 1931 and February 1932, six issues were published, with a small circulation.[28] Yet the magazine deserves attention because it offers insight into Rietveld's network in Utrecht and throughout the Netherlands. The first issue contains a list of 135 names of current and potential staff members and subscribers (no distinction is made), almost all of whom come from Rietveld's network of acquaintances, fellow artists, purchasers and patrons. Many are from Utrecht, of course, and in particular, the group involved in the reform of Kunstliefde is prominently represented. The list includes various patrons of Rietveld's, such as Cornelis Begeer, the Amsterdam pharmacist J.W. Birza, G. ten Doesschate, E.M. Fraenkel, a teacher of classical languages in Utrecht, A.M. Hartog, H.G.J. Schelling and the ceramic painter Sam Schellink (1876-1958). The list also includes friends and acquaintances from the left-wing political scene and artists with socialist views,[29] as well as a substantial number of architects.[30]

Voor de Kunst

It was probably in 1918 that Rietveld joined the other Utrecht artists' association, Voor de Kunst, founded in 1895 by the artist Etha Fles as an alternative to the conservative Kunstliefde. Voor de Kunst had an active programme of exhibitions with the emphasis on contemporary art. While Kunstliefde was intended primarily for artists, the members of Voor de Kunst were all art lovers – for the most part, wealthy members of the upper middle class, intellectuals and business owners. Some belonged to both Voor de Kunst and Kunstliefde, and among them were many of Rietveld's patrons.[31]

In the 1920s, when Kunstliefde was still in a deep slumber, Voor de Kunst was organizing an ambitious programme of six to eight exhibitions a year, few of which featured art from Utrecht. One notable exception came in the spring of 1931, when Voor de Kunst mounted an exhibition of young Utrecht artists. This event was meant to underscore the new vigour of the Utrecht art world, but above all, it reflected the reform of the association's 'competitor' Kunstliefde: eight of the 13 participants belonged to the group of younger artists who had revitalized Kunstliefde one year earlier, a group that included Rietveld.[32] Rietveld even designed the invitation. On the whole, the critics were either moderate in their praise or unimpressed, but the architecture section won their admiration: 'The architecture, in contrast – the new architecture of objective efficiency and "free plasticity" – has a major bastion in Utrecht,' the critic from *De Maasbode* remarked.[33] The *Utrechtsch Dagblad* devoted a separate article to the work of Rietveld, 'whose name is renowned from here to Japan'. Rietveld exhibited a number of designs, including one for four houses on Erasmuslaan, opposite the Schröder House. The construction company Bredero's Bouwbedrijf had built the houses not long before, and the result had moved the critic Cor Schilp to comment: '[This] will go a long way towards overcoming the reservations many people have expressed about this radical architectural reform.'[34] It was Rietveld's first project that did not involve private patronage.

Rietveld may also have been involved in an exhibition of photographs and film stills from the Soviet Union at Voor de Kunst in 1931.[35] He remained on the executive committee until 1938. That same year, Voor de Kunst merged for financial reasons with its old competitor Kunstliefde, continuing its activities as an exhibition committee within the larger society.[36]

Utrechtsche Kunstkring
The Utrechtsche Kunstkring, founded in 1922, organized evenings of music and theatre, lectures and occasional exhibitions. In 1923 Rietveld was involved in organizing a lecture for the Kunstkring by Bruno Taut (1880-1938).[37] In 1924, he contributed to a crafts fair showcasing the state of the art in Dutch design and introducing visitors to the Nieuwe Zakelijkheid, the Dutch branch of the art movement also known as the New Objectivity. The event was an eye-opener for the Utrecht public.[38] A.M. Hammacher, a critic for the *Utrechtsch Dagblad*, wrote in praise of a 'craftsmanlike art that develops organically, in and with life' and has no use for 'whimsical eccentricities and clever tricks'. As examples of this style, he mentioned the work of Rietveld, Vilmos Huszár (1884-1960), Sybold van Ravesteyn and the Utrecht designer Kees Kuiler (1890-1966).[39]

In 1929 Rietveld became a member of the exhibition committee, which brought the touring exhibition 'Neues Bauen' to Utrecht that same year. This exhibition, developed by the Deutscher Werkbund, provided a photographic survey of European architecture in the modern style. In Utrecht, the exhibition was supplemented with local examples of architectural and interior design in this style by Rietveld, Van Ravesteyn, Kuiler, Willem Maas (1897-1950), J.I. Planjer (1891-1966), H.F. Mertens (1885-1960) and Piet Klaarhamer (1874-1954).[40] The exhibition received a great deal of press coverage by journalists such as W. Jos. de Gruyter, Hammacher's successor at the *Utrechtsch Dagblad*.[41]

[34] [C.A.] S[chilp], 'Expositie Utrechtsche Jongeren. Het werk van Rietveld', *Utrechtsch Provinciaal en Stedelijk Dagblad* 30 April 1931.

[35] This exhibition was organized by the Genootschap Nederland-Nieuw Rusland and toured the Netherlands starting in May 1931. In Utrecht, the photographs were included in a larger exhibition organized by Paul Schuitema in collaboration with the architects' association Opbouw. Schuitema made a selection not only of photographs but also of modern graphic art by G. Kiljan, Piet Zwart, Dick Elffers, Schuitema himself and other artists. In 1931, Rietveld was an officer of both the Genootschap Nederland-Nieuw Rusland and Voor de Kunst.

[36] During this period, Rietveld is said to have been a more active member of Voor de Kunst; in 1933, for instance, he opened an Eva Besnyö solo exhibition. Besnyö was the daughter-in-law of Charley Toorop, who counted Rietveld among her circle of friends.

[37] The lecture was entitled 'Wollen und Wirken' (27 September 1923). Taut had come to the Netherlands for an exhibition devoted to his work, organized by the Haagsche Kunstkring, an art association in The Hague. RSA, correspondence between Sybold van Ravesteyn (then probably a member of the Utrechtsche Kunstkring exhibition committee), J.J.P. Oud and Rietveld.

[38] A review of the exhibition prior to the official opening commented that 'this exhibition will be a most remarkable event for Utrecht, the kind of thing that the people of Utrecht have unfortunately had to do without in the past, and that we must have if we are to remain a centre of culture and progress'; Anon., 'De tentoonstelling van den Kunstkring. Aan den vooravond van de opening', *Utrechtsch Provinciaal en Stedelijk Dagblad* 16 April 1924.

[39] Hammacher, 'De tentoonstelling van kunstnijverheid', *Utrechtsch Provinciaal en Stedelijk Dagblad* 20 April 1924.

[40] After its run in Utrecht (and without the extra material included there), the exhibition opened as part of the second show of the A.S.B. Group (Architectuur Schilderkunst Beeldhouwkunst; 'Architecture Painting Sculpture') at Amsterdam's Stedelijk Museum, 2-25 November 1929. The Utrecht architects Rietveld, Van Ravesteyn and Piet Elling were represented, alongside Mart Stam, J.J.P. Oud and Cornelis van Eesteren.

G.Th. Rietveld, Invitation to the exhibition 'Utrechtsche Jongeren', Voor de Kunst, Utrecht, 1931
12 x 8 cm
RSA, Utrecht

G.Th. Rietveld, *De Gemeenschap* (1925) 11

[41] W. Jos. de Gruyter, 'Bouwkundige tentoonstelling van den Utr. Kunstkring. In het gebouw van de Volksuniversiteit', *Utrechtsch Stedelijk en Provinciaal Dagblad* 22, 23 and 24 October 1929.

[42] On the Utrechtsche Filmliga, see Peters 2002. See also Linssen, Schoots and Gunning 1999.

[43] A few years later, from 1934 to 1936, the cinema underwent a much larger-scale renovation and extension. Rietveld designed an apartment on the top floor, which he and his family occupied from 1937 to 1958.

[44] On *De Gemeenschap*, see Van de Haterd 2004 and 2008.

[45] Radermacher Schorer restored Kunstliefde to financial health, took care of the preparatory work for the merger with Voor de Kunst, and nursed *De Gemeenschap* through a difficult period. He was also on the executive committees of many cultural associations, including the Utrechtsche Kunstkring and the Utrechtsche Filmliga. He enjoyed a wide reputation as a man of letters and collector of rare books. See De Boer 1998 and Van den Braber 2002.

[46] After Lucretius. *De Rerum Natura*, book III, line 964 (on card line 977), trans. by W.H.D. House, 1949 New Year's card by Nico Jesse, collection of Museum Meermanno, inv. no. SCHEL 06936a.

[47] In 1924, Van Ravesteyn had designed a bedroom for Radermacher Schorer, now in the collection of the Centraal Museum in Utrecht, along with several tube-frame chairs from the sitting room. On his designs for Radermacher Schorer, see Blotkamp 1977-1978, 40-59 and Scharlemann and Koudijs 2005, 37-39.

[48] J. Engelman, 'Renee Radermacher Schorer in memoriam. Een singulier en dienend mensch', *De Groene Amsterdammer* 11 August 1956.

The Utrechtsche Filmliga and *De Gemeenschap*

In 1927, an Utrecht division of the Filmliga (Film League) was founded. Rietveld served as secretary from its establishment until new officers were elected in 1931. The Filmliga wanted to create opportunities to show films that received too little attention in commercial cinemas. These were generally abstract, experimental films, or films from the Soviet Union that were not shown in the Netherlands for political reasons. The initiative originated in Amsterdam, where such figures as Menno ter Braak and Charley Toorop were involved, and it was brought to Utrecht by Sybold van Ravesteyn. Besides Rietveld, Radermacher Schorer (see below) also agreed to serve on the executive committee. Although some sources state that Rietveld was not without his shortcomings as secretary – he sometimes neglected to strike individuals off the membership roll when they resigned – the screenings in Vreeburg Cinema were a success.[42] Around 1930 the operator of Vreeburg, J. Nijland, asked Rietveld to design the renovation of the cinema. Rietveld radically altered the building's style, making it much more spare and sober, and giving the screening room a far more spacious feel.[43]

The screenings sponsored by the Filmliga were regularly reviewed in the Utrecht-based periodical *De Gemeenschap*. This was a progressive Catholic journal founded in 1924 by a group that included the author and critic Jan Engelman and the architect Willem Maas. In its early period, *De Gemeenschap* devoted a great deal of attention to avant-garde art.[44] For several years, Van Ravesteyn was a member of the editorial board, and in this capacity he was responsible for a number of typographically unusual cover designs. Rietveld designed the cover twice, in 1925 and 1927. The 1925 design was also used as a logo in the journal's letterhead and on invitations and other printed matter, and it made an undeniable contribution to the modern image of *De Gemeenschap*.

René Radermacher Schorer's Salon

In the Utrecht network of artistic pioneers, René Radermacher Schorer's salon played a central role. Radermacher Schorer, an aristocrat and the director of the fire insurance company Utrechtsche Algemeene Brandwaarborg Maatschappij, was a highly influential figure in the city's cultural life in the 1920s, and even more so in the 1930s. He was an officer (usually the treasurer) of just about every Utrecht cultural association, foundation and initiative. His network was not limited to Utrecht, but encompassed the national and international avant-garde.[45]

Radermacher Schorer turned his home into a cultural salon, with a preference for artists who blazed new trails. One of his New Year's cards bore the motto: 'For the old order always passes, thrust out by the new.'[46] This motto certainly applied to the renovation of the sitting room in his townhouse overlooking Wilhelminapark, designed by Sybold van Ravesteyn in 1927. In the most fashionable corner of Utrecht, Van Ravesteyn transformed a dark room with stately furnishings into a bright, airy space with graceful tube-frame chairs.[47] At Radermacher Schorer's receptions, artists rubbed shoulders with local dignitaries and other potential patrons. Jan Engelman described his salon as a 'venue for sampling the latest essences and derivatives'.[48]

G.Th. Rietveld, Interior of Vreeburg
Cinema, Utrecht, c. 1930
RSA, Utrecht

G.Th. Rietveld and T. Schröder-Schräder,
Radio cabinet for M.R. Radermacher Schorer,
1925
Glass, wood and iron
RSA, Utrecht

S. van Ravensteyn, M.R. Radermacher Schorer's salon, 1927
RSA Utrecht

[49] Küper and Van Zijl 1992, cat. no. 102.

[50] The guest books have been preserved in the collection of the Dutch National Library (KB) in The Hague, inv. nos. 134 C 82-87.

[51] On 24 October 1930, Richard Neutra was a guest there after a lecture earlier that day at the Utrechtsche Kunstkring about modern architecture in the USA. Rietveld, his daughter Bep, Truus Schröder and Her Schelling attended the reception at Radermacher Schorer's home. For a description of the lecture, see Anon., 'Hoe bouwt Amerika?', *Utrechtsch Provinciaal en Stedelijk Dagblad* 25 October 1930. For Neutra, Utrecht was an intermediate stop on a European tour, which also took him to the CIAM conference in Brussels in late November. He stayed overnight at the Schröder House.

[52] On 6 March 1933, he played host to the Swiss architect Karl Moser, former president of CIAM, Franz Hausbrand from Laren and Maynard Lyndon from Detroit.

[53] On 22 November 1934, Rietveld attended a dinner at Radermacher Schorer's where one of the other guests was Naum Gabo, who had given a talk for the Utrechtsche Kunstkring two days earlier on the subject of 'kinetic plasticity'.

Rietveld was well acquainted with Radermacher Schorer, since the two of them sat on a number of committees together, and he was a regular at Wilhelminapark 12, often in the company of Truus Schröder-Schräder. In 1925 Rietveld and Schröder-Schräder made Radermacher Schorer a radio set with machinery, tubes and wires that were visible inside a glass case.[49]

Radermacher Schorer's guest books, which he kept from the time that the renovation of his living room was completed, in October 1928, make it easy to reconstruct his circle of friends and acquaintances.[50] He also kept records of committee meetings. Many of Rietveld's friends, contacts and purchasers turn out to have been regular guests at the home of René Radermacher Schorer and his wife. This includes Van Ravesteyn, Charley Toorop and her family, the writer Arthur Lehning (1899-2000), An Harrenstein-Schräder, Leo Brom, J.H. Maronier, the architect W. van Tijen (1894-1974), the designer Elmar Berkovich (1897-1968), the painter Pyke Koch (1901-1991), Willem van Leusden, Van Ravesteyn's wife Dora Hintzen (1893-1975) and Willem Maas. Rietveld also met architects and artists there, such as Richard Neutra (1892-1970),[51] Karl Moser (1866-1936), Maynard Lyndon (1907-1999)[52] and Naum Gabo (1890-1977).[53]

Utrecht was a small city, where artists and other individuals interested in new cultural tendencies had little trouble finding one another. The art associations Kunstliefde and Voor de Kunst helped to bring such people together, and Radermacher Schorer's salon put them in contact with the national and international avant-garde. Rietveld was a strong presence in this network and sometimes played an active, organizing role. He met and grew acquainted with many of his purchasers and patrons through these contacts. Artists, patrons and friends formed a cohesive network that offered Rietveld the inspiration and the opportunity to move forward with his artistic career. ◆

Wolf Tegethoff

Rietveld's Residential Concepts: From Manifesto to Domestic Privacy

Le Corbusier, Villa Stein-de Monzie, Garches, 1926-1927
Driveway seen from the street
Fondation Le Corbusier, Paris

Of all the modern residential buildings erected in the 1920s and 1930s, Rietveld's Schröder House of 1924-1925 is one of the most spectacular, both in a direct meaning and in the figurative sense of being publicly visible and physically present. Villas and houses by Le Corbusier or Ludwig Mies van der Rohe might prove more sumptuous and luxurious, far more technically advanced and more innovative and daring in structure and materials, but before they became publicly accessible in recent years they never achieved Rietveld's recognizability. Photos of the Schröder House and abstract delineations of its façades quickly signified the work of the architect, a recognition which extended to De Stijl architecture and even in general to all Dutch architecture of the Modern Movement of the interwar period.

One reason for the popularity of Rietveld's work may be the simple fact of accessibility; Le Corbusier's villas in Garches and Poissy (Villa Stein-de Monzie of 1926-1927, and Villa Savoye of 1929-1931), for example, both occupy large areas of private land and are barely visible from the street. Mies van der Rohe's Tugendhat House (1929-1930) in Brno only presents its hermetically sealed upper floor plus forecourt and garage to the occasional passer-by, while the dramatically glazed main floor oriented towards the sloping park-like garden remains completely hidden. All three, plus many others were made known by carefully arranged photographs in professional publications, remaining inaccessible to the public for decades.

The Schröder House, by contrast, forms part of an ordinary urban three-storey middleclass development on either side of Prins Hendriklaan, a street that leads through Wilhelmina Park to the old city centre of Utrecht without becoming a major thoroughfare. The building terminates the closed row of moderately sized townhouses (hence its two main fronts), and once sat at the very edge of the city from where the road continued into open countryside. So while not exactly forming a gateway to Utrecht it was, nonetheless, sufficiently visible for anybody who cared to look. From around 1927 few publications on the Modern Movement in

Aerial view of Utrecht's suburbs showing the location of the Schröder House

[1] W. Tegethoff, 'Public Privacy: Privatsphäre und Öffentlichkeit in der Entwicklungsgeschichte des modernen Wohnhauses', in: Burkhardt 2002, 14-39; idem, 'A Modern Residence in Turbulent Times', in: Hammer-Tugendhat and Wolf Tegethoff 2000, 43-97.

[2] Wright 1910; Ashbee 1911.

[3] Bless 1982; Mulder 1994.

[4] On Truus Schröder-Schräder see: A.T. Friedman and M. Casciato, 'Family Matters: The Schröder House, by Gerrit Rietveld and Truus Schröder', in: Friedman 1998, 64-91.

architecture failed to show exteriors of Rietveld's initial architectural work. For obviously similar reasons public attention tended to focus on the formal, if not according to strictly functionalistic doctrine decidedly formalistic handling of the various façade elements and their colourful assemblage, while the amazingly advanced interior arrangement of variable open spaces long went almost unnoticed.

Public Privacy

What does spectacular actually mean and signify when applied to a private residence? Houses, as to a somewhat lesser degree almost all buildings, address both public and private aspects according to the owners' means and social status: typological discriminations such as those between a pretentious city residence and a country house or weekend cottage. Such differences in housing tend to be gradual rather than fundamental. Public aspects refer to everything representational, from the owner's wish to impose himself upon his fellow citizens or just to entertain official guests or friends, all of which will certainly have a strong impact on a building's setting and exterior appearance, dimensions, arrangement and furnishings of those rooms and spaces accessible to visitors. Beyond that, the craving for status and prestige tends to foster the preservation of elements with functions long since obsolete, such as the so called reception room where there is no longer a maid to show in a formal caller, a butler's pantry with no butler, or separate servants' entrances and stairs where the only servant around is the occasional cleaning lady.[1] Radically modern as they may appear at first sight, houses by Le Corbusier or Mies van der Rohe in fact display many remnants of those features usually associated with upperclass standards of the later nineteenth century, an era whose alleged pompousness and outdated social conventions both architects despised. In opposition to such apparently public aspects is a constant yearning for privacy that over two centuries radically changed Western living habits, starting with the English cottage movement of the early nineteenth century and, from around 1910, gaining considerable impetus from an acquaintance with Frank Lloyd Wright's prairie houses, which introduced American middle-class standards to Europeans.[2]

Rietveld's sympathies, judging from his biography,[3] personal leanings, and architectural oeuvre, lay clearly with the less pretentious, the introverted and the intrinsically private aspects of modern living, as did those of Truus Schröder, his client and close collaborator on the design of the house. She never boasted about her key role in introducing modern architecture to the Netherlands and the world beyond, but in her old age she took a private pleasure in watching growing numbers of younger people appreciating her 50-year-old home.[4] But still the question remains: Why did Rietveld choose a formalistic De Stijl exterior for a radically innovative modern open interior – the revolutionary solution which escaped all contemporary attention? Rietveld's first commission certainly served ever after as a showcase for an aspiring young architect. Why then did Rietveld never even attempt to elaborate on this surprisingly successful early masterpiece? Its conception predated Le Corbusier's Villa Savoye and Mies van der Rohe's Tugendhat House in Brno by five years. Despite being much smaller, the Schröder House is nevertheless more than a match for the houses of the other two architects in its definition of private spaces. Leaving aside the question of Truus Schröder's share in the interior design, the architectural structure that makes allowances for the owner's every whim and last-minute change, Rietveld's house patently set new standards for middle-class homes in modern society, many aspects of which seem just as valid today and are open to further exploitation.

Striving for Openness

Rietveld seems to have cared very little about the achievement of his first architectural project and its initial artistic success. Within the Modern Movement, the proliferation of his subsequent residential commissions far outnumbers those of all his colleagues. Had he luxuriated in the wake of the growing publicity of the Schröder House, Rietveld may have gone on to simply reproduce De Stijl houses and furnishings. Wisely, he chose not to, and the break could hardly have been more radical. In his residential buildings of the 1930s Rietveld adopted a sober functionalist attitude, much closer to his Dutch contemporaries Stam, Brinkman and Van der Vlugt, Bijvoet and Duiker, and in a way even to Oud, than his earlier excursion into De Stijl architecture might have suggested.

His 1931 row houses on Erasmuslaan, just east of the Schröder House but now separated from it by an ugly elevated highway, were again conceived in close collaboration with Truus Schröder, who also stepped in as the initial investor. The individual units are quite ample by Dutch middle-class standards. The slightly elevated ground floor provides a continuous living-, dining-, and working-room area, which can be temporarily closed off by folding walls, plus a tiny kitchen space and guest toilet that are all accessible from a stairwell lit by a skylight. The two upper floors provide for up to six bedrooms with one bathroom on the first, and a shower on the second floor. Whether any of the future owners ever really did employ an in-house maid is unknown. The presence of a maid would have imposed severe restrictions on either sides' privacy. Instead of the shielding wall slabs at the Schröder House extending at least to parapet level, all floors are fully glazed on either side of each unit to provide maximum openness. Exposing the interior to passers-by on the street without inviting their curiosity has a certain tradition in the Calvinistic parts of the Netherlands. Here, however, it comes quite naturally, the more so since curtains may be drawn if required. Compared to the sophisticated shielding of each and every space against all others – bedrooms from living areas, servants' quarters from family rooms, forecourt and entrance hall from the rest of the house, that almost became an obsession for Mies van der Rohe in his residential projects of the 1920s and 1930s – Rietveld's handling of how to achieve the desired openness without seriously questioning the sheltering function implicit in the traditional concept of 'home' appears straightforward: he simply does not acknowledge what others considered to be a major problem.

Whether this was subconsciously due to a specifically Dutch Calvinistic tradition or was a deliberate option for a modern lifestyle free of restrictive social conventions cannot be answered. Looking at modern residential buildings from the point of their visual presence in journals, books and exhibitions, though, will lead to quite a different assessment. Whereas fellow architects like Le Corbusier, Mies van der Rohe and many others

L. Mies van der Rohe, Tugendhathuis,
Brno, 1929-1930
Street elevation, garden elevation, hallway
and bathroom
Courtesy Tugendhat family

L. Mies van der Rohe, Tugendhathuis,
Brno, 1929-1930
Ground floor plan

Social Context: Clients and Commissions

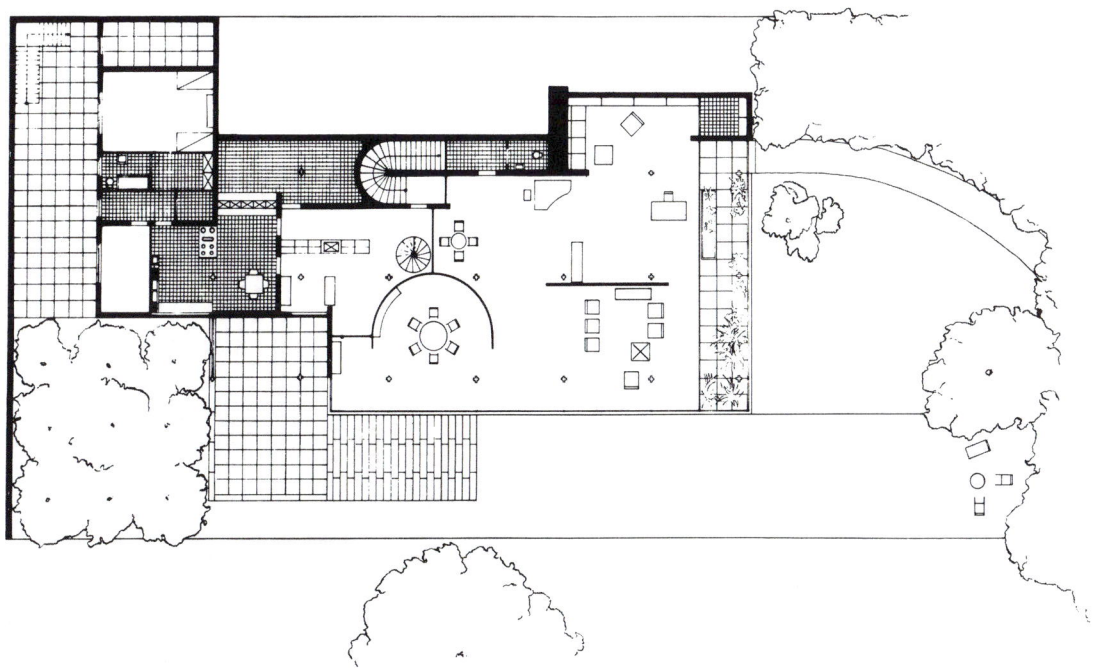

Rietveld's Residential Concepts: From Manifesto to Domestic Privacy

G.Th. Rietveld and T. Schröder-Schräder,
Schröder House, Prins Hendriklaan 50,
Utrecht, 1924
Upstairs interior (photo 1926)
RSA, Utrecht

G.Th. Rietveld and T. Schröder-Schräder,
Dwelling Erasmuslaan, Utrecht, 1931
Ground floor interior
RSA, Utrecht

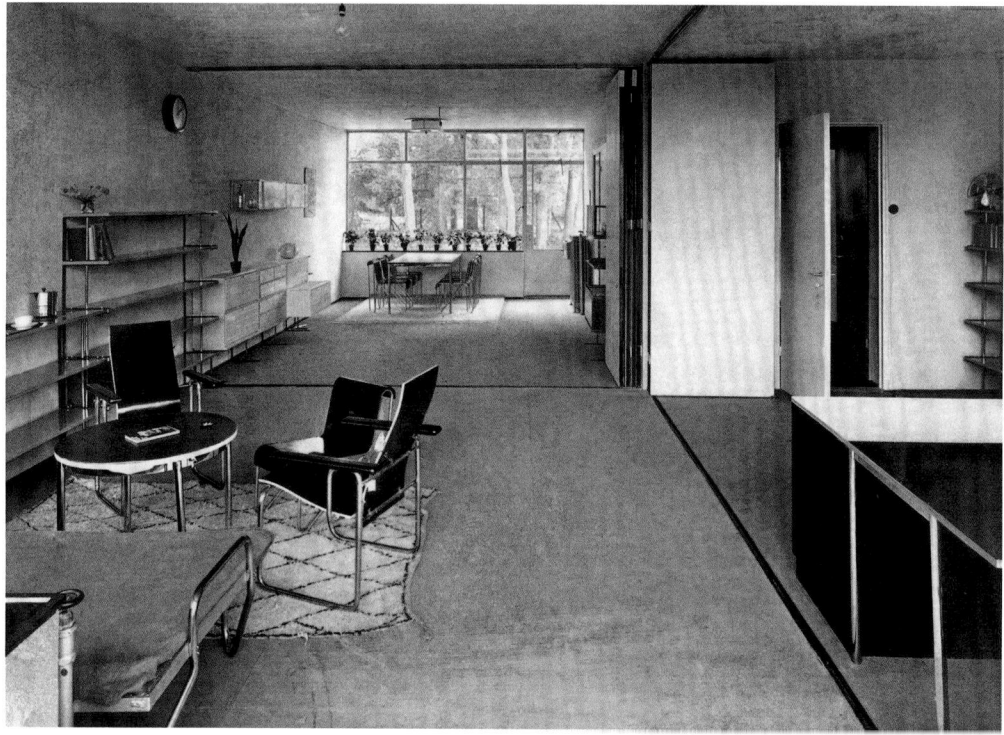

Social Context: Clients and Commissions

infringed heavily upon their respective clients' privacy by lavishly publishing their plans of recently occupied homes down to virtually every detail and corner, bath- and bedrooms not excluded,[5] the mere mentioning of which, hardly more than a century earlier, might have jeopardized an English gentleman's reputation. Contemporary illustrations of Rietveld's interiors are scarce and in the majority of his commissions nonexistent. Again, one may wonder why. Was it Rietveld's personal decision not to promote his career by extensive publishing? Did his clients refuse to expose an essential part of their private sphere to public voyeurism? Or was it simply the dwindling interest of architecture critics and the professional media that considered his later work no longer of broader interest? True enough, the majority of his houses built from the mid 1930s onwards are unpretentious and moderate in scale. The floor plans were generally well conceived, but economically restrained and thus appear rather conventional. Given an absence of public curiosity, the precarious demarcation between exterior representational aspects of a house from its more private interior functions ceases to exist and is no longer an architectural problem.

Family Homes in the Countryside
Renewed international interest in Rietveld's early De Stijl-like furniture design work plus the Schröder House resulted in an amazing career comeback that coloured the whole of the last decade of his life. Rietveld was never short of work but, till then, he had been operating on tight budgets. Only now were the larger commissions that began pouring in funded generously enough to allow for some flexibility and freedom in planning. Most of his subsequent residential buildings – among which should be listed the Van Daalen House in Bergeijk (1956-1958), the Bláha House in Best (1956-1957), the Van den Doel House in Ilpendam (1957-1958), the Van Dantzig House in Santport (1959-1960), and his final work, the Van Slobbe House in Heerlen (1961-1964) – cover a considerable floor area and typologically would have to be listed as 'country houses', a term extremely popular till the beginning of the twentieth century, but outmoded two decades later. Most of those 'family homes in the open countryside' are characterized by a strict separation of living rooms and sleeping quarters almost forming two independent architectural units with a glazed entry hall in between. Differences in floor level and ceiling height accentuate the separate wings (Van Daalen, Bláha, and Van Danzig Houses), while the bedrooms – children's rooms in particular – are occasionally aligned perpendicular to a small corridor (van Daalen and Bláha Houses). The possible reference is to Mies van der Rohe's Hermann Lange House in Krefeld of 1928-1930 although Rietveld could hardly have been familiar with Mies's still unpublished Gericke House project of 1932. The real prototype is the compartment sleeping car of the *Compagnie Internationale des Wagons Lits et Express Européens* (CIWL) operating on the major European international railway lines from the turn of the nineteenth century. When referring back to our original question this will lead to a particularly interesting comparison. Nowhere is privacy more required than in a most luxurious environment that by sheer technical necessity enforces physical proximity with a class of people that defines itself as distinguished, that is, set well apart from the general crowd as well as from its individual fellow members.

[5] B. Colomina, 'The Split Wall: Domestic Voyeurism', in: Risselada 2008, 190-193.

[6] R. Kerr, *The Gentlemen's House. Or, How to Plan English Residences from the Parsonage to the Palace,* London 1864, gives a good, while somewhat hypertrophic survey of the English tradition.

[7] Mies van der Rohe 1931, 241.

[8] Friedman and Casciato, op. cit. (note 4), 64-91.

Modernism and Domestic Convention

Without reducing those well-intentioned hardworking, economically successful (meaning basically wealthy), late-1950s Dutch middle-class clients to the stereotype of the snobbish British of a time long since past, the longevity of enduring domestic conventions needs to be kept in mind. The only house not fitting the overall scheme because of the owners' specific preconceptions bears vivid testimony to the fact: upon explicit request of the clients, the master bedroom of the Van den Doel House lines up directly with the main living room, sharing a rhythmically transposed exterior glass wall, the roof-carrying posts of which blur the interior demarcation line. The division was reduced to a high cupboard unit and a sliding screen of frosted glass. Why didn't Rietveld oppose such an apparently whimsical request from his client? Because French – decidedly not British[6] – aristocratic tradition placed the boudoir or lady's bedroom (which in fact it wasn't) as an intrinsic part of the official sequence of reception rooms. Rietveld apparently had no preconceived notions of what living in the twentieth century should look like. In the Schröder House, he (or maybe Truus) experimented with the concept of open space, but pretty soon must have become aware that the squabbling of little children does nothing to stimulate architectural creativity. He consequently ended up with the conventional living-dining-room unit plus variable reading, writing, or piano-playing facilities already standard in generally more confined mid-twentieth century middle-class homes. Some of his later houses (Bláha, Van Dantzig) have American-type kitchens that open up towards the living-dining-room unit with only a medium-high cupboard, or alternatively some kind of bar or breakfast table as a division. This kind of spatial arrangement became increasingly fashionable with the first wave of Americanization sweeping Western Europe in the 1950s, and may well have answered clients' special wishes. It does, however, signal another major change in the public-private aspects of home and gender relationships; the preparation of food is no longer considered an inferior service function exclusively delegated to the housewife, replacing both cook and maid, but had now become an integral part of daily family life.

Gerrit Rietveld was one of the few modern architects of the first generation who carried out his early quest into the potentials of the single family home well into the post-war period. Unlike Richard Neutra and the architects of the American 'Case Study House Program' who at the time dominated the international scene of residential architecture, Rietveld preferred a moderate approach to the handling of exteriors and interior spaces, even where generous budget allocations would have asked for show. The temptation to create something spectacular, as in his early Schröder House, seems never to have occurred to him again. Nor did he pretend to solve each and every problem generated by the notoriously *gewandelten Lebensumstände* – the fundamental change in living conditions conjured up by Mies van der Rohe in 1931[7] – to which he nonetheless tried to respond.[8] Where Mies and Le Corbusier created series of prototypes and never considered the problem of residential architecture again once the ultimate solution to all world-shaking questions seemed to have been found, Rietveld, in his modest way, strove to simply build good houses adapted to the individual needs of his clients. His devotion to the

G.Th. Rietveld with J.C. Meulenbelt,
Van Dantzig House, Harddraverslaan 60,
Santpoort, 1959-1960
Interior

G.Th. Rietveld, Van den Doel House,
Monnickendammerrijweg 31c, Ilpendam,
1957-1958
View of the bedroom from the living room

Rietveld's Residential Concepts: From Manifesto to Domestic Privacy

L. Mies van der Rohe, Farnsworth House,
Plano, IL, 1945-1951
Museum of Modern Art, New York

modern cause remained uncompromising even where circumstances demanded flexibility in materials and construction, as for example in the Verrijn Stuart House (1940-1941), which in spite of its rough wooden boarding and thatched sloping roof remains nonetheless a modern building. Despite his leading position within the Dutch Modern Movement, Rietveld never pretended to be a star architect, a *master builder*, as Peter Blake had once termed the leading troika of Frank Lloyd Wright, Mies van der Rohe and Le Corbusier.[9] Rietveld's houses are exclusively private homes, neither showcases of the inhabitants' wealth, taste and social standing nor, leaving the early Schröder House once more aside, spectacular manifestos of their architect's creative abilities. ◆

[9] Blake 1960.

Maristella Casciato

Dutch 'Case Study' Houses. Rietveld's Contribution to Modern Living in Perspective

G.Th. Rietveld and T. Schröder-Schräder, Schröder House, Prins Hendriklaan 50, Utrecht, 1924
RSA, Utrecht

[1] On these issues see B. Colomina, 'The Exhibitionist House', in: Ferguson 1998, 127 ff.

Certain artists are destined to conceive a single work of extraordinary relevance and immense success, only to spend the rest of their life chasing after the same elusive inspiration that only once graced them. The embarrassment barely concealed between the lines of some of the writings on the architecture Rietveld designed in the 1950s and 1960s suggests that this might be the case of our creator: a designer who lost, or at least heavily diluted his creative vein after an extremely brilliant debut – albeit one that was enough to consolidate his architectural reputation.

Numerous factors might be listed as causes of this supposed loss of inspiration: the shock of the cruelty of the Second World War and the German invasion of a country known for its tolerance; Rietveld's natural disposition towards the new and his scarce inclination to humour the taste of his ordinary middle-class patrons; the loss of his muse with Truus Schröder's discreet departure from the scene; Rietveld's retreat into an architectural vision based on details, rather than on the play of volumes, to the point that he became a master of understatement.

The key to a reading of Rietveld's creative research as put forward by this essay takes its cue from the apparent discontinuity in the professional itinerary in design as well as in the building practice of this architect/craftsman. My intention is to offer a different interpretation of this discontinuity: namely, to consider the whole of the Dutch designer's production as a consistent process centred on the theme of the home. This subject provided Rietveld with the opportunity to develop a mature and truly authentic workshop practice, one allowing him to experiment with different approaches in different phases of his fertile career, in the course of which he was also influenced by changing home and lifestyle trends produced by the media.[1]

G.Th. Rietveld and T. Schröder-Schräder,
Row of four dwellings, Erasmuslaan 5-11; 1, 3
Utrecht, 1930-1931; 1934
RSA, Utrecht

G.Th. Rietveld, Row of four dwellings for the
Wiener Werkbundsiedlung, Woinovichgasse
14-20, Vienna, 1929-1932
RSA, Utrecht

It is also worth noting that the one-family house, the most common subject of Rietveld's production, represents the pivotal point of the majority of modernism's design practice experiments – besides embodying the preferred and most successful propaganda tool of any programme of home modernization at least in magazines and printed materials.

Rietveld was a prolific designer, who, in the course of a career spanning nearly a half century, had the opportunity to design about a hundred homes; if, among these, we select the most remarkable examples, it becomes easy to identify a line of experimentation, which starts from the famous Schröder House (1924) up to the residential buildings of the 1960s. All these shape an itinerary rich in experiments, resulting in a veritable catalogue of typological variations, which, perhaps, Rietveld modified minimally over the course of the years, but which always displayed a consistent trajectory of research.

Furthermore, Rietveld was used to producing prototypes given his background as a craftsman/cabinetmaker, and his penchant for creating paradigmatic architectural pieces is perceivable in all the homes he brought to completion at the beginning of his career. In the Schröder House in Utrecht, his experimental home *par excellence*, as well as in the adjacent residential buildings on Erasmuslaan (1931) and in the series of four three-storey houses for Vienna's Werkbundsiedlung (1932).[2] These experimental houses were an expression of Rietveld's interest in the prefabrication and modernization of living habitats. They also showed how he applied the principle that was at the heart of the debate championed by the *Nieuwe Bouwen* at the end of the 1920s: namely the service unit (stairwell and toilet) considered as the functional core of the design of low-cost residential structures, imbued with high flexibility.

In further analysis, Rietveld's search for systematic typologies and experimentation in architectural idiom is evidenced not so much by his houses of the 1920s and 1930s, which garnered him the highest critical acclaim and were indeed brilliant, but strongly heterogeneous in their variety of compositional themes; nor by the original integration of regional and vernacular stylistic items which he attempted between the 1930s and the 1940s. Rather, his true mark was articulated in the many houses of the 1950s and early 1960s, less famous and often underestimated – although not by the clients themselves, who in fact rewarded Rietveld for the direction he had taken in those years. Indeed, it seems apposite to suggest a strong analogy – almost a Dutch equivalent – with one of the most intriguing chapters of post-Second World War American architecture, the Californian Case Study House Program.

The question: 'What is a house?' at the origin of John Entenza's initiative born during the turbulent years of the Second World War, provides, in many ways, a very suitable comparison with Rietveld's oeuvre, more specifically when referred to the free-standing single-house projects he worked on after the end of the war.

Entenza, through the magazine *Arts & Architecture* he edited, wanted to provide modern architects with the opportunity to create examples of progressive designs, in the hope that they would have an impact on the taste of the general public and on the building trade. From here came the idea of a programme of experimental projects, bringing on innovations in

[2] See Krischanitz and Kapfinger 1986.

J. Entenza, 'What is a house?', *Arts & Architecture* (July 1944)

J. Entenza, 'Announcement: The Case Study House Program', *Arts & Architecture* (January 1945)

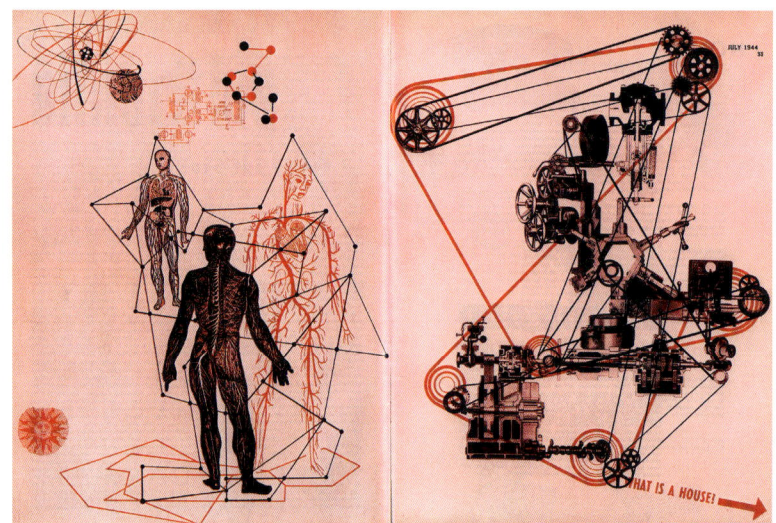

ANNOUNCEMENT

the case study house program

Because most opinion, both profound and light-headed, in terms of post war housing is nothing but speculation in the form of talk and reams of paper, it occurs to us that it might be a good idea to get down to cases and at least make a beginning in the gathering of that mass of material that must eventually result in what we know as "house—post war".

Agreeing that the whole matter is surrounded by conditions over which few of us have any control, certainly we can develop a point of view and do some organized thinking which might come to a practical end. It is with that in mind that we now announce the project we have called THE "CASE STUDY" HOUSE PROGRAM.

The magazine has undertaken to supply an answer insofar as it is possible to correlate the facts and point them in the direction of an end result. We are, within the limits of uncontrollable factors, proposing to begin immediately the study, planning, actual design and construction of eight houses, each to fulfil the specifications of a special living problem in the Southern California area. Eight nationally known architects, chosen not only for their obvious talents, but for their ability to evaluate realistically housing in terms of need, have been commissioned to take a plot of God's green earth and create "good" living conditions for eight American families. They will be free to choose or reject, on a merit basis, the products of national manufacturers offering either old or new materials considered best for the purpose by each architect in his attempt to create contemporary dwelling units. We are quite aware that the meaning of "contemporary" changes by the minute and it is conceivable that each architect might wish to change his idea or a part of his idea when time for actual building arrives. In that case he will, within reason, be permitted to do so. (Incidentally, the eight men have been chosen for, among other things, reasonableness, which they have consistently maintained at a very high level.)

We will try and arrange the over-all plan so that it will make form as well as in social *esprit*, in order to transfer to the market of low-cost residential properties the same compositional improvements that, in the pre-war years, had found their expression in private residential buildings for the affluent.[3] A sizeable community of architects took part in the Case Study House Program promoted by Entenza's magazine, which lasted for about two decades. Some of them, as was the case with Richard Neutra, had already become famous by building extraordinary villas for extremely wealthy Los Angeles patrons; among the others were Charles and Ray Eames,[4] Craig Ellwood, Quincy Jones, Pierre Koenig and Raphael Soriano, just to mention a few. At that time, the beginning of the 1940s, the battle for the modern home was still being fought on a number of fronts, and could not be declared as won yet. Faced with widely-spread eclecticism, hopes for renewal resided in the work of a handful of courageous individuals: Frank Lloyd Wright and his son Lloyd, Rudolph Schindler (active as early as the 1920s, the decade of his first works), Harwell Hamilton Harris and Gregory Ain, who came to the forefront in the following decade. Their projects pointed to a number of shared views: a strictly formal approach, clarity of expression, elegant simplicity, a social agenda, the utopia of the democratic spirit expressed by architecture and the faith in design's mission to model lifestyles in order to create a better world.[5] Twenty-two houses and one apartment were built in the hills around Los Angeles, all produced according to the same ideas: standardization, the adaptability and economy of the floor plan scheme, and the lightness of the prefabricated steel framework (skeleton).[6]

In Rietveld's case, the magazine and the extraordinary cultural catalyst personified by Entenza were missing, as well as the innovative structural concepts behind his programme; however, the Dutch designer's inspirational principles of progressive domestic construction were in tune with those of his California counterpart.

The objective of the Case Study House Program was to design a 'good environment'; equally, all of Rietveld's experience within the 'good design' for a *goed wonen* (good living) movement moved towards the modernization of the living models for a comfortable domestic life'.[7] Especially the one-family houses produced over the course of 15 years, between the end of the 1940s and the death of the architect in 1964, show his commitment to the rationalization of plans and construction forms; the integration of furniture with domestic space, and of the house with the landscape also through the garden. They also reflect a sort of modernist programme, aimed at reinventing the architecture of living according to a style that was both international and Dutch at the same time.[8] What makes these houses interesting as well as influential in the evolution of post-Second World War Dutch architecture is not just, or not only, their globalized attitude, or their inspiration, flavoured with hints of the International Style (a stylistic formula to which the Netherlands had brought a significant contribution): rather, it is their explicit attempt at formulating a kind of discreet popularization of that sophisticated language. In fact, while on one hand we notice the effort to inject residential architecture with some of the style elements typical of avant-garde architecture, those very same stylistic traits are at the same time purified of any ideological motivation, and remain as bearers of formal and functional elegance. It is thus that Rietveld domesticated the language

[3] John Entenza launched the programme in January 1945, see J. Entenza, 'Announcement: The Case Study House Program', in: B. Goldstein (ed.), *Arts & Architecture: The Entenza Years*, Cambridge, Mass., 1990.

[4] Martin Filler has made an interesting point about Case Study House #8 – the Eames's own house of 1947-1949 in Pacific Palisades and their first successful building – that links this residence to the case of Rietveld's early masterpiece. Filler wrote: 'Like his closest twentieth-century counterpart, the Dutch furniture-designer-turned-architect Gerrit Rietveld, Charles Eames built only one great work, and yet that was also enough to consolidate and sustain a major architectural reputation.' *Makers of Modern Architecture* (New York, 2007), 115.

[5] Specifically, Gregory Ain's architectural design represents a strongly similar voice in the context of Rietveld's relationship with space. Ain, who assisted Neutra as well as Schindler, collaborated on the completion of the Neutra VDL (from the name of the Dutch tycoon and philanthropist C.H. van der Leeuw) Research House on Silverlake Boulevard (1932). This marked the beginning of his experimentation on the flexibility of the floor plan, obtained with the use of sliding or folding walls. Just as interesting are his studies on the efficiency of domestic interiors, on the kitchen turned into laboratory and integrated with the living area. On Ain see Denzer 2008. As regards a possible 'Neutra connection', we mustn't overlook the fact that Rietveld's private collection contained a number of volumes on the work on the American-Viennese architect, an extraordinary innovator of modern comfort.

[6] E. McCoy, 'Arts & Architecture: Case Study Houses', in: Smith 1989, 15 ff. The programme ran intermittently for about 15 years, starting soon after its announcement in 1945. While not all 36 designs were built, by 1950 more than ten houses had been already constructed, among which William Wuster: CSH #3; Charles and Ray Eames: Eames House (CSH #8); Charles Eames and Eero Saarinen: Entenza House (CSH #9); Richard Neutra, CSH #13; Craig Ellwood: CSH #17.

[7] The Stichting Goed Wonen was born immediately after the war (1946) as the core of the debate for the *Nieuwe Bouwers*, in particular W. van Tijen and B. Merkelbach, in the context of the reconstruction. Besides the magazine *goed wonen*, first published in 1948 and soon to become the sounding board for the guidelines on the

F.L. Wright, Herbert Jacobs House #1,
Madison, WI, 1936-1937
Perspective drawing and floor plan
The Frank Lloyd Wright Foundation

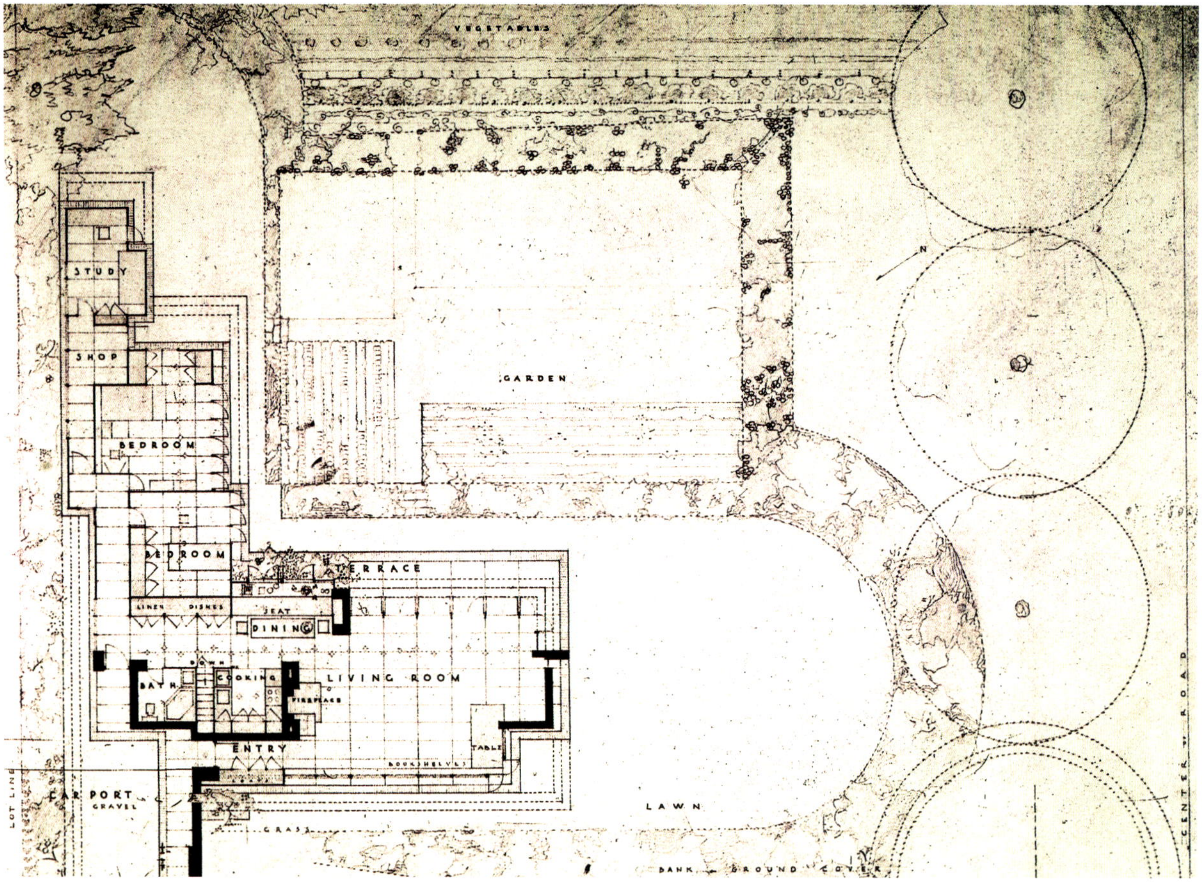

82 Social Context: Clients and Commissions

rules prevalent in buildings conceived for the cultivated bourgeois elite with international tastes, and led them towards a residential modesty that nevertheless still carried authority and persuasion. Rietveld was thus able to mould a sort of 'Dutch Style', made of a popular, middle-class modernity far from any concept of the home as a 'high-art phenomenon'.

For this stance of his, Rietveld found a direct source of inspiration in his De Stijl years, and also in other overseas experiments; above all, in the series of houses designed by Frank Lloyd Wright in the second half of the 1930s, collectively known as Usonian Houses. In these houses Wright, making best use of the critical acclaim he had earned with the Kaufmann House, better known as Fallingwater, and the Johnson Wax Building, returned to one of the themes he had been interested in since the beginnings of his career, but that he never had much of a chance to investigate: domestic economy. The Usonian programme was based on the development of a low-cost building system of houses for a middle-class clientele. Formally, Wright favoured L-shaped plans in those residential buildings and often rejected straight lines, introducing triangles, circles, ellipses and polygons.

The first production in that programme was the Herbert Jacobs House #1 (1936-1937), which remains the most brilliant example of the Usonian ideal, and certainly the most imitated. The master from Wisconsin had thus written about this project in his *The Essential Frank Lloyd Wright*:

> Here is a moderate cost brick and wood house that by new technology of a life time has been greatly extended in scale and comfort . . . There is freedom of movement, and privacy, too, afforded by the general arrangement here, unknown to the current *boxment*.[9]

In his search for 'tomorrow's small house', to quote the title of the famous 1945 show at the Museum of Modern Art, New York, Wright was attuned to what some of his well-respected colleagues, including Marcel Breuer, Gregory Ain or Frederick Kiesler, were promoting in those same years as the 'Idea House'. A number of American museums launched a series of experimental initiatives aimed at giving visibility to these ideals, such as exhibiting life-size model homes. As a result, it's not surprising that, in the early 1950s, the Guggenheims should decide to build a model of a Usonian home on the 5th Avenue lot that would later provide the site for the Guggenheim Museum.[10] Therefore, the emphasis on good-quality architecture at reasonable costs as embraced by Wright was a familiar topic for Rietveld, too.

Het Huis als Ruimte [11] (The Home as Space)

The decade of the 1950s opens with the Stoop House in Velp (1950-1951), starting a new search for a new modernity in the residential model, and clearly echoing references to these experiments. Despite the different language – Wright's predilection for materiality against Rietveld's preference for abstraction – it's not difficult to notice the similarities between the Stoop House and the Herbert Jacobs House: the horizontal layout, the slab roof jutting out on each side, presenting itself as an autonomous architectural

definition of the 'functionele grondslagen van de woning' (functional organization of the house) Stichting Goed Wonen also produced, towards the end of the 1950s, the film *Mens en ruimte* (Man and space, on the occasion of the fiftieth anniversary of Philips Woningbouwvereniging). This became a formidable instrument for the education of the new 'domestic order' and the relationship between man and woman in the management of the home. On the different programmes of the Stichting Goed Wonen see: Van Moorsel 1992.

[8] A comprehensive catalogue of the houses in Rodijk 1991. Kuper also describes some of these houses. See M. Kuper 'Las casas de Rietveld/Rietvelds Houses', in: Kuper, Quist and Ibelings 2006, 34ff.

[9] Frank Lloyd Wright, special issue of *Architectural Forum*, January 1938. With the term *boxment* (italics by the author) Wright hints at his stand 'The Cardboard House' (1931); thus he wrote: 'Most new "modernistic" houses manage to look as though cut from cardboard with scissors . . . The cardboard forms thus made are glued together in boxlike forms . . .' This stand was not very far from the evolution of the Dutch movement De Stijl, as in Van Doesburg's writings from the second half of the 1920s.

[10] The exhibition 'Tomorrow's Small House' was curated by Elizabeth Mock and comprised the building of eight small houses to the scale of 'one inch to one foot'. In the following year, 1949, another building programme of one-family homes was started, also sponsored by the Museum of Modern Art, and the houses set up in the garden of the museum. The first model was the one designed by Marcel Breuer. See the exhibition 'Home Delivery: Fabricating the Modern Dwelling', organized by Barry Bergdoll at the Museum of Modern Art in the course of 2008-2009.

[11] The title proposes again one of the key themes of the debate on the organization of the domestic space as the moving force of the lifestyle of post-Second World War Dutch society. In this context, a lead role was played by the ideas and activities developed around the Stichting Goed Wonen, whose influence was above all strongest in the innovation of interior design in multifamily homes. Despite this, Rietveld made the identity of the house as a space one of his strengths in the research of what he had considered as the main objective of his architectural practice ever since the 1930s: the 'hoedanigheid van de ruimte' (quality of the space). In

element; the chimney emerging from the low body of the building, signposting the ideal centre of the home; the rotation between floor-to-ceiling blind vertical surfaces and glass walls articulated by a regular grid. Rietveld offers an original interpretation of the influential Los Angeles experiments, together with clear references to Wright's style: all these elements are expressed in the minimalism of the building and the economy of semantics typical of all his buildings at that time.

This is the case with the Slegers House (1952-1955), brought to completion for the sculptor Piet Slegers on a plot adjacent to Stoop House. The house has an extremely simple structure, a single floor on an L-shaped plan. A small lower building separates the volumes of the bedrooms from the artist's studio, which incorporates the living-dining area. The front door, giving access to a narrow corridor, functions as a pivot between the two spaces. The building was designed on the basis of a 1-m^2 modular grid, but the geometrical system was so masterfully incorporated in the overall plan that it dissolves in the general composition. The colour scheme is also minimal, highlighting the two parts of the composition: the white-brick body of the rooms is in juxtaposition to the black glass body of the artist studio.

The Driessen House in Arnhem (1953-1954) is a two-storey building comprising two volumes linked by a glass structure, in which the simplifying process goes hand-in-hand with the juxtaposition of different materials: glass, brick and a surface made of large wooden stripes that truly seems to wink at the Usonian residences. This effect is accentuated by the departure from a perpendicular plan with the inclination of one of the two wings, almost as if attempting to embrace the back garden, connecting the house to the land, in a new dynamic of space, lightness, freedom: 'Where does the garden leave off and the house begin?' was the question Wright had provided an answer to with his Usonian model.

This mechanism is repeated in the Visser House, in Bergeijk (1955-1956), a residential property cum art gallery, created to host the contemporary art collection of the owner Martin Visser, himself a furniture designer and art collector. A minimal project, in structure as well as in budget: a sequence of three small volumes, one square, two rectangular, arranged along an uneven line. In this case, Rietveld sees the natural environment as an element of paramount importance – to the point that this can be defined as his first truly site-specific project. He takes into account the rows of trees surrounding the house in order to define the location of the different volumes and their openings. The relationship between the client and the designer is another key element in this residential property. Rietveld also designed a few built-in pieces of furniture and favoured warm colours (yellow, lilac and light blue) for the walls of the communal areas, in relation to their exposure to sunlight. Visser did not like these details as he felt they limited him when selecting which works of art to display. He submitted his doubts to his friend, architect Aldo van Eyck. The latter accused Rietveld of having betrayed the 'significance of pictorial expression' in architecture. The former intended to refer to the long-lasting *querelle* on the artistic essence of the act of building, whose principles, he argued, should never lose their illustrative character. Rietveld's answer sounded like a reproach: 'I recall a conversation with Berlage, he said: you destroy what I built. I feel inclined to say to you: you build on what I destroyed.[12]

---

this respect, it is interesting to observe how he formulates the question of the relationship between dwelling and dweller about 20 years later: 'Zonder ruimte is er voor mij geen "ik" en zonder "ik" is er geen ruimte-onderscheiding' (It is my opinion that no 'I' could be without space and that without 'I' no space differentiation could exist), in Van Moorsel 1992, 63. This philosophy was made explicit also in the multifamily residential buildings that Rietveld designed from the beginning of the 1950s. Certainly among the most interesting is the block of flats in the Hoogaven suburb in Utrecht (1954-1957), in which the floor plan of the living area is conceived in order to achieve a maximum of efficiency (sliding walls and movable furniture) without compromising the comfort of the relationship between the occupier and the space.

[12] The letter is mentioned in Rodijk 1991, 117. Original Dutch: 'Ik herinner me een gesprek met Berlage, hij zei: jij maakt kapot wat ik opbouw. Ik heb the neiging om te zeggen tegen jou: jij bouwt op wat ik kapot maakte.'

G.Th. Rietveld, Stoop House,
Beekhuizenseweg 44, Velp, 1950-1951
RSA, Utrecht

G.Th. Rietveld, Stoop House
Drawings
NAI, Rotterdam

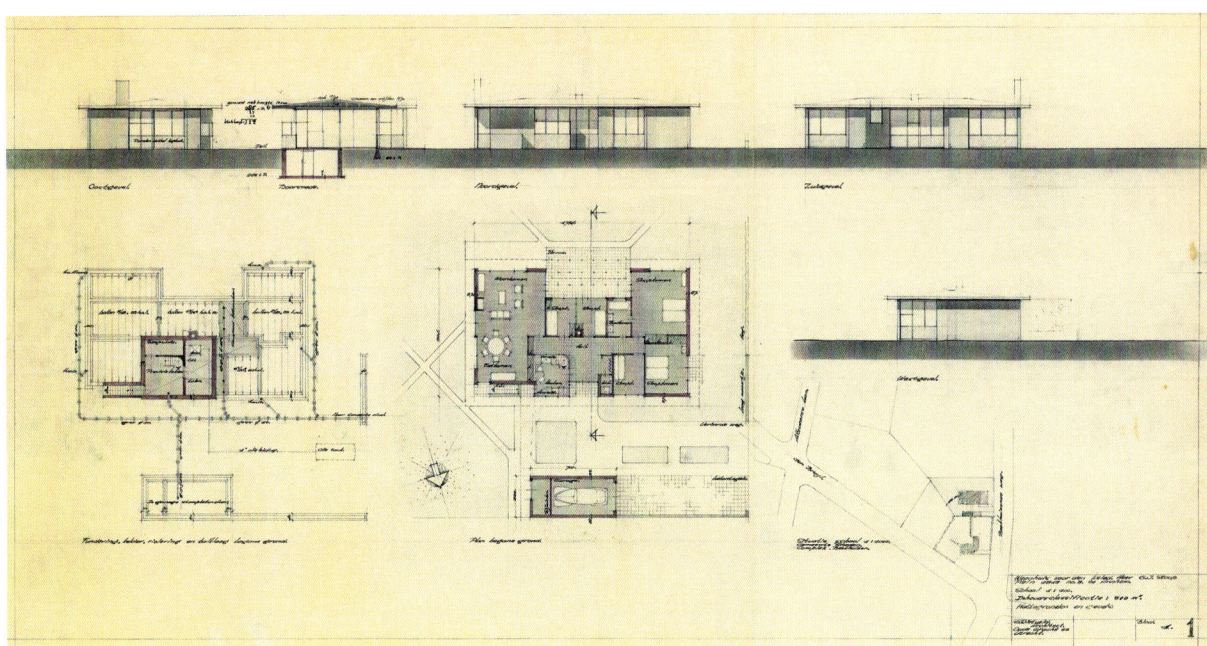

Dutch 'Case Study' Houses. Rietveld's Contribution to Modern Living in Perspective

G.Th. Rietveld, Slegers House,
Den Bruyl 35, Velp, 1952-1955
Photograph and design drawing
RSA, Utrecht

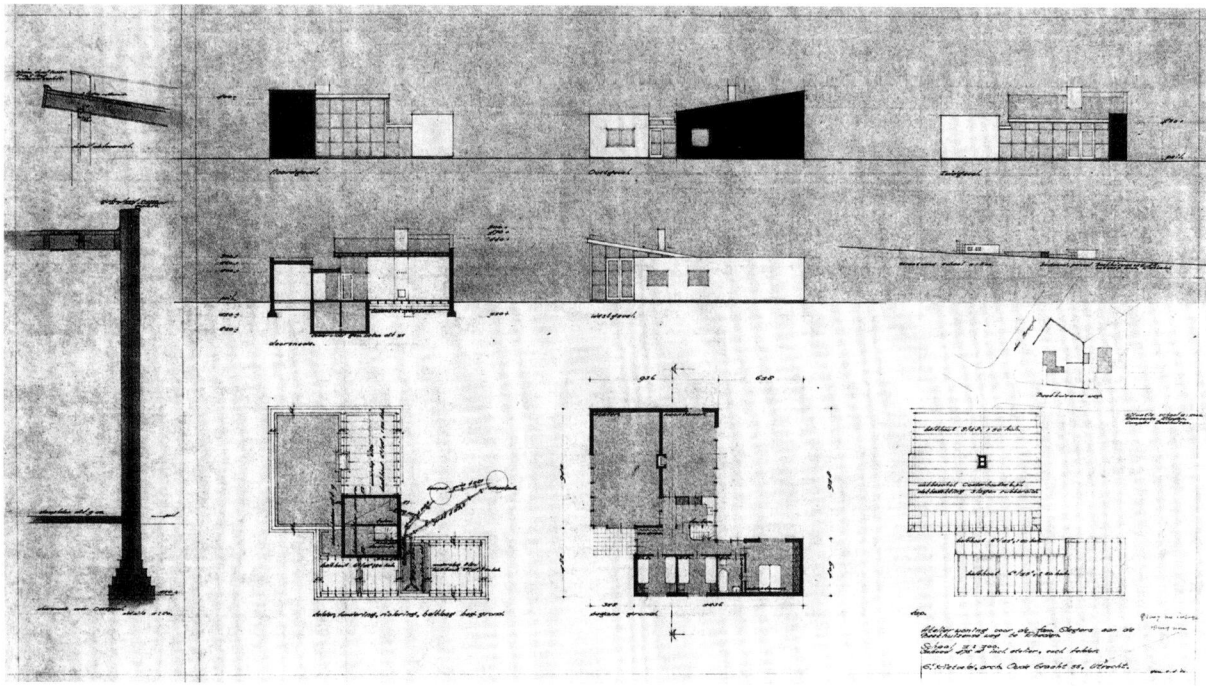

Social Context: Clients and Commissions

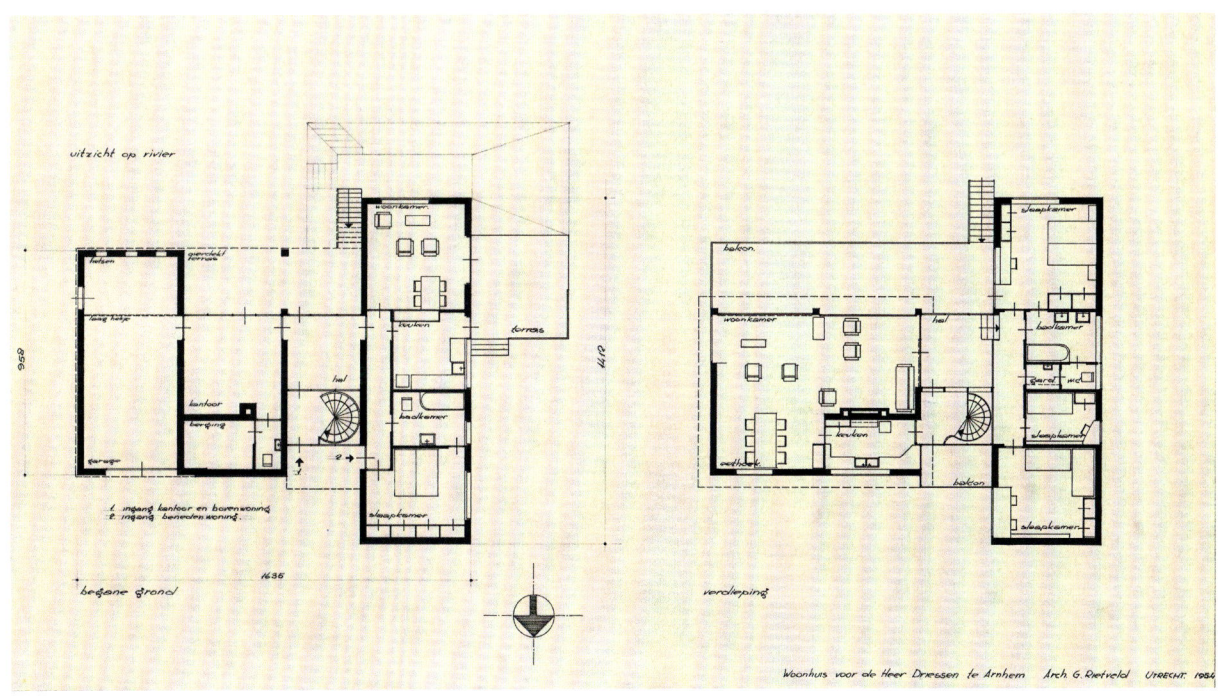

G.Th. Rietveld, Driessen House,
Hulkesteinseweg 21, Arnhem, 1953-1954
Photograph and floorplan
NAI, Rotterdam

G.Th. Rietveld, Visser House,
Eikendreef 2, Bergeijk, 1955-1956
RSA, Utrecht

G. Th. Rietveld, Visser House,
Eikendreef 2, Bergeijk, extension
designed by Aldo van Eyck

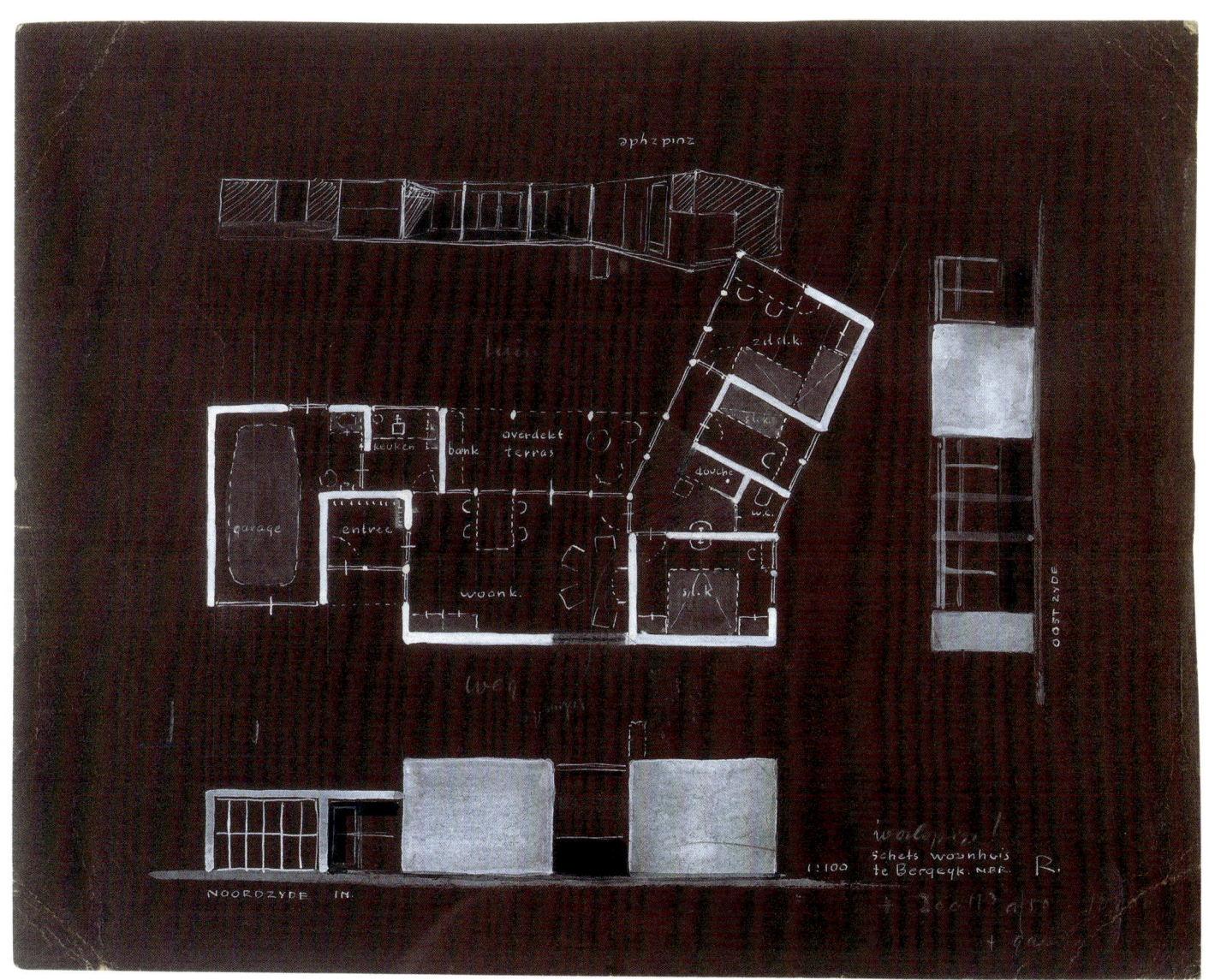

G.Th. Rietveld, Visser House
Design sketch
RSA, Utrecht

[13] The client was one of the directors of the textile company De Ploeg, whose new Bergeijk plants were designed by Rietveld in 1956-1958. The design of the De Ploeg products for furniture and interior textiles was aligned with the search for an aesthetic of consumer products that represented one of the strengths of the philosophy of the Stichting Goed Wonen. See the issues of the magazine *goed wonen* and the book series 'Domestica', published by H. ten Brink in Meppel.

Despite this, Visser ended up asking Aldo van Eyck to alter the design, which the latter did in two different phases: in 1968 with the addition of a circular structure leaning onto the bedroom wing, and in 1974 with a second extension.

During the years that followed, Rietveld favoured more and more the scheme in which the various domestic functions are arranged along linear structures, abandoning his previous predilection for compact volumes. This is what happens in the Van Daalen House in Bergeijk (1956-1958), where four wings extend from the single distribution node in which the entrance to the residence is located.[13] The wings contain the dining room, the sleeping area, the playroom for the children and the garage. This windmill structure guarantees the largest glass surface to each of the rooms, while allowing for a sophisticated compositional trickery involving wall partitions and glass surfaces that slot into one another thanks to slight shifts in the height and alignment of the different wings. Indeed, Rietveld was an old hand at designing this kind of spatial device; however, we can also detect a certain interest for some well-known Miesian buildings.

The Van den Doel House in Ilpendam (1957-1958) was built on a site that appears as quintessentially Dutch: a narrow plot of land flanked by canals in an area of polder, under a sky agitated by restless clouds. In this flat pastoral landscape, Rietveld creates a building with a heavily horizontal layout. With perfect discipline, he forges a composition nodding at an elegant interpretation of Miesian models (see the low fencing wall, a continuation of one of the internal walls, supporting the steps to the entrance) and an evocation of the new sculptural language of the 1920s, made of space and counter- space. This type of volume, in its crispness, demonstrates a total control of the building practice. The hall, the veritable core space, functions as the pivot for all the rooms in the house, in structures of different heights, marked by subtle variations in size, coating and colour. The passage from the compressed space of the entrance to the brightness of the living area, all facing south, highlights the perception of an almost boundless external landscape.

The last works I intend to examine are the Theissing House and the Van Slobbe House, which comprise a happy compendium of all the compositional and spatial features described so far. The Theissing House (1958-1959) was built in Utrecht for one of the heads of the workshop of Bredero Bouwbedrijf. The commission provided the opportunity to experiment with the aesthetical features of B2 concrete blocks, combined with a high degree of economy. A two-storey building on a more or less square floor plan seems to evoke the chauffeur's house Rietveld built about 30 years earlier: a box-like volume progressively disintegrating via the retreating of the façade surfaces and the insertion of glass walls which, on the south side, completely eliminate the masonry.

The Van Slobbe House in Heerlen (1961-1963) is situated on the highest point of a wooded hill dominating the city, a mining and industrial centre in the south of the Netherlands. This house represents the epitome of Rietveld's research. The client, Van Slobbe, one of the directors of the Staatsmijnen (State coal mines), wanted an unpretentious modern house, big enough to accommodate his large family, with a dedicated office and meeting room where he could carry out his work duties. A multifaceted

G.Th. Rietveld, Van Daalen House,
Fazantlaan 14, Bergeijk, 1956-1958
RSA, Utrecht

G.Th. Rietveld, Van Daalen House
Floor plan
NAI, Rotterdam

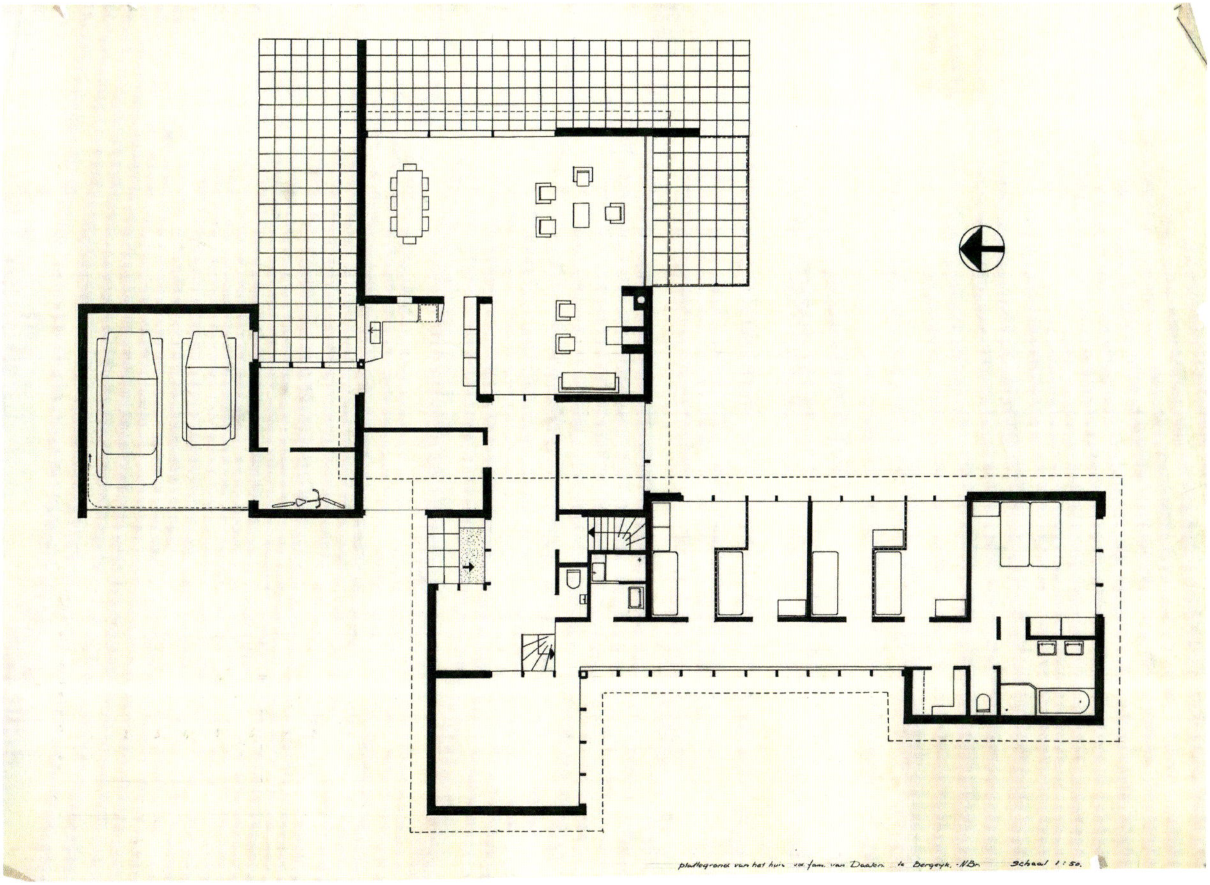

Dutch 'Case Study' Houses. Rietveld's Contribution to Modern Living in Perspective

G.Th. Rietveld, Theissing House,
Breitnerlaan 11, Utrecht, 1958-1959
RSA, Utrecht

G.Th. Rietveld, Theissing House
Drawings
NAI, Rotterdam

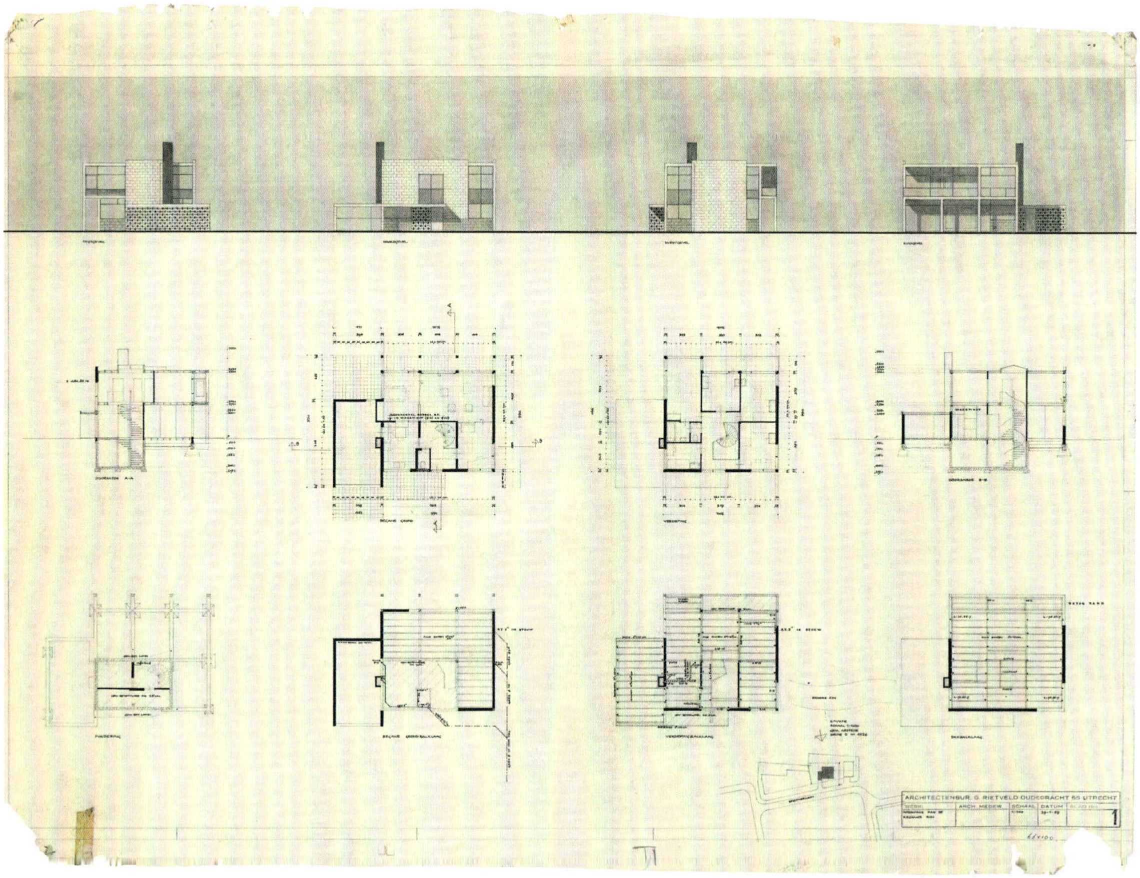

G.Th. Rietveld, Van den Doel House,
Monnickendammerrijweg 31c, Ilpendam,
1957-1958
RSA, Utrecht

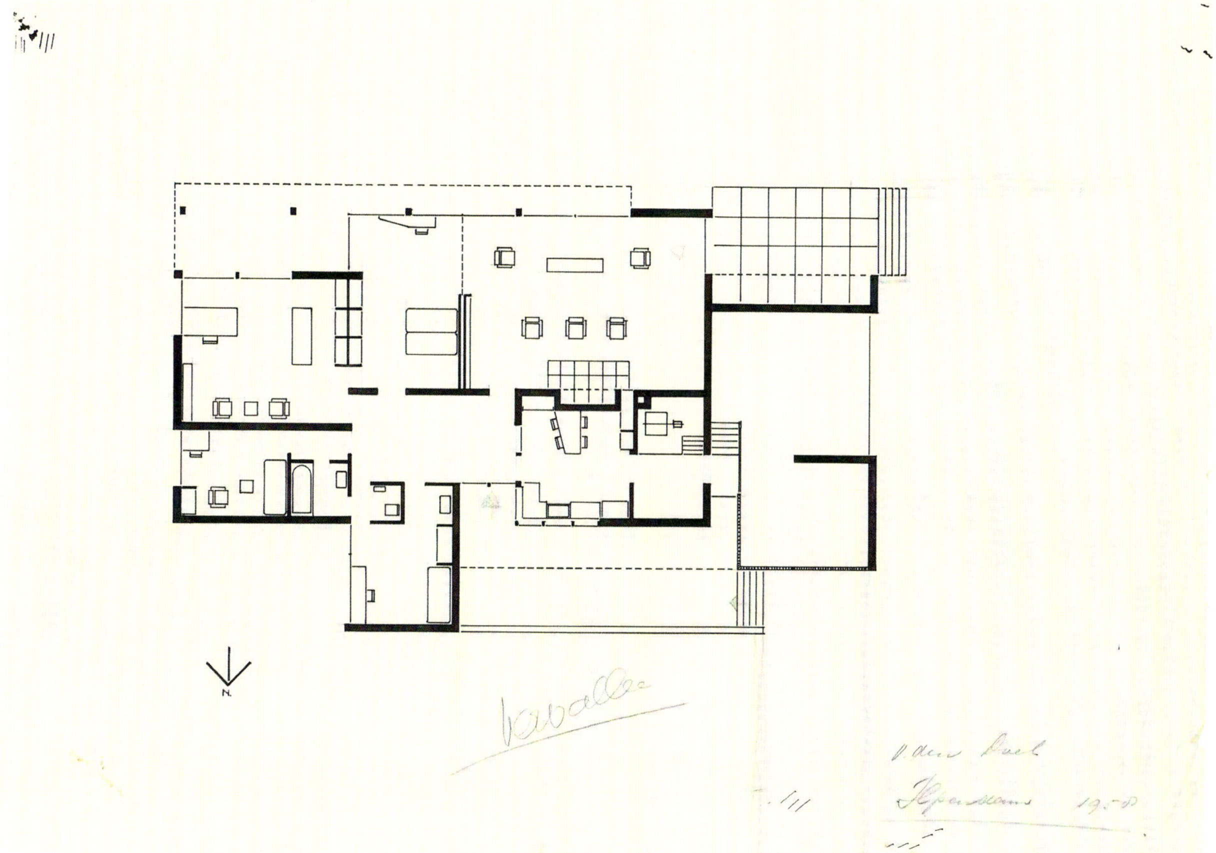

G.Th. Rietveld, Van den Doel House
Floor plan
NAI, Rotterdam

G.Th. Rietveld, Van Slobbe House,
Zandweg 122, Heerlen, 1961-1963
RSA, Utrecht

G.Th. Rietveld, Van Slobbe House
Drawings
NAI, Rotterdam

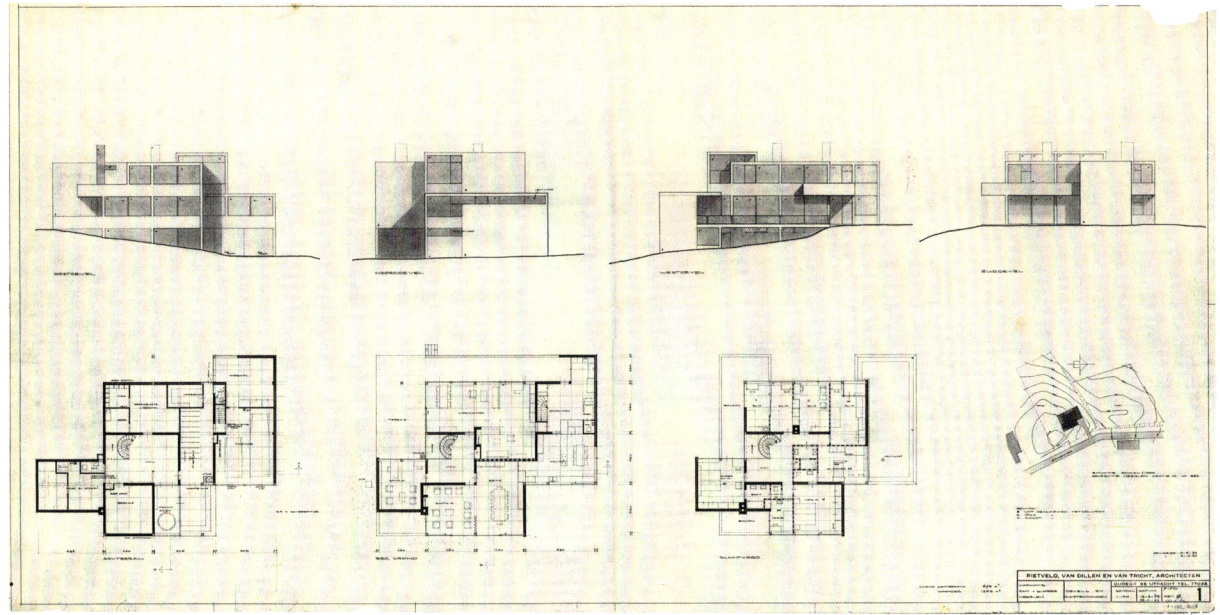

brief to which Rietveld was quite suited, and that prompted him to rethink his experiments from the early 1920s, both in architecture and furniture design: open structures, an emphasis on the strength of linear structures, a dynamic vision of space. The grid of the supporting skeleton in reinforced concrete, emphasized by the sequence of vertical planes that slash through it with the precision of a sharp blade, offers itself unexpectedly in a tectonic order. Arranged on three levels, the house is the result of a series of planes in different materials slotting into one another: glass plates, walls in glazed white bricks, wood surfaces in vivid colours. The house displays spatial dynamics resulting from a complex system of interpenetration of lines, surfaces, volumes – horizontally as well as vertically – apparently emerging from the hill in virtue of its very own vital force.

[14] Schama 1988, 609. nr. p. 95

There is no doubt that the articulation of the volumes as well as the position, leaning along the slope of the hill, both evoke the forms of the Lovell Health House in Los Angeles, although the hills of Limburg are considerably less glamorous than the wooded elevations on the shores of the Pacific.

If Neutra, during his visit to the Netherlands in 1930, had been deeply impressed by the sculptural values of the Schröder House, half a century later Rietveld returned the favour, albeit in the gentle forms that were his stylistic signature. 'To be Dutch still means coming to terms with the moral ambiguities of materialism . . . through the daily living of it', as Simon Schama remarked at the end of his successful tome *The Embarassement of Riches*.[14] ◆

Van den Doel, Ilpendam
90, 93, 121, *122*

Gerrit Rietveld Academy, Amsterdam
117, 124, *126, 128, 130,* 131, 137, *137*

Consultation room A.M. Hartog
140, 141, 189, *190*

Articulating Space: Materials, Techniques and Mass Production

'Factoren van het Zichtbare'
155, 167, *168*, 170, *171*, 173

Centraal Museum Utrecht
144, 163, 172, 173

Philips Pavilion, Brussels
155, *158*, *162*, 163, *164*, *165*, 167, 170, 178

Tube-framed chair
141, *142*, 144, 151, 152

Gropius, Walter
132, 133, 173, 189, 191

Marieke Kuipers

Materialization in Rietveld's Architecture

Gerrit Rietveld, the son of a furniture maker, mastered the profession of architecture by going out and doing it. The fact that he was not academically schooled enabled him to deal freely and undogmatically with commissions for architecture, which he primarily viewed as 'spatial art'. His unconventional approach to building assignments and their materialization enabled him to experimentally develop his mastery as a spatial artist and assembler of steel profiles and concrete blocks.

Training

Rietveld's professional training was deeply rooted in the traditions of the furniture-making trade, which he learned from his father directly after finishing primary school.[1] Heavy artesian labour, particularly woodworking, and style imitations were common practice at that time. From 1904 to 1908, he worked during the day as a designer for the jeweller Carel Begeer and at night attended industrial art school[2] while taking private lessons in architecture from the architect P.J.C. Klaarhamer, who also designed furniture. Thanks to his wide reading and artistic network, Rietveld became acquainted with both a new world of ideas and progressive artists.[3] To Klaarhamer he owed the 'foundation of his professional knowledge' and the Berlagian insight into the importance of the '*dimensional proportions* of space and mass in architecture' and of the 'building as a *logical, functional device*; as a *sound, economical construction* with an appropriate network of pipes; as a *contemporary visual expression* of space and mass, whereby natural materials and colour are important'.[4] Here, in a nutshell, Rietveld gives the key concepts for the physical aspect of his own architecture.

Which textbooks Klaarhamer prescribed and precisely what he taught in terms of building materials and principles of construction is difficult to discover, but he explicitly welcomed new, composite materials like triplex and reinforced concrete as methods of expressing the modern age of machine and community.[5] This ideological overtone was less important to Rietveld, who saw the advantages of triplex in a purely technical and economical light. As a shrink-proof and relatively cheap material, it was suitable for making furniture and scale models, although he considered multiplex even better. Concrete was a much more complicated material because it required precise prior calculations for strength and a formwork that later had to be removed. For smaller building projects, reinforced concrete was often more expensive than traditional brick because of the need to use heavy equipment and to import steel and cement. The biggest disadvantage, however, was that a concrete skeleton construction offered fewer possibilities for adaptations during the building process. This was awkward for a man who was used to working in the field and designing as he went along, a man who usually discussed the finesses of detailing and finishing on the construction site.

Rietveld nonetheless realized his first architectural commission, the decorated front of Cornelis Begeer's jewellery shop (1919), in concrete. At first sight, the stylized figures in the corners of the pilasters look like they are carved out of stone, as does like the double word JUWELIER (jeweller), but they were actually created beforehand in wooden moulds.[6] Technically and typographically, this preparatory treatment more or less dovetailed with the woodcuts Rietveld typically created for his print work

Gerrit Rietveld, designer of light constructions, Utrecht, 1958
RSA, Utrecht

P.J.C. Klaarhamer, Bed made of American pine, 1905
NAI, Rotterdam

[1] Bless 1982, 11-16.

[2] He was enrolled at the 'Kunstindustrieel Onderwijs der Vereeniging Het Utrechtsch Museum van Kunstnijverheid' in Utrecht, where he took classes in drawing and the principles of proportion, style and ornamentation.

[3] Rietveld also followed a series of courses in the period 1911-1915; Bless 1982, 12-27; M. Küper, 'Gerrit Rietveld', in: Blotkamp 1982, 263-284.

[4] G. Rietveld, 'In memoriam P.J.C. Klaarhamer', *Bouwkundig Weekblad* 72 (1954) 13-14, 101. Author's italics.

[5] According to records, Klaarhamer probably referred to publications by E.E. Viollet-le-Duc, H.P. Berlage, J. Ruskin, J.A. van der Kloes and P.W. Scharroo; NAI, Klaarhamer archive, inv. no. 194-197, 211-214.

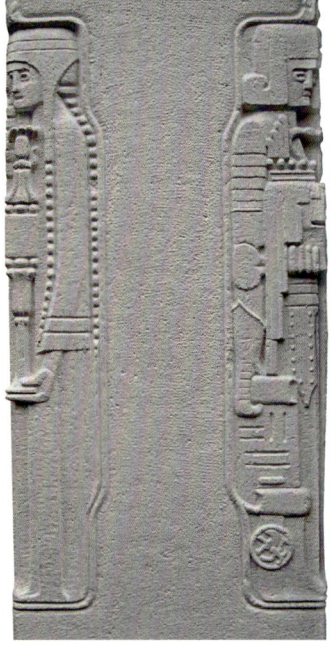

G.Th. Rietveld, Two of the stylized corners of the concrete shop front of Cornelis Begeer jeweller's

Rietveld's first architectural design: ornamental shop front of Cornelis Begeer jeweller's, Oudkerkhof 27, Utrecht, 1919 RSA, Utrecht

[6] Rietveld also designed a new interior, furniture and stationery. The storefront differed slightly from the drawings. In 1920, he received an honorary bronze medal for this; Van Zijl 2001, 01; Küper and Van Zijl 1992, 83, 96-97; also see note 13.

[7] Kuipers 1987, 84-90.

[8] See Rodijk 1991.

[9] M.C. Kuipers, 'Schröderhuis te Utrecht', 'Garage met chauffeurswoning te Utrecht' in: Tieskens, Snoep and Van Wezel 1983, 178-183.

[10] G.Th. Rietveld, 'Notaties over mijn werkwijze', unpublished manuscript for a lecture to be held in 1957 RSA, GR 90.

during this period. Outwardly, it looked like stone; architecturally, however, it was far removed from the austere concrete villas that were already being designed by such architects as Berlage in Santpoort, Robert van 't Hoff in Huis ter Heide, and Klaarhamer; the last one only on paper.[7]

It is hard to say whether this demonstration of artistry and the equating of the material and technique of concrete with that of stone was the client's wish or an idea of the versatile designer, who as yet had had no practical experience in architecture. In any case, shortly after this, Rietveld found his way to a *Nieuwe zakelijkheid* (New Objectivity) in (shop) architecture by using large spans of glass and colour and open spaces. In 1924, he achieved his breakthrough as an architect with the idiosyncratic Schröder House.

Measure and Materials

The majority of Rietveld's architectural assignments consisted of individual dwellings,[8] for which his work was made-to-measure in a double sense: on the one hand, the designs were tailored to the local conditions and the wishes of the users; on the other, they were total concepts of balanced measure and spatial art. He typically developed his designs from the inside out, proceeding from built-in cupboards to outdoor views. For consultations with his clients, he often made simple models in addition to sketches drawn to scale on grid paper.[9] In doing so, he distinguished between the 'spatial view of a building and the choice of construction'.[10] Determining the correct unit of measure was more important than choosing the materials. However, he did consider it necessary to:

> . . . establish in a scientific manner . . . what one must not exclude [from the influences of nature] . . . and what materials and constructions

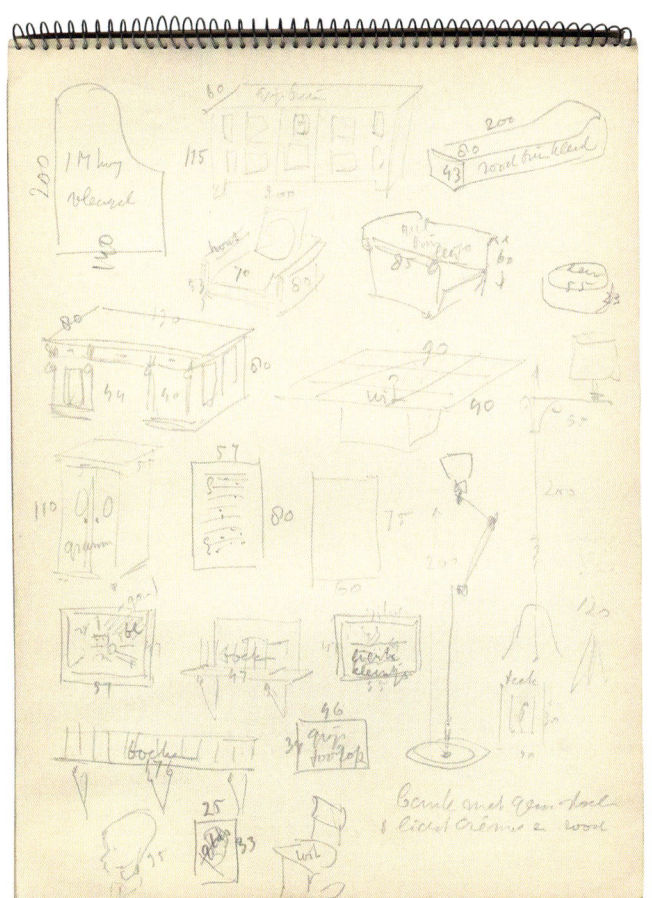
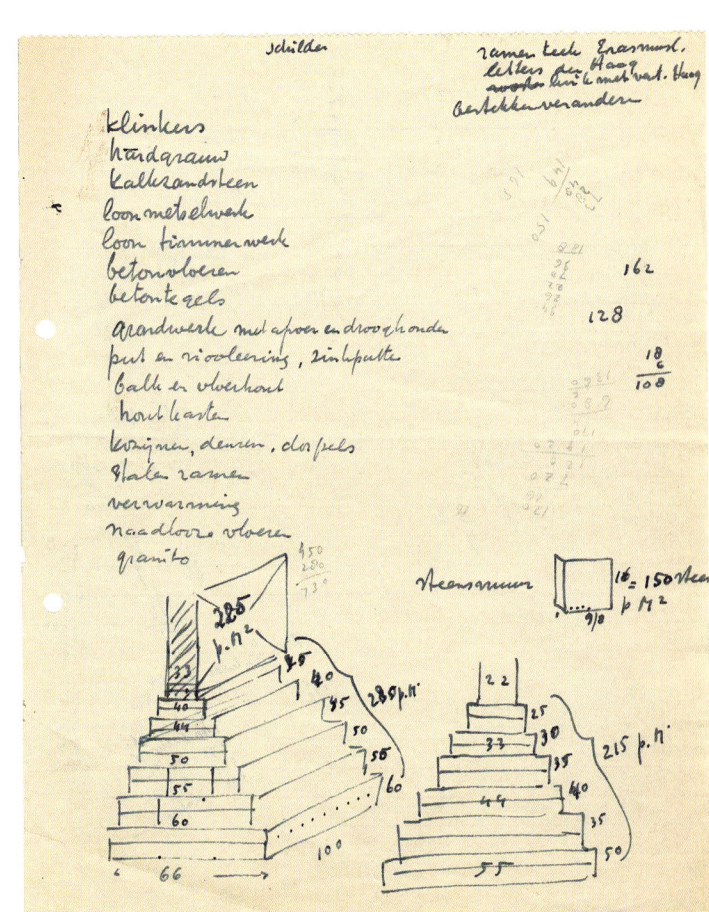

Sketch showing pieces of furniture and
their dimensions, possibly intended to help
with the internal planning of a dwelling,
from an undated sketchbook used by
Gerrit Rietveld
NAI, Rotterdam

G.Th. Rietveld, Practical method
for material analysis
NAI, Rotterdam

Materialization in Rietveld's Architecture

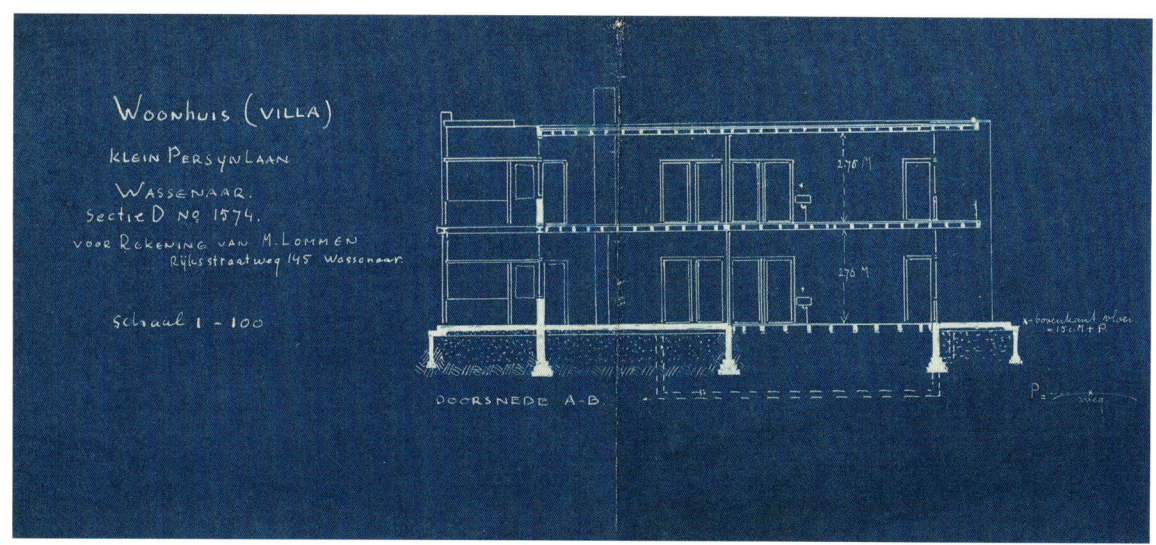

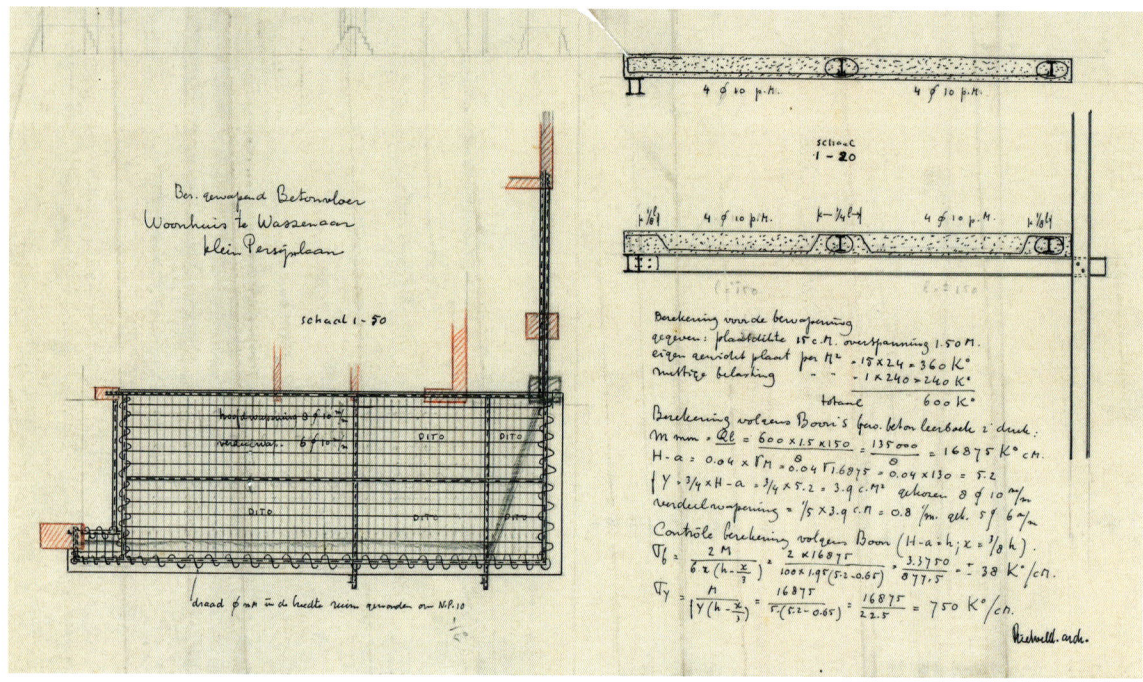

G.Th. Rietveld, Lommen House,
Klein Persijnlaan 39, Wassenaar, 1925
Section and details of the calculation
of concrete structure, with reference to
A.A. Boon's handbook
NAI, Rotterdam

are necessary for demarcating the space that has thus been created in an economically efficient manner. It's not about brick, glass, iron and also not their form . . . It's about the measurements and the amount of space between the materials, around and thereon.[11]

By focusing on the spatial experience of a structure instead of its form, and by defining architecture as spatial demarcation, he broke away from then-current discussions on style, material, technique and art and could treat the building assignment at hand as if making a large piece of furniture, combining separate elements to form an open 'spatial sculpture'. Actually, he wanted a building to function like a tent in which everyone could freely move around and yet be sufficiently protected in all sorts of weather. In this view, the total design had precedent over the choice of building materials. That choice was also determined by price, availability, building regulations and the wishes of the clients.

While his architect colleagues such as J.B. van Loghem and Le Corbusier considered reinforced concrete an essential building material for attaining a new architectural idiom, Rietveld got there by an inventive use of conventional materials. Just as he employed invisible dowels to make his furniture optically appear to float, he also sought ways to keep the plastic effect of materials 'in the background and make the space of primary importance'.[12] The ideal of using materials honestly held by Cuypers, Berlage and the Arts and Crafts Movement did not appeal to him, because he wanted to get away from massive walls and heavy manual labour. Less material also meant lower construction costs. According to Rietveld, lightness was the new truth for architectural innovation and necessary for eliminating the superfluousnesses of the past. As much as possible, he translated this idea into both lightweight constructions and a sophisticated use of daylight. Only when a material contributed to the effect of a modern architectural look – lightness in terms of weight, appearance, openness and colour did he let it speak for itself. He aimed to achieve this with white plasterwork or colourwash above dark skirting boards, large sheets of glass in narrow wooden or steel frames, jutting balconies with light metal railings and virtually borderless flat roofs.

His experimental architecture could not escape local health and building regulations, however. Some building inspectors kept a strict watch on the soundness of the construction. With his second building project, the Lommen House in Wassenaar (1925), Rietveld received a lecture for his cement calculations:

> You put the span at 1.5 m, yet that is not at all certain, because then beam C would serve as the support for the armoured concrete plate, whereas you have meant it as reinforcement. My intention is for you to clearly indicate how you want to support the plate . . . I would like to see everything converted, so that everything is supported on the sandbar, because we are going to build from there, we are not yet able to hang it on air.[13]

Rietveld would certainly have liked to do the latter, as the ultimate denial of the weight of matter.

[11] Rietveld 1932, 1-27: 16 (for the English translation see Küper and Van Zijl 1992, 33-39).

[12] G. Rietveld, 'Het Interieur', 43, RSA, GR 144.

[13] Letter dated 14 October 1925 to Rietveld and drawings in NAI, Rietveld archive inv. no. 2-3. Also see M. Kuper, 'Gerrit Rietveld', in: Blotkamp 1996, 224-227 and Rodijk 1991, 18-19.

G.Th. Rietveld, Nijland House with thatched roof, Hercules Segherslaan 18, Bilthoven, 1940-1942. Made for the son of the owner of the Vreeburg Cinema, it followed the rejection of an earlier design with a flat roof

G.Th. Rietveld, Theissing House, Breitnerlaan 11, Utrecht, 1958-1959 Demonstration of the uses of concrete, 1960

[14] Rodijk 1991, 83-85.

[15] Theissing was professor by special appointment in the science and research of building materials; date of lecture: 14 December 1960. The participating architect was J. van Dillen, who also assisted with the only other house with a concrete skeleton construction, for Van Slobbe in Heerlen (1964). In the 1930s Rietveld had carried out various residential projects with Bredero, partly with steel skeletons; Rodijk 1991, 25-27, 37-39, 143-145 and 164-188; *Cobouw* 18 February 1964, 21; Theissing 1961, 10-13.

In communities situated in rural areas, building codes sometimes led to remarkable roof shapes because the planning authorities did not allow flat roofs. For instance, the slate roof on the Rapsodie House for violinist Zóltan Székely and his wife in Santpoort (1934) acquired a cheerful curve above one of the half-round volumes. And the thatched roofs on the wooden summer cottage for the De Braamakkers (1941) and the neighbouring cottage for Dora van Ravesteyn-Hintzen in Breukelen (1934) had saucy shapes. With the Nijland House in Bilthoven (1940-1942), the broad thatched hip roof was raised above the high wall of glass facing the stairwell, so that, in combination with the façades of green-glazed brick with white stucco and purple brick, it nevertheless retained a certain modern look.[14]

After the war, stuccoed façades became too expensive. Rietveld therefore sometimes entirely or partially colourwashed the brick walls so that the jointing was less obvious. He still associated brick with old-fashioned drudgery, but because of their flat roofs and large surfaces of glass or strong colour combinations and visible steel profiles, these homes nonetheless look unmistakably contemporary. Only the Theissing House in Utrecht (1958-1959) was a deliberate demonstration of the use of concrete: a reinforced concrete skeleton and a varied stacking of B2 concrete blocks. This was not surprising, in fact, for E.M. Theissing was head of the laboratory for Bredero's Bouwbedrijf, where concrete blocks were developed and tested, and also professor by special appointment in building materials at Delft College of Technology. His inaugural lecture was entitled 'Air As Building Material'.[15]

Test Cases for Industrialized Housing Construction

Rietveld had only built two private dwellings in 1927, but he was already thinking in terms of serial construction and mass production so as to be able to offer labourers good and cheap housing, and lighten their workload in constructing them. His third building project, a garage with an apartment for the chauffeur, was meant to be a test case for further industrialization. The entire construction was built 'in three weeks with inexperienced

G.Th. Rietveld, Chauffeur's dwelling,
Waldeck Pyrmontkade 20, Utrecht,
1927-1928
Designed as an experimental prototype for
the increasing industrialization of housing
Photograph and colour design, perspective
and details of the cavity wall construction
NAI, Rotterdam

Materialization in Rietveld's Architecture

workers' with a steel skeleton and 1:3 concrete plates that were just 1 cm shy of the modular dimension of 1 m so that they could conform precisely to that module after being assembled.[16] For the sake of variety, they were mounted both horizontally and vertically, and sprayed through a grid with black and white enamel paint for a visually attractive, waterproof effect. Despite a detailed construction drawing of the cavity walls, insulation sheeting and connecting bolts, the building inspector demanded a layer of brick on the inside.[17]

The flat mastic roof had no overhang, the fastening nuts on the terminating angle brackets worked as modern echoes of the clout nails on upholstered furniture. Together with the rectangular bay window on the upper story, these were the only jutting components in the otherwise flat façades. People in avant-garde circles appreciated the modernity of this experimental dwelling that clearly referred to the Machine Age with its taut lines, colour scheme and use of materials. The client, however, spoke ill of the damp seeping through the walls of the garage apartment and particularly of the leaking roof.[18]

Nonetheless, Rietveld went ahead with flat roofs and his search for an architecturally sound industrialization of housing. Although he preferred 'the totally factory-made house' and had designed a series of *normaalwoningen* (standardized dwellings) with Truus Schröder, he soon discovered that the building industry was not yet ready for industrialization.[19] As an alternative, he developed a prefabricated 'living core' in which the most expensive facilities, such as toilet, shower and kitchen, were concentrated around a spiral staircase in order to save space and costs for labour and materials. The advantage of such
a prefab core was that 'local and unorganized and seasonally-dependent manual work' could be replaced by 'factory work'. He wanted to outfit this prefab core with 'iron construction walls, ceilings and floors in materials that insulate against moisture, temperature and sound' and to 'ship the whole thing as a package to be opened after the basic structure is entirely finished.[20] He worked out many variations of this idea but manufacturers were not interested in producing it.

Due to the special circumstances of the Second World War, Rietveld received an unexpected chance to work directly on an industrial housing project. The initiative came from Bredero's Bouwbedrijf (BBB), which had acquired extensive experience during the 1920s with serial housing construction in concrete blocks, following the Olbertz system. In 1941 director Adriaan Bredero, despite the great business risk, erected a new factory along the Kanaaldijk near Maarssen for the production of concrete elements.[21] He had received special permission to construct an experimental complex of 210 concrete dwellings in Geleen.[22] Businessman that he was, Bredero not only foresaw a great housing shortage and a scarcity of traditional building materials, but also a potential national and international growth market for concrete housing as soon as the war would be over. In hope of that recovery, in May of 1943 he invited Rietveld and other architects for 'further study and preparation of our montage building methods and collaboration on their eventual realization'.[23] Bredero energetically included two sets of standards with central guidelines for housing construction, although this met with heavy criticism.[24]

---

[16] Here he mentions 1926 as the year of construction and also refers to the experiments in Frankfurt; G.Th. Rietveld, 'Rationele vormgeving', lecture given on the occasion of the end of the academic year for the Haagsche Academie and MTS in the Hague, May 1953, 7, typescript RSA, GR 63; also see Küper and Van Zijl, 1992, 28-31.

[17] The garage and upstairs apartment was situated at the Waldeck Pyrmontkade 10 and intended for the chauffeur of H. van der Vuurst de Vries, who had a house at the back of the property (Julianalaan 10) which he previously had had Rietveld renovate; Van Zijl, 2001, 09; M. Kuper, 'Gerrit Rietveld' in: Blotkamp 1996, 227-229; also see note 10 and NAI, Rietveld archive, inv. no. 4-7.

[18] See Van Loghem 1932, 115.

[19] Rietveld 1927 (a), 89-92.

[20] Drawings and texts in NAI, Rietveld archive, inv. no. 16-17.

[21] BBB, *Woonhuizen in montagebouw*, Utrecht 1942, brochure in NAI, Dudok archive, inv. no. d159; BBB, *Constructiedetails van het B.B.B. montagebouw-systeem*, Utrecht (1942), Utrecht City Archives, inv. no. 525, where there are also brochures in English, French and German; Kuipers 1987; B. van Santen, *Bredero's Bouwbedrijf 1921-1947* in: Bekkers 2005, 15-58.

[22] This experiment was exempted from the general building freeze that went into effect on 1 July 1942. The construction was delayed; in 1944 only 122 dwellings had been realized; see 'Monografie Nieuwe systemen in de woningbouw', *Bouw*, March 1948, 21-22, 33-34; also see note 21.

[23] The other architects were J.H. van den Broek, W.M. Dudok, W. van Tijen and P. Zanstra for plans in, respectively, Eindhoven, Arnhem, Rotterdam and Amsterdam; among others incidentally taking part in the meetings was H. van der Kaa, head of the Public Housing Department; notes in NAI, Dudok archive, inv. no. d159 and Rietveld archive, inv. no. 127.

[24] During the occupation, various measures were taken to further the normalization of housing construction, such as the Normaalbladen N 894 and 895; see Bosma and Wagenaar 1995, 215; Siraa 1989.

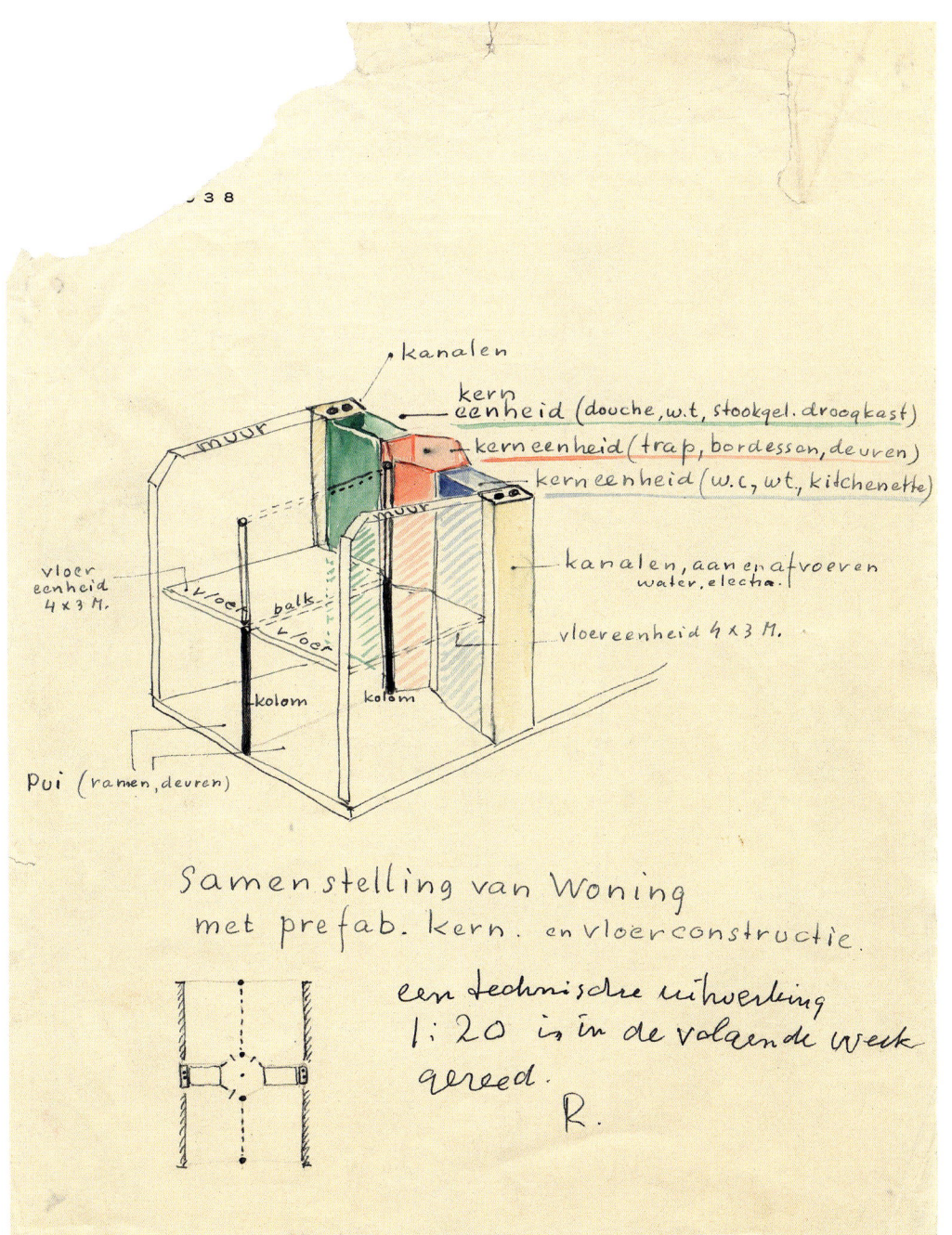

G.Th. Rietveld, Design of a dwelling with
a prefab core and floor construction
21 x 27 cm
NAI, Rotterdam

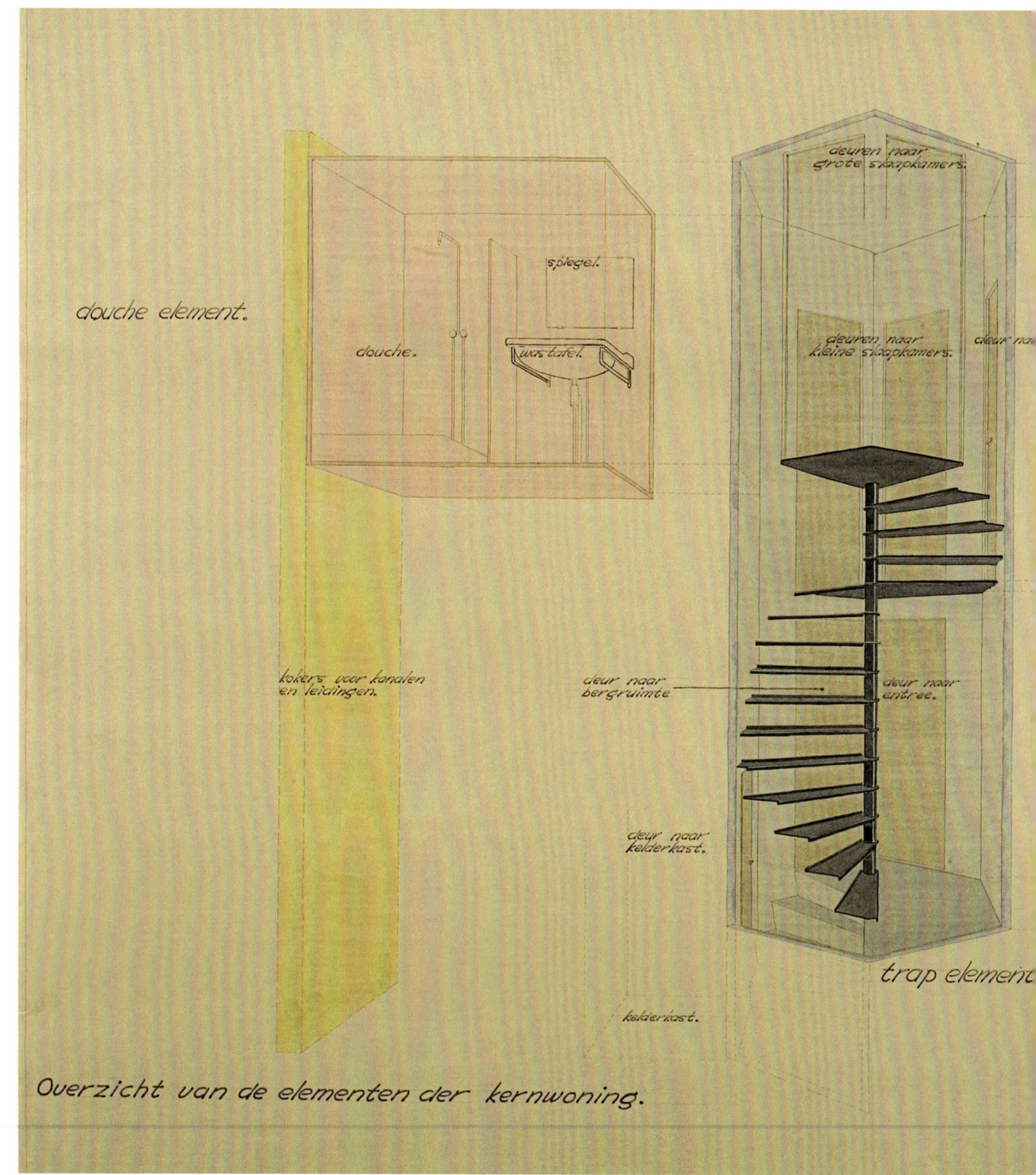

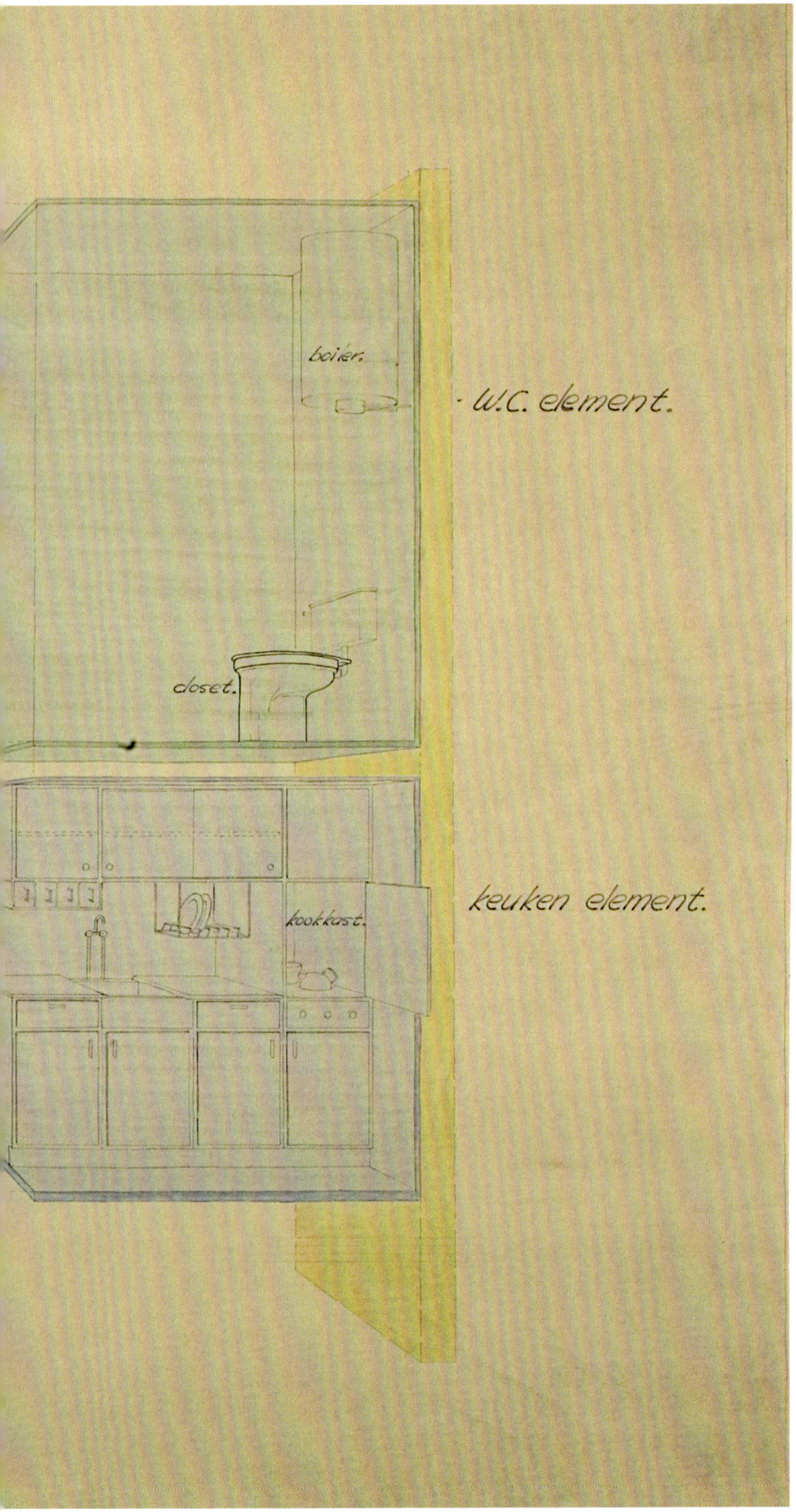

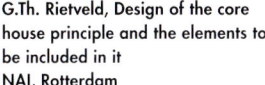

G.Th. Rietveld, Design of the core house principle and the elements to be included in it
NAI, Rotterdam

G.Th. Rietveld, Dwellings on Robijnhof, combining modern and traditional construction techniques in a rhythmic pattern

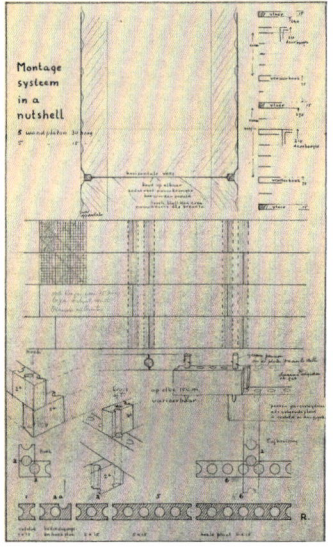

G.Th. Rietveld, Rietveld's version of the BBB assembly system of prefab concrete elements in a proportional system
NAI, Rotterdam

25 See note 24.

26 Notes in NAI, Rietveld archive, inv. no. 127.

27 G. Rietveld, 'Vakantiehuisjes voor het personeel van de superphosfaatfabriek "Albatros" en van De Vries Robbé', goed wonen 4 (1951) 7, pages not numbered.

For BBB, it was advantageous to implement further standardization of sizes, floor plans, walls, façade structures and the like, because this meant that fewer adaptations were needed to meet the requirements of local building regulations and the market possibilities for standard products were greater. Bredero wanted to technically and aesthetically improve his montage system – a stacking of prefab concrete blocks for low-rise buildings – in an open discussion with architects in order to later be able to apply it on a large scale. Presumably he already had the intention of applying for a patent at this time, but that cat only came out of the bag at a later stage. All of those who had been invited joined in. Only Rietveld asked whether this would cause problems with the Kultuurkamer (the German-installed Chamber of Culture).[25] After having been reassured, he was assigned a project in Gorinchem-Noord. Contributing to the thinking on efficiency, detailing and finishing in specific terms, he designed a montage system with concrete elements of 15 x 30 x 90 cm and iron connecting pins. His choice of this particular decimal measurement, independent of existing sizes of bricks or concrete blocks, was characteristic of Rietveld's preference for balanced proportion.

In preparation, he examined the BBB housing in Geleen. Then he began designing, starting from the idea that a plasterer would only be necessary to repair any damages that might eventually occur in the interiors. For the interior walls, comprised of ready-made elements, he wanted to have 'fresh colours, whereby the colour is toned down by the colour of the cement', and not wallpaper. As to how the outer walls would be perceived, he equated 'concrete . . . with natural stone'. According to Rietveld, concrete images could be very beautiful 'as long as there is enough plasticity in them'; conversely, W.M. Dudok, one of the other architects involved, proposed putting vertical strips of brick on the blocks while in the factory.[26]

For the gently sloping saddle roofs required in Gorinchem, which according to Bredero were necessary for good heat insulation and eventual expansion of the space, Rietveld made detailed sketches of concrete tiles and their mounting. From the largest to the smallest detail, he wanted to maintain his architectural direction over the ultimate composition in order to prevent the dwellings from becoming too monotonous and their layout too impractical. In the end, due to the increasingly problematic conditions of the war, the Gorinchem construction project was not realized.

The experiments did, however, lead to the creation of B2 concrete blocks and Rietveld's fascination for their possibilities for architectural variation. They had the advantages of being faster to work with and having a modern look. A disadvantage was their limited resistance to dampness. Therefore Rietveld could only use exterior walls of concrete blocks with dwellings that were not lived in year-round, such as the vacation cottages in Markelo (1951).[27] For normal housing, it was still better from a structural point of view to build the exterior layer of the cavity wall in brick. When after the war Rietveld finally received commissions for social housing, the designs were primarily executed with brick façades to which were attached, as a relative novelty, continuous frames with colourful parapet panels, and flat or ribbed concrete edges at the floor line of each storey, such as in the Robijnhof in Utrecht.

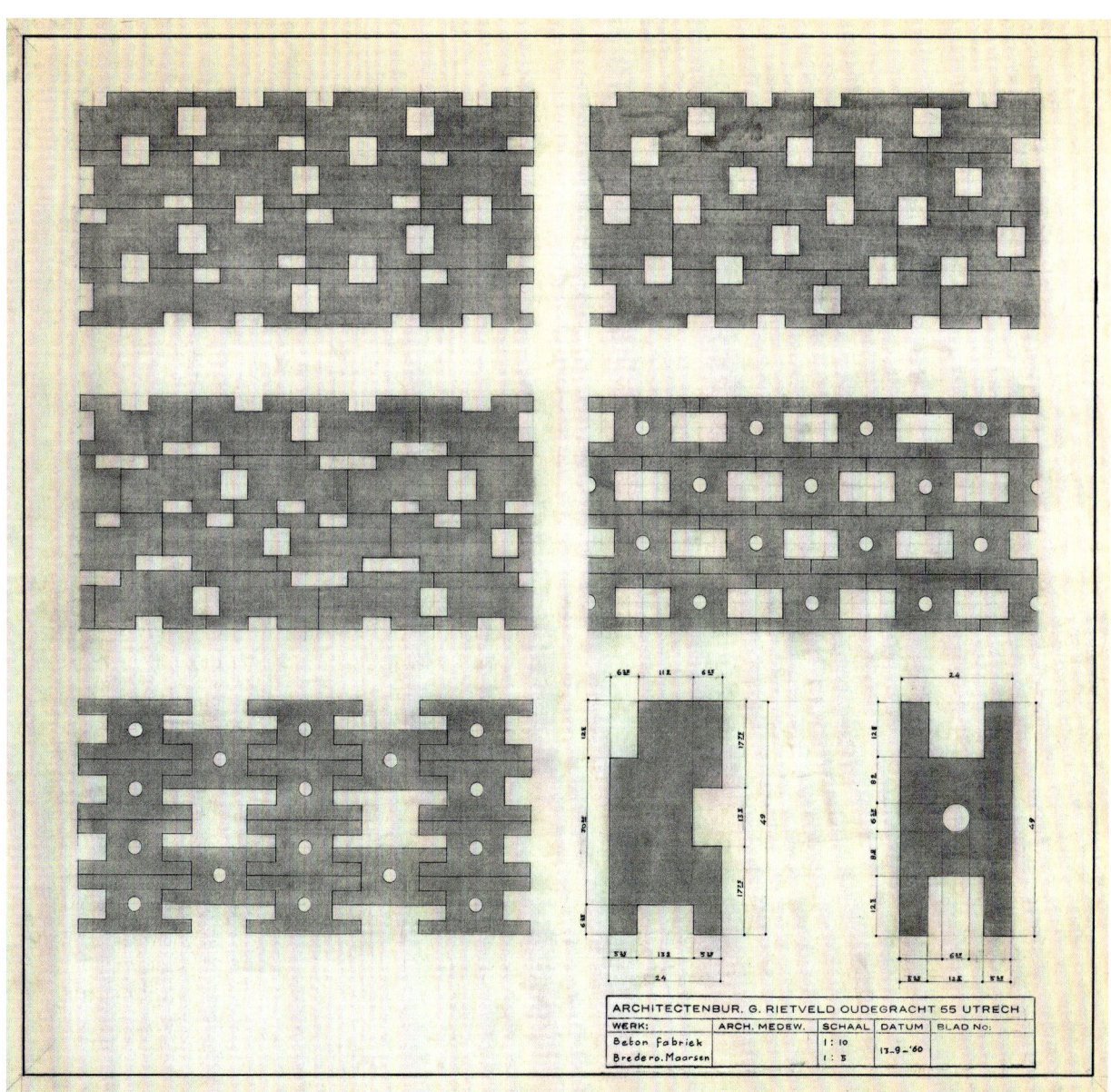

One of Rietveld's many studies for the design of hollow concrete blocks and their different placement options, 1960
NAI, Rotterdam

Materialization in Rietveld's Architecture

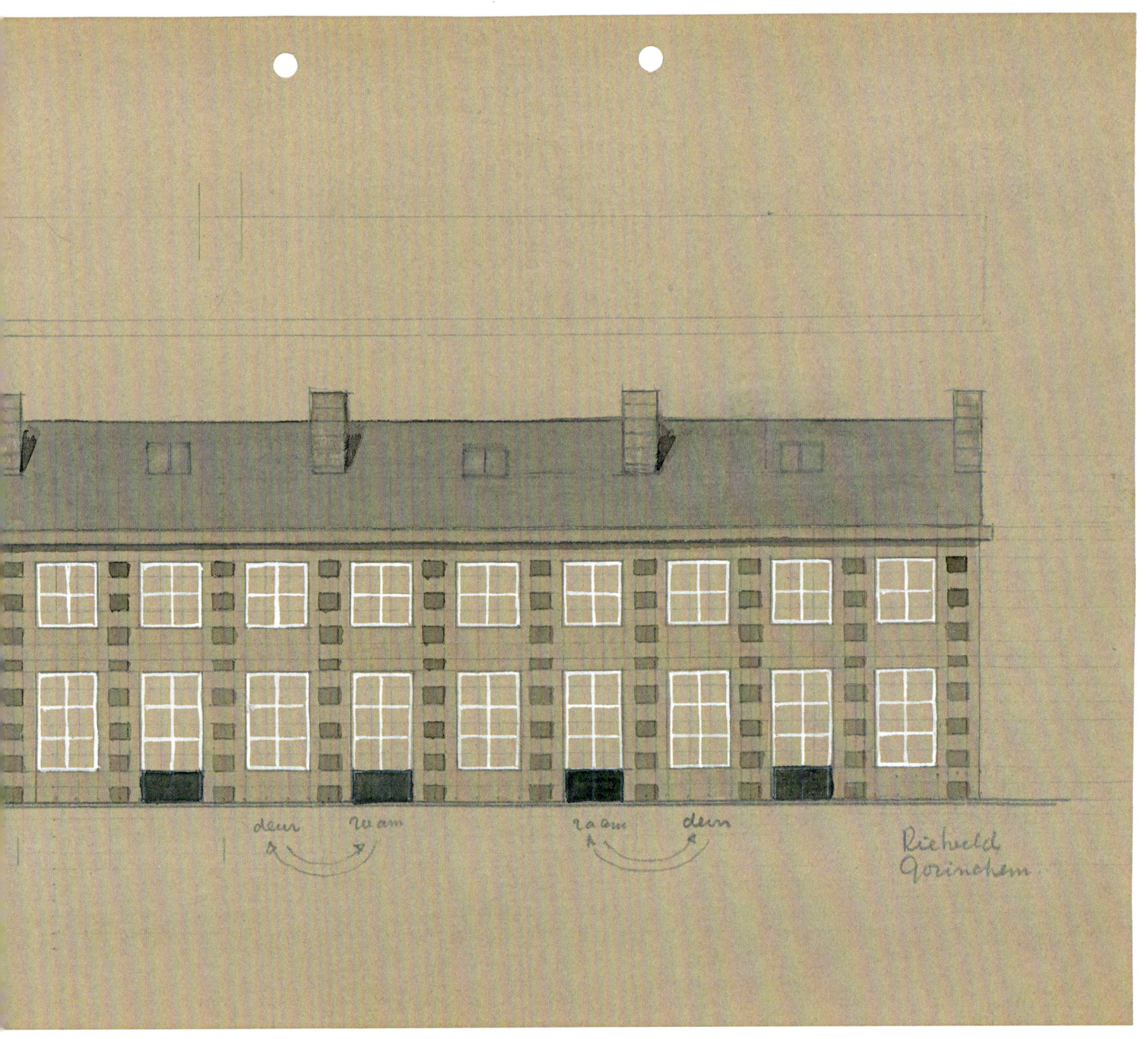

BBB dwellings in Gorinchem-Noord, with Rietveld indicating that the doors and windows can be swapped around
NAI, Rotterdam

Materialization in Rietveld's Architecture **113**

G.Th. Rietveld, Schrale Beton Offices,
Willemsvaart 21, Zwolle, 1957
RSA, Utrecht

G.Th. Rietveld and H.J. Nolte, the
Mgr. M.I. Verriet Institute on the island
of Curaçao under construction, with
locally made concrete blocks and steel
columns and reed slabs imported from
the Netherlands, 1949-1952
NAI, Rotterdam

G.Th. Rietveld, Sonsbeek Pavilion, Arnhem,
1955
RSA, Utrecht

The Building as a Sound, Economical Construction

Not until after the Second World War did Rietveld receive commissions for larger buildings than individual homes. The jump in scale required for designing such an edifice as a logical and economically constructed device implied greater complexity in the structural aspects and the building process itself, the logistics and on-site supervision. Moreover, the specifications for such projects had stiffer technical requirements. The one-to-one way of working between architect and client or architect and contractor was no longer sufficient, so Rietveld was forced to either expand his studio or work with other architects.[28]

A special case in this regard was his involvement with the Mgr. M.I. Verriet Institute on the island of Curaçao (1949-1952), for which he collaborated with a local architect, Henk Nolte.[29] The design and construction process was extra complicated because their consultations primarily took place by telegram, airmail or overseas surface mail. Most of the building material was custom built elsewhere and assembled on the spot by unskilled labourers. The steel columns shipped from the Netherlands were precisely placed on intersections of the chequered floor pattern, with square sections of 4 x 4 m harmonizing with the gently sloping roof of thatched panels from a firm based in Oosterhout.[30] The rainwater caught by the roof was sent to a freshwater reservoir beneath the kitchen. The only local building material consisted of hollow, machine-cast concrete blocks for the cavity walls.[31] On top of this were placed 110 reinforced opaque windows in the dormitories. At both ends and near the central service pavilion, walls of custom-made wooden shutters with 8,000 adjustable slats were installed. This manually operated form of natural ventilation and tempering of the light was cheaper at that time than ready-made blinds and air-conditioning. Rietveld had discussed the colour palette a few months previously, on his way to Mexico, with the Curaçaoan painter Lucila Engels-Boskaljon.[32] He was well aware that the effect of colours in the bright tropical light was different than in the Netherlands and that white was therefore less suitable.[33]

Following upon the Verriet Institute was the equally adventurous and open Sonsbeek Pavilion for an exhibition of sculpture in Arnhem (1954), which combined an original decorative use of canted B2 blocks and awnings with a meandering route in open contact with nature. This was the prelude to large and more enclosed exhibition spaces for art, such as the Netherlands Biennial Pavilion in Venice (1953-1954) with its plaster façades, and the Zonnehof in Amersfoort (1958-1959) with its blue-and-white glazed brick. Structurally, he partly used wooden joisting and an inner cavity wall of concrete blocks in order to make an economically efficient construction of the whole.[34]

Almost simultaneously, Rietveld worked on entirely different types of buildings, including the new office for Schrale Beton in Zwolle. As a way of advertising the products of this building contractor, he completely covered the office walls of B2 blocks with square brushed-concrete tiles. These he specially designed in varied sizes within the same 'metre pattern'. Entirely in keeping with this were large panes of glass that appeared to make the white ridge beams above them float in the air. In reality, they were supported by an inner steel construction. Rietveld carefully directed

[28] Rodijk 1991, 9-10, 220-222.

[29] Rietveld was invited to this during the STICUSA study trip to the Antilles and Surinam; Gill 1999, 94-96, 100-103; M. Küper, 'Het Mgr. Verriet Institute, Curaçao' in: Küper and Van Zijl 1988,127-143.

[30] D. Hoogstraten & Zoon in Zeist provided the steel construction and also calculated the effects of lighter trusses. On 2 November 1951, 72 packages of iron girders and ironwork were shipped per the S.S. Breda of the KNSM, together with the Oosterhout cane panels. That was two weeks after the official laying of the first stone for the home; drawings and correspondence in NAI, Rietveld archive, inv. no. 196-200.

[31] Size 15, respectively 10 x 20 x 40 cm; correspondence in NAI, Rietveld archive, inv. no. 196-200.

[32] Rietveld had become acquainted with her during his first trip with Doctor Chris Engels, who was closely involved in the building of the institute; drawings in NAI, Rietveld archive, inv. no.196-200; G. Rietveld, 'Curaçao', *Katholieke gezondheidszorg* 5 (1951), May, 198-199; Anonymous, 'De gebrekkige kinderen in een Tehuis als een paleis', *Beurs- en Nieuwsberichten van Curaçao* 15 November 1952.

[33] Gill 1999, 102-105, 133-134.

[34] Drawing in NAI, Rietveld archive, inv. nos. 63-66.

G.Th. Rietveld with G. Beltman, De Ploeg,
Riethovensedijk 20, Bergeijk, 1956-1958
The factory under construction
RSA, Utrecht

Rietveld (2nd from left) and others visiting
the construction site of textile factory
De Ploeg, featuring various uses of
concrete, 1958
RSA, Utrecht

what could and could not be seen, the use of colour, the furniture, and the finishing of the interior spaces, right down to the doorknobs. For the 'eye of the entranceway' he designed a kind of 'hollow knob', although he considered flat discs also good. Just as long as boring old wood was avoided, he left the definitive choice of form and material (aluminium, copper or iron) up to the director, Binnert Schröder, the son of Truus Schröder.[35]

Foresight
Rietveld's commissions for the De Ploeg Textile Factory in Bergeijk and two applied arts schools with glass curtain walls in Arnhem and Amsterdam prove how much his prestige as an architect had grown. In 1964 that was even crowned by an honorary doctorate from Delft College of Technology. In an accompanying interview, Rietveld returned to industrialized construction and warned:

> Architects will have to be on the alert if they are not to be brushed aside by technical developments. They will have to make sure that the architectural form does not become lost. They will have to study the possibilities offered by mass production. If not, the process could easily develop further without them.[36]

In that sense, too, his view was prescient. Although he continued to call himself a proponent of prefabrication, he designed many elements for his projects himself and also warned of the risks of unremitting materialism and the waste that could result from industrialization and mass production.[37] Ultimately, he considered architecture an art; and by using the right measurements, a good architect could achieve a crystal clarity that was independent of the materials used. ◆

The glass curtain walls of the Gerrit Rietveld Academy of Art and Design, Amsterdam

[35] *Bouwt in beton BAB* June 1959, 12; *Rietveld aan de Willemsvaart*, Zwolle 2007; drawing in NAI, Rietveld archive, inv. no. 557 and correspondence and drawings in the still unordered Schrale archive in RSA.

[36] G.Th. Rietveld, 'Wij staan nog maar aan het begin', *Cobouw* 18 February 1964, 21.

[37] G.Th. Rietveld, *Handwerk*, manuscript in RSA, GR 31.

Hielkje Zijlstra

Flat Roofs and Open Corners

G.Th. Rietveld with G. Beltman, De Ploeg, Riethovensedijk 20, Bergeijk, 1956-1958
The eaves of the entrance portico. The space is defined by the column and the roof surface. The open eaves, formed by a standard I-beam of which the recessed part has been painted black, actually deny any sense of definition and stress the continuity between the interior and exterior

[1] Rietveld 1927 (a), 92.

The simple principles that Gerrit Rietveld brought to his buildings and that he often expounded prove to be rather more complicated when put into practice. From his first small-scale architectural designs to his last major buildings, Rietveld always tried to define space. He articulated spaces and let them flow into one another, both internally and externally, as his trademark flat roofs and open corners demonstrate. By detailing the intersection of two planes as an open corner, as he did with the famous corner window in the Schröder House, he enhanced the sense of space.

Rietveld wanted to achieve this definition of space through the use of materials and sought simplicity in the solution, which is not to be confused with the simplest solution, as this quotation illustrates:

> Architecture makes it possible to define space and nothing more; (even the materials needed for this make their presence felt more by their position in space than by their individual shapes). Meeting the need for protection from the elements actually makes it possible to realize such a definition of space.[1]

The entrance portico of the De Ploeg Textile Factory in Bergeijk, for example, was articulated by the detail of the eaves, which both defined and continued the space. Rietveld's ideas about a sustainable approach remain pertinent today:

> In the near future technological developments will be far greater than those made possible by steam and electricity and many new

[2] Rietveld 1958, 258-259 (for the English translation see Küper and Van Zijl 1992, 51-55).

[3] R. Stenvert, 'Dak met plat van papier: het ontstaan van het platte dak', in: Emmens 1996, 113-121.

[4] Rothuizen 1916, 1; Rothuizen 1920, 1; Rotshuizen 1950, 1. In 1939 the author changed his name to Rotshuizen.

[5] Rietveld 1927 (a), 90.

materials will become available. Bearing this in mind, I have a very personal wish. Do not overload the environment, it does not benefit anyone, and remember that the earth's natural resources were not all created and designated for us; therefore they can never be conducive to our prosperity without many damaging consequences, which may well turn out to be greater than the benefits. Learn to enjoy the wealth of restraint! Does not the appreciation of the very smallest (the atomic nucleus) also hold the key to the power of restraint? Similarly, restraint holds the key to all creative work.'[2]

This vision shaped the way in which he planned his projects down to the smallest detail. The attention to detail that Rietveld lavished on the intersection of planes – conceived and developed on the basis of simplicity – inevitably culminated in an aesthetic form. Yet unlike his contemporaries in America, such as Ludwig Mies van der Rohe, he never set out to achieve this.

The Flat Roof as a Hallmark of Modernity

The flat roof, which Rietveld favoured in his house designs, became more and more prevalent in Dutch architecture in the 1930s with the advent of the *Nieuwe Bouwen* (the Dutch manifestation of the Modern Movement in architecture).[3] However, the handbooks did not regard this type of roof as appropriate for the Netherlands. The Arnhem-based architect E.J. Rothuizen (1888-1979) wrote in his book *Het dak* (The Roof) in 1916: 'In this country, the weather conditions demand a pitched roof. Whereas in the tropics flat roofs provide the best cover, in this country – which has a high level of annual rainfall – water needs to be drained off fast.' In the chapter 'Concrete roofs' Rothuizen focused exclusively on pitched roofs.

In the second edition in 1920 he supplemented this chapter with 'prefabricated systems (applied to pitched roofs)'. Roof tar and 'cement mastic' are applied to pitched roof surfaces. A completely revised third edition appeared in 1950. In it he slightly modified the preface: 'To all intents and purposes, the weather conditions in this country call for a pitched roof. Any rain water that falls onto it is quickly drained off.'[4] Even though he described a few examples of flat roofs and covered the concept of roof terraces, his heart was not in it. Rietveld distanced himself from these conservative views and, starting in 1924 with the Schröder House, expressed his preference for the flat roof in combination with rectangular planes and masses.

Apparent Simplicity in the Construction of the Flat Roof

As a furniture maker by trade Rietveld was capable of ascertaining the rationale behind a construction through building, so that what looks like decoration may actually have structural origins: 'For example, the upholstered panels . . . of a Dutch Renaissance cabinet are ingenious constructions conceived to protect the ½ inch board of which the door was made from getting warped.'[5]

Rietveld's architecture is epitomized by the positioning of planes. Throughout his entire career he wanted to have perfectly smooth planes

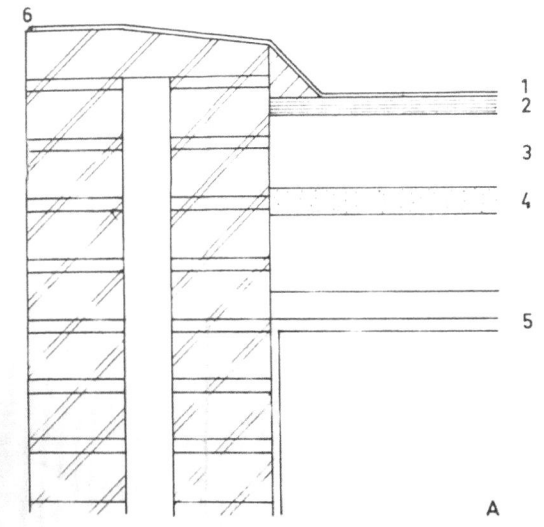
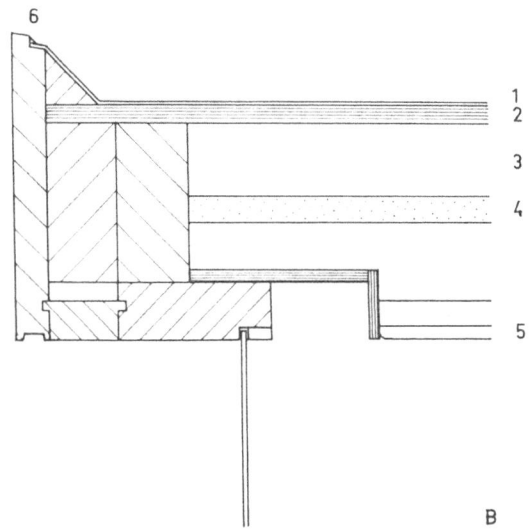

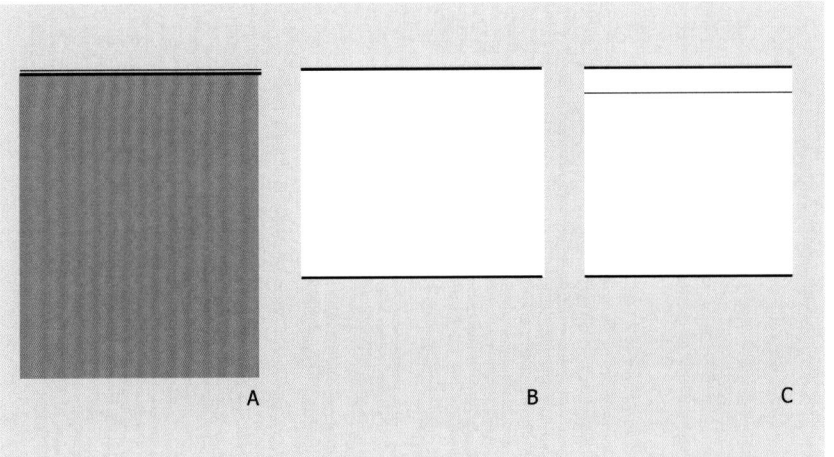

View of the façade surfaces that go with the above sections A and B and the position of the flashing that was fitted later on section B, in orthographic projection

that were not crowned by visible eaves. Brick surfaces and (glass) panels underneath a roof overhang would be flush-fitted. This resulted in smooth planes without a frame, formed by flashing (roof coping) and window sections. These seemingly simple architectural details were in fact difficult to make and soon became defective because rain water managed to seep in between the different materials.

Rietveld drew his designs himself and wrote down how and with what materials the components should be made. From the very first sketch he left no doubt about how the planes were positioned in relation to one another and how they had to be constructed. Later

Flat Roofs and Open Corners

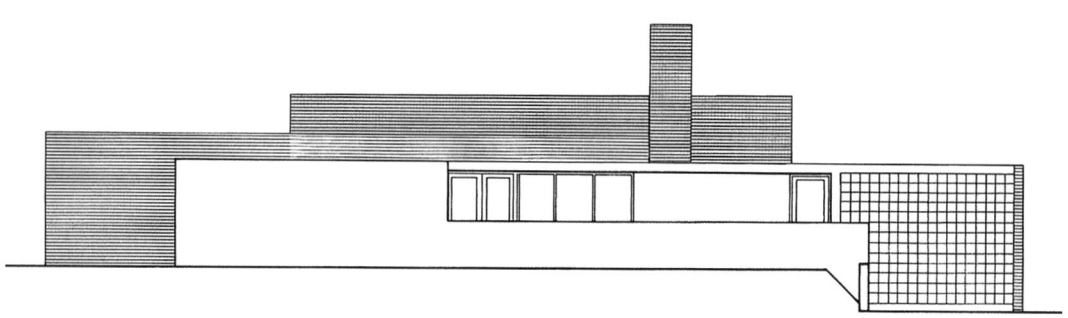

G.Th. Rietveld, Van den Doel House,
Monnickendammerrijweg 31c, Ilpendam,
1957-1958
Photograph and drawing of North façade

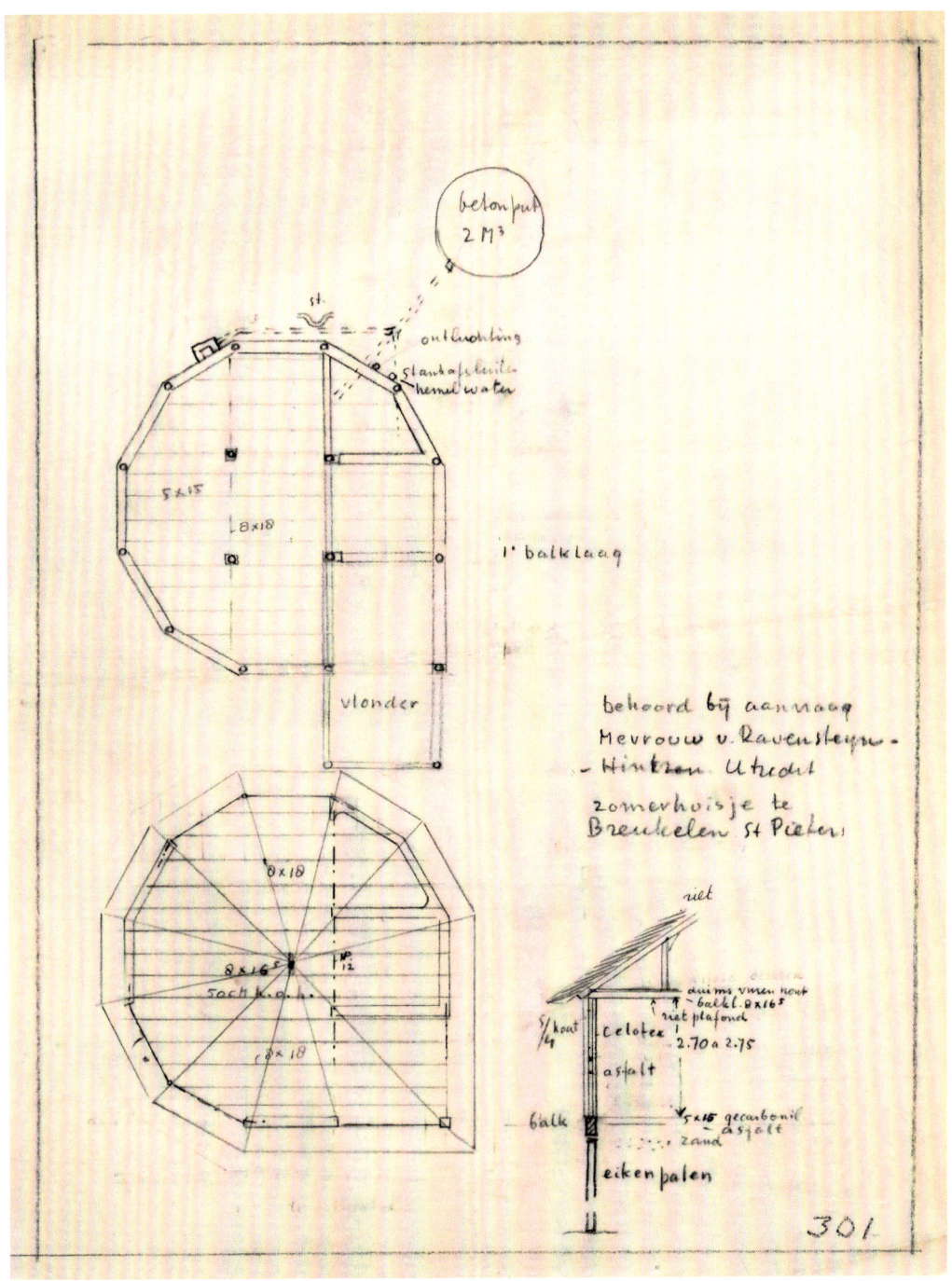

G.Th. Rietveld, Van Ravesteyn-Hintzen Summerhouse, Section F no. 1635, Breukelen St. Pieters, 1934-1935
A drawing by Rietveld in which he outlines the construction method
RSA, Utrecht

Flat Roofs and Open Corners

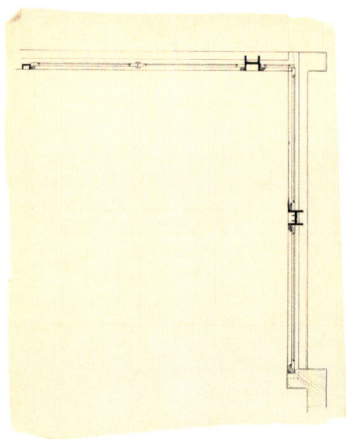

G.Th. Rietveld and T. Schröder-Schräder, Schröder House, Prins Hendriklaan 50, Utrecht, 1924
Detail drawing of the open-corner window (horizontal section)
RSA, Utrecht

[6] Because of a change in location and administrative wrangling, the ultimate design was not completed until 1957.

[7] Mulder 1994, 151.

photographs of the Van den Doel House in Ilpendam (1957-1958) show that the eaves have flashing. This was fitted later to keep rain water out and overhangs the plane, adding an extra line to the picture.

The Intersection of Two Planes in the Open Corner

When finishing the eaves Rietveld alternated between barely visible and a highly expressive form that used a standard I-beam to create an open corner. This open detail made its first explicit appearance in the Schröder House. Planes here retain their autonomy. The autonomy of the roof surface that appears to float above the first floor is reinforced by the perpendicular windows below. The culmination of the open corner is found in the intersection of the two windows that open out through the corner. When both windows are open, the corner disappears completely. Rietveld achieved this by squarely fitting the rotating parts together. Although this is obviously a poor solution in terms of wind and water proofing, from an architectural perspective the intersection of these windows remains the epitome of the 'open corner'.

Rietveld elaborated his ideas about the open corner and the flat roof towards the end of his career in his larger works, the so-called curtain walls of the applied art schools in Amsterdam and Arnhem. Their outer surfaces have been further abstracted into an envelope, in which the floors and the roof surface are visible through the glass but disappear as such behind the façades. Rietveld managed to join three different planes at the corners of these two buildings with a minimum of material (just glass and metal sections). The detailing of the overall plane was paramount. This resulted in such great transparency that the corners of the building in particular are experienced as extremely spacious.

Curtain Walls as Envelopes: The Applied Arts Schools

In 1951 Rietveld was commissioned to design the Institute for Applied Arts, the later Gerrit Rietveld Academy in Amsterdam.[6] That same year, the board of the applied arts school in Arnhem also asked Rietveld to design its building. The briefs were very similar and both design processes proceeded in parallel. The designs had a great deal in common and the buildings also bear a striking similarity in their detailing. Both buildings are based on uniform modules measuring 2.10 m (along both horizontal and vertical axes), with the locations responsible for the differences between the floor plans. The floor plan in Arnhem is more open than the one in Amsterdam.

Rietveld wanted 'to create a neutral background for education, because art cannot be taught and artists in the making should not be influenced or distracted by their surroundings'.[7] He opted for a prefabricated concrete skeleton with a glass envelope. In collaboration with the structural engineer he devised a support structure that could be used for both schools and which would include as many factory-made components as possible. The envelope was one of the first proper curtain walls in the Netherlands: glass sheets that are hung around the skeleton like a curtain. Façades are not visibly stacked on top of one another and no spandrel panels were used. The façades consist of glass surfaces measuring 2.10 x 1.05 m that are connected by slender metal sections,

G.Th. Rietveld and T. Schröder-Schräder,
Schröder House, Prins Hendriklaan 50,
Utrecht, 1924
The open-corner window
RSA, Utrecht

Flat Roofs and Open Corners

125

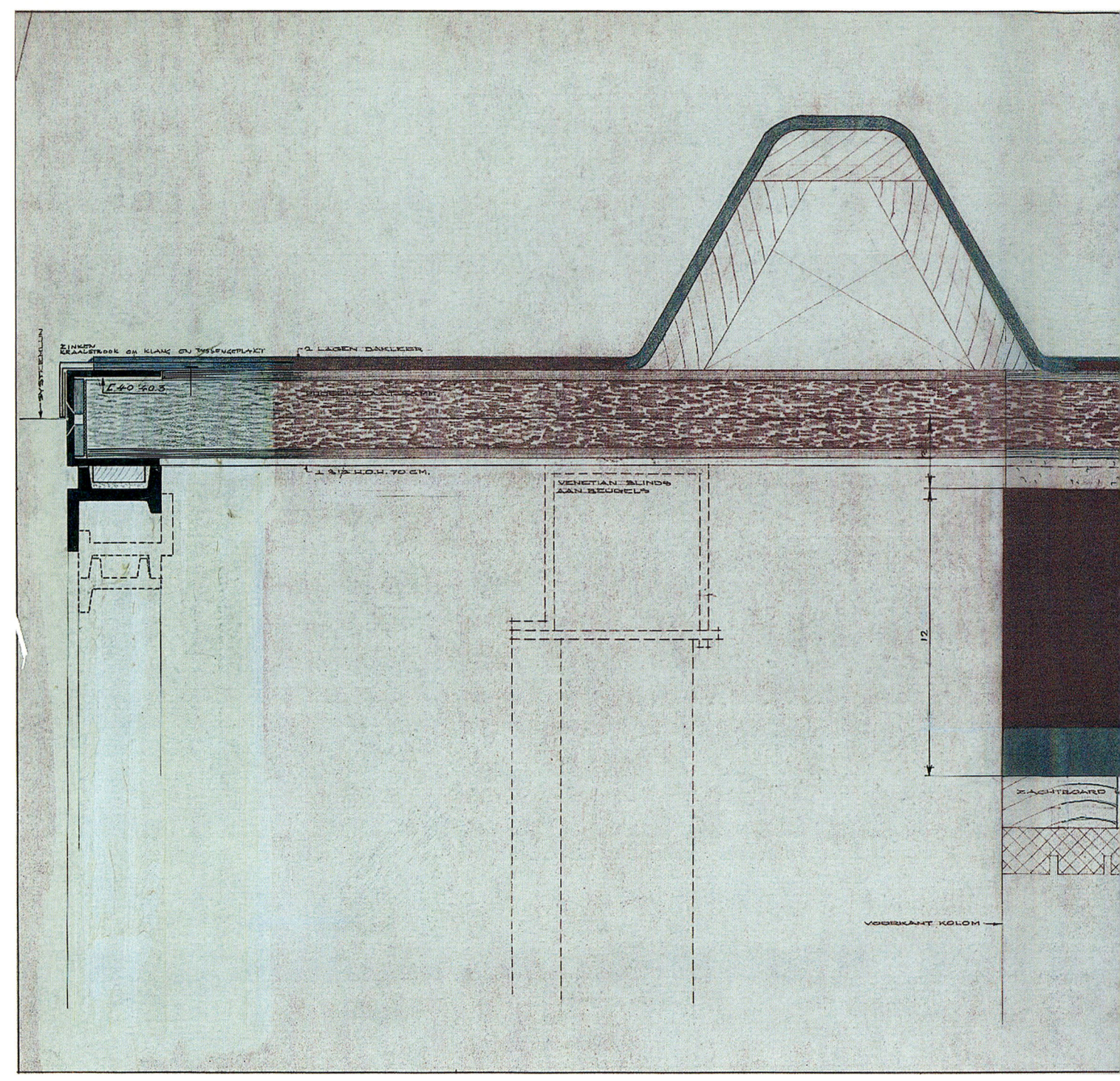

G.Th. Rietveld with J. van Dillen and J. van Tricht, Fine Arts Academy, Gerrit Rietveld Academy, Fred. Roeskestraat 96, Amsterdam, 1956-1967
Detail of the intersection of the roof surface and the façade surface. The roof edge has been reduced to a steel profile with the thickness of a glass profile (drawing February 1960)
NAI, Rotterdam

Articulating Space: Materials, Techniques and Mass Production

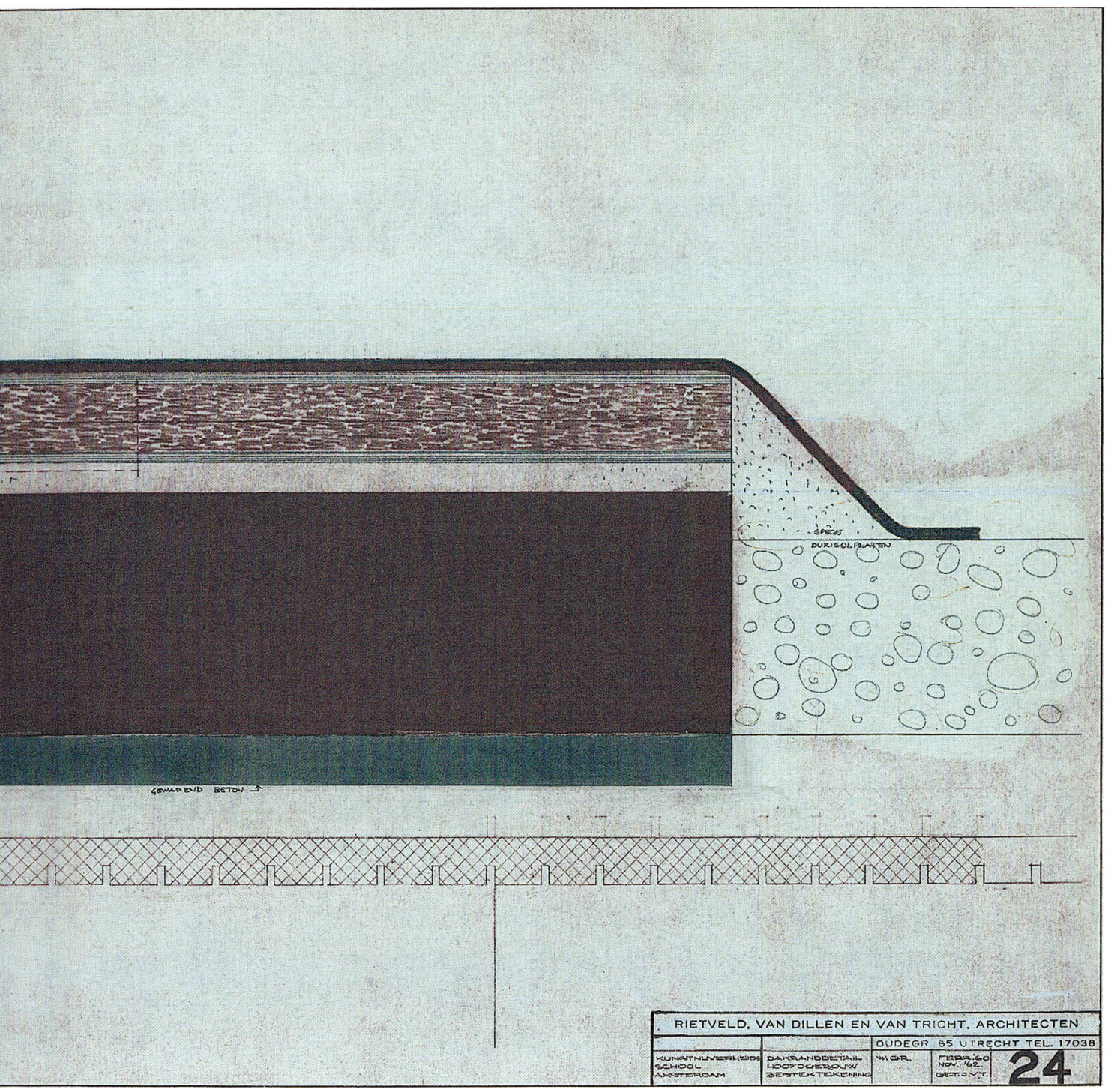

Flat Roofs and Open Corners

G.Th. Rietveld with J. van Dillen and
J. van Tricht, Fine Arts Academy,
Gerrit Rietveld Academy
Elevations and sections (drawing 4,
4 September 1957)
NAI, Rotterdam

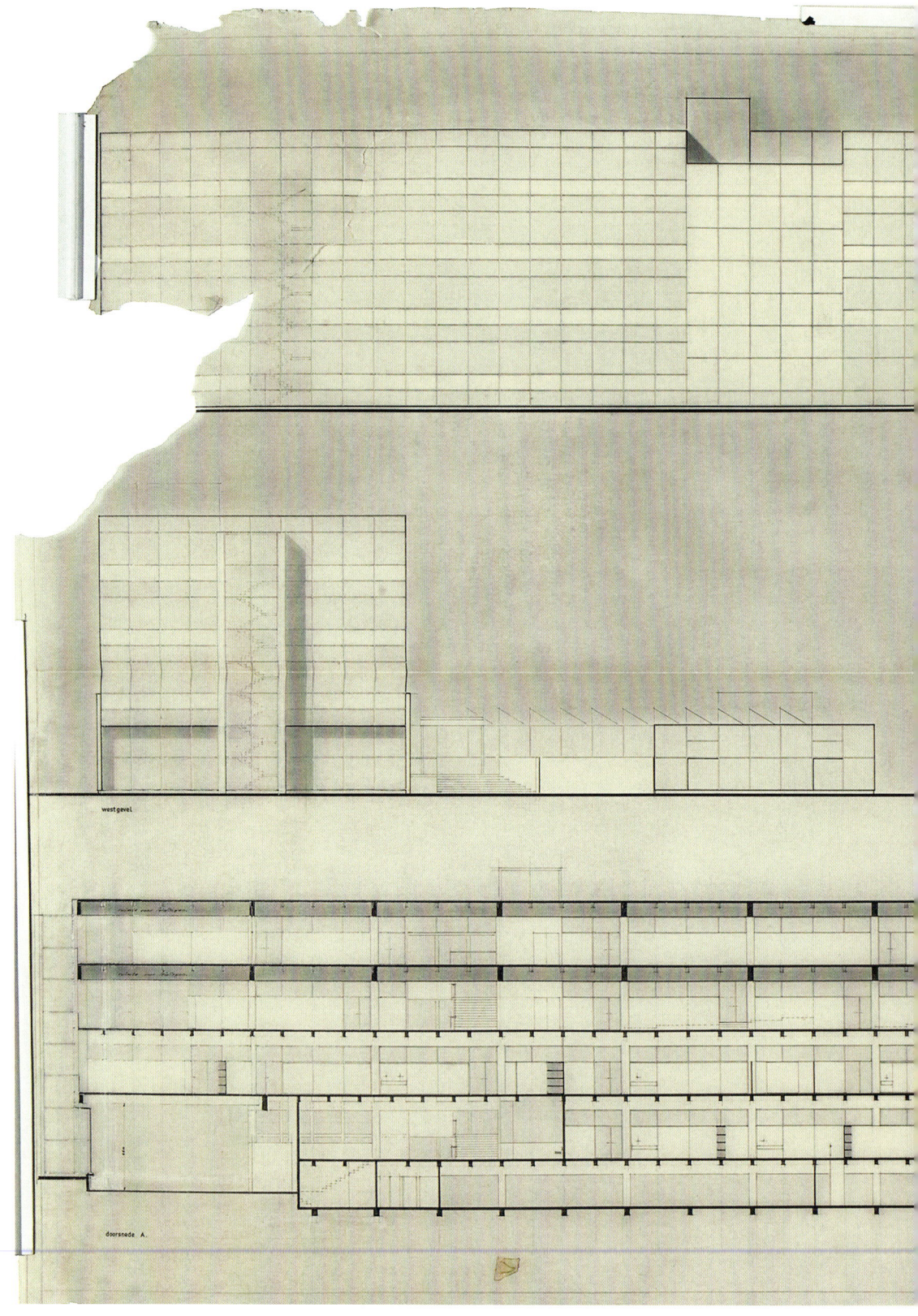

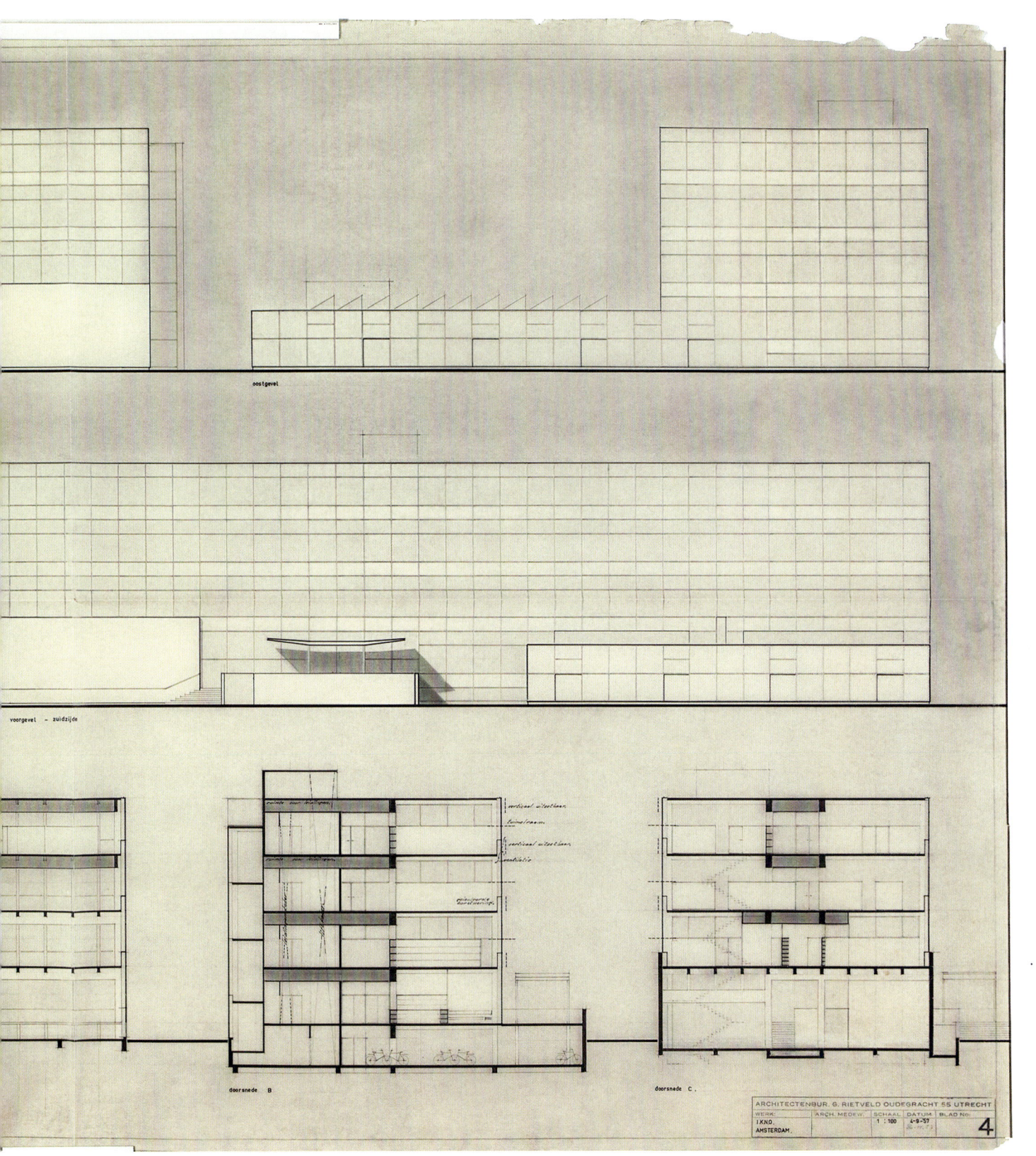

Flat Roofs and Open Corners

G.Th. Rietveld with J. van Dillen and J. van Tricht, Fine Arts Academy, Gerrit Rietveld Academy
The underlying construction is visible through the transparent façade

G.Th. Rietveld with J. van Dillen, Fine Arts Academy, Onderlangs 9, Arnhem, 1958-1963
The façade of the Academy in Arnhem after the renovation. The reflective double glazing and the deeper sections have reduced the façade's original transparency

Articulating Space: Materials, Techniques and Mass Production

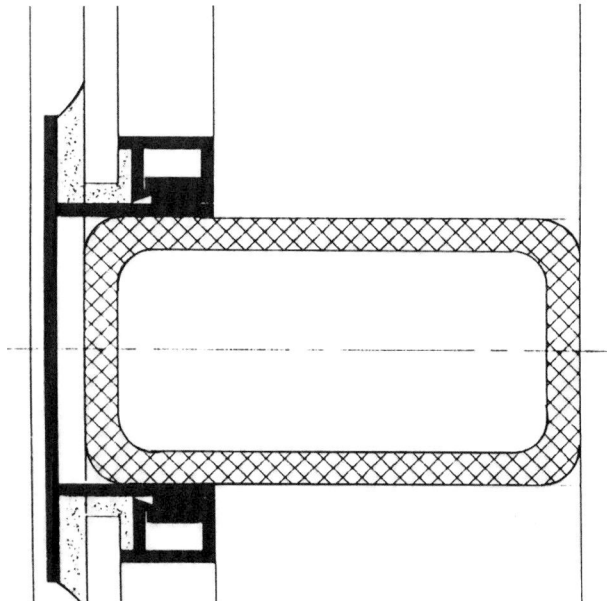
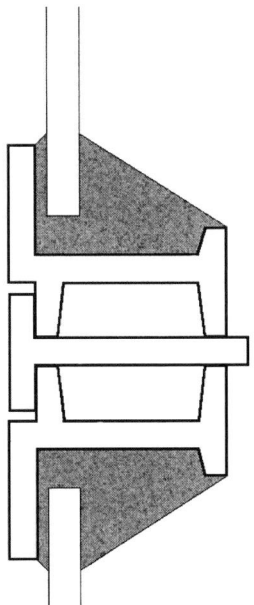

with the glass suspended 40 cm in front of the support structure. The foundation was straightforward and the description of the materials for the planning application easily fit on a single sheet of paper.

But the façade in Arnhem caused problems. When the building opened in 1963 there were leaks. These were dealt with by resealing the glass sections along the entire façade. Construction in Amsterdam did not commence until 1964, so that the Arnhem building served as a test case. But Rietveld died that year and his colleagues Johan van Dillen and Johan van Tricht took charge of the office. Given the experiences in Arnhem, the façade was a frequent topic of discussion. Back in 1963 Rietveld had actually threatened to resign the Amsterdam commission if a façade system other than the one that he and the Wiener company had devised was to be adopted. In the end he asked the Braat company from Delft to develop the façade according to the then prevalent 'chair system'. Braat managed to produce a façade which, despite stacking, measured up to Rietveld's expectations in terms of appearance and technology. The building officially opened in 1967.

Rietveld's façades in Arnhem and Amsterdam were unique in the Netherlands at the time: extremely slender systems with smooth façade surfaces, in which the window sections form an autonomous frame, but the individual window frames are not stacked. The underlying support structure is visible, but does not interfere with the detailing of the façade itself.

The original façade details of the academies in Arnhem (left) and Amsterdam (right). In Arnhem the curtain wall consisted of a steel profile with an aluminium frame on the outside and in Amsterdam of steel 'chair profiles' by the Braat company. In Arnhem the stacking was completely invisible from the outside whereas in Amsterdam it could be seen

W. Gropius, Bauhaus, Dessau, 1925-1926
The glass façade is a neutral plane
suspended between a platform and eaves
made of a stony material
Bauhaus-Archiv, Berlin

Rietveld probably derived inspiration for his façade solutions from Dutch examples such as the Schunck department store in Heerlen (1936-1942) by Frits Peutz and the Van Nelle Factory (1925-1931) in Rotterdam by Brinkman and Van der Vlugt, but the curtain wall proper only materializes in all its simplicity in a design by Rietveld himself. The glass panels in Schunck's building are clearly different in size, as a result of which the corners in particular are more closed and the roof is clearly visible. The Van Nelle Factory sports spandrel panels that make the façade less neutral than Rietveld aspired to in his academies. The façade of Walter Gropius's Bauhaus (1925-1926) in Dessau is also fitted with a curtain wall, but here the platform and eaves are made of a stony material.[8] The façade opening itself has been realized as a neutral, suspended construction.

Simplicity as a Driving Force

With simplicity as his guiding principle, Rietveld tried to take a very pragmatic approach to the realization of his systems. This approach explains his comments in 1953 on the façades of two recently completed buildings in New York: Lever House, built in 1951-1952 by Skidmore, Owings and Merrill (SOM), and the United Nations Building, built in 1949-1950 by Wallace Harrison. He had this to say about the use of prefab components in architecture:

> I would like to express my views on one final issue, namely the question: how advisable is it to build with machine-made components? Lever House in New York, which is almost entirely built of machine-made components, shows that it is possible and that it can be very beautiful. Although closer inspection reveals some concrete floors, stone veneers and stucco ceilings, the building is a uniform product of stainless steel sections and two kinds of glass, which is beautiful and has just as good a claim to the name architecture – or the art of building, if you will – as that which we are wont to call good architecture. This building is much better than the United Nations Building, where the prefab elements are less consistently applied. But a building erected for a large corporation in America does not prove that it is advisable for us to head in the same direction; it is plain to see that is prohibitively expensive for us to build and maintain something like that.[9]

Rietveld objected to the excessive complexity of a building's design. If aesthetics took precedence over simplicity and affordability, he would opt for another solution. The detailing of Lever House was too complex and too expensive in Rietveld's view to serve as an example. The much-lauded opencorner detailing that Mies van der Rohe applied, and which became SOM's signature, is therefore not comparable to Rietveld's detailing of the open corners of his academy buildings. Although Rietveld may have appreciated Mies van der Rohe's detailing of, for example, the Lake Shore Drive Apartments in Chicago (1948-1951), just as he appreciated Lever House, they did not serve as an example, because they were driven by aesthetics rather than the inherent simplicity of the solution. In

F.P.J. Peutz, Schunck Building, Heerlen, 1933-1935
At the corners, at floor level and along the eaves the sections are thicker than the glass sections elsewhere

J.A. Brinkman and L.C. van der Vlugt, with M. Stam, Van Nelle Factory, Rotterdam, 1925-1931
Closed panels have been applied under the windows and the design of the eaves is striking
NAI, Rotterdam

[8] Probst and Schädlich 1986, 76-87.

[9] G.Th. Rietveld, *Rationele Vormgeving. Lezing gehouden bij de gelegenheid van de leerjaarbeëindiging der Haagsche Academie en M.T.S. te Den Haag*, May 1953. RSA, version later revised by Rietveld.

Flat Roofs and Open Corners

Skidmore, Owings and Merrill (SOM), Lever House, New York, 1951-1952
Closed, green-tinted panels are used here under the windows
Details of the low-rise: The glass panels under the windows are faced in stone on the inside and even a stone-clad façade has open-corner detailing

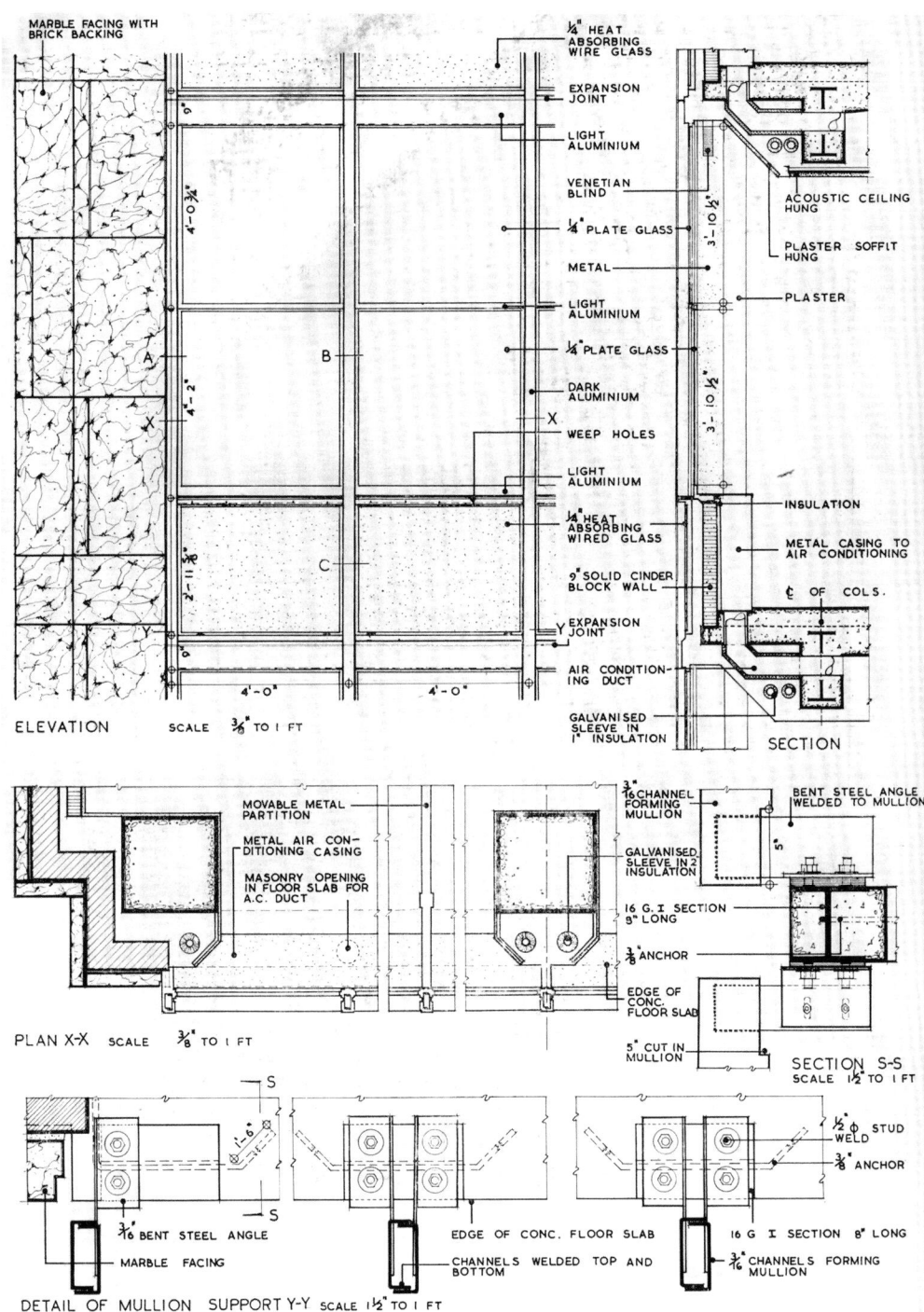

Flat Roofs and Open Corners

L. Mies van der Rohe, 860-880 Lake Shore Drive Apartments, Chicago, 1948-1951
Horizontal section. The steel column is clad in concrete and then wrapped with a steel plate on the outside. The two I-beams on the outside of this column, which are a defining feature, only have an aesthetic function

L. Mies van der Rohe, Federal Center, Chicago, 1959-1964
The open-corner detail

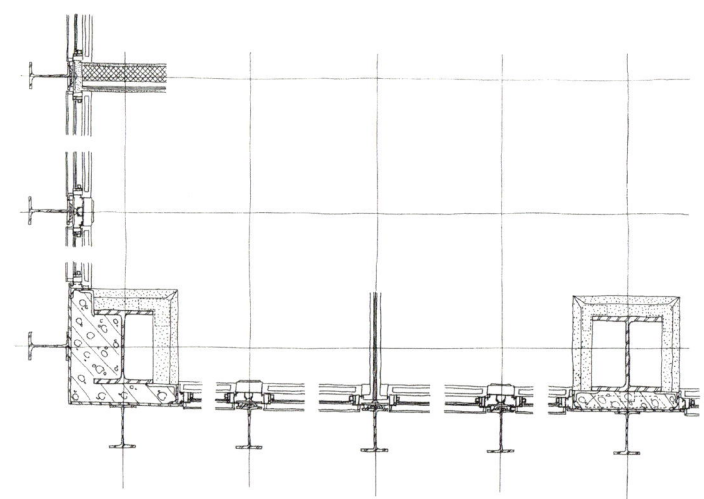

136   Articulating Space: Materials, Techniques and Mass Production

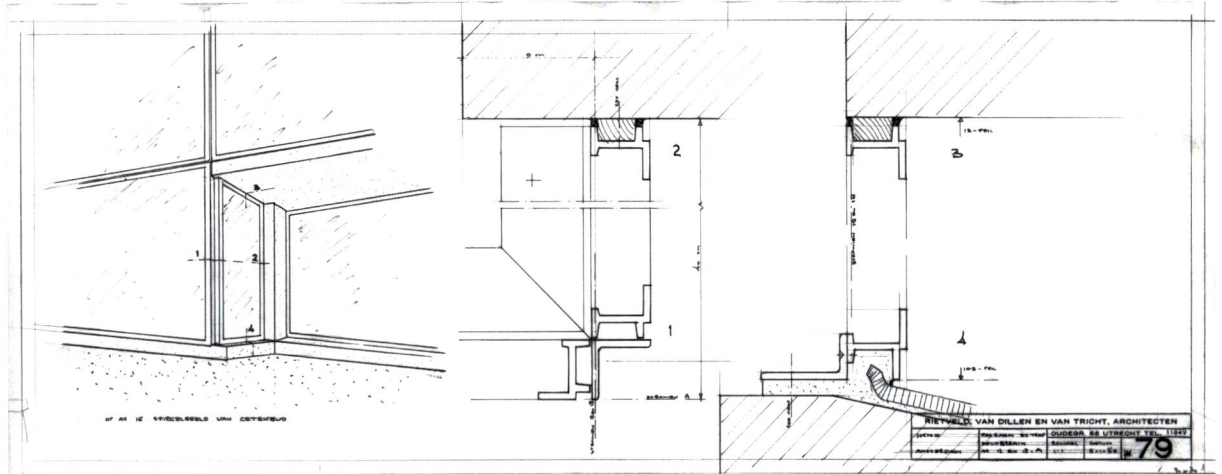

both the Lake Shore Drive Apartments and the later Federal Center (1959-1964) in Chicago the columns of the support structure were positioned in the corners of the buildings. They were also clad in extra steel casing to suggest simplicity in the use of materials. But in reality they hid a complex, composite construction.[10]

Rietveld took a completely different approach to the detailing of the façades of, say, the Academy in Amsterdam. He actually tried to use as little material as possible for the vertical (wall and roof) and horizontal (wall and wall) axes of the corners. The columns were taken out of the corners and the glass sections fitted squarely together. The detailing of the corners had nothing to conceal. In that respect, Rietveld was much closer to Mies van der Rohe's ideal 'less is more' than Mies himself. ◆

G.Th. Rietveld with J. van Dillen and J. van Tricht, Fine Arts Academy, Gerrit Rietveld Academy
The open-corner detail (horizontal section), in which Rietveld only uses the steel chair profiles and a diagonal (drawing 79, 1 January 1965)
NAI, Rotterdam

[10] Blaser 1986, 122-133; Molema 2005, 20-23.

Jurjen Creman & Otakar Máčel

The Hopmi Chair and Rietveld's Other Pre-War Tubular Furniture

M. Breuer, Interior of the Piscator House, Berlin with Model no. B6, 1926-1927
Steel tubing, plywood and paint
RSA, Utrecht

M. Stam, Model no. S33, 1926
Steel tubing, fabric and paint

Until the 1920s, it was more or less a given that furniture was made of wood. Metal furniture was only used to furnish hospitals, schools, offices, factories and other utilitarian buildings. Its functional character, its associations of hygiene and above all its aesthetic potential appealed two avant-garde architects. And as an industrial product a chromed tubular-steel piece of furniture also complemented the image of modernity – the German word for the steel tube, *Prezisionsrohr*, evokes the then much-admired machine aesthetic.

The modern architects were looking for furniture that matched their architecture. For want of such furniture and stimulated by the poor economic climate, which had an adverse effect on the building sector, they began to design their own.[1] And even though most of them had little or no experience of metal, this lack of knowledge may have actually stimulated their urge to experiment. Bauhaus teacher Marcel Breuer, head of the wood workshop at the Bauhaus where he had also received his training, turned to the apprentice workshop at the Junkers factory for help with the design of steel furniture, because the metal workshop, led by László Moholy-Nagy, did not work on furniture.[2] Ludwig Mies van der Rohe, the Rasch brothers, Mart Stam – the first Dutchman to design a tubular-steel chair – and others who had started designing tubular chairs around 1925 were all unfamiliar with the material. The designer-manufacturer Willem H. Gispen on the other hand, the first to manufacture tubular furniture in the Netherlands and familiar with the practical issues surrounding steel furniture, exercised a lot more restraint and waited until 1930 before he started producing the so-called 'diagonal chairs' that he had first exhibited three years earlier.[3]

The success of the first modern tube chairs, designed by Breuer in 1925-1926, triggered a wave of tubular-steel furniture in the Netherlands

[1] C. Wilk, 'Sitting on Air', in: Wilk 2006, 225-249: 227.

[2] O. Máčel, 'Marcel Breuer – "inventor of bent tubular steel furniture"', in: Von Vegesack and Remmele 2003, 52-115: 67-69.

[3] Gispen brought the prototypes of the 'diagonal chair' that he exhibited in November 1927 into production in 1930. See Koch 2005, 148.

G.Th. Rietveld, Armchair for
A.M. Hartog, 1927
Steel tubing, iron, wood, paint
CMU, Utrecht

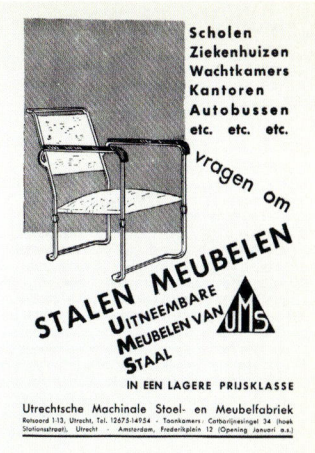

UMS advertisement for steel furniture, 1932

G.Th. Rietveld and T. Schröder-Schräder, Interior of show home on Erasmuslaan, 1931
RSA, Utrecht

and Germany.[4] The industrial-looking tubular furniture, which promised the large-scale production of standardized furniture, fostered the belief in a better world through cheaper, more efficient production.[5] The designs of this tubular furniture still conformed to the traditional dichotomy of a structural frame and body-supporting elements. The wood of the frame was replaced with steel tubing, while the back and the seat were made of fabric, leather or wood.

As a furniture maker Rietveld too had worked almost exclusively in wood until the mid-1920s. His first metal chair is probably the gas-pipe armchair for general practitioner A.M. Hartog in Maarssen, which was created before 1927.[6] It is a chair conceived with wood in mind, with four legs, a leather seat and leather straps for the back. Rietveld used T-shaped connectors, presumably because he was not able to bend the tube. In this respect the armchair boasts a traditional method of construction: the T-shaped connectors replace the classic wooden ones. It is not known whether Rietveld was familiar with the gas-pipe chair that Stam created in Rotterdam in the autumn of 1926. Rietveld probably did not opt for welded connections because he wanted to make the chair himself. As a result he was unable to capitalize on the special properties of metal.

Rietveld's First Tubular Furniture

In 1927 Rietveld appeared to be embracing a new design challenge with the tube-framed chair.[7] By capitalizing on the flexibility of metal he was able to realize a design with one continuous line.[8] The chair consists of two continuous frames that support the seat/back on either side. The first version with solid iron bars features welded components and an unbroken tubular line. Another version with thick-walled tubing and a seat/back of fibreboard has overlapping ends and an open tubular line. From November

[4] Wilk, op cit. (note 1), 228.

[5] Ibid., 230.

[6] M. Kuper: 'Gerrit Rietveld', in: Blotkamp 1996, 195-240: 203-204.

[7] Küper and Van Zijl 1992, 117-118; Vöge 1993, 74-75.

[8] For more on the line principle see Van Geest and Mácel 1986.

G.Th. Rietveld, Tube-framed chair, 1927
Wood, iron, fibreboard
RSA, Utrecht

Upright chair, c. 1928-1930
Steel tube, plywood and paint,
81 x 40.2 x 50 cm
CMU, Utrecht

G.Th. Rietveld, Armchair 'First Model', 1927
Birch and plywood, 83 x 69 x 94 cm
Stedelijk Museum Amsterdam

[9] The results of the research into the material and technological composition, carried out in 2006, suggest that this chair is probably a post-war construction.

[10] Vöge 1993, 103, fig. 176. Vöge dates the chair to around 1935 because Rietveld made a sketch of the crate chair on the same piece of paper.

[11] Küper and Van Schijndel 1987, 4-11: 7.

[12] The chair came from the Lanjouw family, for whom Rietveld had designed a few pieces of furniture for their house in Utrecht. This was followed in 1940 by a commission for a holiday home (Küper and Van Zijl 1992, 201) and in 1956 for the conversion of the garage at their home in Bilthoven (Küper and Van Zijl 1992, 275). The family gave the second chair to an acquaintance and it has been in Switzerland ever since. In 2009 the consignment for approval became a donation.

1927 onwards, the chair was made of a single slim steel tube whose ends were welded together, so that the supporting element forms a fully closed circuit. The fibreboard of the seat/back was replaced with plywood. It is not known whether Rietveld designed the tube-framed chair before the Weissenhof Exhibition in Stuttgart in June 1927. It was the first exhibition to show steel tube chairs made of one continuous tubular line.

It would seem that Rietveld did not just derive inspiration from the new material. The supporting metal sides of the tube-framed chair form legs as it were, whereas a sledge base would have been a more obvious choice for a tubular steel chair. Besides, the tube-framed chair can also be made of wood. Rietveld made a plywood chair which also has two supporting leg-like sides around a seat/back in one piece. The wood version of this 'First Model' suggests that the design of the tube-framed chair is a variation on Rietveld's experimental one-piece chairs.[9] These designs seek to produce a chair from a single piece of material and include the fibre-board Birza Chair of 1927, the Zigzag Chair, an early version of which was made of fibreboard in 1932, and the later aluminium armchair.

A number of later tube chairs have a continuous tubular line between the front legs, which forms the batten on which the seat rests. Breuer's chair B6, which was manufactured at Standard-Möbel in 1927, boasts a similar design. The principle harks back to the traditional construction of many wooden chairs. Rietveld used it for the upright chair (1928-1930), for an armchair presented by Metz & Co at an exhibition in Paris in 1930, as well as for a chair designed for the *Nieuw Amsterdam* ocean liner (1937) and for a chair and armchair with fibreboard seat and back which, until recently, was only known from a drawing published by Peter Vöge.[10] The Metz & Co armchair and the design for the armchair with fibreboard seat and back both have a continuous tubular frame. This is quite rare for tubular furniture at the time. And these two chairs are all the more exceptional because the seat is supported at the back by a piece of tubing that runs from armrest to armrest. This principle can be traced back to Rietveld's Red-Blue Chair, except that it is made of metal. If we imagine the Red-Blue Chair without some of its cross connections and draw its main features as a fluid line we end up with a similar frame. Another Rietveld lounge chair, designed around 1928, is actually a literal translation of the Red-Blue Chair in steel tubing, but without a continuous tubular line.

A tubular-steel version of the Zigzag Chair dates from 1932-1933. Its design is based on a single line. The chair looks exceptional, with diagonally crossing tubes and sharp curves. The peculiar construction caused problems because the welded intersection of the legs and the sharp curves at the front of the seat could not always support the load. This is probably the reason why Metz & Co had the chair in production for only a short period of time.[11]

The Hopmi Chair

In 2008 the Centraal Museum Utrecht received a remarkable consignment on approval: a plastic bag containing the components of a tubular-steel chair.[12] According to the owners, the children of Mr and Mrs Lanjouw, the chair had been designed by Rietveld and formed part of a set of two chairs. Once assembled, the chair turned out to be a version of the armchair

G.Th. Rietveld, Design drawing of a chair for luxury cabin on the *Nieuw Amsterdam*, Holland America Line, 1937
NAI Rotterdam

The Hopmi Chair and Rietveld's Other Pre-War Tubular Furniture

G.Th. Rietveld, Armchair, c. 1928-1930
Steel tubing, birch, plywood,
83 x 59 x 87 cm
CMU, Utrecht

G.Th. Rietveld, Armchair, 1925
Deal, five-ply wood, 94 x 61.1 x 62.8 cm
CMU, Utrecht

G.Th. Rietveld, Mees House, The Hague
with Zigzag Chair with steel tubing,
c. 1932
Steel tubing and cord
RSA, Utrecht

The Hopmi Chair and Rietveld's Other Pre-War Tubular Furniture   **147**

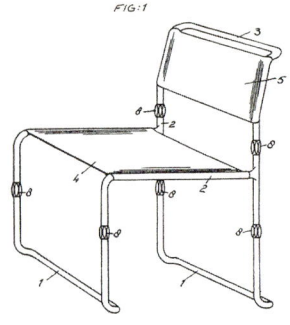
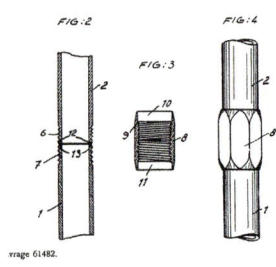

Drawing from the patent application
for the torpedo bolt used for the
Hopmi Chair, 1932
Nederlands Octrooibureau, The Hague

G.Th. Rietveld, Hopmi Chair,
c. 1932-1934
Steel tubing, plywood, 90 x 47 x 50 cm
CMU, Utrecht

148   Articulating Space: Materials, Techniques and Mass Production

with fibreboard seat and back. The Rietveld Schröder Archive was found to have a drawing with sketches of various pieces of furniture intended for the Lanjouw family. Some of these items can be seen on photographs from the 1930s of the interior of their home on Homeruslaan in Utrecht.

The model in question is a tubular chair with armrests, sledge legs and a seat and back of moulded plywood. Labels underneath the chair reveal that the chair was made by N.V. Hollandse Patent Metaalindustrie (Hopmi), a factory in Utrecht that specialized in locks and bicycle parts. This factory had a patent on a type of screwed joint, the so-called 'torpedo bolt' with which the tubes of the chair could be easily connected. Together with the Utrechtse Machinale Stoel- en Meubelfabriek (UMS, later Pastoe) Hopmi produced chairs, desks and school furniture made of tubular steel and plywood. In the early 1930s the two companies tried to capitalize on the popularity of tubular-steel furniture. The woodwork and upholstery were done by UMS, while Hopmi was responsible for the metal. The tube furniture by Hopmi and UMS was first shown at the autumn exhibition in Utrecht in 1932.[13] Most of the pieces had been designed by architect H.F. Mertens (1885-1960). The company also published a catalogue with the tubular-steel furniture.[14] It features a lot of chairs, tables and a desk, but also system furniture, such as school furniture, bus seats and cinema seats designed by Rietveld. These tip-up seats, made of aluminium-coated steel tubing with a blue-painted wooden back and seat, were designed for the first renovation of the Vreeburg Cinema in 1932.[15]

The Hopmi furniture is not noted for its design. What makes the chairs special is the frame that can be taken to pieces: the tubular parts are connected to one another with screw bolts.[16] Hopmi considered this invention significant enough to apply for a patent in 1932. In the patent application the company alludes to the improvement of the production process, because the furniture is made of smaller, more uniform components that are easier to handle. The application also mentions the advantages of more economic storage and transport of the completed items.[17] Two years later the patent was granted. Given that the label underneath the legs of Rietveld's Hopmi Chair says that the patent application is pending, the design can probably be dated to between 1932 and 1934.

The frame of the Hopmi Chair with armrests consists of four U-shaped tubular components and two J-shaped pieces of steel tubing that are connected with screw thread and torpedo bolts. Two U-shaped tubes form sledge legs, which are recognizable as such because at the bottom the steel is forced inward, so that only the tips of the sledge leg touch the floor. The other U-shaped tubular components each sport two holes for attaching the seat with screws. The two J-shaped tubular components each have two welded flanges with screw holes to attach the back.

Rietveld's Contribution: Module and Simplicity

Using the patented screwed joint, Rietveld managed to produce an extremely compact and efficient piece of furniture. He reduced the chair's frame to six elements for which he needed only two different forms. The result is a logical and well thought-out frame. Other Hopmi designs with torpedo bolts are often more complex, with a frame made of lots of different parts. The fact that this furniture can be taken apart appears to

G.Th. Rietveld, Disassembled Hopmi Chair

[13] Vreeburg and Martens 1983, 28.

[14] *Hopmi Stalen Meubelen: De meubelen met de torpedo-moer: de eenigst goede buisverbinding*, catalogue n.d., n.p. A photograph of the chairs for the Vreeburg Cinema can be found on page 11 and is captioned 'arch. Rietveld'. With thanks to Ad van den Bruinhorst for his help in finding the catalogue.

[15] Anonymous, 'Bioscoop Vreeburg. Een ingrijpende verbouwing om in- en uitwendig aspect te verbeteren. Plannen van den architect G. Rietveld', *Utrechtsch Provinciaal & Stedelijk Dagblad*, 26 August 1932. We would like to thank Vera de Lange for bringing this to our attention.

[16] Vreeburg and Martens 1983, 28.

[17] NL Patent Office, no. 33644, citing 'Metal piece of furniture or similar item'.

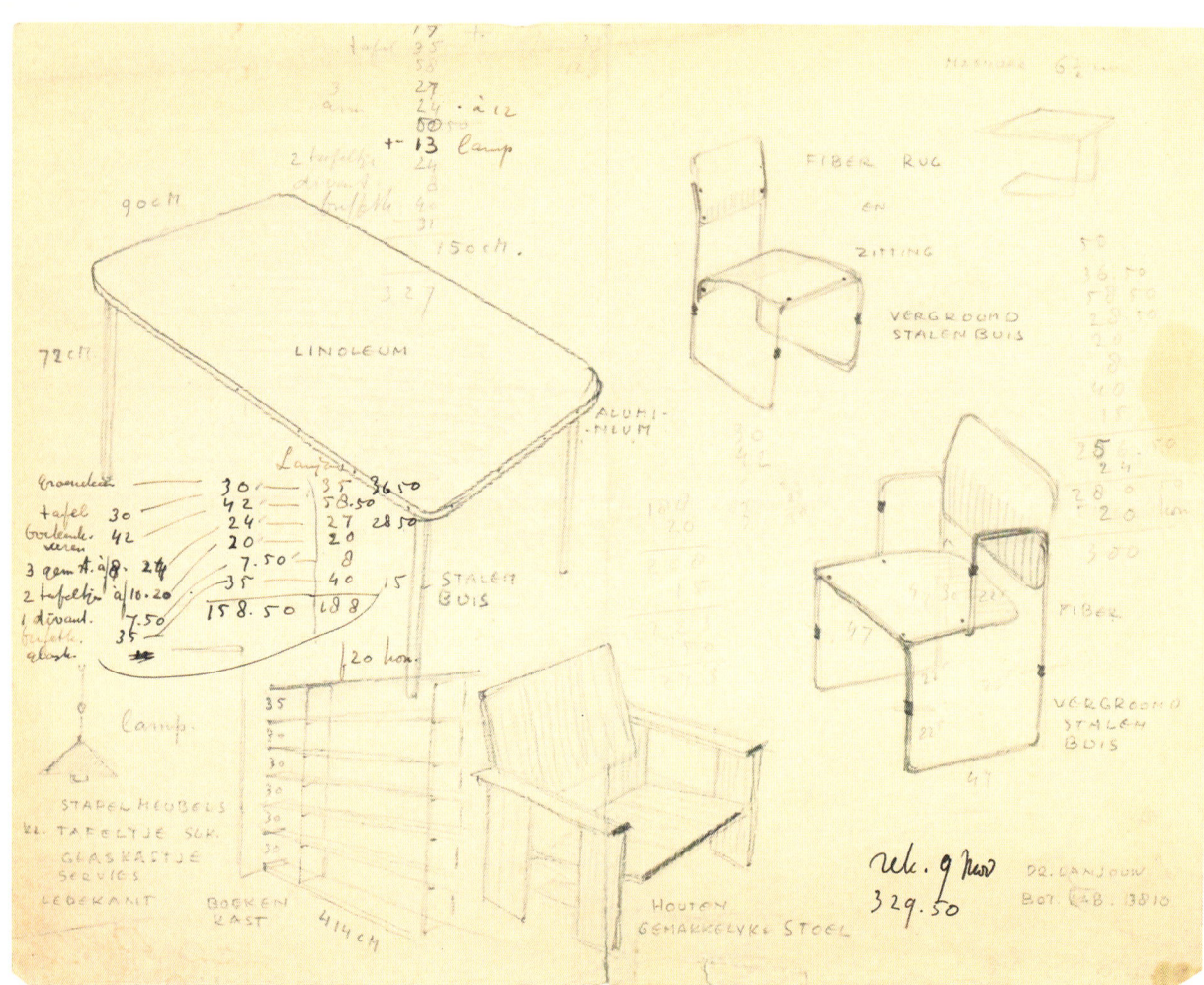

G.Th. Rietveld, Drawing Hopmi Chair
and Crate Chair
RSA, Utrecht

have little added benefit. Rietveld also brought the seat and back down to two identical squares with rounded corners. Only the sharpness of the angles varies. Thanks to clever proportioning, the separate parts fit seamlessly and the chair can be packed up very compactly.[18]

For the Hopmi Chair Rietveld recycled a technique that he had used ten years earlier and that was ahead of its time. The sharply angled back and slightly angled seat of the Hopmi Chair are virtually identical to those of the armchair of 1925. Some other pieces of furniture that Rietveld designed between 1925 and 1930 feature angled and bent plywood seats and backs, including the tube-framed chair, the stick chair and variations on military chairs. By laminating several layers of plywood (by bonding them in different directions) he could fix the new plywood sheet in a curved or angled form. As soon as the glue is dry, the bonded product remains in the desired shape. It looks as if Rietveld was one of the first to apply this method of plywood lamination. The German designers Heinz and Bodo Rasch were the only others to use this production method. Between 1922 and 1928 they developed various new pieces of furniture in their workshop that drew heavily on the lamination of plywood and they published their findings in the booklet *Der Stuhl* in 1928.[19]

During the research into the Hopmi Chair with armrests a version without armrests surfaced.[20] Its plywood seat had broken in two and it looked as if the back was not the original. The back of this particular version is made of 6 mm fibreboard, which corresponds with the drawing. The backrest has been fitted with an additional tube. This is probably not an original feature. The frame of this chair, also fitted with the patented Hopmi screw bolts, is even simpler than that of the model with armrests: instead of six, it consists of four components, three of which sport the same U-shape.

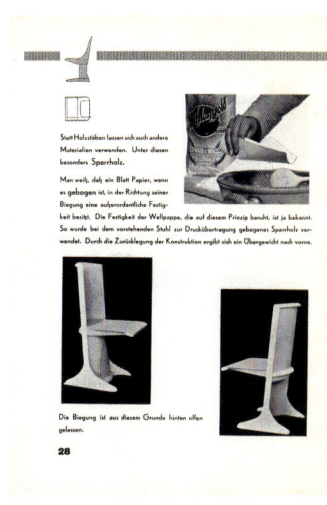

H. and B. Rasch, *Der Stuhl*, Stuttgart 1928, 28

[18] J. Creman, Restauration Report Hopmi Chair (Centraal Museum Utrecht 2010).

[19] Rasch 1928. Truus Schröder owned a copy of the book.

[20] This chair is part of the B. Mulder collection in Utrecht.

Prototype
All parts of the version without armrests are chromed, as indicated on the drawing. Interestingly, only the J-shaped parts of the Hopmi Chair with armrests are chromed, whereas the U-shaped tubes are coated in aluminium-coloured spray-paint. This chrome is in such a bad state that it is probably the original chroming. The original Hopmi transfers underneath the sledge legs suggest that the aluminium-coloured coating is also original. Hopmi's furniture catalogue mentions both chrome and paint as potential finishings. It is so unusual for a single piece of furniture to have two different finishing layers that it is probably not a production error, but more likely a prototype. The plywood of the back and seat also differs from the fibreboard mentioned on the drawing for the Lanjouw family. Whether it was possible to attach wooden armrests to the bare steel armrests, the way Rietveld did with the chromed tube armchair for Metz & Co, is unclear. Both options feature in the Hopmi catalogue, and it tends to be the utilitarian furniture that lacks this luxury.

The Significance of Rietveld's Metal Furniture and the Hopmi Chair
Rietveld experimented with different materials in order to realize his ideas about form and mass production. This is true for both the influential tube-framed chair and for the Zigzag Chair. Rietveld often led the way with

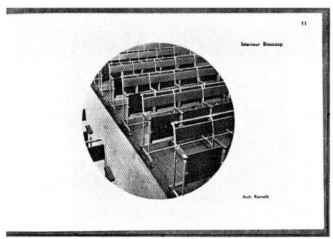

Hopmi catalogue, 1934, 11
Collection A. Holtmaat

these experiments; he created his first tubular chair in 1927 during the early days of this new furniture trend. The tube-framed chair won praise in 1928 for its simplicity and for being the first chair with a one-piece seat and back. It looks as if the metal parts of these pieces of furniture were not directly inspired by the specific material properties. But when Rietveld makes a one-piece seat and back the property of the material is actually one of the key aspects. In these instances he probably experimented with the possibilities offered by the material knowing that he wanted to create a single-piece chair.

The Hopmi Chair is another testament to Rietveld's urge to experiment. He made a design based on a new technique, which facilitated transport and rapid assembly. The way in which Rietveld capitalized on the fact that the Hopmi Chairs could be easily disassembled may well be his most significant contribution. But despite this innovative feature the chair was probably not taken into production, because it is absent from the company catalogue. Shortly afterwards Rietveld introduced this new trend – self-assembly furniture – to his crate furniture, which Metz & Co sold as do-it-yourself kits. In both cases he aspired to beautiful, restrained and affordable furniture for the masses. ◆

Interior of the Lanjouw family home
with Hopmi Chair
Courtesy Lanjouw estate

//Marie-Thérèse van Thoor

Factors of the Visible. Rietveld's Ideas about the Renewal of Architecture

Shop-windows, fairs, stand construction, exhibition layouts and pavilions are important components of Gerrit Rietveld's oeuvre. He called this 'freer architecture', designed with greater spontaneity.[1] Though these designs are highly diverse in nature and quality, some of them, including display windows and pavilions for visual art, are successful examples of the spatiality Rietveld was striving for.

From the 1920s Rietveld wrote and lectured about architecture, and continued to do so for the rest of his life.[2] The concept of space was the central theme in his work. He defined architecture as the delimitation of space. In its purest form architecture would, in his view, be almost invisible and have as little outward form as possible. In ideal buildings, interior and exterior would flow imperceptibly into one another and the architecture would consist of nothing but floors, walls and coverings that delimit the space and render it visible. In his own designs Rietveld often used sliding walls, canopies, partitions and glass. The 'free' designs for exhibition pavilions offered him perhaps the best opportunity to realize his ideas about pure, essential architecture. In the Sonsbeek Pavilion (1955), Rietveld used elementary architectonic means to realize a minimally delimited space, which functioned simultaneously as a backdrop for sculptures and as part of the surrounding unlimited landscape. The Dutch Biennale Pavilion in Venice (1954), though necessarily more enclosed because of the climate, is also an open space stripped down to the essentials.

In the 1950s Rietveld produced various designs for exhibitions, events and interiors that provide us with plenty of information about his outlook on architecture and space. For example, he ventured onto the international stage of the Brussels World's Fair in 1958, where he even had to measure up to no less a figure than Le Corbusier. About a decade earlier he had produced an intriguing design for an exhibition with the title 'Factoren van het Zichtbare' (Factors of the Visible).

The Philips Pavilion in Brussels, 1958

At Expo 58 in Brussels, the Netherlands used a contemporary presentation to distance itself explicitly from its traditional image as the land of clogs, tulips, windmills and cocoa. Together with Joop van den Broek (1898-1978), Jaap Bakema (1914-1981) and Joost Boks (1904-1986), Rietveld was responsible for the Dutch Pavilion, a complex of buildings and a tract of polder landscape where the theme of 'water as enemy and as ally of the Dutch nation' was represented.[3] Like Shell and Unilever, Philips would have preferred to construct its own pavilion in the section for international organizations. However, the enterprise ended up renting a section of the Dutch terrain through the agency of the Dutch entry's secretary-general, H.F. van Walsem, a former Philips director. Van Walsem realized that the Philips Pavilion could have a positive effect on the Dutch presentation, a shift 'away from the cocoa and the cigars'.[4] By that point, in late 1955, the engineer L.C. Kalff, General Art Director of Philips, had probably already informed him that the company was not intending to exhibit any products in its pavilion but was planning to stage a spectacle of light, colour, sound and rhythm using its in-house expertise and resources.[5] For the implementation of his plans Kalff had immediately set his sights on Le Corbusier (1887-1965), at that point still to be teamed up with the composer Benjamin

[1] Bakema et al. 1958, 6.

[2] For example Rietveld 1932 (for the English translation see Küper and Van Zijl 1992, 33-39); 'Het bouwen van Jaarbeursstands is nog in een primitief stadium', typescript 1956, RSA, GR 127; 'Wat is de zin van tentoonstellen?', typescript 1958, RSA, GR 86; 'Voordracht gehouden door architect G. Rietveld op 20 februari 1959 te Delft', NAI, Rietveld archive. See also Küper and Van Zijl 1992, 380-381.

[3] Van Thoor 1998; Everts 1960.

[4] Nationaal archief, Tweede Afdeling, archive Stichting Wereldtentoonstelling Brussel 1958, Afdeling Nederland (hereafter NA-II, Brussel 1958), inv. no. 2: minutes 2 November 1955.

[5] M. Treib describes, with reference to a conversation with B. Lootsma, how Philips had heard rumours that IBM would be able to present a colour television in Brussels. According to Treib, Philips opted for a different concept because the company could not compete in that sphere. Treib 1996, 11; Van Dam 2006, 77.

G.Th. Rietveld, Sonsbeek Pavilion, Arnhem, 1955
RSA, Utrecht

G.Th. Rietveld, Dutch Pavilion for the Venice Biennale, Venice, 1954
RSA, Utrecht

G.Th. Rietveld, Model of the concept interior of an 'ideal flat' for Expo 58, 1956
RSA, Utrecht

G.Th. Rietveld, J. Rietveld and W. Rietveld, Concept interior of an 'ideal flat', Brussels, 1958

Britten, who was replaced by Edgard Varèse later on, and the sculptor Ossip Zadkine.[6] The Dutch architects and advisers, following the lead of J.J.P. Oud [7], were nevertheless of the opinion that the pavilion had to be built by a Dutchman and that the involvement of an architect of Le Corbusier's stature would be sure to eclipse the Dutch contributors.

The lack of specific sources makes it impossible to reconstruct precisely how they intended to elaborate the brief.[8] It seems that, owing to Van Walsem's intercession, they provisionally opted for a diplomatic middle course. Le Corbusier was to design the interior, the so-called electronic art work, while one of the Dutch architects would concentrate on the exterior, which Le Corbusier was still indifferent about at that point. In February 1956, at his first meeting with Kalff, Le Corbusier had been especially captivated by the idea of a multimedia project, for which he was keen to write the scenario. In *Le poème électronique. Le Corbusier*, a booklet about the presentation compiled by Jean Petit, Le Corbusier stated that Kalff had asked him to design the Philips Pavilion: 'You will be free to make whatever façade you wish,' said Kalff, to which Le Corbusier responded, 'I will not make any Philips façade, I will make you an electric poem. It will all happen on the inside: sound, light, colour, rhythm. Perhaps a scaffolding might be the only outside.'[9]

Designs by Rietveld
The Philips Pavilion had still been part of the Netherlands' entry in the initial designs produced independently by Boks, Van den Broek & Bakema and Rietveld in January and February 1956.[10] Rietveld integrated Philips into his first draft, a coloured-in aerial perspective, in the form of a tall tower. As usual, he annotated the drawing with explanations and comments: designations such as 'water', 'trees', 'flowers' or 'industry' and 'sculptural work', as well as suggestions for materials, such as 'B2 blocks with cavities, also big gaps in such a big wall' next to the hall for trade and commerce, and clarifications about the site's topography, such as 'terrain slopes down towards the right by 10 m[etres] (at least), so I made buildings to the right taller', which he jotted at the top of the drawing. For the second round Rietveld modified his design and switched the position of a few components.

On 1 March 1956, the committee, advisers and architects decided that the proposal by Boks would serve as the basis for the plan's elaboration, which would be completed by the whole team, 'architectengroep brussel '58 boks, van den broek – bakema, peutz en rietveld'.[11] The architects did, however, divide oversight of the various sections among themselves. Rietveld was placed in charge of the pavilions for light and heavy industry, for which he not only devised the layout but also designed a model interior for an 'ideal flat' and three types of chairs.[12] The Philips Pavilion was eventually realized to the rear of the halls that Rietveld was overseeing. Rietveld had not been appointed as the designer of this pavilion's exterior yet, but was probably approached shortly thereafter.[13] M. Treib quotes from notes by Kalff, which reveal that in late February he had already spoken with Le Corbusier about the possibility of collaborating with a Dutch architect (Rietveld).[14] Rietveld's name must have been circulating for a while already.[15]

---

[6] Treib 1996, 2-3.

[7] The other adviser was B. Merkelbach.

[8] The written sources are not specific enough or contain only indirect references. NA-II, Brussel 1958: inv. no. 1, minutes 1 March 1956 (here there is a direct reference to telephone conversations). Treib 1996, 2-3; Van Thoor 1998, 174.

[9] Le Corbusier, 'Our Work', in: Petit 1958.

[10] Van Thoor 1998. NA-II, Brussel 1958, inv. no. 64; NAI, Rietveld Archive, inv. no. 667.

[11] Frits Peutz was part of the original team of architects, but withdrew later on. See Van Thoor 1998, 180.

[12] NA-II, Brussel 1958, inv. no. 1: minutes 1 March 1956. For the layout Rietveld was assisted by his sons, Jan and Wim, and by J. Bons. See also Wever and Koch 2008.

[13] Rietveld was mentioned as the building's designer in reports and correspondence in March. NA-II, Brussel 1958, inv. no. 1: minutes 26 March 1956; inv. no. 2: (reference to a) letter from Philips, 23 March 1956.

[14] Treib 1996, 2-3, where he refers to internal Philips memoranda.

[15] According to P. Wever, a letter from Kalff dated 23 March 1956 can be seen as the specific request to Rietveld to design the pavilion's exterior. P. Wever, 'Le Corbusier versus de Nederlandse architecten, "de gedeukte fluitketel van Philips" slaat een deuk in het Nederlands prestige', in: Koch 2008, 115.

G.Th. Rietveld, First design for the Dutch Pavilion at the World Exhibition in Brussels, 1956
Pencil on paper, 22 x 27 cm
NAI, Rotterdam

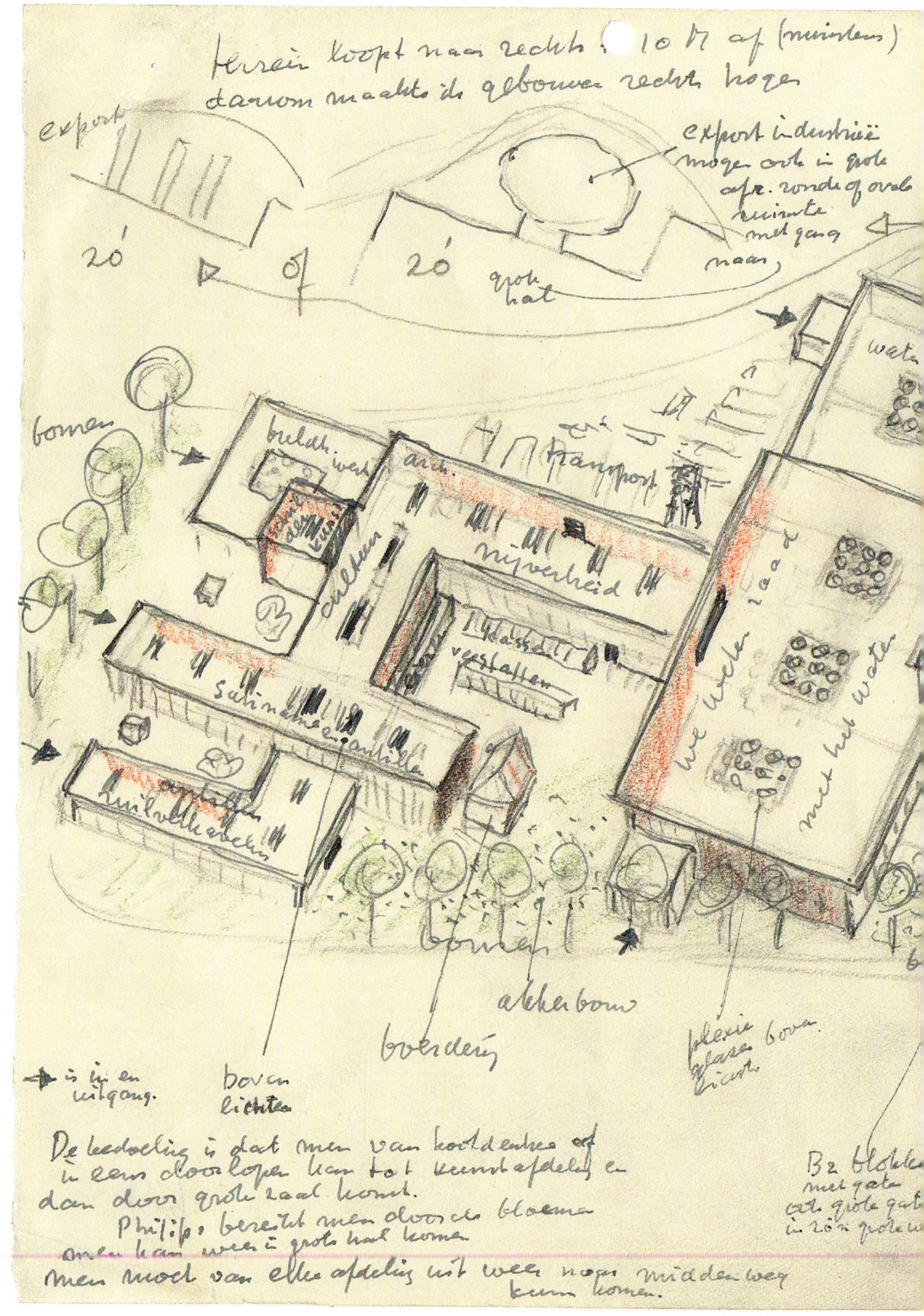

G.Th. Rietveld, Preliminary design for the
Philips Pavilion, 1956
Pencil on tracing paper, 16 x 23 cm
NAI, Rotterdam

J. Bons, Mural design for the exhibition
'Así es Holanda', Mexico City, 1952

The committee for the Dutch entry had initially wanted to award the commission for the entire Dutch complex to Rietveld, because they knew they could depend on him to produce an original and sound design. There was, however, some doubt as to whether his modest architecture practice could handle such a commission.[16] Rietveld was the most senior of the Dutch architects and, as noted, he had the requisite experience with the design of trade fairs and exhibitions. Perhaps the committee deemed him to be the person best able to collaborate with an architect like Le Corbusier.

There are two design sketches and a small model by Rietveld for the Philips Pavilion.[17] The sketches are neither signed nor dated, but were probably produced in March or April 1956. The first bears the text 'Philips pav. Brussel '58' and gives the scale as '1:200'. Rietveld drew the pavilion from above and gives an indication of the planned interior in yellow coloured pencil amid the thicker black lines of the structure. It does not have the form of a stomach – the concept Le Corbusier talked about later on – but is composed of three polygonal sections that are arranged like windmill sails around a core. The building has two entrances and an exit at a higher level. Lines are drawn all around the three sections and, going by a small sketch to the side, these are steps, for '600 to 700 people – standing room' to be able to experience the show. This was how Rietveld translated Kalff's basic principles for the pavilion. Kalff wanted to present the technological spectacle in brief performances of approximately eight minutes in a building able to cope with 20,000 visitors a day, through which groups of 600 to 700 visitors could stream in and out. The space was to be covered by a prism-like structure of three pentagonal figures with a hexagonal figure superimposed in the middle. The highest point of this hexagonal pyramid is set above the pavilion's core. This hexagon was probably Rietveld's interpretation of Kalff's concept of a cupola, in which elements of the show would be presented kaleidoscopically. The model shows how Rietveld envisaged this design in three dimensions.

The second sketch, 'Philips pavilion Brussel '58', gives some idea of the pavilion's appearance, looking towards one of the two entrances.[18] This perspective drawing indicates that the building is suspended from a load-bearing structure with its three apexes located above the three pentagons. The pavilion therefore most closely resembles a tent, as was also the case with the sketch models by Iannis Xenakis, who was assisting Le Corbusier, for the pavilion that was eventually realized.[19] The surfaces are shaded in different colours and provided with textual and graphic annotations. To the left stands the caption 'Philips light' with a drawing of a large eye and by the entrance on the right-hand side it states 'Philips colour' and depicts a triangular prism refracting sunlight into the primary colours. Alongside this it states 'Philips' with a light bulb and an arrow pointing towards the right-hand facet, which has the text 'Philips Sound' and a depiction of an ear. The motifs display a striking resemblance to a mural that Rietveld commissioned from Jan Bons for the 'Así es Holanda' (This is Holland) presentation in Mexico City in 1952.[20] There, too, the scenes on the wall referred to Philips, one of the companies represented. Rietveld had produced various designs for this exhibition, such as sketches for the layout, an information booth (entrance) and a tower of flags. His collaboration with Bons, which began in 1948 at the Royal Trade Fair in

[16] This was a topic of discussion in December 1955. Van Thoor 1998, 163.

[17] One drawing is located in the RSA, inv. no. 167 A 001. The other is in the NAI, Rietveld archive, inv. no. 668. See also Küper and Van Zijl 1992, 292; Van Thoor 1998, 173; Koch 2008, 112; Wever and Koch 2008, 52. The model, collection CM inv. no. 31245, was part of a recently inventoried donation to the Centraal Museum.

[18] The reverse side of the sketch in the NAI is marked 'E. Eskes Rie . . .', which suggests that it was in the possession of Elisabeth Eskes-Rietveld, one of Rietveld's children.

[19] See Treib 1996, 41.

[20] Wever, op. cit. (note 15), 114-116.

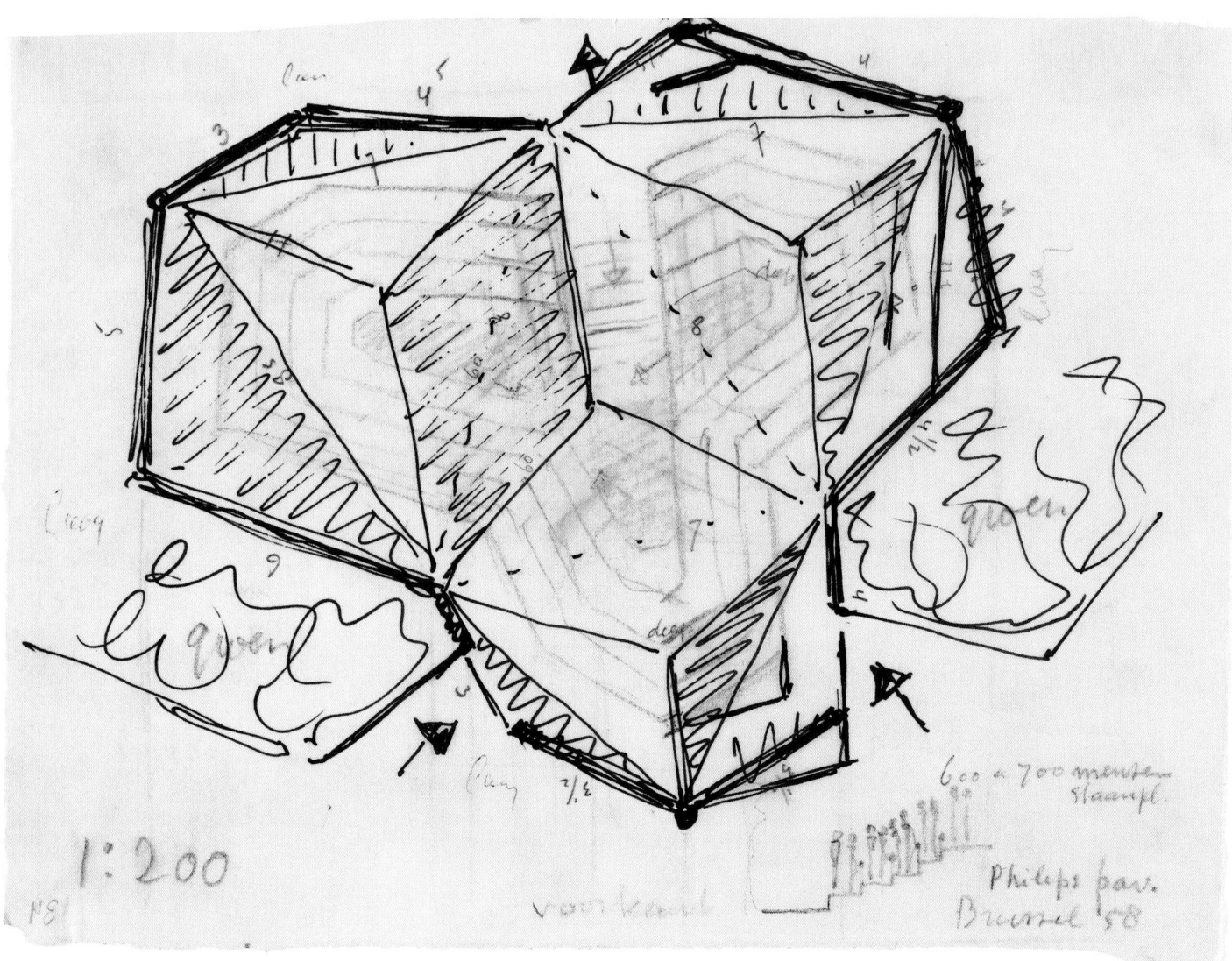

G.Th. Rietveld, Preliminary design for the
Philips Pavilion, 1956
Pencil on paper, 15.5 x 22 cm
RSA, Utrecht

G.Th. Rietveld, Model for the Philips
Pavilion, 1956
4 x 18.5 x 15.7 cm
CMU, Utrecht

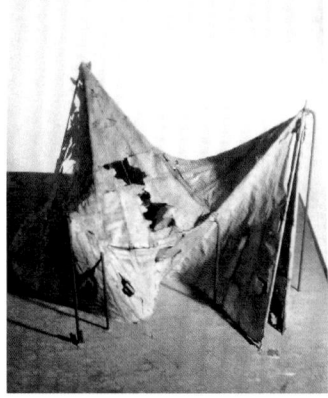

I. Xenakis, Model of Le Corbusier's second design for the Philips Pavilion, 1957
Philips, Eindhoven

Le Corbusier and I. Xenakis, Philips Pavilion (background), Brussels, 1958
Nationaal Archief, The Hague

166 Articulating Space: Materials, Techniques and Mass Production

Utrecht and was followed by projects including the Holland Fair in Philadelphia (1950), was continued in Brussels with the textiles section.[21]

Le Corbusier Continues Solo
In April 1956 Rietveld and Kalff visited Le Corbusier, who on that occasion made it known that he was after all keen to design the exterior of the Philips pavilion as well, for the sake of unity of interior and exterior.[22] Because the views in the Dutch camp were at variance with this there was a second meeting in June, though the outcome was the same.[23] In an interview, Rietveld related how Le Corbusier drew a little sketch during one of these meetings and said:

> Rietveld, I am making an interior which does not have an exterior. It is just like a stomach: that is how they enter and that is how they exit. It should seem as if you are about to enter an abattoir. You go inside: pow, a blow to the head and away.[24]

Later on Rietveld wrote that he had left a design and the small sketch model he had taken along 'in the box',[25] though in conversations about the pavilion he undoubtedly set forth his own ideas for the Philips presentation to Le Corbusier and Kalff.

Rietveld eventually stepped aside, deferring to Le Corbusier. In June he wrote to Kalff that Le Corbusier probably thought he knew everything, but that his ideas about the art of painting and music were actually rather commonplace.[26] Kalff's reaction reveals that he had not wanted to give Le Corbusier *carte blanche* but was in fact keen to keep the Rietveld options open.[27] Rietveld explained in an interview:

> I had the design in my bag . . . But he's a tough cookie, you know. He boxes everyone aside. A nice chap nevertheless, an incredible chap . . . I've also got some decency in me . . . I found it pretty unpleasant, but it has done me no harm. With a foreign colleague you have to be as agreeable as possible.[28]

Ideas about Presentation and Space
In the Rietveld Schröder Archives there are four small sketches by Rietveld with the heading 'Factoren van het Zichtbare' (Factors of the Visible) dating from 1948 to 1950.[29] They display striking similarities to Rietveld's designs for the Philips Pavilion. One of the four sketches was jotted on an envelope and depicts a leaf-like plan with the entrance and exit marked.[30] The other three present ideas for the layout of an exhibition, which begins with a portal in Renaissance style, proceeds via 'attempts to break free from the classics' and ends with displays devoted to the present day.

Interesting aspects of these sketches, especially in the most detailed one, are Rietveld's comments and suggestions for the selection of works to be exhibited.[31] Here he distinguishes between the 'elements of the audible: sound and movement', and the 'elements of the visible: space, colour and form'. According to a diagram to the top right of the sheet, the 'perceptible, the senses' is divided into 'hearing, sight and smell-taste', and via 'movement, space, colour and form' sight is subdivided into 'in, around,

G.Th. Rietveld, Design for 'Factoren van het Zichtbare', 1948-1950
Pencil on paper, 12 x 15 cm
RSA, Utrecht

[21] See P. Wever, 'De textielafdeling van Gerrit Rietveld en Jan Bons, van sprookjesachtige plastiek tot apenrots', in: Koch 2008, 87-109.

[22] NA-II, Brussel 1958, inv. no. 8: (with reference to) minutes 24 April 1956.

[23] NAI, Rietveld Archive, inv. no. 671, diverse correspondence; Treib 1996, 14; Van Thoor 1998, 174; Wever, op. cit. (note 15), 116.

[24] Bibeb 1958.

[25] Wever, op. cit. (note 15), 116.

[26] Treib 1996, 14.

[27] NAI, Rietveld archive, inv. no. 671, letter from Kalff to Rietveld, 15 June 1956. The Philips Pavilion is generally associated with Le Corbusier alone, but besides input from Varèse, Zadkine and Kalff (or Philips) the design for the structure was by I. Xenakis.

[28] Bibeb 1958.

[29] RSA, inv. no. 882 A 001-004. The stamp on the envelope bears the postmark 30 August 1948.

[30] The foliate or finger-like plan is similar to one of Rietveld's sketches for the village of Nagele from 1948. According to Rietveld's jottings on the sketch this was 'an attempt to create a village as one unit'. See Berg et al. 2004, 142.

[31] The drawing in question is 882 A 003.

G.Th. Rietveld, Design for 'Factoren van het Zichtbare' (Factors of the Visible), 1948-1950
Pencil on paper, 21 x 27.2 cm
RSA, Utrecht

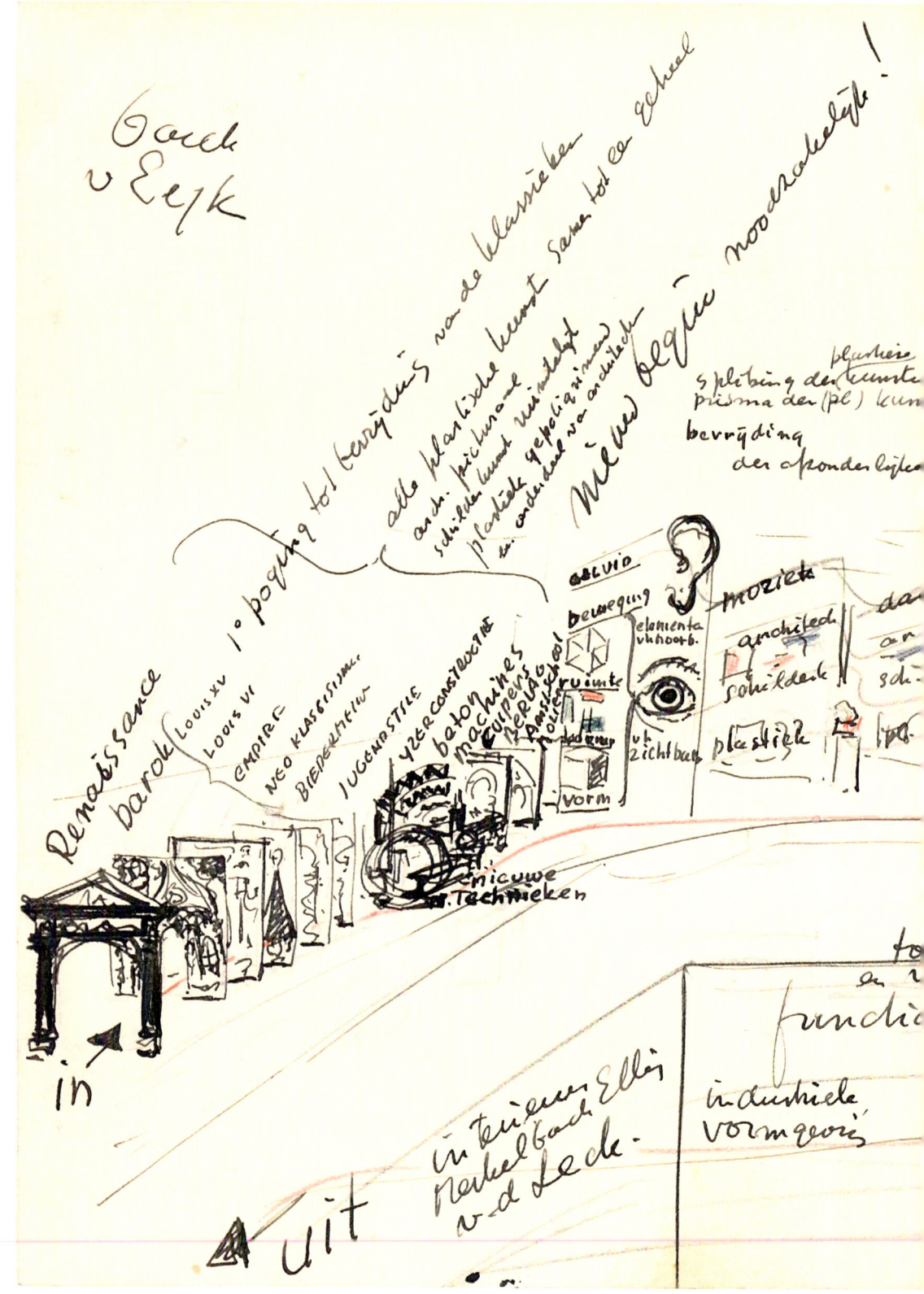

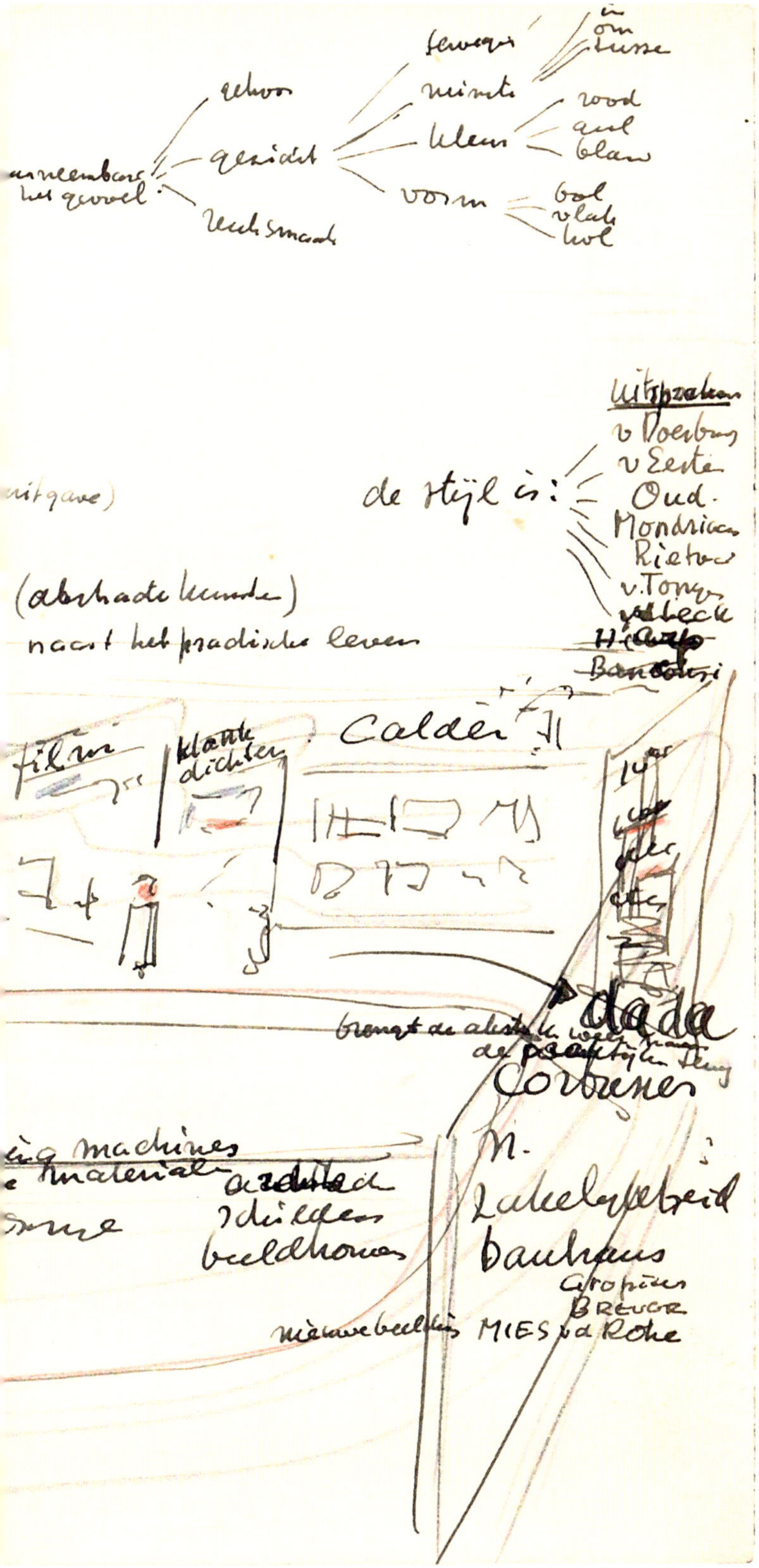

Handwritten notes (in Dutch), partially legible:

- gehoor
- gezicht
- reukssmaak
- beweging
- ruimte
- richting
- kleur — rood, geel, blauw
- vorm — bol, vlak, hol

onneembare / het gevoel

(uitgave)

de stijl is:
- Uitspraken
- v Doesburg
- v Eesteren
- Oud
- Mondriaan
- Rietveld
- v Tongerloo
- ~~Lebeck~~
- ~~Huszar~~
- ~~Brancusi~~

(abstracte kunst)
naast het praktische leven

film | klank dichter | Calder

dada
Corbusier
M.
Lubetkin?
bauhaus
Gropius
Breuer
MIES v.d. Rohe

machines
materiaal
architect
schilders
beeldhouwer
nieuwe beelding

Factors of the Visible. Rietveld's Ideas about the Renewal of Architecture

[32] 'Wat is architectuur en wat is kleur en waar ligt hun ontmoeting?', a lecture by Rietveld delivered in Antwerp on 15 November 1963 (NAI, Rietveld, Van Dillen en Van Tricht archive).

[33] Rietveld 1932 (for the English translation see Küper and Van Zijl 1992, 33-39).

[34] 'Voordracht gehouden door architect G. Rietveld op 20 februari 1959 te Delft', NAI, Rietveld archive.

between', 'red, yellow, blue' and 'convex, flat, concave'. Movement, space, colour and form are also designated as 'factors of the visible' in one of the other three sketches.

Rietveld also spoke about the sensory experience of architecture in a lecture he gave in 1963. 'An unlimited, empty space is not visible,' he argued, given that material and especially colour are required for a space to be visible, because the light reflected by material is always in colour.[32] These statements are in essence no different to those he had formulated 30 years earlier in 'Nieuwe Zakelijkheid in de Nederlandse architectuur' (New Objectivity in Dutch architecture).[33] This text from 1932, in which the renewal of architecture and the concept of space and delimitation are pivotal, also addresses the recurring theme of the emptiness 'around' and 'above' architecture. The faculties of sight, hearing and taste (including smell) are necessary to perceive these spaces. Rietveld dissects sight into the sense of colour, space and form in this text as well. In 1959, during the period when he had readopted the De Stijl train of thought, Rietveld stated that, in the movement's pursuit of a universal formal idiom, De Stijl had already differentiated the elements of sight into the qualities of colour (red, yellow, blue), form (convex, flat, concave) and space (in, around, between).[34] The 'Factoren van het Zichtbare' can therefore be seen as an elaboration of ideas about the senses and architecture which had occupied Rietveld for many years.

The depictions of the eye and the ear in the 'Factoren van het Zichtbare' drawings correspond with those in the perspective sketch and the model for the Philips Pavilion. Moreover, the prism demonstrates the refraction of light. It seems as if the cubes from the 'Factoren van het Zichtbare' were transformed into the polygonal forms of the Philips Pavilion's roof. The artistic disciplines of 'music, dance, film and sound poetry' were appended to those of 'architecture, painting and sculpture' that are mentioned on the exhibition's partitions. Rietveld had in fact applied his ideas for the factors of the visible to Philips, in his sketches and the model for the pavilion in Brussels and even earlier, in the graphic designs for Mexico City. A presentation by Philips, the light bulb manufacturer, gave him the opportunity to present his ideas about the visible and hence about spatiality, too. It is, after all, the reflection of light that renders pure space truly visible.

Rietveld's Contribution to the Renewal of Architecture
Rietveld was never able to realize an exhibition entitled 'Factoren van het Zichtbare', which is unfortunate, because besides unfolding his outlook on the senses, the most detailed sketch conveys something about other themes and ideas he was interested in. All things considered, Rietveld must have already formed a very clear mental picture of the exhibition, because the sketch provides plenty of information about its content, sequencing and layout. The presentation of architectural styles ranging from Renaissance, baroque and Louis styles to the Art Nouveau at the beginning is followed by new materials (concrete, steel) and technologies (machines), and leads on to Cuypers, Berlage and the Amsterdam School. Via the explanation about the elements of the audible and the visible, the arts are then separated and presented individually. The practical application of 'abstract art and architecture' is presented on the other side of the

G.Th. Rietveld, design for 'Factoren van het Zichtbare' (Factors of the Visible), 1948-1950
Pencil on paper, 27.2 x 21 cm
RSA, Utrecht

Exhibition 'Rietveld. Bijdrage tot
vernieuwing der bouwkunst', Centraal
Museum Utrecht, 1958
RSA, Utrecht

space. Here we see names and movements such as 'dada, Corbusier, N. Objectivity, Bauhaus, Gropius, Breuer, Mies v.d. Rohe, deployment of machines and new materials [as a header], functionalism, industrial design, neo-plasticism' and 'interior, Merkelbach, Elling, v.d. Leck' towards the exit. Above the pictorial elements stand comments in the vein of 'liberation from the classics', 'separation of the arts' and 'new start required'. One noteworthy feature is a list with names of members of De Stijl with the note instruction 'figure out' above it. The exhibition concept is wholly in keeping with Rietveld's ideas about architecture and space, as expounded in the above-mentioned texts from 1932 and 1959 as well as elsewhere.

The most important threads and concepts from Rietveld's texts and from the 'Factoren van het Zichtbare' were eventually encapsulated in the 'Rietveld. Bijdrage tot vernieuwing der bouwkunst' (Rietveld. Contribution to the renewal of architecture) exhibition, a retrospective staged by the Centraal Museum in Utrecht in 1958 on the occasion of Rietveld's 70th birthday.[35] It presented an idiosyncratic perspective of Rietveld's work in a chronological overview spanning the period from circa 1900 to the present that he had compiled himself. Rietveld's oeuvre was presented in nine galleries, in part using tried and tested themes such as renewal, New Objectivity, Functionalism and 'freer' architecture. One gallery presented work by Dutch and foreign contemporaries: W. Gropius, Le Corbusier, H. van de Velde, F.L. Wright, H.P. Berlage, W.M. Dudok, J.J.P. Oud and the Amsterdam School. The gallery entitled 'Zoeken naar een visueel a-b-c der ruimte (± 1915- ± 1924)' (Searching for a visual A-B-C of space (± 1915- ± 1924)) was devoted to Rietveld's work during his De Stijl period, yet he did not exhibit a single work by his De Stijl affiliates. In the speech Rietveld delivered at the opening, which he had to repeat because of overwhelming interest, he addressed the familiar aspects of his work and rationale. In conclusion he quoted an aphorism by the Chinese philosopher Lao-Tse: 'Through the limitation of the unlimited, truth becomes reality.'[36] Perhaps that was what Rietveld wanted to contribute to the renewal of architecture. ◆

[35] Bakema et al., 1958.

[36] 'Tweede min of meer herhaalde lezing Hr. Rietveld tijdens de architectuurtentoonstelling in het Centraal Museum te Utrecht', typescript, 1958, RSA, GR 102. See also Bless 1982, 220-239.

Dietrich Neumann

Artificial Lighting as a Design Task for the Modern Architect

The various possibilities of artificial lighting will form no small part of the task of our profession . . .[1] Gerrit Rietveld, 1947

> A nocturnal journey from Rotterdam to Delft is always a particularly unique experience, when from far away already Brinkman and van der Vluchts [sic] building of the tea, coffee- and tobacco factory van der [sic] Nelle emerges from the dark landscape, drawing in your gaze, like a magnet, until the train finally rushes right along its 8 stories of wide and long bands of light.[2]

What German art historian Richard Klapheck[3] described – mesmerized – in 1938, had long been one of the most iconic images of the new 'architecture of light' (*Lichtarchitektur*) as it was called in Europe, or an 'architecture of the night' in the words of American architect Raymond Hood. Soon after the factory had opened in 1930, its famous nocturnal photograph appeared in countless publications around the world,[4] helping to spread an awareness of the new design parameters that electric light offered.[5]

Gerrit Rietveld used this image in 1932[6] – not to illustrate nocturnal illumination as such, but to underscore his argument. He explained that the factory was 'the best building in Holland in the new functionalist style' namely 'only a shelter, floor, roof and insulation system to serve the company'.[7] The nocturnal view helped Rietveld to make his point succinctly, as it eliminated distracting details and reduced architecture to its essential elements. More than a quarter of a century before, Julius Meier-Graefe was perhaps the first to notice this quality in architectural illumination:

> With its help all the small and small-minded embellishments vanish, ghost-like, in the dark. What remains are the large outlines, the enormous masses of this creation. All by itself, the night presents what we expect from the new architecture: concentration and greatness.[8]

With the arrival of modern architecture, architects and critics had discovered another benefit of electric light in buildings: large windows would make the unornamented ceilings, structural elements and deep spaces inside visible as soon as evening fell and the lit interior became brighter than the outside. During the day, any window glass above eye level reflected the luminous sky or the bright façades across the street and were therefore opaque. At night, thanks to interior illumination, a building could gain transparency, depth and structural readability and thus confirm and illustrate the modernist credo of its architect.

The German Werkbund magazine *Die Form*, for example, noticed: 'The nocturnal view shows clearly and unmistakably that the facade is only the skeleton for the inner distribution of spaces and that its design is determined by the spatial organism within.'[9] While, astonishingly, this particular fact was hardly discussed in the contemporary debates about light architecture, which focused mainly on the integration of luminous advertising and its stylistic impact, in the 1920s architects increasingly considered the nocturnal appearance of their buildings and had them photographed at night for publication.

---

[1] G. Rietveld, 'Het Interieur' (Interiors), 1947 typescript for a lecture held in 1948 at the Academy of Fine Arts in Rotterdam; in: Küper and Van Zijl 1992, 40-47: 44.

[2] Klapheck 1938, 96; I would like to thank Dr Rudi Fischer, Munich, for telling me about this citation.

[3] Richard Klapheck (1883-1939) was a professor in the history of art at the Düsseldorf Art Academy. He lost his job in 1934 when the National Socialists took over power in Germany.

[4] See for example: Howells 1930, 474-475.

[5] Klapheck might have been lucky to see the building illuminated. According to Gillian Darley, all the lights were left on at night only on Tuesdays and Fridays, as the energy prices were still very high in the 1930s. On other nights only those rooms in which work was conducted were illuminated, leading to a much less unified and less dramatic impression.

[6] See Küper and Van Zijl 1992, 32.

[7] Ibid, 37.

[8] Meier-Graefe 1900.

[9] 'Das Deukonhaus von Erich Mendelsohn', *Die Form* 2 (1928), 43-48.

J.A. Brinkman, L.C. van der Vlugt with
M. Stam, Van Nelle Factory, Rotterdam,
1925-1931
NAI, Rotterdam

Light column during 'Edison lichtweek',
Amsterdam, 1929

D. Roosenburg, N.V. Philips Gloeilampenfabrieken, Eindhoven, 1928

[10] 'Prosperous Lamp Factories in the Netherlands', in: *Commerce Reports*, Washington, DC, 7 July 1916, 67.

[11] Heerding 1986, vol. 2, 291ff.

[12] Kalff 1937, 8-12; Kalff 1943; Kalff et al. 1958; Kalff 1958, 37-42. See also the recent bibliography on Kalff: Van Dam 2006.

Rietveld and the Architecture of the Night

Rietveld's career coincided with the emancipation of electric light as an essential tool for architects and the widespread debates about its role in the future. While Rietveld hardly participated in these discussions, his own projects certainly can be understood as deliberate and mindful contributions to the emerging vocabulary of a nocturnal architecture.

It is no coincidence that several of the most spectacular applications of electric light in architecture came from the Netherlands. The N.V. Philips Gloeilampenfabrieken of Eindhoven had consolidated its role among other lamp producers in Europe and the USA. Its factory headquarters in Eindhoven by architect Dirk Roosenburg, built in 1927, would be frequently published in luminous night shots, and Amsterdam would hold its annual light festival from 1929 onwards. The Netherland's domestic market for incandescent lamps could be served by locally made products.[10] Agreements with General Electric in the USA helped to consolidate Philips' strong, independent position among its closest rivals, GE in the USA and Osram in Germany (jointly owned by Siemens and AEG).[11] In 1924 Philips had hired a young designer, Louis C. Kalff, fresh from art school, who soon steered Philips towards better product design and the creation of a corporate identity. Kalff established Philips' first advertising studio in 1929 and, in the same year, an office for lighting advice. He was also a prolific lamp designer and published several articles and a book on architectural illumination.[12] He was responsible for the illumination of the Dutch pavilion at the

V. Karfík, Bata shoe shop, Amsterdam, 1930

[13] After Xenakis 1958-1959; For Rietveld's involvement at the beginning of the design process: Van Thoor 2008.

[14] Küper and Van Zijl 1992, 270.

[15] Rogers and Powell 1935, 69; It is also the frontispiece of Neumann 2002.

Barcelona World's Fair (1929) and created light installations at the Colonial Exhibitions in Antwerp (1930) and Paris (1931). After discussing a Philips pavilion for the Brussels World's Fair in 1958 with Rietveld, Kalff's ideas culminated in the close cooperation with Iannis Xenakis and Le Corbusier.[13]

Light and Space

The 1920s saw an increased use of photography in architecture journals and a growing interest in nocturnal imagery. Night-time photography engaged in a dialogue with architecture and began to formulate an aesthetic vocabulary at a time when it could be achieved only through the photographer's intervention. His arsenal of portable lights, long or multiple exposures and manipulation of the development process created an imagery that predated and informed the eventual approach of many lighting designers. The nocturnal photo of Vladimír Karfík's Bata Store in Amsterdam is a good example. The lighting seems to have come from a few moveable, temporary light sources.

Rietveld's conversion of the interior design store Zaudy in the German town of Wesel (1928) is a case in point. The photographer brought in portable artificial light and worked with long exposure times and a careful treatment of the image during the development process. Close examination of the showrooms behind the glass façade on the upper floors reveals that their illumination does not stem from the actual ceiling lights, but rather from hidden, temporary light sources – the shadows of the actual, but unused ceiling lamps are clearly visible, but the desired effect of rendering the depths of the building's spaces has been achieved. This is typical for the time, because the image presented is a very unusual, elaborately staged moment, which would, in all likelihood, never be repeated.

Almost 30 years later, Rietveld's Schrale Beton building in Zwolle (1957, with J.C. Meulenbelt), clearly illustrates the next phase in which less or no staging was necessary. While the large glass panes of the second-floor windows would reflect the sky during the day, at night the building's ceilings, brightly illuminated by strips of suspended light bulbs, offered views deep inside the building.

An even more complicated night view has been made of the Julianahal at the Royal Trade Fair in Utrecht. In designing it with a team of others between 1953 and 1956, Rietveld adopted the recently introduced recessed ceiling lights, which provide a pattern of bright spots on the ceiling.[14] The lights themselves are recessed deeply, and baffled rings keep light from escaping sideways. The resulting focused light pools on the floor or pavement shine back upwards to the ceiling and thus provide a glare-free and welcoming atmosphere.

The Vreeburg Cinema and Absolute Architecture of Light

The façade as an independent luminous screen is a different theme in nocturnal architecture. Rietveld's Vreeburg Cinema in Utrecht of 1936 had probably learned from the structure that was called the 'most famous of all luminous buildings',[15] namely Jan Willem Eduard Buijs and Joan B. Lürsen's building for the Dutch socialist cooperative De Volharding (The Perseverance) in The Hague of 1928. Architect Jan Buijs, a member of the Dutch Socialist Party SDAP, who had previously built only private resi-

G.Th. Rietveld, Conversion Zaudy Shop,
Brückstrasse, Wesel, Germany, 1928
RSA, Utrecht

G.Th. Rietveld, Offices Schrale Beton,
Willemsvaart, Zwolle, 1957
RSA, Utrecht

G.Th. Rietveld with groep '53,
Julianahal Royal Trade Fair, Graadt
van Roggenweg, Utrecht, 1953-1956
RSA, Utrecht

[16] Rehorst 1985, 159.

[17] Pfeffer 1928, 1-5.

[18] E. May, 'Städtebau und Lichtreklame', in: Lotz 1928, 44-47.

dences, drew on formal ideas from De Stijl, Willem Dudok and Russian constructivism as well as the much discussed German concept of *Lichtreklame*, a combination of advertising, light and architecture. He stated at the building's opening that he intended to create a structure 'that seemed to consist of light'.[16]

The areas above the large plate-glass windows consisted entirely of opal glass panels, and glass bricks made up the elevator shaft and staircase tower, as well as the horizontal band above the ground-floor windows. By day, the opal glass appeared as an opaque white. At night, interior lights silhouetted letters that were placed behind the glass (which could be accessed via slim 28-inch wide gangways). However, befitting a socialist cooperative, the texts in the façades did not advertise consumer products, but spelled out the benefits that the cooperative bestowed on its 16,000 members. The fact that the letters could be read at night only, and were very cumbersome to change did not matter much for this particular client, but proved impractical for advertising purposes and thus were not repeated elsewhere.

Rietveld's response to this solution and its shortcomings was his new façade of the Vreeburg Cinema in Utrecht of 1936. Here, letters that needed to be changed regularly for new announcements were placed in front of the luminous glass panels above the entrance, where they were easily reachable. The name of the cinema, however – not likely to change – was etched on the inside surface of square opal glass panels and became visible at night only, when the panels were lit from behind and the theatre was at its busiest. Less frequently published than the De Volharding, the Vreeburg Cinema façade is a next step in the contemporary debate about the integration of advertising.

Berlin's AEG happily joined the debate and predicted a future luminous architecture:

> At first luminous advertising merged continuously with the buildings that carried it. Soon, however, certain architectural elements were left out altogether in favor of artistically valuable light carriers. Entire buildings were designed for this luminous art . . . And we already see beginnings pointing towards a great future: towards an absolute architecture of light.[17]

German architect Hugo Häring wrote: 'Advertising is about to replace the architecture . . .' and welcomed the integration of writing into a façade and a new consideration for its architectural features. For most European architects, the American approach to advertising, familiar from countless illustrations in lighting magazines, was the 'classic counterexample: 'The eye is unable to read any letters, or distinguish individual form, it is blinded instead by the overbearing amount of glimmering lights, countless luminous elements that cancel out each other's effects . . .' architect Ernst May wrote about the 'luminous advertising on Broadway in New York'.[18] Instead, May recommended panels of translucent glass lit from behind, and mentioned in particular the 'luminous façade' of the De Volharding in The Hague. In 1928 Mies van der Rohe developed two somewhat similar designs for the Adam department store in Berlin and a bank building in

J. Buijs and J.B. Lürsen, De Volharding, The Hague, 1928

G.Th. Rietveld, Conversion of Vreeburg
Cinema with two apartments on top,
Vredenburg, Utrecht, 1934-1936
RSA, Utrecht

Stuttgart. Both remained unexecuted, but shared the idea of a luminous, translucent box, wrapped in opal glass and offering plenty of space for the application of advertisements on the outside. Mies wrote: 'In the evening it represents a powerful body of light and you have no difficulties in affixing advertising [which] . . . will have a fairy-tale effect.'[19]

Rietveld continued to be interested in the concept and applied it again in 1940, when he designed a translucent façade with integrated letters for the lunchroom and ice-cream factory Van Beurden.[20] But it is not only the façade of the Vreeburg Cinema that made it one of his most important commissions of that period. Just as important is the apartment he designed for himself and his wife on the top floor. In a brilliant attempt to emulate film's capacity to manipulate and tie together time and space, Rietveld asked his friend and photographer Nico Jesse to document his apartment in a series of individual photographs taken in all directions and assembled into a continuous panorama. It was the only sensible way to capture an arrangement that essentially consisted of one large room, housing a broad range of family functions. While the photos had been taken consecutively, once they were aligned and connected with each other, they provided the illusion of one continuous, panoramic image, and no progress of time – an impression that was then joyfully undermined by the fact that Rietveld and his wife show up several times in this panorama,

[19] L. Mies van der Rohe, 'The Adam Building', in: Neumeyer 1991, 305.

[20] Küper and Van Zijl 1992, 203.

[21] Van Tijen 1964, 1-6B; Van Tijen was also referring to an 'ideal house' Rietveld sketched and modeled for himself. He quoted Rietveld: 'in that house that you wanted to build, but never would build; the house with one fountain, one light and one fire.' It is most likely that this is a reference to the dwelling for an architect (1946), Küper and Van Zijl 1992, 221. I would like to thank Rob Dettingmeijer for the reference to this citation.

[22] Küper and Van Zijl 1992, 186; NAI, Rietveld archive, inv. no. 699 (1939).

simultaneously inhabiting different parts of the space. When Rietveld became an honorary member of the Society of Dutch architects, his friend Van Tijen, who had visited this apartment, called it 'a purifying space of pure living humanity'.[21] This photographic experiment was an indication for Rietveld's continuing search for a better way of depicting space. At the same time, he began to develop speculative drawings for a 'stereoscopic cinema'[22] allowing the viewing of three-dimensional films – a fascination that stayed with him for the rest of his life.

N. Jesse, Composite panorama of Rietveld's apartment above the Vreeburg Cinema, c. 1947
RSA, Utrecht

The Luminous Ceiling
Simultaneous to the backlit opal-glass panels in façades, they began to show up on interior ceilings. Evenly luminous and uninterrupted ceiling planes had already been imagined by architects in the 1920s. For example, Mies van der Rohe and Lilly Reich stretched white canvas above their cool modernist *Glasraum* interior at the Stuttgart Werkbund exhibition in 1927, and lit it evenly from above. They might have been inspired by solutions for the theatre (the stage at the Hellerau theatre, for example) and for photo and film studios.

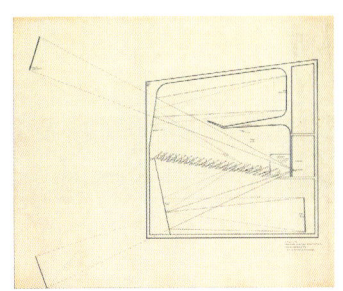

G.Th. Rietveld, Design stereoscopic cinema, 1938
Ink on tracing paper, 79.5 x 96 cm
NAI, Rotterdam

Artificial Lighting as a Design Task for the Modern Architect

L. Mies van der Rohe, Unrealized design
for Adam Department Store, 1928
Photo montage, airbrushed gouache on
gelatine silver print
Museum of Modern Art, New York

G.Th. Rietveld, Design for the conversion of lunchroom and ice-cream factory Van Beurden, Vredenburg, Utrecht, 1940
Pencil on tracing paper, 35 x 32 cm
NAI, Rotterdam

L. Mies van der Rohe and L. Reich, *Glasraum* for exhibition 'Die neue Wohnung', Stuttgart, 1927
Museum of Modern Art, New York

G.Th. Rietveld, Conversion of auditorium Rijksakademie van Beeldende Kunsten, Stadhouderskade 86, Amsterdam, 1954-1958
RSA, Utrecht

Rietveld was one of the very first to apply luminous ceilings in interiors, such as a room in one of the Erasmuslaan buildings of 1931 or a year later in the bathroom for L. Brom, to best simulate the conditions of daylight. In 1938 in the Verrijn Stuart House the utilitarian application looks like a voluminous sculptural object between the study and sitting area.[23] It took another decade before luminous ceilings became commercially available and were mass produced by firms such as Lightolier and others and widely applied in buildings such as SOM's Hanover Manufacturer's Trust or the Seagram Building in New York City by Ludwig Mies van der Rohe.

When, in 1958, Rietveld converted the exhibition hall and auditorium of the Rijksacademie voor Beeldende Kunsten, he developed a luminous ceiling that combined daylight and nocturnal lighting; between vertical glass fins underneath the skylights he placed fluorescent lights. At night, their light would be distributed sideways through the opal-glass fins, creating lighting conditions that were almost perfectly controlled and still gave the impression that light was being filtered down from the sky.[24]

Lamp Designs

Luminous ceilings turned an entire segment of architecture into a lamp, or at least a glowing object that could make individual lamps superfluous. Rietveld, however, knew about the power of individual lights, and their space-forming ability.

Rietveld designed only a small number of lamps, each one of which, however, clearly demonstrates his interest in reducing an object to its essential, logical parts.

Rietveld's probably most widely known lamp was his hanging lamp of 1922.[25] In the three-tube version, the luminous lines seem to represent the three dimensions, a second version has one additional vertical tube. The three or four tubes hang freely and separately. A draft from an open window, however, would send them into a swinging motion, and towards potential breakage. The light bulbs Rietveld used were the recently re-leased double ended tubular opal light bulbs with a bayonet cap, each 29 cm long. The wooden end pieces containing the bayonet mounts and wire connection were designed by Rietveld and custom made by the manufacturing firm of Gerard A.van den Groenen. In 1922, Rietveld also built a four-piece variation for general practitioner A.M. Hartog's consultation room.[26]

Clearly, the three or four vertical lights, hanging independently from each other, were a perfect response to the arrangement of the slats in his furniture pieces since 1918. The central approach of working with the most essential and basic part of the lamp, namely the light bulb, had fascinated Rietveld before. When he renovated the apartment of Truus Schröder-Schräder at Utrecht's Biltstraat 135 in 1921, he hung a cluster of four individual light bulbs from the ceiling on their wires, and tried to lower their potential movement by encasing the vertical wires in metal tubes.

Walter Gropius's office at the Bauhaus in Weimar of circa 1924 contained a hanging lamp that worked with very similar elements, and was, in all likelihood, inspired by Rietveld's creation; the same opal tubular light bulbs and black cubes at their ends. The comparison is worthwhile and quite telling. While the light bulbs in Rietveld's lamp are clearly treated as separate entities, in Gropius' director's office in Weimar, four lamps are

G.Th. Rietveld, Conversion of Verrijn Stuart House, Emmalaan 6, Utrecht, 1938
NAI, Rotterdam

[23] Küper and Van Zijl 1992, 134, 142, 187. For Erasmuslaan also see: Rodijk 1991, 25-26.

[24] Küper and Van Zijl 1992, 286. He was well aware of the impossibility to imitate daylight perfectly: 'Elk soort kunstlicht verandert de kleur. Aan bepaalde veranderingen der kleur kan men wennen, zodat de attractie van de felle belichting het wint van het hinderlijke der kleurmisleiding.' [Every kind of artificial light changes color. One can get used to certain aspects of changes of colour, so the attraction of vivid lighting takes precedence over the troublesome aspect of deceiving colors.] G. Th. Rietveld, 'Stands en hun inrichting vroeger en nu', in: Sandfort 1956, 48-54: 51.

[25] Küper and Van Zijl 1992, 88; It assembled three (or, in a slightly later version four) tubular bulbs whose two ends were attached to identical black wooden cubes from which electric wires emerged, connecting them to a black ceiling plate, ca. 104 cm above. Each of the tubes with its wooden end pieces is c. 29 cm long.

[26] Küper and Van Zijl, 1992, 87.

G.Th. Rietveld, interior with hanging lamp, A.M. Hartog Surgery, Emmaweg 1, Maarssen, 1922
RSA/CMU, Utrecht

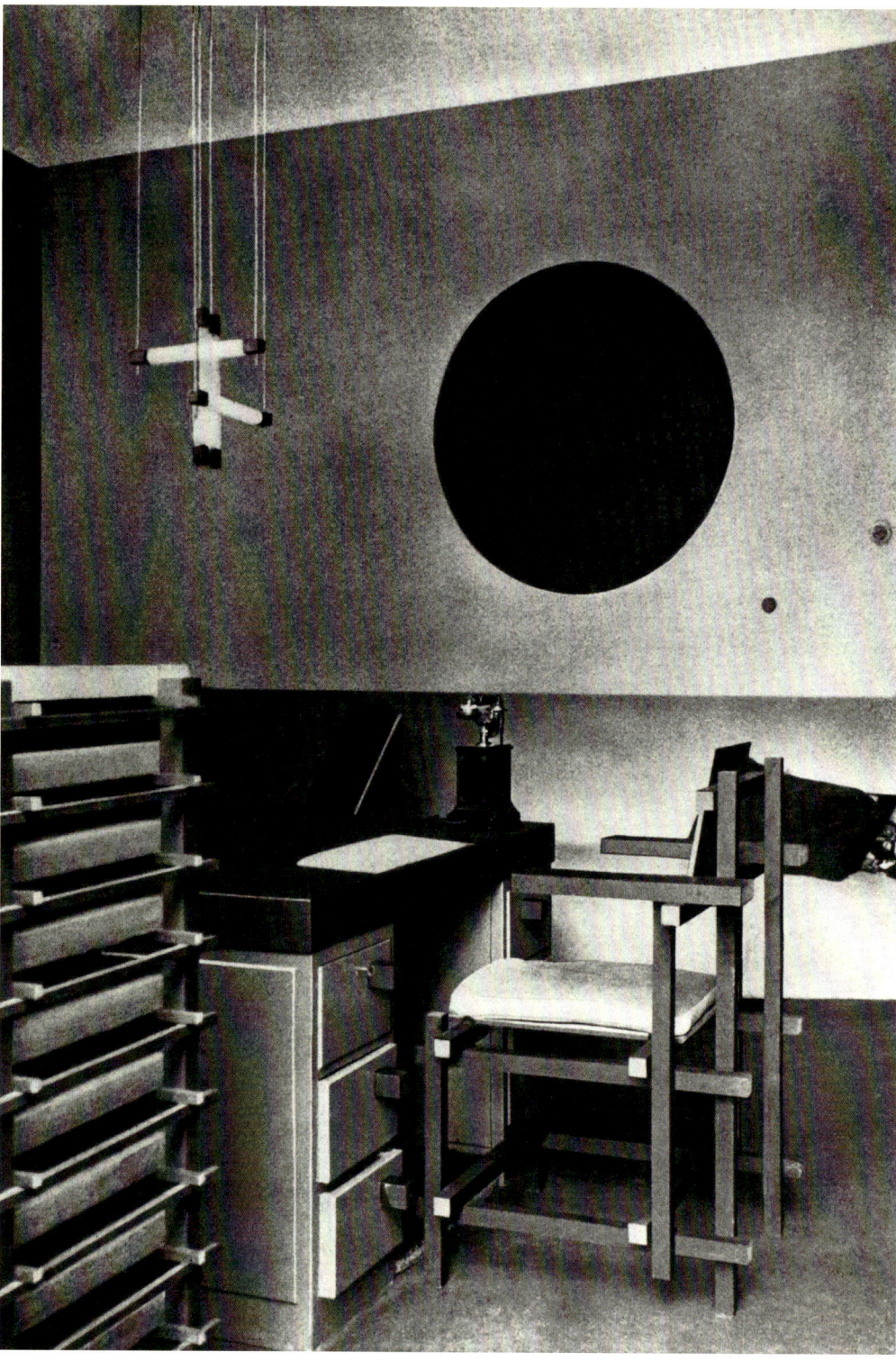

connected at their ends to form a three dimensional sculpture. Metal tubes containing the wires suspend them not just from the ceiling, but also create firm connections to the walls. A space defining overhead wire sculpture is the result, surpassing in scope and purpose Rietveld's essential arrangement of four bulbs providing light.

In 1925, Rietveld created a table lamp from a long metal tube, and two short thick tubes and a spherical glass bulb, whose upper half (in some examples two thirds) is painted black. This directs the light of this table lamp downwards onto the table surface and shields the user from glare. This simple idea wasn't patented until much later in the USA by Clarence Birdseye.[27] The simple table lamp shows up in a number of Rietveld's developments and furniture pieces, such as the transparent Radio Cabinet with Truus Schröder-Schräder of 1925, or in the photo of a modular cupboard in the same year.[28]

In his pictures of his own apartment in Vreeburg, his 1935 experimental lamp using a slender opal glass box of great simplicity and elegance is visible. He used variations of this opaque lighting on many occasions. Rietveld's lamp and lighting designs make clear how closely informed he was about the progress in this field. Often his solutions predate a general broad application. Rietveld reliably avoided repetition in his own formal vocabulary as much as in his technological solutions. His lighting designs seem like deliberately singular interventions in the ongoing debate, driven by his life-long quest for a 'joyful liberation from all that is superfluous'.[29] ◆

W. Gropius et al., Hanging lamp in Walter Gropius's boardroom, Bauhaus Weimar, 1924-1925
Bauhaus-Archiv, Berlin

G.Th. Rietveld, Table lamp, 1925
CMU, Utrecht

[27] See US Patent no 2142104, application July 29, 1935 'Electric Lamp'.

[28] Küper and Van Zijl 1992, 106, 109.

[29] Küper and Van Zijl 1992, 38.

Schröder House, Utrecht
197, 204-206, 207, 216, *216*, 219, 225, 239, 240, 244, 253, 254

Huszár, Vilmos
195, 208-211, 216

Moscow
213, 215, 217, 219, 220, 222-225, 233

De Stijl and Styles

Dutch Pavilion, Venice Biennale
244

Van Doesburg, Theo
195, 196, 198, 201, 202, 207, 208,
209, 211, 213, 216, 234, 235, 244

Sonsbeek Pavilion, Arnhem
244, 246

Oud, J.J.P.
195, 196, 198, 202, 207, 208, 211,
213, 216, 225, 233, 234, 239

Marijke Kuper

Rietveld and De Stijl

De Stijl has many faces. De Stijl encompasses an idea, a movement, a periodical and, ultimately, a visual language. The accent is constantly shifting from one meaning to another. In his book *De Stijl*, the art historian Paul Overy writes: 'Each account of De Stijl, including this one, produces a new "De Stijl" which is in itself historically located and constructed.'[1] Similarly, in 1927, Theo van Doesburg – initiator, promoter and mastermind of De Stijl – had written that the idea of De Stijl was more than a finished, dogmatic and entirely static insight.[2] Accordingly, within this *mouvement perpétuelle*, as Van Doesburg called it, every member could at some point in time find something that appealed to him and could give shape to the idea of De Stijl in his own way.

The founding members and collaborators were the poet Antony Kok; the painters Vilmos Huszár, Bart van der Leck and Piet Mondrian; and the architects J.J.P. Oud and Jan Wils. The architect Robert van 't Hoff and the sculptor/painter Georges Vantongerloo joined somewhat later. Gerrit Rietveld was the final member to join this group in its early period.[3] These individuals found common ground, sometimes imaginary and sometimes real. The first De Stijl manifesto begins with the words: 'There is an old and a new consciousness of the times.' The signatories, the founders of neoplasticism, called on all those who believed in the reform of art and culture to destroy tradition and dogmas.[4] This article presents several illustrations of how Rietveld interpreted and fleshed out this 'new consciousness of the times'.

It must have been in the first half of 1919 that Van 't Hoff introduced Rietveld – or his work, at any rate – to Van Doesburg.[5] Rietveld's exposure to the members of De Stijl and their work and ideas came at the start of a new stage in his life, which was accompanied by a surge of creative energy. Rietveld's affiliation with De Stijl brought him into contact with prominent members of the international avant-garde, such as Bruno Taut, Walter Gropius, Kurt Schwitters, El Lissitzky and László Moholy-Nagy. Rietveld expanded his horizons far beyond his birthplace of Utrecht, where life moved at a stultifying pace.[6] His work was exhibited from Paris to Berlin and published in myriad professional journals outside the Netherlands.[7]

Meanwhile, De Stijl benefited from the involvement of an artist whose architectural and furniture designs truly expressed a 'new consciousness of the times'. The ideal of De Stijl was to integrate life and work, and Rietveld gave form to this ideal in his work. The results were so compelling that the entire movement could bask in his reflected glory; even many decades later, in 2006, his Red-Blue Chair was chosen to represent De Stijl in the Cultural Canon of the Netherlands.

Two years after the founding of the periodical in 1917, Rietveld became involved with De Stijl, and he remained in the group until the last issue was published in 1928. In a chronological list of 'principal contributors' dating from 1927, Rietveld's name is consistently paired in later years with 'Schräder'.[8] The collaboration between Rietveld and Truus Schröder-Schräder on the design and building of her house in 1924 led them to form a partnership, 'Schröder & Rietveld arch-atelier', working out of that very house.[9] The construction of this house and the new partnership ushered in a new stage of development for Rietveld, in which his approach to architecture and design became more pragmatic. In 1925, Rietveld complained in a

---

[1] Overy 1991, 17.

[2] Van Doesburg 1927. This anniversary series, with multiple issues in a single publication, was not published before 1928; Ottevanger 2008, 510-511.

[3] On the founding of De Stijl, see Blotkamp 1986. In this collection, on Rietveld's relationship with De Stijl, see in particular the article M. Küper, 'Gerrit Rietveld', in Blotkamp et al. 1986; see also M. Kuper: 'Gerrit Rietveld', in: Blotkamp 1996, 196-240.

[4] Van Doesburg et al. 1918, 2-3.

[5] On the first contact between Rietveld and De Stijl, see M. Küper, 'Gerrit Rietveld', in Blotkamp et al. 1986, 262-263.

[6] NAI, Oud archive, letter from Rietveld to Oud, 19 August 1930. Rietveld attributed the fact that everything moved so slowly in Utrecht to conservatism: 'The truth is, they like things just the way they are.'

[7] Küper and Van Zijl 1992, 356-357 and 363-364.

[8] Van Doesburg 1927, 59-62.

[9] M. Kuper, 'Rietveld at Work: Recollections of Colleagues, Pupils and Clients', in: Oku 2009, 220-227: 221-222.

G.Th. Rietveld, Contribution to the anniversary issue of *De Stijl* 7 (1927), 79-84, 46

[10] NAI, Rietveld archive, postcard from Rietveld to Hammacher, postmarked 15 June 1925.

[11] NAI, Oud archive, letter from Rietveld to Oud, 8 July 1931.

[12] NAI, Oud archive, letter from Rietveld to Oud, 18 February 1952.

[13] RKD, Van Doesburg archive, letter from Rietveld to Van Doesburg, 7 October 1919.

[14] NAI, Rietveld archive, draft of a lecture for the Art Historical Institute at Utrecht University, 1960, inv. no. 753. Translator's note: Rietveld uses a variation on the expression 'lijkt nergens op', which literally means 'resembles nothing', but has the idiomatic sense of 'is disgraceful' or 'is wretched in quality'. By taking the idiom in its literal sense, he and the other members of De Stijl transformed a criticism into a compliment.

postcard to the art critic Bram Hammacher that the new demand for the work of 'our school' – undoubtedly referring to De Stijl – made life more difficult for him than the earlier resistance had. 'There's also something to be said for agonizing. Now they're flinging areas of colour and cubes about too wildly for my taste.'[10] Rietveld turned down an invitation to contribute an article to the commemorative issue of *De Stijl* published after the death of Van Doesburg in 1931 by a number of members and former members of the movement. 'It seems as though all that were in the past,' he confided to Oud.[11]

De Stijl

Looking back at the time when he had come into contact with De Stijl, Rietveld saw himself as 'a strait-laced little man'. He went on to clarify that this was not part of his nature, but the result of 'all sorts of circumstances'.[12] This evokes an image of Rietveld as a man whose everyday bourgeois rut was holding him back from fulfilling his ideals and ambitions. For Rietveld, De Stijl was a way out of his intellectual isolation. 'The most gratifying thing is to realize that, while I have always stood alone, there are others who felt and thought the same way,' he wrote to Van Doesburg in 1919.[13] Rietveld was not particularly communicative about his thoughts and feelings, especially not in his De Stijl period. No more has survived than occasional comments in letters, a few statements and retrospective remarks. The richest source of information is his work, which shows an authenticity in his De Stijl period that promises great things for the future.

Rietveld saw the work of De Stijl, including his own, not as a style but as preliminary to a style. He gave life to the idea of De Stijl by breaking free of tradition and routine, of outdated production methods and archaic forms, of a habitual, unconscious way of life. In 1960, Rietveld discussed the visual effect of this approach, giving an explanation that was concise and not without humour: 'If we made something that people said, in all seriousness, "looked like nothing on earth", we took that as the greatest possible compliment.'[14] Yet his motivation was not to rebel against the old, but to create something that expressed the essential spirit of the age. This 'something' went beyond art, design and architecture, which were merely modes of expression that pointed to the consciousness of society. Rietveld did not have a well-defined conception of the appearance of the new. The first step towards creating the new visible was to analyse seeing itself. Visual perception was reduced to elementary perception, categorized into colours, forms and space, which Rietveld associated with the visual sensitivity that he saw as fundamental to the character of the painter, sculptor and architect.

In 1926 Rietveld wrote a unique, unpublished four-point manifesto setting out his ideas about the relationship between art, sculpture and architecture.

> 1. Neo-Plasticism captures in a system of forms the rules and the order that it sees in the life of our times. 2. For the architect, form is the delimitation of space; for the sculptor, the delimitation of material; and for the painter, the delimitation of colour. 3. Colour, not intended here in the sense of pigment, but seen in terms of the workings of our tripartite sense of colour, is the painter's material, and what matters (as in the

G.Th. Rietveld, Red-Blue Chair, design c. 1918, photograph taken in the Schröder House
CMU, Utrecht

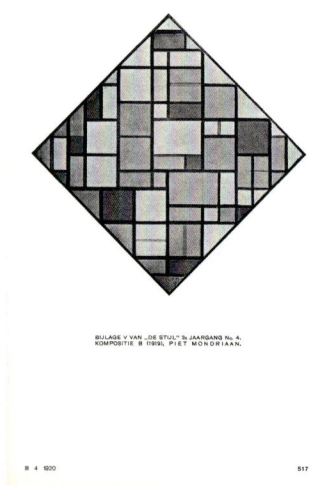

P. Mondriaan, *Compositie met kleurvlakken* depicted in *De Stijl* as 'Kompositie B', 1919

[15] RSA, typescript, dated 'Dec. 1926 Holland', signed 'w.g. [was getekend = was signed] Rietveld'. Translator's note: In item 4 of the manifesto, 'give plastic form to' is a translation of *beelden*. The use of the unconventional verb *beelden*, normally found only in the participial form *beeldend* (visual, plastic, expressive), should undoubtedly be seen in connection with *Nieuwe Beelding*, one of the Dutch terms for neoplasticism.

[16] RKD, Van Doesburg archive, letter from Rietveld to Van Doesburg, 28 February 1920.

[17] Van Doesburg's comparison also involves a sculpture by Georges Vantongerloo and a factory design by Oud. Van Doesburg 1920, 44-46.

[18] RKD, letters from Mondrian to Van Doesburg, 6 January 1920 and 11 April 1920, with thanks to Els Hoek.

[19] Georges Vantongerloo archive, Haus Bill, Zumikon, copyright: A. Thomas Schmid/pro litteris, letter from Van Doesburg to Vantongerloo, undated [late November 1919], with thanks to A. Thomas Schmid.

[20] Van Doesburg 1919, n.p.; Georges Vantongerloo archive, Haus Bill, Zumikon, copyright: A. Thomas Schmid/pro litteris, letter from Vantongerloo to Van Doesburg, 10 December 1919, with thanks to A. Thomas Schmid.

case of an architect or sculptor) are the dimensions and proportions of the delimitation and division. 4. This expression of style gives plastic form to the greatest common denominator of our times, in a simple, clear way . . . By seeking the proper manifestation of the necessary things, the architect too captures the essence of the times.[15]

Rietveld attached great importance to visual impressions. This fact once led him to compare his own work to Mondrian's, a comparison later reiterated by many others, beginning with Van Doesburg. Rietveld wrote to Van Doesburg in February 1920:

> Yesterday I received *De Stijl*, which included a reproduction of a Mondrian that, for me particularly, was suddenly of great value. You see, I had made 10 chairs (without seats or backs) and stacked them up, and because all the proportions are fairly simple, the stack's surprising yet calm construction of lines (rods) pleased me. But now here comes *De Stijl* and all at once I see the value of such a composition, then you suddenly see clearly again that it is more than a quantity of little planes and lines brought into balance, but, as a plane, in its plasticism [*beelding*], says something to you without words.[16]

Soon afterwards, in the March issue of *De Stijl*, Van Doesburg drew a parallel between Rietveld's furniture and the Mondrian painting that Rietveld had been referring to, 'Kompositie B'.[17] Mondrian was sceptical. At first he had been favourably impressed by Rietveld's furniture, but a few months later, in April 1920, he opined that Rietveld's work had a 'contrived' quality.[18] Mondrian found a fervent ally in Georges Vantongerloo, who even saw Rietveld's work as opposed to the ideas of De Stijl. Van Doesburg was mystified:

> I know no equal to these purely plastically expressive [*beeldende*] pieces of furniture. What is more, I have met him personally. He takes a very pure stance, and that includes his views. We can expect him to produce wonderful things in *de Stijl*![19]

Vantongerloo was not convinced. He considered Rietveld's work a starting point, 'a skeleton (frame)', and believed that Van Doesburg's suggestion that it was similar to sculpture was utterly misguided, because Rietveld's furniture had absolutely nothing to do with relationships between volumes.[20]

The Chair

The chair for which Rietveld had ten frames stacked in his workshop was very probably what later went down in history as the Red-Blue Chair. This armchair, which is described throughout the literature as having been designed and initially produced in 1918, is the first Rietveld design to form a convincing reflection of his aspirations. The chair, originally made of unpainted beechwood with slanted side panels under the armrests, was displayed in public for the first time at an exhibition in Haarlem in September 1919.[21] Around the same time, a photograph of it was published in the

G.Th. Rietveld, Armchair, owned by
Piet Elling, design c. 1919, realized
c. 1921
CMU, Utrecht

G.Th. Rietveld, Armchair, design c. 1918, realization c. 1919

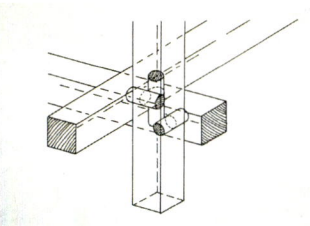

Joint made of three beams and three separate dowels
RSA, Utrecht

Gerrit Rietveld in his armchair next to his workshop on Adriaen van Ostadelaan 93, Utrecht, photo c. 1919
RSA, Utrecht

periodicals *De Stijl* and *De Hollandsche Revue*.[22] This initial version is known only from photographs. The chair represents Rietveld's interpretation of the contemporary age. It was designed for standardization and mechanical production (though this has sometimes been denied in the literature, because it was executed in different sizes), in line with what was expected and possible at that time.[23] Standard machine-sawed one-inch planks were sawn into two panels, two boards used as armrests, and thirteen slats joined in the simplest possible way, with dowels. Neither the fact that the chairs were made in Rietveld's own workshop, nor the fact that the length of the panels and slats differs from version to version, resulting in narrower, broader, higher or lower chairs, in any way detracts from the intention. Rietveld made his chairs in series. In discussion with Bram Hammacher, who was interested in buying a chair from him, Rietveld used the term 'factory price' for a first series of 12 chairs, with a much lower price for the following series.[24]

The use of dowels was deliberate and allowed the vertical and horizontal elements to be joined laterally. Rietveld's comments underscore this point:

> The construction of the chair makes it easier to connect the parts to one another undamaged, and as much as possible to prevent any one part from largely covering or dominating another one, so that the chair as a whole is for the most part free and clear in space and form triumphs over material.[25]

That evocative final phrase is packed with significance. The chair is a composition of lines and planes in space, which give the impression of being separate from one another. In a highly unconventional move, the seat and the back are separated by empty space from the armrests and the vertical elements of the rear legs. It is the idea behind this spatial and compositional

[21] Though not mentioned in the catalogue, this chair was included in the exhibition 'Aesthetisch Uitgevoerde Gebruiksvoorwerpen', which ran from 22 September to 29 October 1919 at the Museum van Kunstnijverheid (Museum of Applied Arts) in Haarlem.

[22] Van Doesburg 1919, n.p.; Anonymous 1919, 578.

[23] Troy 1988, 8-10: 9.

[24] NAI, Rietveld archive, postcard from Rietveld to Hammacher, postmarked 15 June 1925.

[25] The quote does not come from a description of the armchair but one of a child's chair constructed in the same fashion, with simple dowel joints. Rietveld 1919, 102.

Rietveld and De Stijl

W. van Leusden, Design for public transport shelter and design for a urinal, 1922, depicted in *L'Architecture Vivante* 5 (autumn 1925), figure 19

[26] Centre Canadien d'Architecture (CCA), Montreal/Canada, letter from Rietveld to Oud, 18 March 1922. With thanks to C. MacWhirter of the CCA.

[27] The architect Albert Boeken praised the design, saying it flouted convention and was radical and ruthless; see Boeken 1922, 476-478: 477.

[28] On the collaboration between Rietveld and Schröder, see L. Büller and F. den Oudsten, 'Interview met Truus Schröder', in: Overy et al. 1988, 42-104: 52-73; M. Kuper, 'Gerrit Rietveld', in: Blotkamp 1996, 222, and M. Kuper, 'Rietveld at Work: Recollections of Colleagues, Pupils and Clients', in: Oku 2009.

[29] Staal 1938, 88.

[30] Rietveld 1948, 199-201: 200 (for the English translation see Küper and Van Zijl 1992, 40-47).

[31] Van Eyck 1958, 34-42: 37.

characteristic that detaches this chair from tradition. Rietveld evaluated his pieces of furniture as spatial objects in their own right, but also in relation to the spaces in which they were found. Their formal dissection and reduction to mere lines and planes with space between them cries out for comparison with Van der Leck's paintings. Beginning in 1916, Van der Leck worked on paintings in which form was reduced to geometric figures in black, red, yellow and blue drifting over a white background – lines and planes in relation to space. The analogy is reinforced by the fact that the Red-Blue Chair consists of lines and planes in these same colours.

Architecture

The gravity-defying impression of isolated elements, seemingly tossed together by chance, and the powerful spatial impact of Rietveld's armchair were carried over into his architectural designs. The alteration of the interior and front of the Goud- en Zilversmidscompagnie (Association of Gold and Silversmiths, 1921) was, in a functional and a visual sense, proof of his ability literally to give form to space. He was asked to design a shop front that, though less than 5 m wide, included a display window, a grand entrance, a shop door, and a front door.[26] By opening up the shop front and using transparent, cubical volumes to define the border between the outside and inside (its 'delimitation') in a varied way, Rietveld made up in depth what he lacked in breadth. The illumination of the interior made the ceiling appear to extend from the inside to the outside, underneath a compartment thrusting out over the sidewalk that contained the roll-up steel shutters. In the interior, Rietveld redecorated the long, narrow room with purple carpeting and glass display cases. He connected the walls, ceiling and floor with continuous rectangles, probably in white, black and shades of grey.[27]

Three years later, in an inspiring collaboration with Truus Schröder, Rietveld designed Schröder's house on Prins Hendriklaan in Utrecht.[28] This time, he did not use transparent volumes, but a set of laterally connected planes and lines with space flowing between them, in a design like that of his famous chair. All three of the façades, both individually and in combination, achieve an equilibrium between horizontal and vertical, open and closed, line and plane. The planes are white, black and grey and the lines red, yellow and blue. This work, too, invited associations with visual art, expressed evocatively by the architect Arthur Staal, who spoke of 'a painting in concrete: grey, white and red'.[29] The upper floor, designed as a living and sleeping area, has an open plan. Sliding panels are used to partition the space into rooms. The colour scheme of the interior, with red, yellow and blue planes, is livelier than that of the exterior. Rietveld gave concrete form to the ideas of De Stijl as Van Doesburg had only ever dreamed of doing. And it was not only the unconventional external features of his design that made it so groundbreaking. Rietveld also gave new content to the idea of dwelling, based on an active, conscious approach to life, and he often said that 'dwelling is also a verb' (in Dutch, a *werkwoord*, or 'work-word').[30]

'Gosh, it's terrific, it's canonical,' the English architect Peter Smithson cried when his Dutch associate Aldo van Eyck brought him face to face with the house.[31] That made two canonical works in just over five years: the chair and the house, which was added to the UNESCO list of World Heritage Sites in 2000.

ARCHITEKT G. RIETVELD.   INTÉRIEUR N. V. GOUD EN ZILVERSMIDSCOMPIE AMSTERDAM

G.Th. Rietveld, Conversion of shop front and interior Goud en Zilversmids Compagnie, Kalverstraat 107, Amsterdam, 1921-1923
RSA, Utrecht

G.Th. Rietveld and T. Schröder-Schräder,
Schröder House, Prins Hendriklaan 50,
Utrecht, 1924

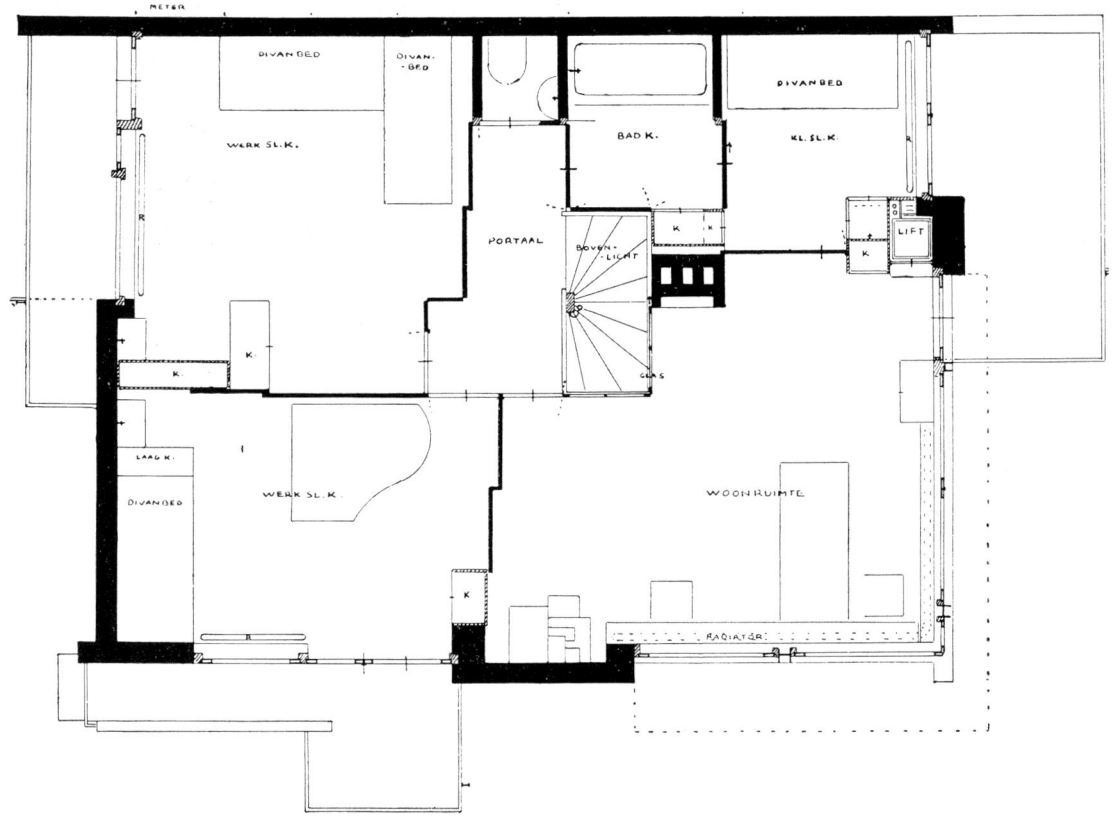

SCHRÖDER EN RIETVELD, ARCH. VERDIEPING WOONHUIS UTRECHT. 1922
DEZE VERDIEPING KAN, VOOR ZOOVER DIT NOODIG IS, DOOR MIDDEL VAN SCHUIFWANDEN INGEDEELD WORDEN IN ÉÉN WOONRUIMTE, DRIE SLAAPKAMERS, PORTAAL EN BADKAMER. DE RUIMTE ALS GEHEEL IS LICHT GEHOUDEN; WEINIG KLEUR. PLATTEGROND EN FOTO GEVEN DE RUIMTE MET DE SCHUIFWANDEN UITGESCHOVEN.

G.Th. Rietveld and T. Schröder-Schräder,
Schröder House
Upstairs floor plan depicted in
Wendingen 8 (1927), 2, 12
NAI, Rotterdam

G.Th. Rietveld and T. Schröder-Schräder,
Schröder House, Prins Hendriklaan 50,
Utrecht, 1924
Interior

Rietveld was certainly indebted to De Stijl to some degree. He had moved beyond his strait-laced origins, and his artistic discussions with his new friends and his exposure to their work had stimulated his creativity. He drew inspiration from the unexecuted work of fellow designers such as Oud, Van Doesburg, Van Eesteren and the graphic designer and painter Willem van Leusden, who was loosely affiliated with De Stijl.[32] Van Doesburg and Oud each claimed a somewhat disproportionate influence on Rietveld's development: 'The architectural projects that you know I have been working on (in collaboration with Eesteren), along with everything I discussed in my last talks in Jena, have now been executed magnificently in Holland by my friend Rietveld,' Van Doesburg wrote to Walter Dexel on 17 April 1925.[33] He made similar remarks to the painter César Domela. Van Doesburg considered himself the one who had, in conceptual terms, 'sown the seed' of the new architecture in the Netherlands, though he had not yet had the opportunity to design a building for actual construction. Nonetheless, Van Doesburg was happy to see (in a photograph of the Schröder House) that Rietveld – whom he considered one of the movement's most sincere and gifted architects, in a class with Van Eesteren – had produced 'an excellent house . . . The application of our most up-to-date principles'. Unlike Van Doesburg, Domela (who had joined De Stijl just one year earlier) had seen the actual house, and he had an equally high opinion of it: 'It is a good application of our ideas, and to me it was like an oasis in the desert of Dutch suburban architecture.'[34] Oud did not claim a share of the credit until 30 years later, when he declared that the Schröder House was an extension of his own 1919 designs.[35]

Rietveld Puts His Best De Stijl Foot Forward (To Paraphrase Van Doesburg)[36]

In her study *The De Stijl Environment*, art historian Nancy J. Troy says: 'The history of De Stijl can best be understood through the study of the collaborative efforts that produced so many of the environmental designs.'[37] In this context, Rietveld's significance is highly dependent on how broadly the term 'collaboration' is interpreted. By the nature of his profession, Rietveld's contribution was to make furniture for interiors designed by others, such as the one in Katwijk aan Zee designed for Bart de Ligt (1919) and that of the model home in the district of Spangen (1920), designed by Oud, both of which made use of colour schemes by Van Doesburg. Although there is every reason to assume that Rietveld adapted his furniture designs to the interiors, there is no evidence that he was conceptually involved in creating the overall plan.

At an early stage, Rietveld showed some interest in collaboration, perhaps with a painter.[38] Experience showed, however, that collaborative De Stijl projects tended to lead to conflict. Furthermore, Rietveld was perfectly capable of developing colour schemes for his own projects.[39] It quickly became clear to Van Doesburg that Rietveld was not eager for the De Stijl painters to become involved in his work. 'You must be taking care of the COLOUR yourself; I n-e-v-e-r hear anything about that from you any more,' Van Doesburg wrote to Rietveld after hearing about the house in Utrecht.[40]

Rietveld collaborated with other members of De Stijl only when they invited him to do so. It was in 1923 that he worked most closely with the

[32] M. Küper, 'Gerrit Rietveld', in: Blotkamp et al. 1986 and M. Kuper: 'Gerrit Rietveld', in: Blotkamp 1996.

[33] Vitt 1980, 84-85.

[34] RKD, Van Doesburg archive, letter from Van Doesburg to Domela, 27 August 1925; letter from Domela to Van Doesburg, 26 September 1925. Excerpts from the two letters are included in Van Straaten 1983, 137-138. It is not clear when Van Doesburg finally saw the actual house. On 28 October 1925 he wrote to Van Eesteren that he planned to go to Utrecht to see the house, but that trip never took place, RKD, Van Doesburg archive.

[35] NAI, Oud archive, letter from Oud to J.J. Vriend, dated 15 January 1957 [should probably be 1958].

[36] Van Doesburg 1927, 53-71: 55.

[37] Troy 1983, 6.

[38] M. Küper, 'Gerrit Rietveld', in: Blotkamp et al. 1986, 276.

[39] Rietveld's boyhood dream was to become a painter. In fact, he did try his hand at painting for a very short time and belonged to a number of artists' associations. See Bibeb 1958; Brugmans and Japikse 1938, 1738, and M. Küper, 'Gerrit Rietveld', in: Blotkamp et al. 1986, 261.

[40] RSA, postcard from Van Doesburg to Rietveld, dated '24/3' [1925]. Various publications date this card to 1924: L. Büller en F. den Oudsten, 'Interview met Truus Schröder', in: Overy et al. 1988, 42-203: 65; and Overy 1991, 118. This is unlikely, given that Rietveld lived at Adriaen van Ostadelaan 93, Utrecht, in March 1924 and did not move to Bachstraat 11, Utrecht, the address to which the card was sent, until May 1924. Furthermore, Van Doesburg did not receive Rietveld's new address from Van Eesteren until March 1925, RKD, Van Doesburg archive.

J.J.P. Oud, Interior with colour composition by Theo van Doesburg and furniture by Rietveld in show home in the Spangen neighbourhood of Rotterdam, 1920
CMU, Utrecht

[41] The Exhibition 'Les Architectes du Groupe "de Styl"' ran from 10 October to 15 November 1923 in Léonce Rosenberg's gallery in Paris, L'Effort Moderne. On this project, see e.g. Van Straaten 1983, 116-125; Troy 1983, 103-117; Bock 2001, 151-195; Ottevanger 2008, 429-445.

[42] NAI, Van Eesteren archive, postcard from Rietveld to Van Doesburg, undated [May 1923] and postcard from Rietveld to Van Eesteren, undated [May 1923].

[43] RSA, letter from Van Doesburg to Rietveld, 26 July 1923.

[44] Ex, Hoek and Troy date the design to 1924: Ex and Hoek 1985, 81; Troy 1988, 46 and 207. See also, RSA, postcard from Masthoff and Brugman to Rietveld, postmarked 14 July 1923. Brugman had also asked Rietveld and Van Doesburg to collaborate on a design for another room. But Van Doesburg, who had already designed a colour scheme for another room in Brugman's home, felt that the proposed fee was absurdly low. Rietveld consequently decided to do no more than design the music room, CMU, RSA, letter from Van Doesburg to Rietveld, 26 July 1923.

[45] Buchholz and Roters 1993, 108.

others. Van Doesburg invited him to participate in what was meant to be a large, collective De Stijl project, but was eventually trimmed down to an architecture exhibition that took place in the autumn of 1923 in Paris in the gallery of art collector Léonce Rosenberg.[41] Rietveld wanted to contribute an architectural design of his own for Rosenberg, but only had the time to make a scale model of the Hôtel Particulièr, a design attributed to Van Doesburg and Van Eesteren but which Rietveld referred to consistently in his correspondence as Van Eesteren's design.[42] The exhibition also included a model of the GZC made for the occasion by Rietveld. In addition, Van Doesburg had wanted to exhibit furniture by Rietveld. He promised that cushions would be made for them: 'The French won't plant their bums on a wooden chair.'[43] But the plan was never carried out; Rosenberg did not like Rietveld's furniture.

Rietveld was also involved in two projects with Huszár in 1923, playing a more substantial part than he did in the Rosenberg project. The first was a music/sitting room in the home of the writer Til Brugman in The Hague, in which Rietveld's armchair, a high-backed chair and a low, asymmetrical table were set against the backdrop of Huszár's colour scheme, a 'Space-Colour-Composition in Grey'. Rietveld's colour choices – like the monochrome white for the armchair – were probably made in light of the grey planes on the walls and ceiling. The design is generally dated to 1924, but correspondence with the clients, Brugman and her friend Sienna Masthoff (a singer), shows that the room was completed in the summer of 1923.[44]

In the same period, Huszár, Erich Buchholz, Willy Baumeister and El Lissitzky were invited to design a *Raumlösung* (spatial solution) for the 'Juryfreie Kunstschau Berlin' (Jury-Free Art Exhibition, Berlin); JKB.[45] The plan was to execute the four designs full-scale at the JKB exhibition in October/November 1923, but a shortage of funds made full-scale execution impossible. Huszár had involved Rietveld in the plan from an early stage.

INTÉRIEUR, 1919

V. Huszár, *Space-Colour Composition in Grey*, with furniture by Rietveld in Til Brugman and Sienna Masthoff's interior, The Hague, 1923

Th. van Doesburg, Colour composition for the room in Bart de Ligt's house, with furniture by Rietveld, Katwijk 1919, depicted in *L'Architecture Vivante* 5 (autumn 1925), figure 12

Rietveld and De Stijl

209

G.Th. Rietveld and V. Huszár, *Space-Colour Composition for an exhibition space,* 1923, depicted in *L'Architecture Vivante* 5 (autumn 1924), figure 10-11

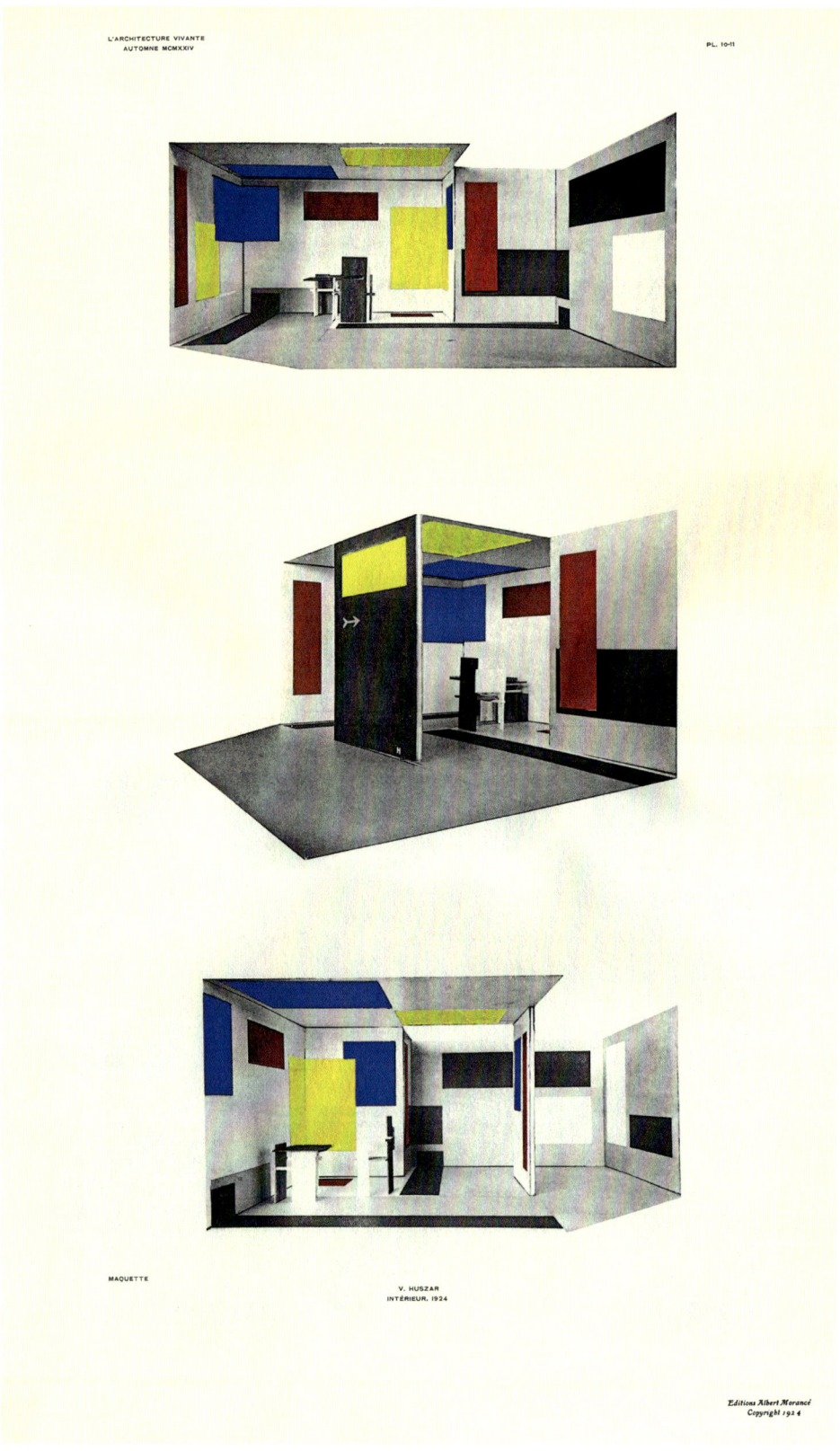

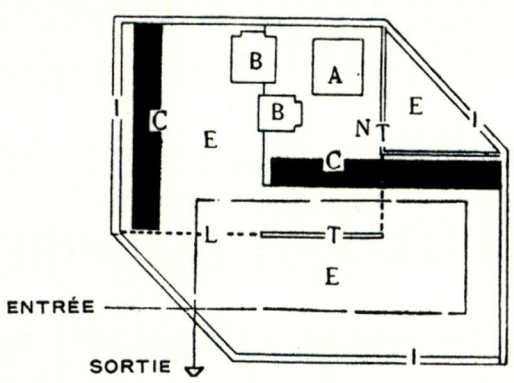

G. Th. Rietveld and V. Huszár, *Space-Colour Composition for an exhibition space*, Floorplan depicted in *L'Architecture Vivante* (autumn 1924) 14

Rietveld supplied the design and a scale model of the 9 x 9-m exhibition space.[46] Huszár developed the pattern of coloured areas for the ceiling, floor and walls.

One of the corners of this space was diagonal, and Rietveld seized the opportunity to make the opposite corner diagonal as well, thus making the entrance to the area more visually intriguing. He then masked the existing diagonal with two perpendicular walls that formed an angle pointing inward. Parallel to the longitudinal axis of one of the walls, he placed a third, freestanding wall, creating a walking route that allowed visitors to move among the coloured surfaces and become a part of the spatial and chromatic composition. Huszár was wild with enthusiasm, calling Rietveld's design superb and astoundingly simple. He asked whether Rietveld wanted to include any furniture.

Huszár had in mind a table and chair, and he wrote to Rietveld, 'May I take care of the colours, then.'[47] Rietveld designed two asymmetrical, sculptural constructions made up of orthogonal planes and lines, which could actually be used as a table and chair. He placed scale models of them in the architectural model. As far as is known, only the chair – which became known as the Berlin Chair – was ever executed by Rietveld in a full-scale version. It is unknown who devised the chair's black, white and grey colour scheme, but it may have been Rietveld's response to the areas of primary colour on the walls and ceiling.

After 1923, the relationship between Rietveld and De Stijl became less active. His work still appeared in the periodical on occasion, but he was no longer as close to Van Doesburg and the other members. One exception was Oud, with whom he developed a lifelong association characterized by mutual respect. Yet Rietveld had also made a favourable impression on most of the other members of De Stijl. Van Doesburg, in particular, had been euphoric about Rietveld and his work from the very start: 'His work was a revelation to all of us here' (1919).[48] ◆

[46] Until now, the attribution of this interior design was always uncertain or incorrect. Troy 1983, 129-132 and Ex and Hoek 1985, 75-78. A postcard from Huszár indicates that the design is Rietveld's work. CMU, RSA, postcard from Huszár to Rietveld, postmarked 1 July 1923.

[47] RSA, postcard from Huszár to Rietveld, postmarked 1 July 1923.

[48] Georges Vantongerloo archive, Haus Bill, Zumikon, copyright: A. Thomas Schmid/pro litteris, letter from Van Doesburg to Vantongerloo, undated [late November 1919], with thanks to A. Thomas Schmid.

Ivan Nevzgodin

Perspective from the East: Rietveld's Impact on the Soviet Union

The years 1920-25 saw an astonishing expansion of the influence of de Stijl, first in Belgium, then in Germany, France, Eastern Europe and even in Russia where it met the earlier but less practicable abstract traditions of Suprematism and Constructivism.[1]

Early Contacts

Rietveld's first direct involvement with the new Bolshevist Russia probably dates from the period shortly after his introduction to De Stijl. In 1919, he and 97 other artists signed a petition to the Dutch parliament requesting that 'all limiting regulations standing in the way of free international communication by mail between artists be lifted' – there was a postal blockade against Russia. Other members of the De Stijl group also signed the petition, although the signatures of J.J.P. Oud and B. van der Leck are missing.[2]

From 1927, Rietveld was a member and secretary of the Utrecht department of the Filmliga, which screened many Russian films. In 1928, he also became a cofounder of the Genootschap Nederland-Nieuw Rusland (Netherlands-New Russia Society) and architectural editor for the associated journal, *Nieuw Rusland* (New Russia), which from 1933 on was called *Cultuur der U.d.S.S.R.* (Culture of the USSR). Rietveld's sympathy for Russia stemmed from a personal, utopian striving for a better world.

Unconsciously Creating 'Blind Architecture'

J.J.P. Oud said in his lecture 'From Modern Painting and Contemporary Techniques to New Architecture' given for the Rotterdamsche Kring in 1927:

> The Russian painter Malevich camouflaged this suicide [of painting] as 'blind architecture', El Lissitzky called it 'Proun': the station where one changes from art to architecture. In the Netherlands, the artist who definitively purchased a transfer ticket – perhaps unconsciously – was Rietveld, in whose furniture and buildings the aesthetic premise in this sense was initially still in the foreground, certainly not entirely to be defended architecturally, yet bringing with it much important impetus.[3]

Malevich himself underscored this viewpoint a year later:

> By this I do not mean to say that the new Western architecture is Suprematist, but I can say that the new Western architecture has chosen the path of the Suprematist architectonics. The new architectural works of artist-architects like Theo van Doesburg, Le Corbusier, Gerrit Thomas Rietveld, Walter Gropius, Arthur Korn and others are typical examples of this.[4]

A remarkably short list – which does, however, include two Dutch artists. Perhaps this was partly influenced by the prominent presence of Rietveld's work at the international exhibition in Moscow in 1927.

There are many similarities between De Stijl's search for innovation and the quest of the Russian avant-garde: the work of Kazimir S. Malevich (1878-1935), such as the Bèta-Architekton (before May 1926), can be

[1] Barr 1952-1953, 10.

[2] For details on this action, see: G. Harmsen, 'De Stijl en de Russische revolutie', in: Friedman 1982, 45-49.

[3] *Nieuwe Rotterdamsche Courant*, morning paper, 23 December 1927.

[4] Malevich 1928, 122.

Stroitel'naja promyshlennost'
(The Building Industry) (December 1926)

Stroitel'stvo Moskvy (Construction of Moscow) featuring Boris A. Sokolov's cabinet design (El Lissitzky studio) (1929)

Mart Stam, Gerrit Rietveld and El Lissitzky
at the Schröder House, 1926
RSA, Utrecht

[5] Gan 1922, 67-69.

[6] 'De mislukte internationale van beeldende kunstenaars te Düsseldorf', *Het Vaderland*, evening paper, 10 June 1922, B, 3.

[7] Lissitzky 1926, 12, 879.

compared with those of Theo van Doesburg and Cornelis van Eesteren (Hôtel Particulièr, scale model by Rietveld, 1923); or the Stair Pole, sculptural interior architecture by Robert van 't Hoff (1918) and the Monument for Leeuwarden by Theo van Doesburg (1917-1918) with Malevich's Zèta-Architekton (before April 1927). Contemporaries in both camps, such as Moisei Ia. Ginzburg (1892-1946), the ideologist of constructivism in Russian architecture, and Theo van Doesburg himself, were aware of this like-mindedness. As early as 1922, Aleksei M. Gan (1893-1942) pointed out, in the first and most well-known Russian book on constructivism, the connection with the De Stijl movement, even calling it 'the constructivism in the West'.[5]

A comparison of the 'Model of the Room Design for the 'Juryfreie Kunstschau Berlin' (1923), by Vilmos Huszár (1884-1960) and Rietveld, with the 'Prounen-Raum for the Great Berlin Art Exhibition' (19 May – 17 September 1923), by Lissitzky, clearly shows that Rietveld also let himself be swept up by this wave of mutual influences. Probably Lissitzky met Huszár before he met Rietveld. Lissitzky had also become acquainted with Van Doesburg before Rietveld and even had carried out a joint, stormy protest action with him.[6] Lissitzky was in the Netherlands for the famous First Russian Art Exhibition in Amsterdam's Stedelijk Museum (29 April – 28 May 1923), but we do not know whether Rietveld saw this revelation of the new Russian art.

The House as Manifesto

The photograph taken in 1926 of Mart Stam and Lissitzky on the doorstep of the Schröder House with Rietveld inside the house is quite special. Here we have the representatives of the *Nieuwe Bouwen* (the Dutch manifestation of the Modern Movement in architecture), De Stijl and Russian constructivism and Suprematism together as a triad. With Lissitzky and Rietveld, the admiration was clearly mutual: in 1926, Lissitzky published Rietveld's works in Russia, in the journal *Stroitel'naia promyshlennost'* (The Building Industry) and Rietveld and Oud did the same for Lissitzky in the Netherlands, publishing his works in *i10*. Lissitzky wrote:

> The house is a two-story house, the usual type of dwelling in the Netherlands, but then designed in a revolutionary style. The entire top floor is one large space, in which the furniture, except for the chairs, is built-in: the cupboards, divans and tables are laid out like houses in a city, so that between them are left streets and squares, as it were, for people to walk in.[7]

Later, Lissitzky's widow recalled:

> We were also privileged to be guests in a house in Utrecht that had been designed and furnished by the architect Gerrit Thomas Rietveld. His furniture and his built-in fittings were exquisite in proportion and workmanship. A huge living area, with enormous glass windows all around it, had a music-and-study corner for several children, a dining area and a library: at night it was transformed into separate cubicles by means of sliding partitions which were pulled out from the wall.

Rietveld, first a cabinet-maker, then a furniture-designer, was an artist in his own line, and to our mind especially deserving of admiration for his modesty and simplicity. Lissitzky was able to make sketches of many exciting possibilities suggested to him, which were of great advantage to him in his teaching at Vkhutemas and which he later discussed in an article on contemporary furniture.[8]

In 1926, Lissitzky had also seen the interior of the house of doctor Reinder Johan Harrenstein (1888-1971) in Amsterdam. Harrenstein was married to An Schräder, Truus Schröder-Schräder's sister. His house on the Weteringschans was used as a meeting place by pro-Russian intellectuals and artists. Afterwards, Lissitzky published a photograph of the Harrensteins' bedroom in Amsterdam and of two lamps by Rietveld in his article 'Kultura zhil'ia' (Housing Culture). The transformation of a space by means of sliding walls was one of the architectural means that Lissitzky would later use in his designs for exhibitions.

Upon returning to Russia, Lissitzky taught at the Wood and Metal Working Department of the VKhUTEIN (Higher Art and Technical Institute) in Moscow. There he tried to introduce the first course on interior architecture in the Soviet Union, giving students assignments to design furniture for housing for the masses. One of the assignments was to design the furnishings for a small room for two people. Lissitzky was a proponent of built-in furniture – and we indeed find clear influences of Rietveld's experiments in the work of his students; a good example is the design made by his student Boris A. Sokolov (1906-?) of a cupboard that can be accessed from the kitchen and the dining room simultaneously.[9]

A Soviet Variation on Rietveld in Prefab Concrete
In Russia, just as in the Netherlands, Rietveld is sometimes considered the greatest of architects and sometimes only a marginal one, or even not mentioned at all. This contrasting assessment sets him apart from other avant-garde Dutch architects. Did Rietveld's artistic integrity and pursuit of experimentation make him difficult to imitate, and therefore less popular? Attempts to copy Rietveld not infrequently ended up as sheer banality. Remarkably enough, in 1928 one of the first architectural imitations of Rietveld in the Soviet Union was presented by the Constructivist journal SA (*Sovremennaia arkhitektura*, Modern Architecture), and in the most well-known French journal, *L'Architecture Vivante*.[10]

In 1927, Mikola (Nikolai) V. Kholostenko (1902-1978), one of the most active members of the Ukrainian branch of the Union of Contemporary Architects (OSA, Ob'edinenie Sovremennykh arkhitektorov) and a student at the KHI (Kiev Art Institute), made the design for an agitation centre for the working-class settlements in an industrial district.[11] He chose glass and insulating slabs of concrete as materials for the building. On the ground floor, he designed a cloakroom, a workroom (office), and an apartment for the agitation service director. Upstairs there were two reading rooms and a library. The office and one of the reading rooms had balcony terraces. The roof of the reading room was also used as a terrace. Kholostenko: 'The basis of the architectural composition, both for the groundplans and the façades, lies in the characteristic peculiarities of the construction of the

[8] Lissitzky-Küppers 1967, 74.

[9] Lobov 1929, 9.

[10] Kholostenko 1928 (a), 62.

[11] See: Kholostenko 1928 (b), 34. In German, the caption reads: 'Agitations- und Propaganda Pavilion', in French it is more neutral: 'Centre intellectuel ouvrier'.

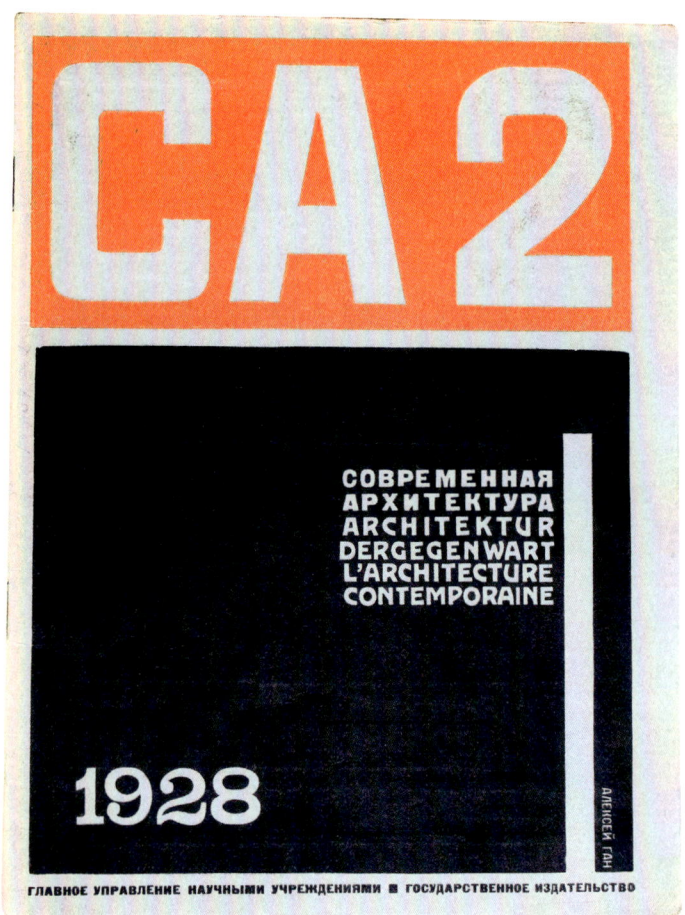

SA (1928) 2

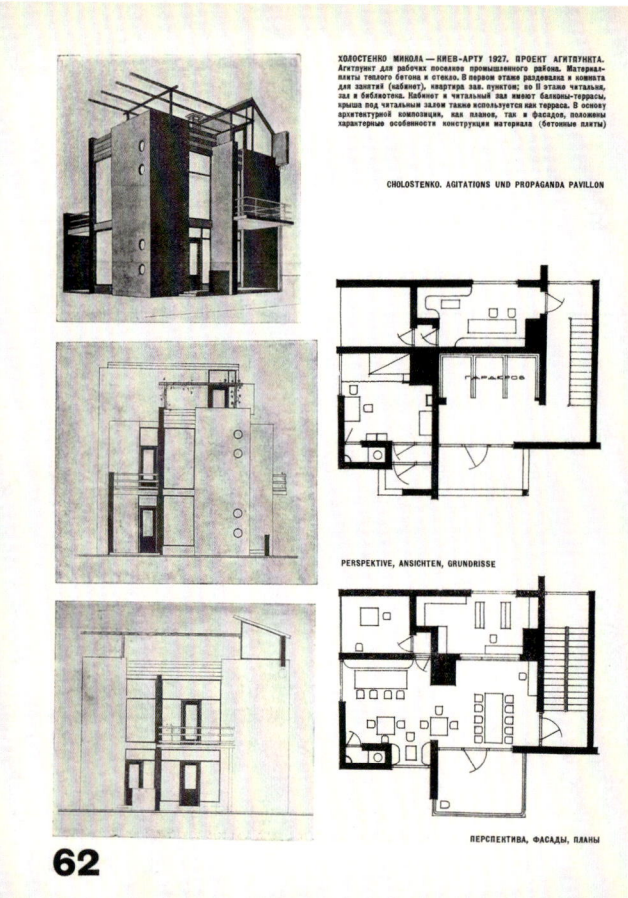

SA (1928) 2, 62
M.V. Kholostenko, Design for an agitation centre for the working-class settlements in an industrial district, 1927

material (concrete slabs).'[12] This is clearly a less realistic choice of material than Rietveld's. The floor plans for this little building show that Kholostenko had not understood Rietveld's principles very well. Kholostenko was not interested in the space and spatial transformations, which indeed would have been an obvious theme for an agitation pavilion. In comparison with Rietveld, the floor plan is too unwieldy. The student Kholostenko paid much more attention to the façades – after all, what was important was the propaganda.[13]

Rietveld and the Soviet Idea of the House of the Future

Rietveld had an idealistic idea of designing a contemporary type of standardized, normal working-class housing. His attempt, in collaboration with Truus Schröder, to place a questionnaire on new housing demands in *i10* ultimately failed.[14] However, the Russian constructivists of the OSA did manage to publish both a questionnaire, a survey and even the results of a competition for a new type of working-class housing in their journal *SA* in 1927.[15]

Rietveld's experiments with furniture, flexibility and spatial transformation probably attracted the attention of the famed Aleksandr M. Rodchenko (1891-1956). In 1927 he made the sets for the film *Albidum* by cineast Leonid Obolenskii (1902-1991). For this he designed rational office furniture, a table and a chair. They look remarkably similar to Rietveld's work, although Rodchenko undoubtedly was absolutely original when it came to his own art. In 1927-1928, the film director Grigorii P. Shirokov (1901-1976) made the popular-science film *Kak ty zhivesh?'* (How do you live?), for which Gleb I. Glushenko (1901-1967) designed a model working-class home of the future. This was a compact apartment consisting of one open space with sliding walls and built-in furniture. The image of this future Soviet working-class home reflected Rietveld's principles. In the article 'The Rationalization of Housing' in the journal *Communal Work*, L. Vygodskii used the Schröder House as an example of spatial transformation for new Soviet dwellings.[16] Rietveld's influence also can clearly be traced in the furniture designs made in 1931 by the Leningrad IZORAM.[17]

Dutch-Russian Exhibitions

Another aspect of Rietveld's relation with Russia was the international exhibitions. From June to August of 1927, he was the most important foreign participant in the famous exhibition of modern architecture in Moscow. The constructivist group, OSA, was the initiator of this exhibition. In addition to the photographs of the Schröder House, Rietveld also submitted photographs of the refurbishing of the E. Wessels & Son leather shop at Oude Kerkhof 15 in Utrecht, the Lommen House at Klein Persijnlaan 39 in Wassenaar and the interior of the Harrenstein House in Amsterdam.

In 1929, Rietveld became involved in organizing the exhibition 'Graphic and Book Art from the Soviet Union' in the Stedelijk Museum in Amsterdam.[18] A year later, he was the only Dutch architect featured at the international exhibition 'Socialist Art Today' in that same museum (8 November – 8 December 1930), organized by the Dutch Socialist Artists' Circle (SKK), which was founded in 1927. For this exhibition, the Netherlands-New Russia Society brought a great deal of interesting material from the Soviet

G.I. Glushenko, Design of a model worker's dwelling of the future, 1927-1928 *Pionery sovetskogo dizaina*, Moscow 1995, 256

[12] Kholostenko 1928 (a), 62.

[13] The rest of Kholostenko's life was less exciting. After finishing his studies in 1929, this now almost forgotten Ukrainian architect erected a few buildings in Kiev; after the Second World War, he was actively involved with the preservation of monuments and historic buildings.

[14] See the essay by Dolf Broekhuizen in this publication.

[15] *SA, Sovremennaia arkhitektura* (Modern Architecture) (1927) 1, 21-26; (1927) 4-5, 142-147.

[16] Vygodskii 1929, 94-98: 96. The map of the upstairs level of the Schröder House shown here is taken from Lissitzky 1926, 877-881: 879.

[17] IZORAM, *Izobrazitel'noe iskusstvo rabochei molodezhi* (Art of Working Class Youth).

[18] For the catalogue, see: *Grafiek en boekkunst uit de Sovjet-Unie: tentoonstelling Stedelijk Museum Amsterdam, 21.4-13.5.29*, Amsterdam 1929.

SA 3 (1927), cover, 89, 91, 93
with Rietveld designs exhibited in
Moscow in 1927

СПРАВА: РИТВЕЛЬД (ГОЛЛАНДИЯ, УТРЕХТ). ЖИЛОЙ ДОМ. RIETVELD (UTRECHT). WOHNHAUS. ВНИЗУ: РИТВЕЛЬД. МАГАЗИН В УТРЕХТЕ. RIETVELD. LEDERLADEN IN UTRECHT

РИТВЕЛЬД. ГОЛЛАНДИЯ. ЖИЛОЙ ДОМ. ИНТЕРЬЕРЫ
RIETVELD. (UTRECHT) WOHNHAUS. INTERIEURE

ERSTE AUSSTELLUNG DER ARCHITEKTUR DER GEGENWART. AUSLÄNDISCHE SEKTION

ERSTE AUSSTELLUNG DER ARCHITEKTUR DER GEGENWART. AUSLÄNDISCHE SEKTION

ПЕРВАЯ ВЫСТАВКА СА. МОСКВА. ИНОСТРАННЫЙ ОТДЕЛ

ПЕРВАЯ ВЫСТАВКА СОВРЕМЕННОЙ АРХИТЕКТУРЫ. МОСКВА. ИНОСТРАННЫЙ ОТДЕЛ

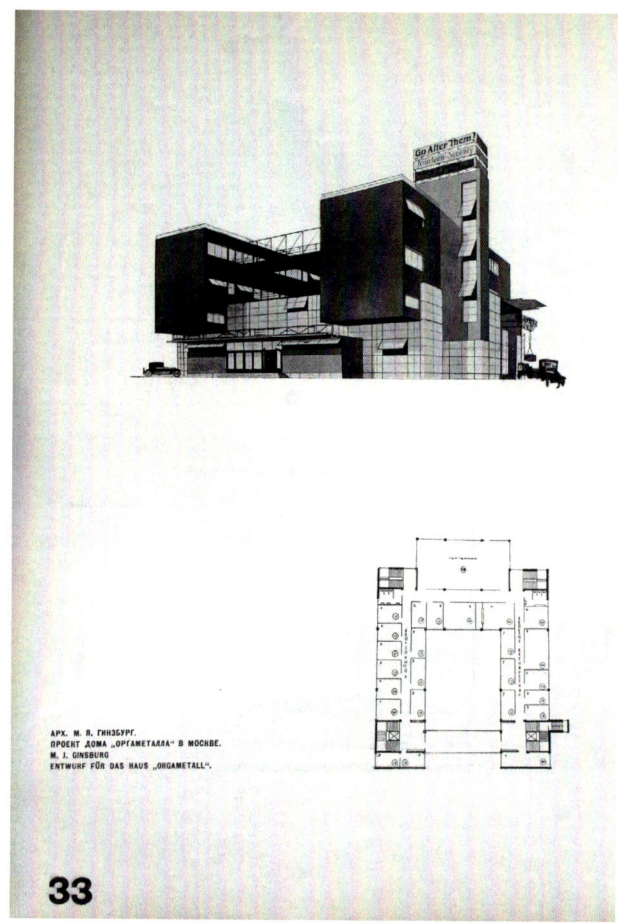

The Moscow architecture association
yearbook (anniversary edition 1928), 5,
cover and 33
M. Ginzburg, Competition design for
ORGAMETALL in Moscow, 1926-1927 (33)

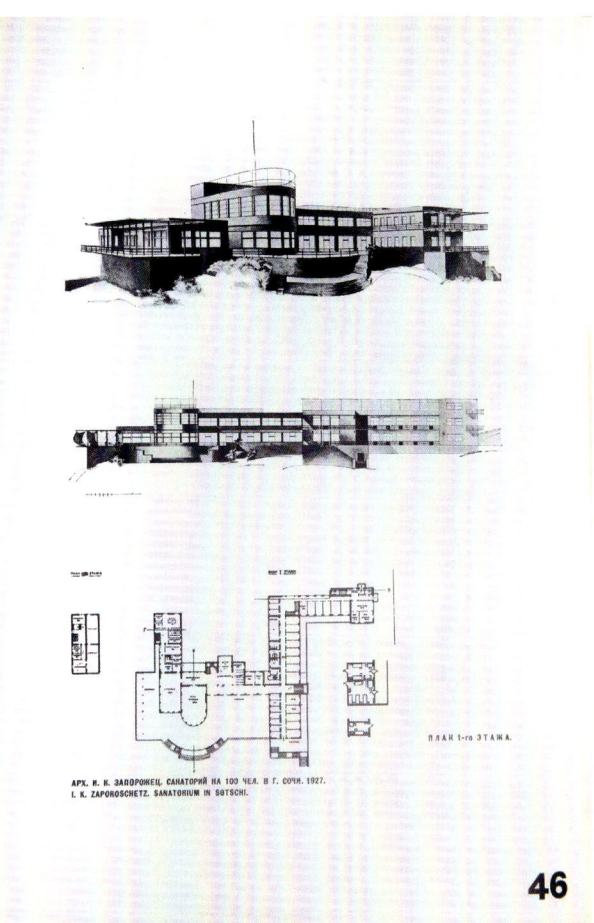

The Moscow architecture association yearbook (anniversary edition 1928), 5, 24 and 46
B.M. Velikovskii, design for Gostorg in Moscow, 1925-1927 (24) and
I.K. Zaporozhets, design for a sanatorium in Sochi, 1927 (46), both selected by Rietveld for his article in *Nieuw Rusland*

[19] The Soviet part of the exhibition: IZORAM, Art of Working Class Youth, 383-386; Montage, placards, 387-404; Architectural montage with *'facts about new buildings and socialist cities'*, 405-410; Film, 411-417.

[20] See the essay by Dolf Broekhuizen in this publication.

[21] Rietveld 1929, 10-11.

[22] Steinmann 1979, 113. In 1933, CIAM met aboard ship, the *SS Patris II*, which sailed from Marseille to Athens.

Union with the help of the VOKS (the 'all-Russian association for cultural relations abroad').[19] Later, in 1932, Rietveld, along with Peter Alma and Hildo Krop, was a member of the committee of a travelling exhibition of contemporary Dutch art in Moscow, Leningrad (the Hermitage) and Kharkiv. The exhibition's organization in the Netherlands was financed from Moscow.

Rietveld as Architectural Editor of *Nieuw Rusland*

In addition to being busy with exhibitions, Rietveld was architectural editor of the journal *Nieuw Rusland* (New Russia) later called the *Cultuur der U.d.S.S.R.* (Culture of the USSR) published by the Netherlands-New Russia Society, later the Netherlands-USSR Society. How closely Rietveld was involved with the journal's editorial staff is unclear. In several issues, he was even given the wrong initial, 'C. Rietveld'. He only wrote one article for the journal himself, but then again, he did not publish very much before the Second World War.[20] In 1929, Rietveld wrote a review of the jubilee issue of Moscow's architectural society. He characterized new Soviet works as 'functional architecture, not specifically Russian' and was mainly critical:

> In Russia . . . they enthusiastically go ahead with the new; no matter what architecture journal you get hold of, the functional solution is what has been sought everywhere. However, this enthusiasm does not seem to have precluded a certain trend: concrete floors on pillars, round endings, alternated by the use of units – concrete, iron and glass. The cliché aspect that one finds in almost all reproductions does not in itself seem wrong to me, but the fact that people seem more fulfilled by the building materials and technical-looking constructions than by the spaces they must to allocate, is, no matter how justified it might be construction-wise, not correct in terms of architecture. Perhaps that's why this architecture, despite all the enthusiasm, seems oppressive and rather lifeless.[21]

Rietveld regularly gave Ben Merkelbach (1901-1961), one of the founders of the architecture association De 8, the opportunity to publish an article in the journal. The fact that Rietveld was well aware of what was going on in the Soviet architecture world is evidenced by articles that the journal published, such as one by Aleksei N. Tolstoy (1883-1945) which had been translated into Dutch. With this text, Tolstoy paved the way for social realism's entrance into Soviet architecture.

The Suspect Society

Remarkably, Rietveld remained a member of the Netherlands-USSR Society in the late 1930s, the darkest period of Stalinism. The development of Soviet architecture was increasingly being steered in another direction by those at the top. This led to neoclassicist extravagance, which must have elicited little sympathy from Rietveld. The Congrès International d'Architecture Moderne (CIAM) never was held in Moscow, because it was becoming increasingly clear that modern architects were no longer welcome.[22] Having a subscription to the journal *Cultuur der U.d.S.S.R.* and being a member of the society were becoming more and more suspect in the Netherlands. First the journal was forbidden in the military barracks, and finally the Dutch government considered members of the society politically suspect by definition. Perhaps Rietveld's involvement with this pro-Soviet Russian society was the reason why the US government refused to give him an entry visa in 1956.[23]

Growing Criticism

In the Soviet Union, more and more of the reactions to Rietveld's work were critical. The most influential Soviet art and architecture critic, Ivan (János) L. Mácza (1893-1974), wrote in 1929: 'The Suprematist surface areas, "constructed" from iron-concrete slabs by Le Corbusier and Rietveld, are only justified by their aesthetic principles, not by the space, nor by the material.'[24] Mácza was wrong about Rietveld's building materials; perhaps he got his information from Walter Gropius, who described the Rietveld-Schröder creation as 'house in Utrecht, concrete, iron, glass'.[25]

In addition to the flood of foreign and Soviet journals with articles on the West, the collection of essays in *Arkhitektura sovremennogo Zapada* (The Architecture of the Contemporary West), edited by David E. Arkin (1899-1957) which was published in Moscow in 1932, is a good example of how well-informed Soviet architects were of developments in the West. Included in this book were texts by Le Corbusier, Bruno Taut, J.J.P. Oud, Walter Gropius, Ludwig Hilberseimer, László Moholy-Nagy, Frank Lloyd Wright, Richard Neutra and Ernst May. Rietveld's work was not mentioned. In the same year, however, the Schröder House was given a place in Moisei Ginzburg's manuscript of the book *Dwelling*.[26] Ginzburg, as a practicing architect, perhaps had more appreciation for Rietveld's experiments than Arkin, an architecture critic who considered Rietveld to be passé.

The Sympathizer from the Constructivist Corner

The Soviet architecture historian Anderei V. Ikonnikov (1926-2001) opined in 1982: 'The dogmatic doctrines of the De Stijl group were not fruitful in themselves. This is confirmed by the limited creative results achieved by an architecture that followed the principles of De Stijl in an orthodox manner.'[27] This view is at odds with that of architecture historian Nadezhda L. Krasheninnikova (1892-1985). For almost half a century, she was an enthusiastic ambassador for Dutch and Belgian architecture in the Soviet Union. Virtually on her own, she created an image of Dutch architecture for Russian people. Krasheninnikova was not only a personality in the area of Russian architecture of the twentieth century, but also the author of the only Russian-language book to give an overview of Dutch architecture of the twentieth century.[28] In this publication, Rietveld is considered the most important master. It is therefore not surprising that Krasheninnikova visited Rietveld in the summer of 1961 to have him clear up a few difficult points in the history of the early years of De Stijl. In doing so, he gave her a tour through the Schröder House. Rietveld also showed her other works of his; after his death, Truus Schröder even sent photos of them to Moscow. ◆

[23] Bless 1982, 150.

[24] *Iskusstvo epokhi zrelogo kapitalizma na Zapade* (Art from the Era of Mature Capitalism in the West), Moscow: Publishers of the Communist Academy, 1929, 215.

[25] Gropius 1925, 76-77.

[26] The book was published two years later. See: Ginzburg 1934.

[27] Ikonnikov 1982, 64.

[28] Krasheninnikova 1971. Nadezhda Krasheninnikova was herself a member of the group of Moscow Constructivists (OSA) and is without doubt worth a separate book. She was helped in the Netherlands by two teachers from the architecture department of the TH Delft (Technische Hogeschool Delft, Delft College of Technology, the predecessor of Delft University of Technology), Max Risselada and Gerrit Oorthuys. Her travel impressions have determined Rietveld's place in the Russian version of architecture history.

Ida van Zijl

De Stijl as Style

G.Th. Rietveld, Verrijn Stuart Summer House, Section F no. 1701, Breukelen St. Pieters, 1940-1941
RSA, Utrecht

[1] Lecture by architect G. Rietveld on 20 February 1959 in Delft, RSA GR 81.

[2] I. van Zijl, 'De Mondial in Rietvelds oeuvre', in: Venneman and De Kroon 2006, 40-45.

Rietveld's Work in the First Few Years after the Second World War

'20 years ago I would never have spoken of "de Stijl", which was all but forgotten at the time,' Rietveld told his audience in Delft on 20 February 1959.[1] Even for Rietveld himself De Stijl had seemed a thing of the past. Over the years, he had developed a progressively free approach to materials and forms and had spent the 1940s designing buildings and furniture that bore little resemblance to his De Stijl furniture or to the work of the *Nieuwe Bouwen* (the Dutch manifestation of the Modern Movement in architecture).

During the first five years after the Second World War, Rietveld's furniture designs were extremely varied and gave little evidence of a distinctive style. All kinds of influences, among them the shortage of materials, new production methods and foreign examples, played a role. His Danish Chair appears to have been influenced by the curved wooden chair by Americans Charles (1907-1978) and Ray Eames (1912-1988). These two designers and their compatriot Henry Bertoia (1915-1978) may have inspired Rietveld to create a steel wire chair. His only cane chair also dates from this period. They are joined by a great many sketches of models for industrial production that never got beyond the drawing board.[2]

The Verrijn Stuart Summer House by the Loosdrechtse Plassen recreation area (1940-1941) and the Mgr. Verriet Institute on Curaçao (1949-1952) also show a Rietveld with whom many are unfamiliar. It suggests that his architectural output might have been equally varied if he had had the opportunity to build more, but in the years after the Second World War Rietveld had trouble finding work.

There are several causes for this. First of all, building efforts were directed at reconstruction and the alleviation of the immense housing shortage, while Rietveld had failed to carve out a strong position in the public housing sector before the war, despite his affinity with this line of work and some brilliant ideas in this field. His political persuasion formed

Ch. and R. Eames, Chair of curved wood,
1945-1946
Birch and plywood,
67.5 x 55.5 x 61 cm
Stedelijk Museum Amsterdam

G.Th. Rietveld, Danish Chair, c. 1948-1950
Five-ply wood,
61.5 x 61.5 x 59 cm
CMU, Utrecht

H. Bertoia, Steel wire chair, 1952
Vinyl-coated metal, cushion with synthetic
fabric cover, 57.5 x 85.5 x 71 cm
Stedelijk Museum Amsterdam

G.Th. Rietveld, Wire Chair, 1950
Steel wire, 86 x 40 x 41 cm
CMU, Utrecht

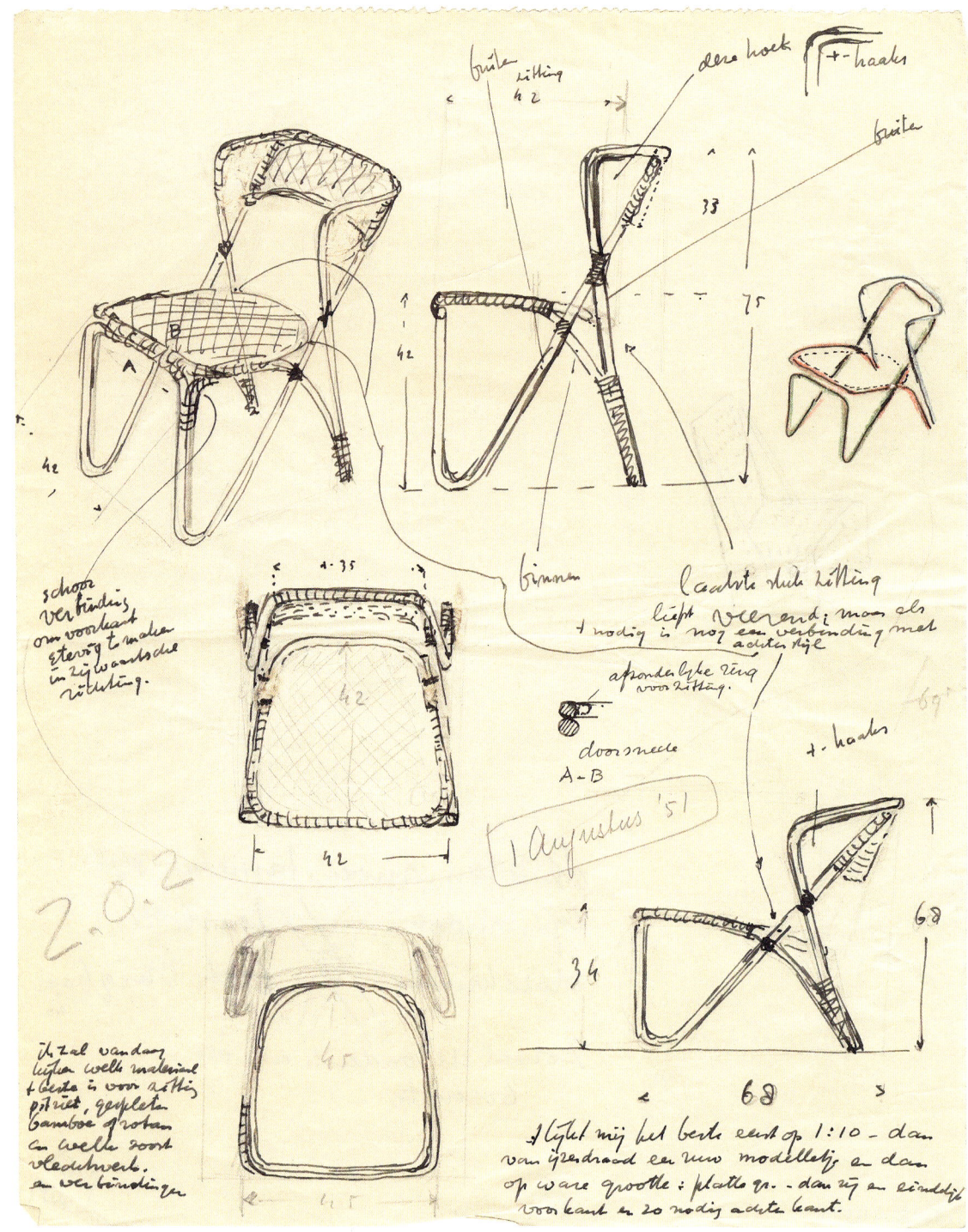

G.Th. Rietveld, Preliminary designs for
rattan chairs, c. 1935-1940
Ink on paper
26 x 21 cm
NAI, Rotterdam

another obstacle. Fairly soon after the war, anti-communist sentiment grew strong in the Netherlands, which was reflected by the authorities in both official and unofficial ways. Many saw Rietveld as a fellow-traveller because of his pre-war involvement in the Vereniging Nederland-Nieuw Rusland (Netherlands-New Russia Society), which explains why he was passed over for the directorship of the Institute for Applied Arts (the later Gerrit Rietveld Academy) in the late 1940s.[3] No major projects came his way; most of his commissions involved the design of exhibitions and exhibition areas and a few houses for private clients.[4] This changed in the early 1950s when De Stijl gained in popularity and the national character of this avant-garde movement became increasingly important.[5] Not only was Rietveld seen as one of the foremost representatives of this movement but, unlike Oud, he had never turned his back on De Stijl.

The Making of De Stijl
The De Stijl exhibitions at the Stedelijk Museum in Amsterdam in 1951 and at the Museum of Modern Art (MoMA) in New York in 1952 were not initiated by the Dutch, but took place at the special request of the American museum. It was a direct result of a remarkable development in previous decades.[6] New York replaced pre-war Paris as the focal point of developments in the visual arts. As American abstract art came to be seen as the true heir to the pre-war avant-garde, the input of Eastern Europe and the international communist movement faded into the background. From this point of view, the avant-garde was inextricably linked with the Free West. In the 1930s and 1940s Nazi Germany had posed the biggest threat, but during the Cold War it was replaced by Russia. A similar process took place within the disciplines of architecture and design. Paradoxically, the left-wing avant-garde's passionate faith in industrial production for the benefit of the masses proved to be an added weapon, because this ideal was being realized in the capitalist economy of the Free West.[7]

Rietveld appears to have been unaware of this 'battle for the hearts', which triggered an ideological reorientation of European artists and intellectuals on many fronts.[8] In 1947 and 1949 he visited the USA and, like so many other Europeans, was deeply impressed with its material wealth and the American way of life.[9] On 5 May 1947 he wrote from Holland (Michigan) to Truus Schröder:

> dear Truus . . . I forgot to tell you about this book that I bought and read whenever I have a moment – it's a novel about the new architecture – very well written . . . I'm completely engrossed in it, because I recognize many of our own aspirations in it and compare them. I will have to return to New York soon for an appointment with the dir. of the Mus. o Mod. Arts [Director of the Museum of Modern Arts] – because that's far more important than this work . . . What strikes me is the equality of the people, no servility, there is no need – they need each other – and the funny thing is: . . . what appears to be forgotten in the Netherl. [Netherlands] the abstract style appears to be in demand in some circles here; they are ready for it and seem to know how to work it much better than we do.[10]

[3] Slothouber 1997, 16-20. The issue dragged on for two years.

[4] Willem Sandberg, general director of the Stedelijk Museum Amsterdam, later recalled that they tried to fix Rietveld up with jobs by giving him commissions for exhibition designs. Leeuw Marcar 2004, 274-275.

[5] Jaffé 1956.

[6] Guilbert 1983.

[7] The 'kitchen debate' between Richard Nixon, then Vice President of the USA, and the Russian leader Nikita Khrushchev in 1959 is a famous moment in this psychological and cultural conflict: standing in front of an American kitchen at the 'American National Exhibition' in Moscow in 1959, Nixon challenged his Russian counterpart to compete not in an arms race but in the production of consumer goods. For the literature on this occasion see: Crowley and Pavitt 2008.

[8] Guilbert's first chapter is tellingly called 'New York, 1935-1941: The De-Marxization of the Intelligentsia'. Guilbert 1983, 17-47.

[9] De Rijk 2007, 360-386.

[10] Van Zijl 1998-1999. Rietveld was referring to Ayn Rand's *The Fountainhead*, which was first published in 1943 (NAI, Oud archive, inv. no. B 107). The book is a great example of how elements of the modernist jargon, the modernist visual imagery and the modernist ideology are used for a conservative, purely individualistic philosophy.

[11] NAI, Van Eesteren archive, inv. no. X760. See also Broekhuizen and Van Moorsel, who have described in detail the roles played by Oud and Nelly van Doesburg respectively in the realization of the De Stijl exhibitions. Broekhuizen 2000, 285-298; Van Moorsel 2000, 239-245. D.F. Lunsingh Scheurleer was secretary of the Rijkscommissie voor de Musea (national commission for museums).

[12] Barr 1974, 140-162: 141. 'De Stijl, one of the longest lived and most influential groups of modern artists, was formed in Holland during the war.'

[13] SMA, De Stijl exhibition archive 1951, letter from Johnson to Sandberg and copy of letter from Sandberg to Johnson 7 and 13 August 1947.

[14] Jaffé 1956.

[15] Van Moorsel 2000, 239.

[16] Meeting at J.H. van den Broek's home in Rotterdam on 11 June 1948, concerning the organization of an exhibition about the De Stijl group. SMA, De Stijl exhibition archive, folder 3430.

Rietveld was in the USA to design the 'Centenary Holland' exhibition, a commission that he did not enjoy very much, as the same letter shows. His appointment at the Museum of Modern Art (MoMA) was with Philip Johnson and concerned the De Stijl exhibition that Johnson had discussed a few months earlier with Hans van Weerden-Griek, head of exhibitions and visual education at The Netherlands Information Bureau (New York).[11] In a letter dated 5 February 1947 to D.F. Lunsingh Scheurleer, inspector-general of movable heritage, Van Weerden-Griek reports on the conversation.

> I showed Mr Johnson this material [about modern Dutch architecture], which I regret to say, did not impress him very much. As you possibly know, the Museum of Modern Art is always 'very avant garde' in its attitude, and they always try to obtain exhibitions which prove their particular view point . . . It is felt in this country that one of the most important and far reaching influences that Dutch thought and art has had in the contemporary world emanated from the 'De Styl' group . . . It would be of major interest to the Museum of Modern Art to make an important historical exhibition which would not only relate the history of this movement, but of their influences throughout the world in other media, such as architecture, painting, sculpture, industrial design, etc. etc.

This is in fact the view taken by Alfred Barr, Director of Collections at MoMA, who in his book *Cubism and Abstract Art* credited De Stijl with an important role in the development of modern art.[12]

The Dutch were only too happy to accept the suggestion from New York. The exhibition was to be a collaborative project between MoMA and the Stedelijk Museum Amsterdam. However, the two parties failed to reach an agreement about the content of the exhibition. The correspondence between Philip Johnson and Willem Sandberg shows that the main area of contention was the Dutch character of De Stijl. To Johnson De Stijl was of major international interest and he did not want the show to be reduced to a 'one-country exhibition'. Sandberg wanted an exhibition that would present De Stijl as '"the Dutch contribution to the new architecture", to begin with the Style-movement and to finish about 1935'.[13] The theoretical underpinnings for the Dutch character of De Stijl have been provided by the likes of H.L.C. Jaffé, deputy director of the Stedelijk Museum and Sandberg's right-hand man.[14] The two parties agreed to compromise and produce two editions. Philip Johnson was to curate the New York exhibition while in Amsterdam the responsibility lay with a commission chaired by J.H. van den Broek.[15] The Amsterdam version was officially known as 'a pilot'. During the first meeting at Van den Broek's home, J.J.P. Oud and Cornelis van Eesteren questioned the point of such an exhibition. They had no time to join in the preparations, but were willing to give advice and open up their archives. Rietveld believed 'that the De Stijl group had been abandoned too soon and that it was not just a historical phenomenon, but that it continued to influence young architects. He would be happy to draw up a design for the exhibition and to implement it.'[16]

The proposal that Rietveld submitted a few months later was called 'Outline of a design for: an exhibition of works by members of the "De Stijl Group" and their influence on contemporary architecture and other plastic arts, at "The Museum of Modern Art" in New York, USA'. In the document, dated 1 October 1948, he writes:

> The only way de stijl could break free from the completely worn-out tradition of the time was by establishing foundations for the visual arts as a profession, by specialisation, e.g. the visual arts free from literary influences. Literature free from visual elements, colour, form and conceptualization of space separate and independent from trends; in order to achieve this, the colour sensations would have to be reduced to primary sensations (primary colours and forms – a primary sense of space). Most saw this not as an end in itself, but as a truly new idiom.

Following a description of the themes and the objects to be shown, he concludes with the sentence: 'The whole must be composed like free-form architecture (pure spatial art, a balance between planes and rods in the 3 dimensions).'[17] Rietveld's stance here reflects his own development rather than the ideas of De Stijl, as disseminated in the eponymous journal for instance.

When the plans were fleshed out three years later, the other members of the committee criticized the timeline, the selection of works and the presentation. It was an implicit rejection of Rietveld's view of De Stijl. His 'white room' came in for particular criticism. This room 'will reflect the idea of De Stijl; white models, up on the walls, floor plan in relief (white)', Rietveld's proposal read.[18] Van Eesteren, who did not attend this meeting, voiced such fierce opposition to the white room that the idea was dropped, to Rietveld's displeasure. Later he scribbled the following comment on a draft of the museum texts: 'dear Jaffé . . . everything seems clear and attractive and will certainly contribute to a good reception . . . I still regret not forcing through the model room; did you ever hear from Van Eesteren what he thinks of the exhibition?'[19]

On another point the dispute was settled in Rietveld's favour. On 5 May 1951 he listed for Van den Broek which original works had been preserved and concluded:

> This is it. Putting these on the wall and in 5 display cases would create the impression of the tarnished remains of a hastily repressed, pathetic, dilettante and exaggerated attempt to pave the way for a new style; we certainly cannot exhibit this disgrace. (except for the paintings, which look reasonably good).[20]

He therefore proposed to restore a number of pieces, to set up the exhibition in the spirit of De Stijl and to conclude it with the contemporary architecture that had taken its inspiration from De Stijl. He developed these ideas in a detailed floor plan and a model. Rietveld failed to mention that a great many pieces would have to be reproduced. The bill for the replicas – an estimated 2,500 guilders – would be footed by the Stedelijk Museum, which would get to keep the pieces afterwards. Again, this met with fierce opposition from Van Eesteren, who believed that the exhibition ought to be distinctly historical and could therefore only feature historically authentic material. Sandberg reproached Van Eesteren for making a decent representation of Van Doesburg's work impossible and allowed Rietveld to go ahead.[21]

[17] Typescript, NAI, Van den Broek archive, inv. no. 586.1.

[18] Minutes of the meeting of the preparatory committee for an exhibition about the so-called De Stijl group, held on Saturday 28 April at 12.30 at the Stedelijk Museum in Amsterdam. NAI, Van den Broek archive, inv. no. 586.1.

[19] Typescript De Stijl 1917-1931. SMA, De Stijl exhibition archive, folder 3429.

[20] SMA, De Stijl exhibition archive, folder 3427, letter Rieetveld to van den Broek, 5 May 1951.

[21] NAI, Van Eesteren archive, inv. no. X 760, letter from Sandberg to Van Eesteren, 1 July 1951.

G.Th. Rietveld, Model for the design of the exhibition 'De Stijl 1917-1928'
RSA, Utrecht

G.Th. Rietveld, Drawing of the floor plan for the exhibition 'De Stijl 1917-1928', Stedelijk Museum Amsterdam, featuring the white room, 1951
Pencil on paper
RSA, Utrecht

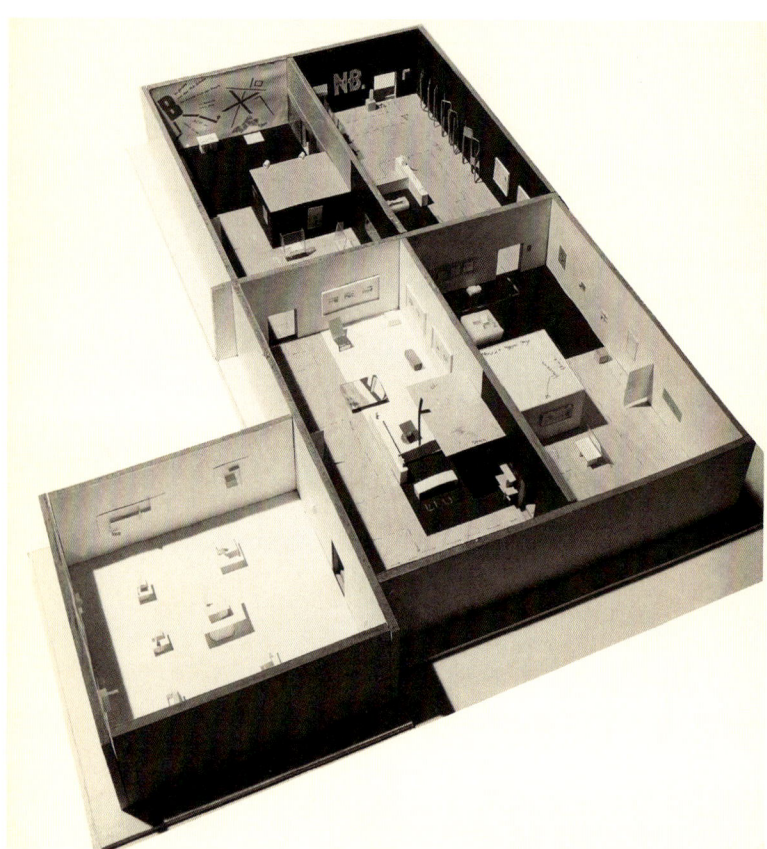

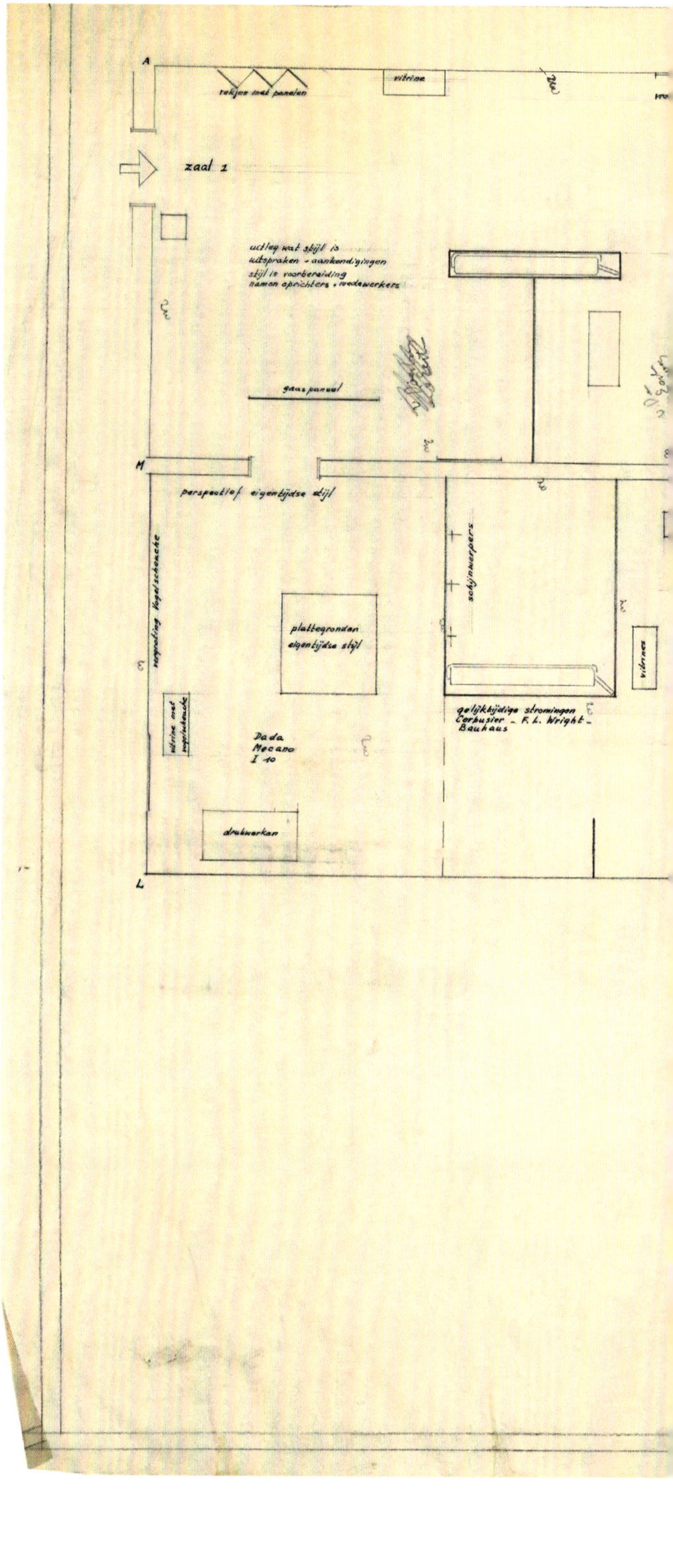

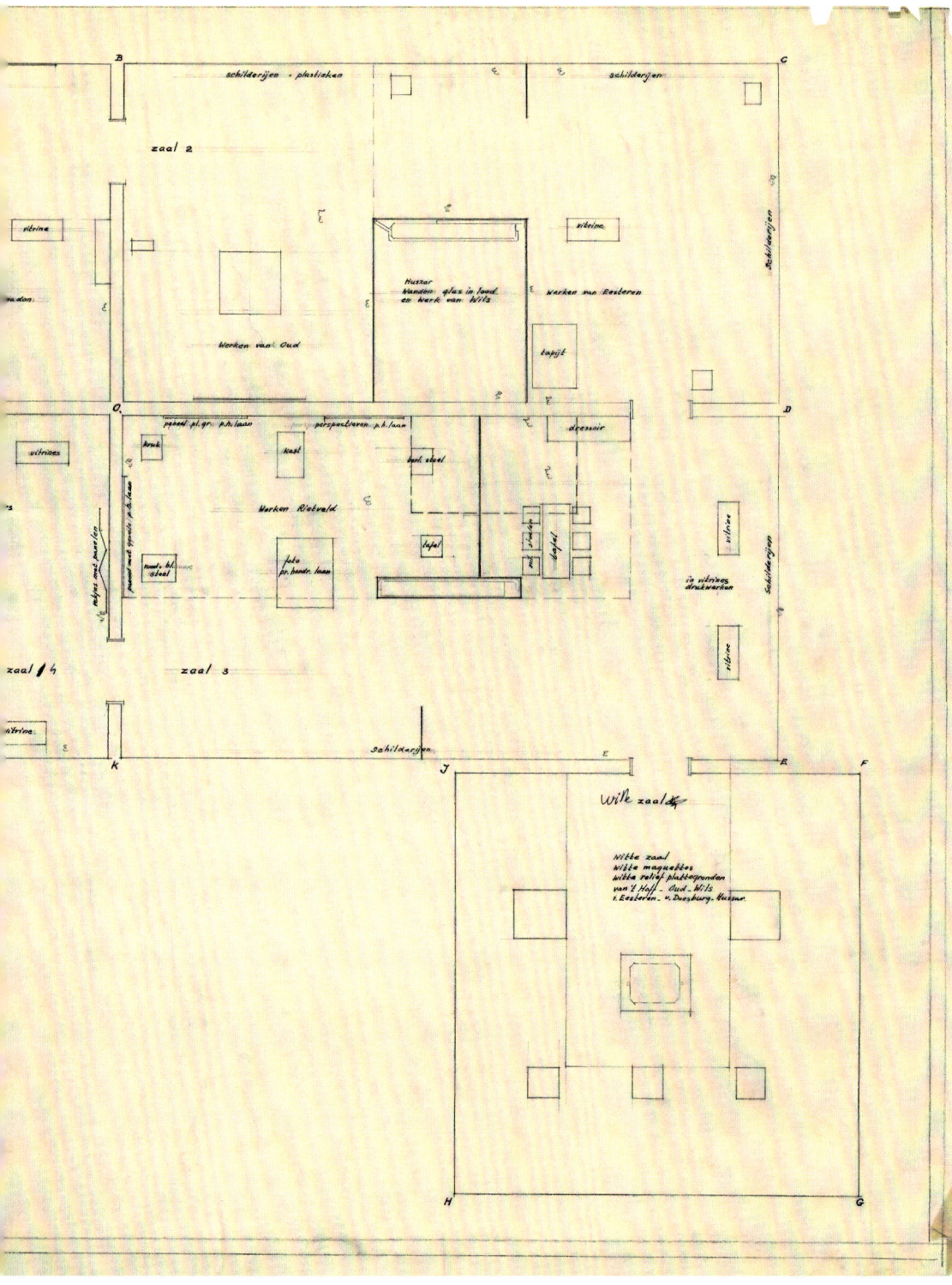

G.Th. Rietveld, Design for the exhibition
'De Stijl 1917-1928', Museum of Modern
Art, New York, 1951
RSA, Utrecht

G.Th. Rietveld, Sideboard, reconstruction for the De Stijl exhibition, Stedelijk Museum Amsterdam, 1951
Birch, 104 x 200 x 45 cm
RSA/CMU, Utrecht

[22] 'Brief report on the meeting concerning the organization of De Stijl exhibitions in Italy and Germany in 1960/61, held on 21 January 1960 at the Ministry of Education, Culture and Science'. NAI, Oud archive, inv. no. 27.

[23] RSA, letter P. Bucarelli to Rietveld, 22 October 1960. Thanks to R. Dettingmeijer who drew my attention to this letter.

In the end the exhibition layout followed Rietveld's proposed configuration of planes and rods. Quite a few items were reconstructed. The buffet of 1919, the model of a dowel joint, a miniaturized version of the modular cupboard from the Schröder House and the silk-screen prints on which the articulation and colours of the interiors and façades of the Schröder House were reproduced were not authentic but reproductions and propagated Rietveld's own view of De Stijl.

Tailored versions of the De Stijl exhibition of 1951-1952 toured several more countries around the world in the years that followed and Rietveld was nearly always involved in the design and layout. This proved to be no guarantee of quality. Van Eesteren was no longer interested after the exhibition in Amsterdam in 1951 and in due course Oud became fed up as well. A meeting about possible De Stijl exhibitions in Italy and Germany took place on 21 January 1960. A.M.W.J. Hammacher, the director of Rijksmuseum Kröller-Müller, chaired the meeting, which was attended by Rietveld as well as Oud, Van Eesteren and Jaffé. The three architects still did not see eye to eye and all three questioned the point of organizing a De Stijl exhibition. Rietveld eventually came round when Hammacher suggested that 'the existing differences will be clearer and easier to understand if we show the individual developments side by side. Would Messrs Jaffé and Rietveld be prepared to take responsibility for such a design?' They agreed to do so.[22] The result was an exhibition that featured a selection from the complete oeuvres of Oud, Rietveld and Van Eesteren, up to and including their most recent projects, while the other members of De Stijl were only represented by works from the period 1914-1930. The bickering about the plans extended to the design for the poster. On 22 October Rietveld received a request, via the Dutch Institute in Rome, from the director of the Galleria Nazionale d'Arte Moderna, where the exhibition was to be held. She asked for the year 1930 to be dropped from the design, 'because the artists who were part of De Stijl as well as the De Stijl experts are in utter disagreement about the year in which the movement "died".'[23] Rietveld readily complied with the request.

De Stijl as Style

G.Th. Rietveld and H. Schröder, Coloured collotype of the eastern façade of the Schröder House, Utrecht, 1951
Paint, paper, cardboard, 49.5 x 64.5 cm
RSA, Utrecht

G.Th. Rietveld, Drawing of the interior of the Schröder House, with the living and dining area, c. 1951
13.5 x 16 cm
RSA, Utrecht

G.Th. Rietveld and H. Schröder, Coloured collotype of the interior of the Schröder House, with the girls' sleeping area, 1951
Paint on thick grey paper, 49 x 65 cm
RSA, Utrecht

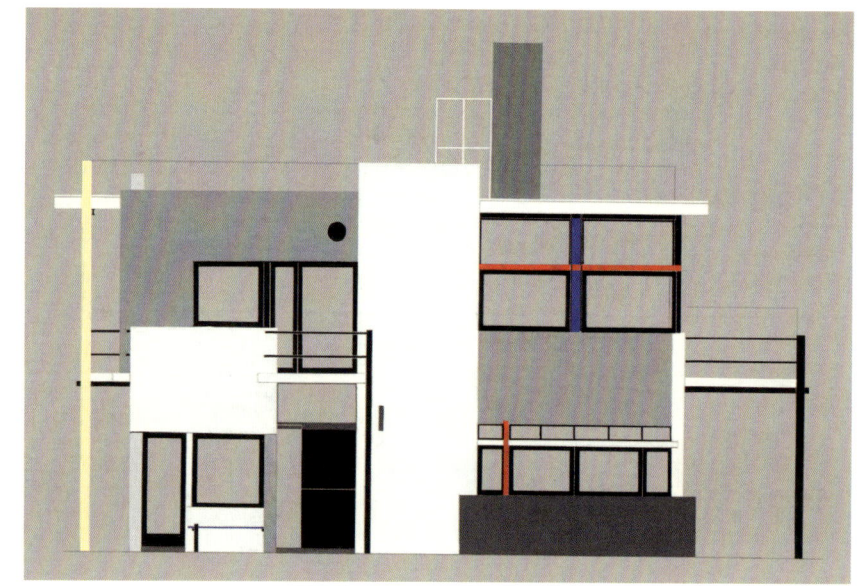

De Stijl as Style

G.Th. Rietveld, Design of exhibition poster for the exhibition 'De Stijl 1917-1930', Galleria Nazionale d'Arte Moderna, Rome, 1960
Paint on paper, 72 x 72 cm
RSA, Utrecht

G.Th. Rietveld, Exhibition poster for the exhibition 'De Stijl 1917-1930', Galleria Nazionale d'Arte Moderna, Rome, 1960
Paint on paper, 72 x 72 cm
RSA, Utrecht

Gerrit Rietveld in front of the entrance to the Dutch Biennial Pavilion, 1954
RSA, Utrecht

24 Overy 1988, 61.

25 Giedion 1956, 88.

26 Rietveld, lecture Delft 1959, op. cit. (note 1).

27 See R. Dettingmeijer's article in this publication.

28 Singelenberg points this out in: P. Singelenberg, 'Ruimte, licht en kunst', in: Doctor 1995, 9-12: 10.

29 Overy 1988, 84.

30 See Hielkje Zijlstra's article in this publication.

Rietveld's 'Stijl'

Rietveld's involvement in the De Stijl exhibitions had a remarkable effect. He had always maintained that De Stijl represented a phase in the renaissance of the visual arts and architecture, but until the 1950s he frequently distanced himself from the movement and emphasized the autonomous development of his work. Thus, he used to present the Schröder House as a logical extension of his furniture experiments in earlier years.[24] When De Stijl took centre stage again he was more or less forced to articulate his own ideas about the meaning of the movement. During the preparations for the De Stijl exhibitions in Amsterdam and New York he adopted a very clear stance. He was indignant when, at a preliminary conference in 1951, Sigfried Giedion suggested a link between the Dutch mentality and tradition and the formal aspects of the work of Mondrian and Van Doesburg.[25] He countered it with the idiosyncratic vision of architecture that he had formulated and published back in the 1920s. From the 1950s onwards he would present these views under the heading '"De Stijl" as an attempt at universal formal syntax'.[26] But this view of the matter was not taken seriously by anyone. For decades, any discussion of De Stijl would follow the path mapped out by Barr, Giedion and Jaffé.[27]

But more significant than Rietveld's views on De Stijl is the effect that the renewed interest in the movement had on his reputation as an architect and on his work of the last ten years of his life. It looks as if Rietveld took inspiration from the 'stylistic tools' of his earlier work. Both the stacking of geometric volumes, as seen in the Goud- en Zilversmidscompagnie (Association of Gold and Silversmiths, 1921) as well as the seemingly free-floating planes of the Schröder House, and the primary colours return in his late oeuvre.

The first commission to clearly reflect Rietveld's rehabilitation as an architect is that for the construction of the Dutch pavilion in Venice (1953-1954).[28] Its design is based on three short rectangular blocks and one longer block at right angles with one of the shorter elements. The steps leading up to the entry zone are placed at an invitingly oblique angle. The approach harks back to Rietveld's early shop conversions. Not inviting but nevertheless a fine example of the stacking of geometric volumes is the front elevation of the house in Ilpendam (1957-1958). Rietveld, incidentally, considered it to be one of his best houses, not because of its closed façade, but because of the rear elevation that was made almost entirely of glass and offered a panoramic view of the polder.[29] The sculpture pavilion for Sonsbeek of 1955 brings to mind the Berlin Chair. The pavilion consists of low, partially closed galleries, high walls and a flat roof. It is a brilliant, justly praised configuration of open, half-open and closed planes, varying in size and structure, intimate but always in harmony with its surroundings. During the latter half of the 1950s the De Stijl colours also staged a cheerful comeback in Rietveld's work. In the press room for the Unesco building (1957-1958) in Paris Rietveld reverted to a tried-and-tested recipe: the application of primary colours to articulate and define an interior space.

This is not to say that Rietveld merely repeated himself after 1955. He produced variations on the visual idiom that he had established around 1920, but he also took inspiration from stylistic elements from other modernist architects.[30] This resulted in a form of architecture that evokes

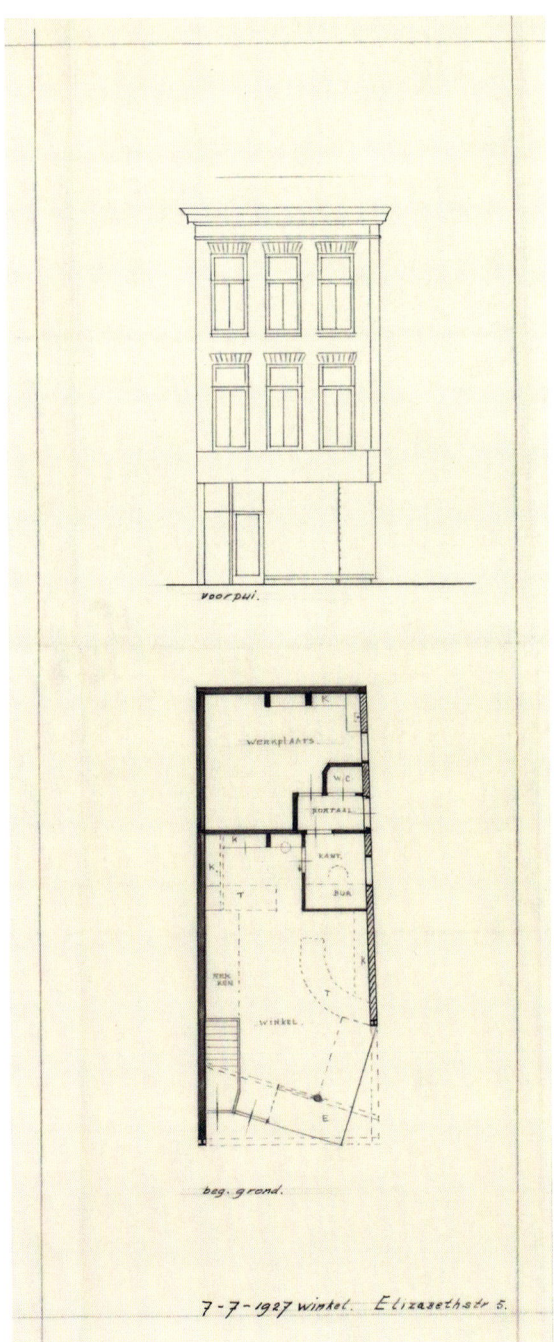

G.Th. Rietveld, Conversion of shop and shoemaker's workshop Record, Utrecht, 1927
Photograph 1927 and drawing featuring the façade and floor plan
Pencil and ink on tracing paper, 45 x 32 cm
RSA, Utrecht

De Stijl as Style

G.Th. Rietveld, Sonsbeek Pavilion,
Arnhem, 1955
RSA, Utrecht

G.Th. Rietveld, Berlin Chair, 1923
Five-ply wood, beech, paint,
106.2 x 75.3 x 58.3 cm
CMU, Utrecht

G.Th. Rietveld, Layout press room
UNESCO building, Paris, 1957-1958
Illustration from brochure
RSA, Utrecht

G.Th. Rietveld, Conversion and interior design of Steltman Jeweller's, Paleisstraat 2, The Hague, 1963-1965
RSA, Utrecht

[31] Ibelings 1991.

[32] Van Dijk 1990, 8-12.

[33] The commission dates from 1963, the shop was completed in 1965.

the halcyon days of modernism while at the same time carrying a distinctive, post-war signature. This particular incarnation of Rietveld sits very well with the ideological development that turned modernism into a value-free source of inspiration.[31] It is a style, according to architecture critic Hans van Dijk, which is still taught at Dutch schools.[32]

This formal approach has also come to dominate the interpretation and presentation of Rietveld's work. In 1963 Rietveld refurbished jewellery shop Steltman in The Hague.[33] He designed new furniture and display cases for the sales area, all in black and white. Two chairs – each other's mirror image – stand in front of the counter, which is finished in white leather. When two people come to choose a piece of jewellery they sit down on the chairs on either side of the black surface on the counter on which the jewellery is displayed. By entering into a relationship with each other and with the surrounding space, the two autonomous elements together form a kind of open-structured sofa.

The Steltman Chair has since assumed a life of its own, independent from this interior. The chair has undergone the same metamorphosis as the slatted armchair, Rietveld's first revolutionary design. Isolated from their original purpose and context, these pieces of furniture are presented by passionate admirers as pure sculpture and Rietveld as the eternal standard bearer of De Stijl. ◆

De Stijl as Style

Wright, Frank Lloyd
253, 254

America
252-256

Modern Movement
253, 254

Approaches to Rietveld

Functionalism
254

Red-Blue Chair
253, 256

'Cubism and Abstract Art'
254

Anthony Alofsin

Rietveld's Influence in America: The Chair and the House

Gerrit Rietveld's impact on contemporary architecture and architecture history in the USA shows the problematic nature of influence itself.[1] Once asserted we believe influence is a reliable explanation of the transmission of ideas. But proving influence is a more complex phenomenon, a condition without certitude or verifiability. Rietveld's Red-Blue Chair, first made unpainted in 1918, published in 1919, and polychromed by 1923, and the Schröder House, built in Utrecht in 1924, are standard icons in surveys of modern architecture. Their images have been transmitted via reproductions to architects who, though increasingly unfamiliar with the history of modern architecture, recognize both the name and the images, and see in them the core elements of modernism: abstraction, materiality and planarity. However, the fundamental generative idea of Rietveld's work, which emphasized sensorial experience through the perception of clear forms, has remained relatively obscure as has the full range of his architectural production, which continued up to his death in 1964. In other words, a paradox is operative with Rietveld: among the most three dimensional of designers, his contribution has been reduced to a virtual one dimension that focuses on a chair and a single building.

A number of factors contribute to the paradox of Rietveld's influence outside of the Netherlands. He only published his writings in Dutch so the theories were little known. The particular nature of the historiography of modern architecture, the first phase in the 1920s and 1930s and the second in the 1970s and 1980s, gave primacy to individuals who fit the polemic of the moment, and ignored those who did not. But more germane is the fact that Rietveld was a victim of early success.[2] The immediate recognition of the chair and the house as the physical manifestations of the long-sought new language of modern architecture provided him with a role in the Modern Movement, but his role was that of a secondary player. His innovation was folded into the De Stijl movement, and his work and ideas were absorbed in the general history of modern architecture and in architectural practice generally. While this condition described the European scene it also characterizes Rietveld's reception in the USA.

Before looking at Rietveld's influence in America, the potential connections between Frank Lloyd Wright and the Dutch Modern Movement need brief consideration.[3] H.P. Berlage's role in introducing Wright not only to the Dutch, but more broadly to German speaking areas of Europe has been established.[4] It is tempting to make assertions of influence of Wright on the Dutch, but these claims tend to be facile and speculative. While Rietveld must have known of Wright's rectilinear and planar aesthetic, through, as some writers claim, his connection to Robert van 't Hoff, Wright's ardent imitator, Rietveld's design orientation also benefited from precedents of furniture by Berlage as well as his training under P.J.C. Klaarhamer. While visual similarities exist, drawing a straight line between Wright's rectilinear furniture and the work of Rietveld is reductive.[5] Conversely, we should ask if Rietveld influenced Wright, as the American was closely in touch with Dutch Modern Movement, particularly through its expressionist wing spearheaded by H.Th. Wijdeveld. Rietveld's direct impact on Wright is unlikely as he had developed his planar aesthetic long before Rietveld's initial furniture designs, and Wright was moving in different aesthetic and technical directions during the 1920s.[6] More likely, Wright, Rietveld, Oud and even Le Corbusier were working to a large degree in parallel. Rather than simplistically influence one or the other, they sought similar and dissimilar goals, all of which, shared, in varying degrees, interests in abstraction, a social programme for architecture, and visions of creating a new modern way of life.

Instead of exerting a direct influence in America, Rietveld's work was transmitted through a process of absorption that mirrored the larger development of De Stijl itself as it was consumed by the Bauhaus

[1] On influence, see Alofsin 1993, 1-8. I thank Elise Wasser, my research assistant, who compiled material for this essay.

[2] For a similar perspective, see Ibelings 2006.

[3] On Wright and the Dutch, A. Alofsin, 'Frank Lloyd Wright and the Dutch Connection', in: Bergeijk 2008; A. Alofsin, 'Wright, Influence, and the World at Large', in: Eggener 2004, 281-293; Alofsin 1999.

[4] Alofsin 1993, 305, and note 40, 327.

[5] Warnke 1991, 120.

[6] For Wright's expansion of his system of rotational design from building to ground plans, see Alofsin 1993, 280-286; for his Textile Block designs in the 1920s, see Sweeney 1994 and De Long 1996.

[7] Brown 1958, 33; the exhibition catalogue *In Focus: Gerrit Rietveld, Designer*, Hartford, CT (Wadsworth Atheneum Museum of Modern Art) 1980 provides a date of 1920 with note that the original with an additional light was designed for the Maarssen Clinic of Dr. Hartog, and that the three-lamp version was placed by Rietveld in the Schröder House in 1924.

[8] For the complex history of the International Style exhibition, see Riley and Perrella 1992. Riley indicates that a photograph of Rietveld's Schröder house did appear in a second section of the exhibition, 'The Extent of Modern Architecture', as part of work influenced by the European avant-garde; for a reproduction of the house, see 171. Initiated in June 1930 with Henry-Russell Hitchcock and Philip Johnson as a plan for a popular book on modern architecture, the proposal expanded at MoMA into an exhibition. It opened as 'Modern Architecture – International Exhibition', on 9 February 1932 and traveled. For Hitchcock's assessment of the Schröder House in 1929, see Brown 1958, 58-59.

[9] In the accompanying book, *The International Style*, Oud's work remained primary, but Brinkman and Van Der Vlugt's Van Nelle Tobacco, Tea and Coffee Factory in Rotterdam (1928-1930) was added.

[10] For Barr's exhibition in 1936, see Overy 1994.

[11] For a review of Brown's book, see Hitchcock 1959; for Rietveld's theories, see Brown 1965.

[12] Exhibitions included, 'De Stijl 1917-1928', Museum of Modern Art, New York, 1952; 'De Stijl: 1918-1931', Walker Art Center, Minneapolis, Hirschhorn Museum and Sculpture Garden, Washington, DC, 1982; 'Gerrit Rietveld: A Centenary', Barry Freedman Ltd., New York, Struve Gallery, Chicago, 1988, Dayton Art Institute, 1989.

[13] Johnson 1980.

[14] See Ibelings 2006.

[15] Trachtenberg and Hyman 1986, 526.

under Gropius during 1920s and by the invention of the International Style in the 1930s. Van Doesburg's assault on the Bauhaus and his efforts to co-opt the Bauhaus student body are known, but the full extent of the Bauhaus's appropriation of De Stijl aesthetics and principles is not fully grasped. Gropius's triumph was not the broad dissemination of a teaching method, but the conflation of multiple strands of the Modern Movement into a popular conception, which reigns today, of a Bauhaus Style. Certainly, such as style could not have existed without the contributions of De Stijl. With respect to Rietveld, his contributions beyond the chair and the house were quickly ignored. Gropius is identified as the designer of the lamps in the Bauhaus director's office in Weimar in 1923, but they are derived directly from Rietveld's designs of 1922 for a hanging lamp, which was published in *De Stijl* in 1923.[7]

By 1932, the Schröder House had begun its canonization, but Rietveld was already on the road to marginality. Although Henry Russell Hitchcock mentioned the house in his *Modern Architecture* of 1929, he, Alfred Barr, Jr and Philip Johnson omitted Rietveld from the main galleries of the landmark exhibition at the Museum of Modern Art that introduced the style to America.[8] Rietveld's work did appear in the exhibition catalogue, *Modern Architects*, and the accompanying book, *The International Style*. The curators assigned J.J.P. Oud the role of representing the Dutch movement.[9] Illustrations of the chair and the house did appear in Barr's 1936 exhibition at the Museum of Modern Art, 'Cubism and Abstract Art', which served both to confirm and to limit Rietveld's contribution.[10]

In the post-war period a broader interest in Rietveld was subsumed into a vague and general perception in the USA that the Dutch movement had lost its cutting edge. The stagnation of Rietveld's reputation continued until 1958 when the American Theodore M. Brown published the first monograph on the architect. Written in Utrecht originally as Brown's doctoral dissertation while Rietveld was alive, the book remains a remarkably perceptive account of the architect's ideas, his individuality and the broad scope of this work, including a full range of his buildings into the 1950s. Brown succeeded in revealing not only Rietveld's theory, which Brown perceptibly saw as unevolving from 1919 to 1964, but also a far more extensive corpus of work than anyone outside the Netherlands knew of.[11]

Regardless of the fact that Rietveld's interest was in form, the psychology of perception and architecture's improving the quality of life, he was perpetually presented as a functionalist at a time when functionalism reigned as the only viable modernism. His work was seem as emblematic of concrete, glass and steel, but materials were only a means of manifesting an ideology, not as an end in themselves as they were in reductive functionalist practices.

When exhibited in the USA from the 1950s onwards, his work appeared under the rubric of De Stijl or furniture design.[12] Typical of the tendency was the Wadsworth Atheneum's exhibition in 1980. In his preface to the exhibition catalogue, Phillip Johnson reiterated the standard lumping together of Rietveld with neoplasticism and De Stijl and pointed to his furniture as the most influential factor on art, architecture and design.[13] Even with the appearance of critical histories of modern architecture, Rietveld received the same treatment, focusing on the chair, the house, De Stijl and materiality.[14] General histories of architecture repeated a similar line as seen in Marvin Trachtenberg and Isabelle Hyman's obligatory bow to the Schröder House in their survey *Architecture from Prehistory to Post-Modernism/The Western Tradition*. After a formalist description of the Schröder House, the authors assert: 'Rietveld was neither an artist nor an architect, but a gifted avant-garde furniture designer who took up architecture. At the Schröder House we observe how much the cabinet maker he remained.'[15]

The perception of Rietveld in America began, however, to change later in the

Gerrit Rietveld with model of a core house, 1941
RSA, Utrecht

[16] Closer scrutiny and fresh scholarship helped sharpen our understanding of the De Stijl movement. See, for instance, Blotkamp 1986.

[17] Troy 1988, 8-10: 9.

[18] Küper and Van Zijl 1992; The exhibition 'Gerrit Rietveld 1888-1964' was organized by the Centraal Museum Utrecht and the Netherlands Architecture Institute, Rotterdam, in Utrecht, opened in Utrecht 1992-1993 and traveled to Paris, Centre Pompidou, 23 June-27 September 1993.

1980s. As postmodernism and deconstructivism waned a void opened allowing a reconsideration of modernism that saw many forgotten figures re-emerge and a broader interest in secondary players like Rietveld.[16] While the 1988 exhibition 'Gerrit Rietveld: A Centenary', organized by Barry Freedman, focused on Rietveld's designs – not his architecture – it had glimmers of a revision of the fixed view. In presenting over 30 different designs it intended to move interest beyond the Red-Blue Chair, and Nancy Troy, the American scholar whose career has dramatically expanded an awareness of De Stijl outside of the Netherlands, provided a fresh perception on Rietveld: his appeal comes from his furniture bridging the gap between 'High art and mere design.'[17] In 1992 the first major international exhibition on Rietveld, opening in Utrecht and travelling to Paris, provided an opportunity to look more comprehensively at Rietveld's career, and the exhibition catalogue served as a fully updated reference on the architect and his work.[18]

Despite these expansions in the awareness of Rietveld's oeuvre, the Red-Blue moved from being a commercial commodity to a fetish object. In the context of contemporary architectural practice, there is no way to parse the complexities of neo-modernism finely enough to show Rietveld's distinct influence. His ideas and aesthetic remain conflated within the general iterations of ideas that had roots in purist and neoplasticist practices. The Bauhaus, Le Corbusier, Oud and a panoply of functionalists are currently merged into a vague neo-modernism. Beyond metaphormic blobs, the old modernism has been repackaged to define modern as anything with flat roofs, planarity, great expenses of glass, and material and structural bravura. Somewhere deep within are the innovative works of Rietveld motivated by a unitary concept.

The revision of the historiography of modern architecture now enters a third phase in the midst of a disruptive global economic crisis that requires a refocusing of the lens through which we look at the history of modern architecture in the twentieth century. Historians and critics will revise the revision of an earlier generation of critical histories. The time is appropriate, therefore, for the full examination of Rietveld's accomplishments, encompassing not only furniture, but his theories and decades of architectural production. This ongoing reassessment may even work itself into the architectural discourse in America which searches for heroes to fill the void as star architects decline and the profession finds itself in an economic tail spin. As architects lose clients and seek to redefine themselves, the skills of a mere furniture maker may be more valuable than ever. ◆

Ole Bouman

Honest Designs

Considered by many during his lifetime to be a remarkable man, Rietveld was also quite familiar, one of us. His genius lay in the fact that he managed to turn this familiarity into something quite remarkable. Not for him the usual hypocrisy of pretending that the special is quite ordinary; that the design merely honours the wishes or the tastes of the ordinary people. No, throughout his life he adhered to the belief that the ordinary can take on a sublime quality if it is handled with extreme honesty; don't spin a story to make it look better, but produce a design that is so fundamental that it allows people to become part of your story.

His outlook on life was: know your limitations and respect them. It is rare for an artist to build such a splendid oeuvre on such an acute awareness of sin. It informs every single aspect of his work, beginning with his work ethic. By working hard you make the most of life; you owe it to your creator. And above all, you must do it yourself; never accept more work than you can manage on your own. Passing the buck to someone else is a sign of sloth or pride or both and is to be avoided at all times. When you make something, do not use more means than strictly required. There is no need. And do not make it more complicated than necessary. Keep it simple and straightforward. Show everybody how it is made, so that it is easy to repair or reproduce. The design is really nothing but a way of leading by example. The users of his objects are certainly not inferior to the artist. Let alone a necessary evil, as some designers would argue. On the contrary, the user is the judge. The user is in fact a higher power, because in use a truth emerges with which no aesthetic pleasure can compete. Though extended use the user ultimately knows everything there is to know about the quality of the designer. In order not to be found wanting, the artist/designer must do his utmost.

The work is first and foremost for the here and now. It proves its worth in everyday life, not in a fancy story or a compelling theory, which is why there are none. Every now and then a few words are said about the work, but never in justification or self-promotion. It is the way it is. Don't be fooled. Don't represent things better than they are; honesty is the best policy. And that means no personality cult, no clique of young students or over-zealous media that hang on the master's every word like an oracle. None of that. The designer keeps a low profile and does what he does best: designing what is needed. He does not make a big deal out of it; he does not have to save the world; he does not make any claims that he cannot substantiate with the work of his own hands. In that respect his entire life's work is a powerful stance against the (oh so) human vice of exaggeration.

The Dutch reader has been presented with quite a few truisms by now. Is this Rietveld – decent, austere, pragmatic, frugal and industrious – the Dutch national character personified? No, this is only one side of him. His personality was multifaceted. But as an art-historical icon of the twentieth century Rietveld gives this country exactly what it has needed again and again since the late Middle Ages: righteous men who draw on the gift of art or of eloquence to urge the congregation to think. This is the level of austerity that makes us proud: not as an end in itself, but as a means to achieving a spiritual purity that gives meaning to life. And with every piece of furniture and with every building Rietveld first and foremost aspired to give meaning. Without being fully aware of it, he captured his own people. He made architectural genre works, which do their job with every daily encounter. And at the same time they admonish: wealth is in the mind, not in one's purse or in aesthetics. This wealth is also the most democratic thing there is, because everybody can have good thoughts.

In recent years the above script for understanding our culture and its testators has lost some of its popularity. We were becoming fed up with the reformation ethics, even when it was aesthetically translated into an accomplished and autonomous oeuvre that appeared to be free of religion.

Rietveld and employees in his studio at
55 Oudegracht, Utrecht, c. 1958
RSA, Utrecht

Art was scared to death of dogma. De Stijl – this was something for the masses or for merchandizing. Besides, the postmodern frame of mind preferred baroque hybrid forms and hybrid colours to the simplicity of the platonic, primary essences. But Rietveld's work has since taken on a new relevance. Those who let all the aforementioned virtues sink in become aware of the underlying and still pertinent message to mankind: stop doing everything on credit!

Suddenly Rietveld's work regains its reputation as a vital expression of the wealth embedded in poverty, or at least in unpretentiousness. For beauty and inspiration you need not dip into the purse of the future. Not financially, by spending money that has yet to be earned; not materially, by using raw materials that are finite, and not rhetorically, by telling a story that reality cannot measure up to. Rietveld's designs strike the contemporary consumer as extremely austere because they are 'merely' rooted in reality, not in wishes or desires. Rietveld utilized every single means at his disposal, found meaning in the smallest space, fashioned something valuable from virtually nothing. He created an oeuvre that was averse to any kind of pretence. He showed that this need not result in something dismal. On the contrary: it created, and continues to create, space and awareness.

This leaves the question of whether the renewed interest in an oeuvre for its relevant ideas is powerful enough to contribute to its present-day vitality. It is one thing to realize that Rietveld's work is valuable, but quite another to claim that this value can be embodied in contemporary cultural production. We are not quite there yet. Within the public debate austerity is still about abstract regulation or personal lifestyle choices. The new austerity is often characterized as a new 'slow life' movement or 'the new luxury', not as a paradigm shift that will undermine the concept of 'new' itself. For now Rietveld remains primarily a point of reference that may inspire feelings but that does not yet teach us any lessons.

If the signs do not deceive us, the need for this austerity will increase rapidly. Due care to technique and choice of materials, traditional working methods, the possibility of reuse and thus a long-term vision – these values are all clearly on the rise. Whether this is a deliberate attempt to improve the quality of life or just an awareness that we must tackle the crisis, as far as I am concerned the Rietveld Year 2010 escapes the randomness of cultural anniversaries and short-lived political interests. Given the urgencies of this day and age it has arrived just in time. ◆

Bibliography

Anonymous, 'Stoel ontwerp-Rietveld', *De Hollandsche Revue*, 24 (1919) 10

Alofsin, A., *Frank Lloyd Wright. The Lost Years (1910-1922)*, Chicago 1993, 1998 (paperback), 2009 (digital edition)

Alofsin, A. (ed.), *Frank Lloyd Wright. Europe and Beyond*, Berkeley 1999

Ashbee, C.R., *Frank Lloyd Wright. Eine Studie zu seiner Würdigung*, Berlin 1911

Bakema, J.B. et al., *Rietveld-tentoonstelling. Bijdrage tot de vernieuwing der bouwkunst*, exhib.cat. Utrecht (Centraal Museum) 1958

Banham, R., *Theory and Design in the First Machine Age*, London 1960 (1), 1972 (5)

Banham, R., *The Age of the Masters. A Personal View of Modern Architecture* (revised edition of *Guide to Modern Architecture*, London 1962), London 1975, 1978 (reprint)

Barr, A.H., *Cubism and Abstract Art*, New York 1936 (1), 1974 (paperback)

Barr Jr., A.H., 'De Stijl', *The Bulletin of the Museum of Modern Art* 20 (1952-1953) 2

Bekkers, W.M.J. et al. (ed.), *Bredero's bouwbedrijf, familiebedrijf – mondiaal bouwconcern – ontvlechting*, Utrecht 2005

Benevolo, L., *Storia dell'architettura moderna*, Bari 1960

Benevolo, L., *Geschichte der Architektur des 19. und 20. Jahrhunderts* (Deutsche Sonderausgabe für die Wissenschafliche Buchgesellschaft Darmstadt), 3 vols., Munich 1988. German translation of *L'ultimo capitolo dell'architettura moderna*, Bari 1985

Berg, J. et al., *Living in the Lowlands. The Dutch Domestic Scene 1850-2004*, exhib.cat. Rotterdam (NAI) 2004

Bergeijk, H. van, *Jan Wils. De Stijl en verder*, Rotterdam 2007

Bergeijk, H. van (ed.), *Amerikaanse dromen. Frank Lloyd Wright en Nederland*, Rotterdam 2008

Beusekom, A. van, 'Gerrit Rietveld en zijn "periodiek in briefvorm" 1931-1932', *Jong Holland* 7 (1991) 1

Bibeb (pseudoniem voor E.M. Lampe-Soutberg), 'Wij maken maar een achtergrond. Gesprek met architect Rietveld', *Vrij Nederland*, 19 April 1958

Blake, P., *The Master Builders. Le Corbusier, Mies van der Rohe, Frank Lloyd Wright*, New York 1960

Blaser, W., *Mies van der Rohe*, Rotterdam 1986

Blau, E. and N.J. Troy (eds.), *Architecture and Cubism*, Cambridge, MA/London 1997

Bless, F., *Rietveld 1888-1964. Een biografie*, Amsterdam/Baarn 1982

Blotkamp, C. (ed.), *De vervolgjaren van De Stijl 1922-1932*, Amsterdam/Antwerp 1996

Blotkamp, C. et al., *De beginjaren van de Stijl 1917-1922*, Utrecht 1982

Blotkamp, C. et al., *De Stijl. The Formative Years 1917-1922*, Cambridge, MA/London 1986. Translated and revised edition of *De beginjaren van De Stijl 1917-1922*, Utrecht 1982

Blotkamp, H. et al., *S. van Ravesteyn*, exhib.cat. Amsterdam (Stichting Architectuur Museum) and Utrecht (Centraal Museum) 1977-1978

Bock, M. (ed.), *Cornelis van Eesteren, architect-urbanist*, 4 vols., Rotterdam [etc.]; vol. 1: M. Bock, V. van Rossem and K. Somer, *Bouwkunst, stijl, stedebouw. Van Eesteren en de avant-garde*, Rotterdam/The Hague 2001; vol. 2: V. van Rossem, *Het Algemeen Uitbreidingsplan van Amsterdam. Geschiedenis en ontwerp* (diss. Amsterdam), Rotterdam/The Hague 1993; vol. 3: K. Somer, *C.I.A.M. De Internationale Congressen voor het Nieuwe Bouwen* (diss. Groningen), Rotterdam 2007; vol. 4: Z. Hemel, *Het landschap van de IJsselmeerpolders. Planning, inrichting en vormgeving* (diss. Amsterdam), Rotterdam 1994

Boeken, A., 'Eenige opmerkingen over de winkelverbouwing Kalverstraat 107 te Amsterdam. Architect G. Rietveld', *Bouwkundig Weekblad* 43 (1922) 49

Boekraad, C. et al., *Het Nieuwe Bouwen, De Stijl. De Nieuwe Beelding in de architectuur/Neo Plasticism in Architecture*, exhib.cat. Delft (Delft University of Technology)/The Hague (Gemeentemuseum Den Haag) 1983

Boer, T. de et al., *M.R. Radermacher Schorer 1888-1956. Minnaar van het 'schoone' boek*, Amsterdam/The Hague 1998

Bolland, G.J.P.J., *Zuivere rede*, Leiden 1904

Bolland, G.J.P.J., *Het schoone en de kunst*, Amsterdam 1906

Bosma, K. and C. Wagenaar (eds.), *Een geruisloze doorbraak. De geschiedenis van architectuur en stedenbouw tijdens de Duitse bezetting en wederopbouw na 1945 in Nederland*, Rotterdam 1995

Braber, H. van den, *Geven om te krijgen. Literair mecenaat in Nederland tussen 1900 en 1940*, n. pl. 2002

Broekhuizen, D., *De Stijl toen – J.J.P. Oud nu. De bijdrage van architect J. J. P. Oud aan herdenken, herstellen en bouwen in Nederland (1938-1963)*, Rotterdam 2000

Brown, Th.M., *The Work of G. Rietveld Architect* (diss. Utrecht), Cambridge, MA 1958

Brown, Th.M., 'Rietveld's egocentric vision', *Journal of the Society of Architectural Historians* 24 (1965) 4, 292-296

Brown, Th.M., 'Mondrian and Rietveld. The devining rod and the compass', *Kunsthistorisch Jaarboek* 19, Leiden 1968, 205-214

Brugmans, H. and N. Japikse, *Persoonlijkheden in het Koninkrijk der Nederlanden in woord en beeld*, Amsterdam 1938

Buchholz, M. and E. Roters, *Erich Buchholz*, Berlin 1993

Bullock, N., 'First the Kitchen Then the Facade', *AA Files* (May 1984)

Burkhardt, B. (ed.), *Scharoun. Haus Schminke. Die Geschichte einer Instandsetzung* (Baudenkmale der Moderne), Stuttgart 2002

Byars, M., *The Design Encyclopedia*, London/New York 1994 (1), 2004 (2)

Colenbrander, B. (ed.), *Style. Standard and Signature in Dutch Architecture of the Nineteenth and Twentieth Centuries*, Rotterdam 1993

Crowley D. and J. Pavitt, *Cold War Modern Design 1945-1970*, London 2008

Dam, P. van, *Ir. Louis C. Kalff 1897-1976. Het artistieke geweten van Philips*, Eindhoven 2006

De Long, D.G., *Frank Lloyd Wright. Designs for an American Landscape (1922-1932)*, New York 1996

De Michelis, M., *Heinrich Tessenow 1876-1950.*

Das architektonische Gesamtwerk, Milan 1991
Denzer, A., *Gregory Ain. The Modern Home as Social Commentary*, New York 2008
Dijk, H. van, 'Het onderwijzersmodernisme; van inspiratiebron tot ballast: de moderne traditie in Nederland', *Archis* 6 (1990)
Doctor, R. (ed.), *De mooiste ruimte die ik ken. Het Nederlandse Biënnalepaviljoen van Gerrit Rietveld in Venetië*, Rotterdam 1995
Doesburg, Th. van, 'Aanteekeningen bij de bijlage. XXII Aanteekening bij een leunstoel van Rietveld', *De Stijl* 2 (1919) 11
Doesburg, Th. van, 'Aanteekeningen bij de bijlagen VI en VII', *De Stijl* 3 (1920) 5
Doesburg, Th. van, '10 jaren Stijl 1917-1927', *De Stijl* anniversary series (XIV) (1927)
Doesburg, Th. van, 'Data en feiten (betreffende de invloedsontwikkeling van "De Stijl" in 't Buitenland) die voor zich spreken', *De Stijl* anniversary series (XIV) (1927)
Doesburg, Th. van et al., 'Manifest I van "De Stijl", 1918' (signed by Van Doesburg, Van 't Hoff, Huszár, Kok, Mondrian, Vantongerloo and Wils), *De Stijl* 2 (1918) 1
Edens, C. (ed.), *Rietvelds Robijnhof. De geschiedenis van een moderne Utrechtse buurt*, Bussum 2009
Eggener, K.L. (ed.), *American Architectural History. A Contemporary Reader*, New York/London 2004
Emmens, K. (ed.), *Monumenten en bouwhistorie. Jaarboek Monumentenzorg 1996*, Zwolle/Zeist 1996
Everts, F.E.C., *Nederland op de Wereldtentoonstelling Brussel 1958. Verslag van de Nederlandse deelneming*, The Hague 1960
Ex, S. and E. Hoek, *Vilmos Huszár. Schilder en ontwerper (1884-1960)*, Utrecht 1985
Eyck, A. van, 'De bal kaatst terug', *Forum* (reprint 1958) 3
Fabre, G. and D. Wintgens-Hötte (eds.), *Van Doesburg & the International Avant-Garde. Constructing a New World*, exhib.cat. Leiden (De Lakenhal) and London (Tate Modern) 2009
Fanelli, G., *Architettura moderna in Olanda 1900-1940*, Florence 1968
Fanelli, G., *Moderne Architectuur in Nederland 1900-1940* (Dutch translation of *Architettura moderna in Olanda 1900-1940* with revised and supplemented bibliography and biographies by W. de Wit), The Hague 1978
Ferguson, R. (ed.), *At the End of the Century. One Hundred Years of Architecture*, Los Angeles 1998
Frampton, K., *Modern Architecture. A Critical History*, London 1980 (1), 2007 (4)
Friedman, A.T., *Women and the Making of the Modern House. A Social and Architectural History*, New York 1998
Friedman, M. (ed.), *De Stijl. Visions of Utopia*, exhib.cat. New York (Walker Art Center) 1982. (Dutch translation: Friedman, M. (ed.), *De Stijl 1917-1931*, exhib.cat. Amsterdam (Stedelijk Museum) and Otterlo (Rijksmuseum Kröller-Möller) 1982)
Gan, A., *Konstruktivizm (Constructivism)*, Tver 1922
Geest, J. van and O. Máčel, *Het museum van de continue lijn*, Amsterdam 1986

Giedion, S., *Space, Time and Architecture. The Growth of a New Tradition*, Cambridge, MA 1941
Giedion, S., *Mechanization Takes Command. A Contribution to Anonymous History*, New York 1948; German edition: *Die Herrschaft der Mechanisierung. Ein Beitrag zur anonymen Geschichte*. Mit einem Nachwort von Stanislaus von Moos, Frankfurt am Main 1987
Giedion, S., *Architektur und Gemeinschaft. Tagebuch einer Entwicklung* (Rowohlts deutsche Enzyklopädie), Hamburg 1956
Gill, R.G., *Een eeuw architectuur op Curaçao. De architectuur en stedenbouw van de twintigste eeuw op Curaçao*, Willemstad 1999
Ginzburg, M.J., *Zjilischje. Opyt piatiletnoj raboty nad problemoj zjilischja* (The Dwelling. The Experience of Working on the Problem of the Dwelling for Five Years), Moscow 1934.
Groenendijk, P. and P. Vollaard, *Architectuurgids Nederland/Architectural Guide to the Netherlands (1900-2000)*, Rotterdam 2006
Gropius, W., *Internationale Architektur* (Bauhausbücher 1), Munich 1925
Guilbert, S., *How New York Stole the Idea of Modern Art. Abstract Expressionism, Freedom and the Cold War*, Chicago 1983
Haag Bletter, R. and M. Robinson, *Adolf Behne. The Modern Functional Building* (Getty texts and documents), Santa Monica 1996
Haar, H. van der et al., *Kerende tijden. 190 jaar Genootschap Kunstliefde*, Utrecht 1997
Hammer-Tugendhat, D. and W. Tegethoff (eds.), *Ludwig Mies van der Rohe. The Tugendhat House*, Vienna/New York 2000
Hartveld, C., *Moderne zakelijkheid. Efficiency in wonen en werken in Nederland 1918-1940*, Amsterdam 1994
Haterd, L. van de, *Om hart en vurigheid. Over schrijvers en kunstenaars van tijdschrift en uitgeverij De Gemeenschap 1925-1941*, Haarlem 2004
Haterd, L. van de, *De waarheid hooger dan de leus. Over de beeldvorming rondom tijdschrift en uitgeverij De Gemeenschap 1925-1941*, Haarlem 2008
Hays, K.M., *Architecture Theory since 1968*, Cambridge, MA 1998 (1), 2000 (2)
Heerding, A., *The History of N.V. Philips Gloeilampenfabrieken. A Company of Many Parts*, Cambridge, MA 1986, vol. 2
Henket, H.-J. and H. Heynen (eds.), *Back from Utopia. The Challenge of the Modern Movement*, Rotterdam 2002
Hitchcock, H-R., *Architecture. Nineteenth and Twentieth Centuries* (Pelican History of Art), Harmondsworth/Baltimore 1958 (1), 1969 (3)
Hitchcock, H-R., 'Review of the Work of G. Rietveld, Architect by Theodore M. Brown', *Journal of the Society of Architectural Historians* 18 (October 1959) 3
Hitchcock, H-R. and Ph. Johnson, *The International Style. Architecture since 1922*, New York 1932, 1966 (with a foreword and appendix by H-R. Hitchcock).
Hofer, S., *Reformarchitektur (1900-1918). Deutsche Baukünstler auf der Suche nach dem nationalen Stil*, Stuttgart/London 2005

Howells, J.M., 'Fundamentals of Architecture as Related to lighting', *Transactions of the Illuminating Engineering Society* 25 (1930) 5, 474-475
Huygen, F. (ed.), *Visies op vormgeving. Het Nederlandse ontwerpen in teksten*, (vol. 1: 1874-1940) Amsterdam 2007, (vol. 2: 1944-2000) Amsterdam 2008
Ibelings, H., *Modernism without Dogma. Architects of a Younger Generation in the Netherlands*, Rotterdam 1991
Ibelings, H., *20th Century Architecture in the Netherlands*, Rotterdam 1995
Ibelings, H., *Architecten in Nederland. Van Cuypers tot Koolhaas*, Amsterdam 2005
Ibelings, H., 'La fama de Rietveld/Rietveld's Fame', *2G Revista Internacional de Arquitectura/International Achitectural Review (Gerrit Th. Rietveld)* (2006) 39-40, 262-264
Ikonnikov, A.V., *Zarubezhnaja arkhitektoera: ot 'novoj arkhitectoery' do postmodernizma* (Foreign Architecture: From 'the New Architecture' to Postmodernism), Moscow 1982
Jaffé, H.L.C., *De Stijl 1917-1931. The Dutch Contribution to Modern Art*, Amsterdam 1956
Jencks, Ch., *Modern Movements in Architecture*, Harmondsworth [etc.] 1973
Johnson, P., 'Introduction', in: *In Focus. Gerrit Rietveld, Designer*, exhib.cat. Hartford, CT (Wadsworth Atheneum Museum of Modern Art) 1980
Juffermans, J., *Met stille trom. Beeldende kunst en Utrecht sinds 1900*, Utrecht 1996 (2)
Kalff, L.C., 'Illumination and Architecture', *Philips Technology Review* 2 (1937) 1
Kalff, L.C., *Kunstlicht und Architektur*, Eindhoven 1943
Kalff, L.C., 'The "Electronic Poem". Performed in the Philips Pavilion at the 1958 Brussels World Fair. A: The Light Effects', *Philips Technical Review* 20 (23 October 1958) 2/3
Kalff, L.C. et al., *Le poème électronique Le Corbusier*, Paris 1958
Kholostenko, M.V., *L'Architecture Vivante* (1928) 22 (b)
Kholostenko, M.V., *SA, Sovremennaia arkhitektura* (Modern Architecture) (1928) 2 (a)
Klapheck, R., *Gussglas. Bedeutung, Herstellung und Verwendung eines deutschen Werk- und Baustoffes*, Düsseldorf 1938
Koch, A., *W.H. Gispen. Serieproducten 1923-1960*, Rotterdam 2005
Koch, A., *Dichtbij klopt het hart der wereld. Nederland op de Expo 58*, Schiedam 2008
Krasheninnikova, N.L., *Sovremennaja arkhitektoera Niderlandov (Gollandija)* (Modern Dutch Architecture [Holland]), Moscow 1971
Krekel-Aalberse, A., *Carel J.A. Begeer 1883-1956*, Assen/Zwolle 2001
Krischanitz, A. and O. Kapfinger, 'Documentazione di un rinnovamento. La Werkbund Siedlung di Vienna', *Casabella* 522 (1986), 46 ff
Kuipers, M.C., *Bouwen in beton. Experimenten in de volkshuisvesting voor 1940*, The Hague 1987
Kultermann, U., *Baukunst der Gegenwart. Dokument des Neuen Bauens in der Welt*, Tübingen 1958

Kultermann, U., 'Rietveld – neu bewertet', in: *Möbel und Decoration* 7 (1959) May

Küper, M. and M. van Schijndel, 'Der Sitzgeist. Over het ontstaan van de zigzagstoel', *Jong Holland* 3 (1987) 2, 4-11

Küper, M. and I. van Zijl, *Rietveld Schröder Archief*, exhib.cat. Utrecht (Centraal Museum) 1988

Küper, M. and I. van Zijl, *Gerrit Th. Rietveld 1888-1964. The Complete Works*, exhib.cat. Utrecht (Centraal Museum) 1992

Kuper, M., W. Quist and H. Ibelings, 'Gerrit Rietveld Casas/Houses', *2G Revista Internacional de Arquitectura/International Achitectural Review (Gerrit Th. Rietveld)* (2006) 39/40

Langmead, D., *Dutch Modernism. Architectural Resources in the English Language*, Westport 1996

Leeuw Marcar, A., *Willem Sandberg. Portret van een kunstenaar*, Rotterdam 2004 (revised edition, Amsterdam 1982)

Leupen, B., W. Deen and C. Grafe (eds.), *Hoe modern is de Nederlandse architectuur?*, Rotterdam 1990

Linssen, C., H. Schoots and T. Gunning, *Het gaat om de film! Een nieuwe geschiedenis van de Nederlandsche Filmliga 1927-1933*, Amsterdam 1999

Lissitzky, E., 'De woningcultuur', *Stroitel'naia promyshlennost* (The Building Industry) (1926) 12

Lissitzky-Küppers, S., *El Lissitzky*, Dresden 1967

Lobov, I., 'Mebel fakulteta po obrabotke dereva i metalla VKhUTEIN' (Furniture by the Wood and Metal Working Department of the VKhUTEIN), *Stroitel'stvo Moskvy* (1929) 10

Loghem, J.B. van, *Bouwen, bauen, bâtir, building. Built to live in, vers une architecture, neues bauen, nieuwe zakelijkheid*, Rotterdam 1932

Lootsma, B., 'Een ode van Philips aan de vooruitgang. Het paviljoen van Le Corbusier, Xenakis and Varèse op de Brusselse wereldtentoonstelling' and 'Le Poème electronique. Het verlangen naar synthese', *Wonen TA/BK* (1984) 2

Lotz, W. (ed.), *Licht und Beleuchtung*, Berlin 1928

Madge, P., 'Controversen rond Rietveld. Van De Stijl tot de Nieuwe Zakelijkheid', *Wonen TA/BK* (1982) 15/16

Malevich, K., 'Zhivopis v probleme arkhitektoery' (The Art of Painting in the Problem of Architecture), *Nova Generatsija* (1928) 2

Meier-Graefe, J., *Die Weltausstellung in Paris 1900 mit zahlreichen photographischen Aufnahmen, farbigen Kunstbeilagen und Plänen*, Paris/Leipzig 1900

Mens, N., *W.G. Witteveen en Rotterdam*, Rotterdam 2007

Mertins, D. and H. Mallgrave, *Walter Curt Behrendt. The Victory of the New Building Style* (Getty Texts and Documents), Los Angeles 2000

Mies van der Rohe, L., 'Die Wohnung unserer Zeit', *Die Form* 6 (1931) 7

Molema, J., 'De standaard in hoogbouw. 860-880 Lake Shore Drive Apartments, fase 1 Chicago (USA) door Mies van der Rohe', *de Architect Detail* (October 2005)

Moorsel, W. van, *Contact en controle. Over het vrouwbeeld van de Stichting Goed Wonen*, Amsterdam 1992

Moorsel, W. van, *Nelly van Doesburg 1899-1975*, Nijmegen 2000

Mulder, B., *Gerrit Thomas Rietveld. Schets van zijn leven, denken en werken*, Nijmegen 1994

Neumann, D., *Architecture of the Night. The Illuminated Building*, Munich [etc.] 2002

Neumeyer, F., *The Artless Word. Mies van der Rohe on the Building Art*, Cambridge, MA 1991

Oku, K., *The architecture of Gerrit Th. Rietveld*, Tokyo 2009

Ottevanger, A., '*De Stijl overal absolute leiding'. De briefwisseling tussen Theo van Doesburg en Anthony Kok*, Bussum 2008

Overy, P., *De Stijl*, London 1969 (1), 1991 (revised edition)

Overy, P., *Het Rietveld Schröder huis*, Houten 1988

Overy, P., 'Equipment for Utopia.', *Art in America* 82 (January 1994) 1, 34-42

Overy, P., *Light, Air & Openness. Modern Architecture between the Wars*, London 2007

Overy, P. et al., *The Rietveld-Schröder House*, Guilford/Cambridge, MA 1988

Peters, F., 'De Utrechtsche Filmliga 1927-1933. Opvattingen over film als kunst in Utrecht' (diss. Universiteit Utrecht), Utrecht 2002

Petit, J., *Le poème électronique. Le Corbusier/The Electronic Poem by Le Corbusier*, Brussels 1958

Pevsner, N., *Pioneers of the Modern Movement from William Morris to Walter Gropius*, London 1936 Pevsner, N., *Pioneers of Modern Design*, New York (Museum of Modern Art) 1949; London/Yale 2005 (revised and extended edition)

Pevsner, N., *An Outline of European Architecture*, Harmondsworth 1943; Baltimore, MD, 1960 (sixth anniversary edition)

Pfeffer, H., 'Im Anfang war das Licht', *Spannung. Die AEG Umschau*, II, 1 (October 1928), 1-5

Probst, H. and Ch. Schädlich, *Walter Gropius, Band 2: Der Architekt und Pädagoge*, Berlin 1986

Rasch, H. and B. Rasch, *Der Stuhl*, Stuttgart 1928

Rebel, B., *Het Nieuwe Bouwen. Het functionalisme in Nederland 1918-1945* (diss. Utrecht), n.pl. 1983

Rehorst, Chr., 'Jan Buijs and De Volharding, The Hague, Holland', *Journal of the Society of Architectural Historians* 45 (May 1985), 147-160

Rietveld, G.Th., 'Aanteekening bij kinderstoel (bijlage nr. XVIII)', *De Stijl* 2 (1919) 9

Rietveld, G.Th., 'Nut, constructie: (schoonheid: kunst)', *i10* 1 (1927) 3 (a)

Rietveld, G.Th., 'G. Rietveld', *De Stijl* 7 (1927) 79/84 (b)

Rietveld, G.Th., 'Inzicht', *i10* 12 (1928) 17/18

Rietveld, G.Th., *Jaarboek der Moskousche architectenvereeniging* [architectuurvereniging] (Jubileumnummer 1928) 5, *Nieuw Rusland* 1 (1929) 2

Rietveld, G.Th., 'De stoel', *De werkende vrouw* 1 (1930) 9 (a)

Rietveld, G.Th., 'Architectuur', *De werkende vrouw* 1 (1930) 11-12 (b)

Rietveld, G.Th., 'Interieur', *Bouwbedrijf* (1930), 25 (c)

Rietveld, G.Th., 'Nieuwe zakelijkheid in de Nederlandsche architectuur', *De Vrije Bladen* 9 (1932) 7

Rietveld, G.Th., 'Het interieur', *Bouwkundig Weekblad* 66 (1948) 25

Rietveld, G.Th., 'Curaçao', *Katholieke gezondheidszorg* 5 (1951) mei, 198-199

Rietveld, G.Th., 'In memoriam P.J.C. Klaarhamer', *Bouwkundig Weekblad* 72 (1954) 13-14

Rietveld, G.Th., 'Feestrede', *Forum* 13 (1958) 8/9

Rijk, T. de, 'Een grand tour naar de Nieuwe Wereld: "Geobsedeerd door locomotieven, sex, gebakken biefstukjes en snelheid"', in: *Het Nederlandse binnenhuis gaat zich te buiten. Internationale invloeden op de Nederlandse wooncultuur* (Leids Kunsthistorisch Jaarboek 14), Leiden 2007

Riley, T. and S. Perrella, *The International Style. Exhibition 15 and the Museum of Modern Art*, New York 1992

Risselada, M. (ed.), *Raumplan versus plan libre. Adolf Loos – Le Corbusier*, Rotterdam 2008

Rodijk, G.H., *De huizen van Rietveld*, Zwolle 1991

Rogers, T.S. and A.L. Powell, 'Exterior Illumination of Buildings', *American Architect Reference Data* 18 (1935), 1-360

Rothuizen, E.J., *Het dak. Handleiding tot het construeren van dakbedekkingen*, Amsterdam 1916, 1920 (2), 1950 (5)

Sandfort, A.J.P.G. (ed.), *40 jaar Jaarbeurs Utrecht*, Utrecht 1956

Santen, J. van et al. (ed.), *Monumenten van Herrezen Nederland* (National Department of Archaeology, Man-Made Landscape and Monuments, top 100 for the Minister of Education, Culture and Science, dr. R.H.A. Plasterk, foreword), Amersfoort 2007

Sartoris, A., *Encyclopédie de l'architecture nouvelle. Tome 2, Ordre et climate nordiques*, Milan 1957

Schaafsma, H., *Gerrit Rietveld. Bouwmeester van een nieuwe tijd*, Utrecht 1959

Schama, S., *The Embarrassment of Riches. An Interpretation of Dutch Culture in the Golden Age*, Berkeley 1988

Scharlemann, M. and J.-D. Koudijs, *S. van Ravesteyn (1889-1983). De meester van de gebogen lijn*, Rotterdam 2005

Siraa, H.T., *Eén miljoen nieuwe woningen. De rol van de rijksoverheid bij wederopbouw, volkshuisvesting, bouwnijverheid en ruimtelijke ordening (1940-1963)*, The Hague 1989

Slothouber, E. (ed.), *De kunstnijverheidsscholen van Gerrit Rietveld/The Artschools of Gerrit Rietveld*, Amsterdam 1997

Smith, E.A.T. (ed.), *Blueprints of Modern Living. History and Legacy of the Case Study Houses*, Cambridge, MA 1989

Staal, A., 'Nog meer abstracte Kunst?', *De 8 en Opbouw* 9 (1938) 9

Steinmann, M. (ed.), *CIAM. Internationale Kongresse für Neues Bauen. Dokumente 1928-1939*, Basel 1979

Straaten, E. van, *Theo van Doesburg 1883-1931*, The Hague 1983

Sweeney, R., *Wright in Hollywood. Visions of a New Architecture*, New York/Cambridge, MA 1994

Szénássy, I.L., *Architectuur in Nederland*

1960-1967, Amsterdam 1969

Tafuri, M., *The Sphere and the Labyrinth. Avant-Gardes and Architecture from Piranesi to the 1970s*, Cambridge, MA 1987. Translated and revised edition of *La sfera e il labirinto: Avanguardie e architettura da Piranesi agli anni '70*, Turin 1980

Tafuri, M. and F. Dal Co, *Modern Architecture*, New York 1979 (series: P.L. Nervi [ed.], *History of World Architecture*, translation of *Architettura contemporanea*, 1976)

Theissing, E.M., 'Lucht als bouwstof', *Cement* 13 (1961) 1

Thoor, M.T.A. van, *Het gebouw van Nederland. Nederlandse paviljoens op de wereldtentoonstellingen 1910-1958*, Zutphen 1998

Thoor, M.T. van, 'Gerrit Rietveld and the Netherlands Participation in Brussels (1958)', in: *Abstracts of Papers, Presented at the Sixty-first Annual Meeting of the Society of Architectural Historians*, Cincinnati, OH, 23-27 April 2008

Tieskens, R.W., D.P. Snoep and G.W.C. van Wezel (eds.), *Het Kleine Bouwen. Vier eeuwen maquettes in Nederland*, Utrecht/Zutphen 1983

Tijen, W. van, 'Rietveld, Molière en – in gedachte – Merkelbach', *Bouwkundig Weekblad* 82 (1964), 1-6B

Trachtenberg, M. and I. Hyman, *Architecture from Prehistory to Post-Modernism. The Western Tradition*, New York 1986

Treib, M., *Space Calculated in Seconds. The Philips Pavilion. Le Corbusier, Edgar Varèse*, Princeton, NJ 1996

Troy, N.J., *De Stijl's Collaborative Ideal. The Colored Abstract Environment, 1916-1926*, Cambridge, MA 1979

Troy, N.J., *The De Stijl Environment*, Cambridge, MA/London, 1983

Troy, N.J., 'Rietveld's Modernism', in: *Gerrit Rietveld. A Centenary Exhibition. Craftsman and Visionary*, exhib.cat. New York (Barry Friedman Ltd.) 1988

Vegesack, A. von and M. Remmele (eds.), *Marcel Breuer. Design and Architecture*, Weil am Rhein 2003

Venneman, J. and M. de Kroon (eds.), *De Mondial. Rietvelds stoel voor de wereld*, Culemborg 2006

Vidler, A., *Histories of the Immediate Present. Inventing Architectural Modernism*, Cambridge, MA 2008

Vitt, W. (ed.), *Hommage à Dexel (1890-1973). Beiträge zum 90. Geburtstag des Künstlers*, Starnberg 1980

Vöge, P., *The Complete Rietveld Furniture*, Rotterdam 1993

Vreeburg, G. and H. Martens, *UMS Pastoe. Een Nederlandse meubelfabriek 1913-1983*, Utrecht 1983

Vygodskii, L., 'Ratsionalizatsiia zjilischjia' (The Rationalization of Housing), *Kommunal'noe delo* (1929) 1

Wagt, W. de, *Piet Elling (1897-1962). Een samenstellende eenheid*, Bussum 2008

Warnke, C.-P., *De Stijl 1917-1931*, Cologne 1991

Wever, P. and A. Koch, 'Tales of the Unexpected. Gerrit Rietveld at Expo 58', *Modernism* 11 (2008) 4

White, M., *De Stijl and Dutch Modernism*, Manchester/New York 2003

Wilk, C. (ed.), *Modernism. Designing a New World 1914-1939*, London 2006

Wright, F.L., *Ausgeführte Bauten und Entwürfe von Frank Lloyd Wright*, Berlin 1910

Xenakis, I., 'The Architectural Design of Corbusier and Xenakis', *Philips Technical Review* 20 (1958-1959), 1, 2-8

Zevi, B., *Storia dell'architettura moderna*, Turin 1950 (1), 1955 (3)

Zevi, B., *Poetica dell'architettura neoplastica. Il linguagio della scomposizione quadridimensionale*, Milan 1953

Zijl, I. van, *Rietveld in Utrecht*, Utrecht 2001

Zijl, I. van (ed.), [Truus Schröder: tentoonstelling per post], Utrecht, 1998-1999 (a starter book in 1998 with five additions, sent by mail, complete by the end of 1999)

Zijl, I. van and B. Mulder, *Het Rietveld Schröderhuis. De voorgeschiedenis, het huis als woning, het huis als monument*, Utrecht 2009

Zijl, I. van and I. de Roode, 'Kinderstoel voor Hendrikus Johannes Witteveen', *Bulletin van de Vereniging Rembrandt* 19 (summer 2009) 2

About the Authors

Anthony Alofsin is an architect, artist and author. He has written eight books about architecture, one work of fiction, *Halflife* (2009), and published over 80 articles, essays and reviews. He is a Fellow of the MacDowell Colony in Peterborough (NH) and won the Vasari Award for his book *When Buildings Speak: Architecture as Language in the Habsburg Empire* (2007).

Ole Bouman is director of the Netherlands Architecture Institute, Rotterdam. He was editor-in-chief of the periodical *Volume*. Bouman has published widely in periodicals such as *Domus*, *Harvard Design Review* and *El Croquis* and is (co-)author of several books. Most recently he published *Architecture of Consequence* (2009). Bouman has curated exhibitions for the Milan Triennale, Manifesta 3 and Boijmans Van Beuningen Museum as well as a series of public events for the reconstruction of the public domain in cities hit by disasters. He regularly lectures at internationally acclaimed universities and cultural institutions.

Dolf Broekhuizen is a freelance architecture historian. He received his doctorate in 2000 with a thesis on the post-war work of architect J.J.P. Oud and his involvement in writing the history of De Stijl. He was co-author of the comprehensive overview of the work of J.J.P. Oud and was one of the organizers of the exhibition on Oud held at the Netherlands Architecture Institute in Rotterdam (2001). In 2010 he was co-author and editor of *Robert van 't Hoff. Architect of a New Society*.

Maristella Casciato is professor of history of architecture at the University of Bologna. From 2000 to 2009 she has served as Chair of DOCOMOMO International. Her scholarly studies focus on the history of twentieth-century European architecture. She is currently engaged in a research project on Pierre Jeanneret. Her recent publications include: 'A New Town Planned Literally from A to Z', in S. von Moos (ed.), *Chandigarh 1956. Le Corbusier, Pierre Jeanneret, Jane B. Drew, E. Maxwell Fry*, with photographs by Ernst Scheidegger (2010).

Jurjen Creman is a furniture restorer who specializes in the restoration, conservation and study of twentieth-century furniture. He was involved in the retrospective of Rietveld's work at the Centraal Museum in 1992-1993. Since then he has worked for a great many museums, auction houses, collectors and dealers of Rietveld furniture. In his own studio he researches and restores Rietveld furniture with special attention to their material and structural properties.

Rob Dettingmeijer taught theory and history of architecture and urban planning for the last 30 years at Utrecht University. His doctoral thesis is titled *Open City, planning development, townplanning, housing and architecture in Rotterdam between the wars* (1988). He is one of the founders of the European Architectural History Network and editor of the Bulletin *KNOB* (Royal Dutch Antiquarian Society).

Roman Koot is an art historian and the head of public services and chief curator at the RKD, the Netherlands Institute for Art History. He researches and publishes on modern visual art. His main area of interest is the configuration and significance of local art scenes. He has published work on modernist trends in Rotterdam during the interwar period and on art in Utrecht. His most recent publication is a monograph on the Utrecht-based graphic design group De Luis (1960-1980).

Marieke Kuipers is professor of cultural heritage at ®MIT/Faculty of Architecture at Delft University of Technology and senior specialist in twentieth-century architectural heritage at the Netherlands Agency for Cultural Heritage. She received her PhD in 1987 for her dissertation on experimental housing in concrete before 1940 and has published widely, in particular on the architectural heritage of the Modern Movement. She has also been involved in the statutory protection of various buildings by Rietveld. Besides, she is vice-chair of the International Specialist Committee on Registers of the international organisation DOCOMOMO.

Marijke Kuper is an art historian and expert on the work of Gerrit Rietveld. Her early research at Utrecht University resulted in contributions to *De Stijl: The Formative Years 1917-1922* (1982) and *De Vervolgjaren van De Stijl 1922-1932* (1996). In 1992 she was joint curator of the Rietveld exhibition at the Central Museum Utrecht and joint editor of the catalogue *Gerrit Th. Rietveld 1888-1964 The Complete Works*. In 2003 she published *2G, Gerrit Th. Rietveld Casas – Houses*.

Otakar Máčel is an architecture historian who works at the IHAAU (Institute of History of Art, Architecture and Urbanism) at the Faculty of Architecture, Delft University of Technology. He obtained his doctorate in 1992 with a thesis on the history of the cantilevered chair and obtained tenure in modern Czech architecture at the Technical University in Prague. He specializes in modern architecture, socialist realism and the history of modern design.

Dietrich Neumann is a professor of the history of modern architecture at Brown University Providence (RI). He has published books and essays on the history of European and American architecture of the twentieth century, among them a book on movie set design (*Film Architecture*, 2000) and architectural illumination (*Luminous Buildings: Night Architecture*, 2006). In 2007 he was chief curator for an exhibition of the same title at the Netherlands Architecture Institute in Rotterdam.

Ivan Nevzgodin is an assistant professor at ®MIT, Faculty of Architecture, Delft University of Technology. He received his doctorate in 2002 in Novosibirsk with a thesis on Dutch-Russian relations in architecture and town planning at the beginning of the twentieth century. In 2004 he obtained his Dutch doctorate at Delft University of Technology. He is (co-)author of several publications on architecture and urbanism in the Netherlands and Russia.

Wolf Tegethoff studied art history, town planning and economic and social history at Bonn University (PhD in 1981) and at Columbia University in New York. He became director of the Zentralinstitut für Kunstgeschichte in Munich in 1991. As a visiting professor he lectured at the universities of Haifa, Bonn and Venice (CA), and, since 2000, has held an honorary professorship at the Ludwig-Maximilians-Universität in Munich. He is the author of *Mies van der Rohe: The Villas and Country House Projects* (1984) as well as of numerous publications on the history of architecture and design in the nineteenth and twentieth centuries.

Marie-Thérèse van Thoor is associate professor at ®MIT, Faculty of Architecture, Delft University of Technology. She received her doctorate in 1998 with the thesis *Het gebouw van Nederland. Nederlandse paviljoens op de wereldtentoonstellingen 1910-1958* (The Netherlands' building. Dutch pavilions at World's Fairs 1910-1958). She is editor-in-chief of the *Bulletin KNOB* and writes regularly about heritage and twentieth-century architecture. She is co-editor-in-chief of the publication on the restoration of the Zonnestraal sanatorium in Hilversum (2010).

Ida van Zijl is a specialist on art, design and architecture. Since 1978 she has been curator of applied arts at the Centraal Museum in Utrecht, that houses the world's largest Rietveld collection and the Rietveld Schröder Archive. In this capacity she is responsible for the preservation and administration of the Schröder House. She has organized numerous exhibitions on applied arts and design and has published many articles and books in the field. From 1983 to 2009 she was deputy director of the Centraal Museum.

Hielkje Zijlstra is an architect. She worked at several architecture firms from 1987 to 2001. In 2006 she obtained her doctorate from Delft University of Technology with her study *Bouwen in Nederland 1940-1970* (Building in the Netherlands 1940-1970). She developed her doctoral research method into the ABCD' research method (Analysing Buildings from Context to Detail in time). In 2006 she became an associate professor at ®MIT (Research Centre for Modification Intervention and Transformation) at the Faculty of Architecture, Delft University of Technology.

This book was published to coincide with the exhibition 'Rietveld's Universe' at the Centraal Museum Utrecht (20 October 2010 – 30 January 2011), mounted by the Centraal Museum, Utrecht and the Netherlands Architecture Institute, Rotterdam and conceived by the Centraal Museum, Utrecht, the department of ®MIT at Delft University of Technology and Utrecht University.

This publication concludes the study 'Rietveld's Universe', a joint project by the Centraal Museum Utrecht, Utrecht University and the department of ®MIT at Delft University of Technology.

The exhibition and publication were made possible with the financial support of the City of Utrecht, the Province of Utrecht, Mondriaan Foundation, Fentener van Vlissingen Fonds, KF Hein Fonds, Prins Bernhard Cultuurfonds, SNS Reaal Fonds, VSB Fonds

Publication:
Text and photographs: Centraal Museum Utrecht, ® MIT TU Delft
Editors: Rob Dettingmeijer, Marie-Thérèse van Thoor, Ida van Zijl
Text editing: Marjan Vrolijk, Sara Stroux, D'laine Camp, Els Brinkman
Photo editor: Iwert Bernakiewicz
Translations: Jane Bemont (Foreword, Introduction, Kuipers, Nevzgodin); Beverly Jackson (Broekhuizen); David McKay (Dettingmeijer, Koot, Kuper); Andrew May (Van Thoor); Piccia Neri (Casciato); Laura Vroomen (Bouman, Creman/Máčel, Van Zijl, Zijlstra)
Design: Lesley Moore, Amsterdam
Lithography and print: Ofset Yapimevi, Istanbul
Paper: 135 grs. Furioso
Project coordination: Barbera van Kooij, NAi Publishers
Publisher: NAi Publishers, Rotterdam

Photo credits:
Illustrations have been obtained from the following archives:
CMU: Centraal Museum, Utrecht
NAI: Nederlands Architectuurinstituut, Rotterdam
RSA: Rietveld Schröder Archive, Utrecht

Index:
B: Bauhaus, Dessau, 1928-1930, photo Atlantic Photo-Co, Bauhaus-Archiv, Berlin
B: G.Th. Rietveld, Visser House, Bergeijk, RSA
C: Le Corbusier portrait, Photographie FLC L4(1)127, © FLC/PICTORIGHT, 2010
D: De Stijl, cover
E: Eames chair: Stedelijk Museum, Amsterdam
G: Walter Gropius, 1926, Bauhaus-Archiv, Berlin ©BPK, Berlin
I: G.Th. Rietveld, Van den Doel House, Ilpendam, RSA
L: El Lissitzky: source: *El Lissitzky, 1890-1941*, Eindhoven: Van Abbe Museum
M: Mies van der Rohe, Adam Department Store, Berlin: ©Museum of Modern Art, New York/Scala, Florence
R: Gerrit Rietveld
R: G.Th. Rietveld, Red-Blue Chair: CMU
R: G.Th. Rietveld, Dutch Pavilion Venice: RSA
R: G.Th. Rietveld and T. Schröder-Schräder, Schroder House: RSA
R: G.Th. Rietveld, Academy, Arnhem, photograph by Hielkje Zijlstra
S: Schelling Family: Schelling Estate
S: Truus Schröder-Schräder: RSA, photograph by Eva Besnyö
U: Gerrit Rietveld next to his workshop, Utrecht, c. 1919, RSA
V: Theo van Doesburg, c. 1920: ICN Amsterdam/Rijswijk
V: Cornelis van Eesteren, NAI
V: M.R. Radermacher Schorer: Nico Jesse/Nederlands Fotomuseum, Rotterdam
V: G.Th. Rietveld, invitation 'Utrechtsche Jongeren': RSA
X: Le Corbusier and I. Xenakis, Philips Pavilion: Nationaal Archief, The Hague

And:
Bauhaus-Archiv, Berlin 132
Bauhaus Archiv/VG Bild-Kunst Bonn, 191 top
Berlinische Galerie 209 right
Eva Besnyö 147 bottom
Jan Bons and Lex Reitsma 162 bottom
Bruschweiler 142, 227
Christie's 231
Jurjen Creman 149
©2010 Fondation Le Corbusier/Pictoright 65
© 2010 The Frank Lloyd Wright Foundation, AZ/Art Resource, NY/Scala, Florence 82
Axel Funke 143
Allard van der Hoek 110 top
Nico Jesse 78 top, 185 top
Marieke Kuipers 100 left, 117
Lanjouw estate 153
F.W. van Malsen 70 bottom
Ernst Moritz 147, 148, 165, 191, 199, 229, 247
Museum of Modern Art, New York 238
Museum of Modern Art, Mies van der Rohe Archive, photo: Heinrich Blessing © 2010 MoMA/Scala, Florence 74
Museum of Modern Art, Mies van der Rohe Archive © 2010 MoMA/Scala, Florence 186
Nationaal archief The Hague 166 right
Ivan Nevzgodin collection 215-223
Jaap d'Oliveira 239
Cas Oorthuys 93 top
Rijckheyt centrum voor regionale geschiedenis Heerlen, J. Cohnen 133 top
®MIT TU Delft 136 top
Henny Rodijk 104 right, 122 bottom
Ton Roelofsma 94 top
Stedelijk Museum Amsterdam 144, 228, 230, 236, 238
Tugendhat Family 68
Jan Versnel 73 bottom, 84 top, 88, 114 top, 122 top, 156, 172, 180, 188
F. v.d. Werf 181
Hans Wilschut 197
Hielkje Zijlstra 119, 121 bottom, 130, 135, 136 bottom
Kim Zwarts 73 top, 197, 204, 206

Acknowledgments
Berry Bergdoll, Museum of Modern Art, New York; Maristella Casciato MAXXI, Rome; Bart Hofstede, Ministry of Foreign Affairs, Berlin; Florian Hufnagel, Neue Sammlung, Munich; Maarten Mevis, Kinkorn; Angelika Nollert, Neues Museum, Nürnberg; Klaus de Rijk, Ministry of Foreign Affairs, Rome; Harm Scheltens, Utrecht Manifest; Tim Vermeulen, Stichting Premsela/DDFA; Willem van Zeeland, Rietveldjaar 2010

© 2010 The authors and NAi Publishers
All rights reserved. No part of this publication
may be reproduced, stored in a retrieval system,
or transmitted in any form or by any means,
electronic, mechanical, photocopying, recording
or otherwise, without the prior written permission
of the publisher.

For works of visual artists affiliated with a
CISAC-organization the copyrights have been
settled with Pictoright in Amsterdam.
© 2010, c/o Pictoright Amsterdam

Although every effort was made to find the
copyright holders for the illustrations used,
it has not been possible to trace them all.
Interested parties are requested to contact
NAi Publishers, Mauritsweg 23, 3012 JR
Rotterdam, The Netherlands.

NAi Publishers is an internationally orientated
publisher specialized in developing, producing
and distributing books on architecture, visual
arts and related disciplines.
www.naipublishers.nl info@naipublishers.nl

ISBN 978-90-5662-746-1
Dutch edition: ISBN 978-90-5662-745-4
Printed and bound in Turkey

Available in North, South and Central America
through D.A.P./Distributed Art Publishers Inc,
155 Sixth Avenue 2nd Floor, New York, NY
10013-1507, tel +1 212 627 1999,
fax +1 212 627 9484, dap@dapinc.com

Available in the United Kingdom and Ireland
through Art Data, 12 Bell Industrial Estate,
50 Cunnington Street, London W4 5HB,
tel +44 208 747 1061, fax +44 208 742 2319,
orders@artdata.co.uk